13

STORY & CHARACTER & FORMATION

The girls soccer team for Saitama Prefectural High School Warabi Seinan—a notoriously weak team once derided as the Wallabies—is about to be reborn. Sumire Suō, a girl with overwhelming speed as a winger. Midori Soshizaki, a defensive midfielder, strong enough to have been recruited to the national youth team. And Nozomi Onda, a midfielder who charms all who watch her. With the addition of these players and help from the new coach, the legendary Naoko Nōmi, the perpetual underdogs begin to move forward.

After losing to the reigning champions, Urawa Hōsei, in the Saitama Preliminaries for the national high school tournament, the Wallabies sign up for the JKFB Interleague tournament, where they will face the strongest schools in the Kanto region.

In the semifinals, they struggle against a powerful defensive block and ace player, Tae Kokubu, but they ultimately defeat Eisen Funabashi and advance to the finals! Their next opponent is one of the two strongest teams in the high school girls soccer realm: Kōrenkan High School.

The curtain rises on a spectacular start to this tournament's final match!! Faced against the hybrid soccer style of the same athletes that won the inter-high championship, including scoring queen Mika Kurusu and prodigy wingback Ume Fujie, the Wallabies lose the first point all too quickly. Add to that Soshizaki's removal from the game, and the first half ends with our team at an overwhelming disadvantage. Meanwhile, Head Coach Fukatsu implements a new strategy: he has Suō and Shiratori change positions! The plan works, and the Wallabies bring the score 3-2, with them now only one point behind. Can our heroines keep it up and defeat Kōrenkan?!

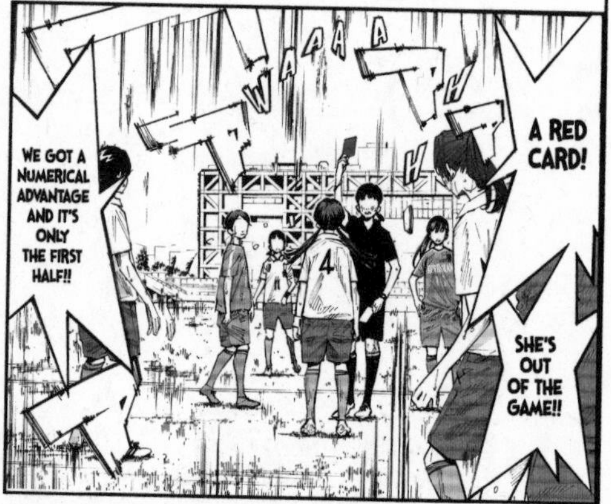
A RED CARD!
SHE'S OUT OF THE GAME!!
WAAAAAH
WE GOT A NUMERICAL ADVANTAGE AND IT'S ONLY THE FIRST HALF!!

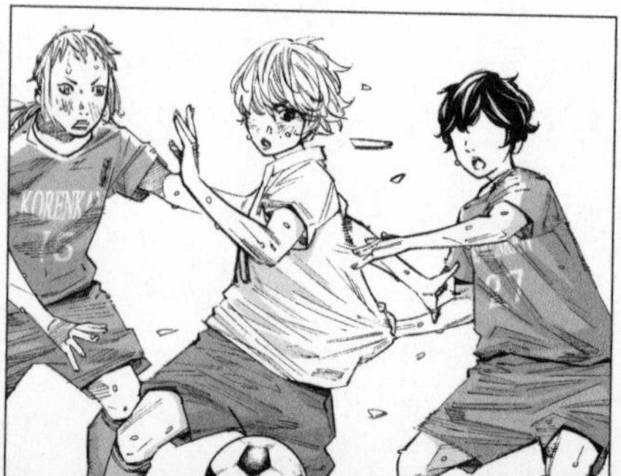

Warabi Seinan High School Formation

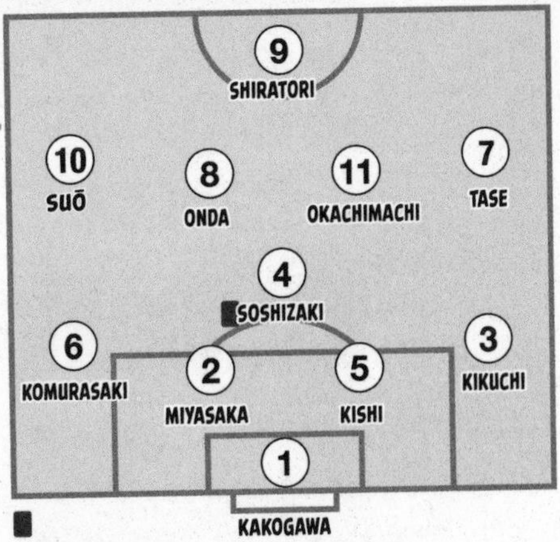
9
SHIRATORI
10
SUŌ
8
ONDA
11
OKACHIMACHI
7
TASE
4
SOSHIZAKI
6
KOMURASAKI
2
MIYASAKA
5
KISHI
3
KIKUCHI
1
KAKOGAWA

4—1—4—1

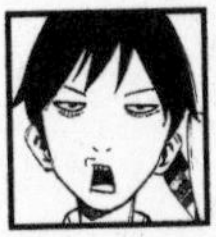

HEAD COACH: FUKATSU

A lazy sack of bones who is always reading horse racing magazines.

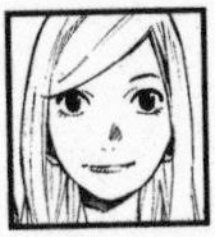

COACH: NAOKO NŌMI

A legend in Japanese girls soccer. Has now retired and become a coach at Warabi Seinan.

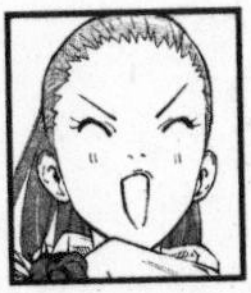

(9) AYA SHIRATORI (1ST-YEAR)

The excessively loud self-proclaimed center forward. Is a bit of a clown, but is able to make most of her shots when feet aren't involved.

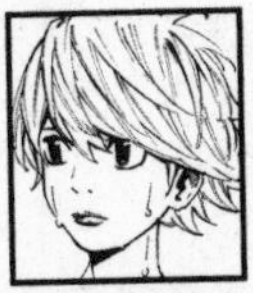

(10) SUMIRE SUŌ (1ST-YEAR)

A winger with overwhelming speed. She doesn't talk much, but when she does, it isn't nice.

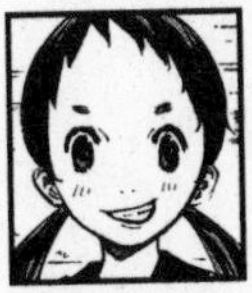

(4) MIDORI SOSHIZAKI (1ST-YEAR)

Played defensive midfielder for Todakita Middle School, which landed third in the country. Surprisingly geeky.

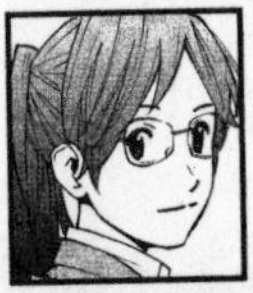

(2) MAKOTO MIYASAKA (2ND-YEAR)

A reliable second-year who leads the team's defense.

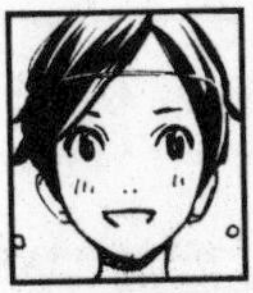

(7) ERIKO TASE (2ND-YEAR)

Team captain. A kind and responsible girl who is the glue that holds this very disparate team together.

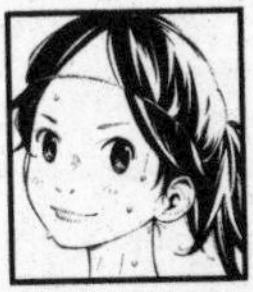

(8) NOZOMI ONDA (1ST-YEAR)

A charismatic midfielder who played for a boys team in middle school.

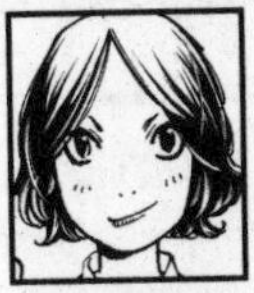

(3) RUI KIKUCHI (2ND-YEAR)

In charge of designing the team uniforms.

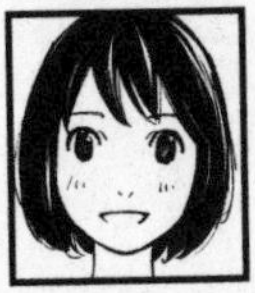

(13) SAWA ECHIZEN (1ST-YEAR)

Joined the team as a manager, but has recently started playing on the team as well.

Kōrenkan High School Formation

3—4—3

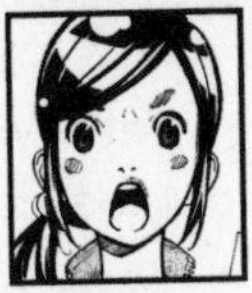

UMI FUJIE (3RD-YEAR)

No longer plays due to a leg injury, but was a central figure in building the current team.

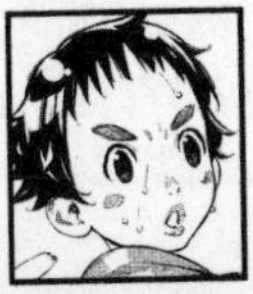

(21) UME FUJIE (1ST-YEAR)

Umi's younger sister. She may be small, but she's a brilliant wingback with several tricks up her sleeve.

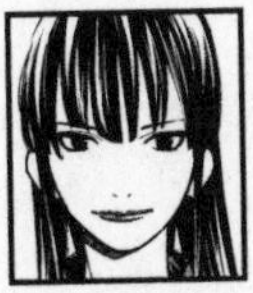

(11) MIKA KURUSU (2ND-YEAR)

The scoring queen of the inter-high tournament. The high school has a fan club for her, and she is actually extremely self-centered.

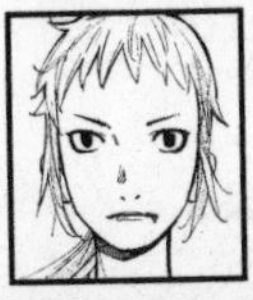

(15) REI KUTANI (1ST-YEAR)

Kōrenkan's duelist. Appears to have a grudge against Onda since the futsal tournament....

CONTENTS

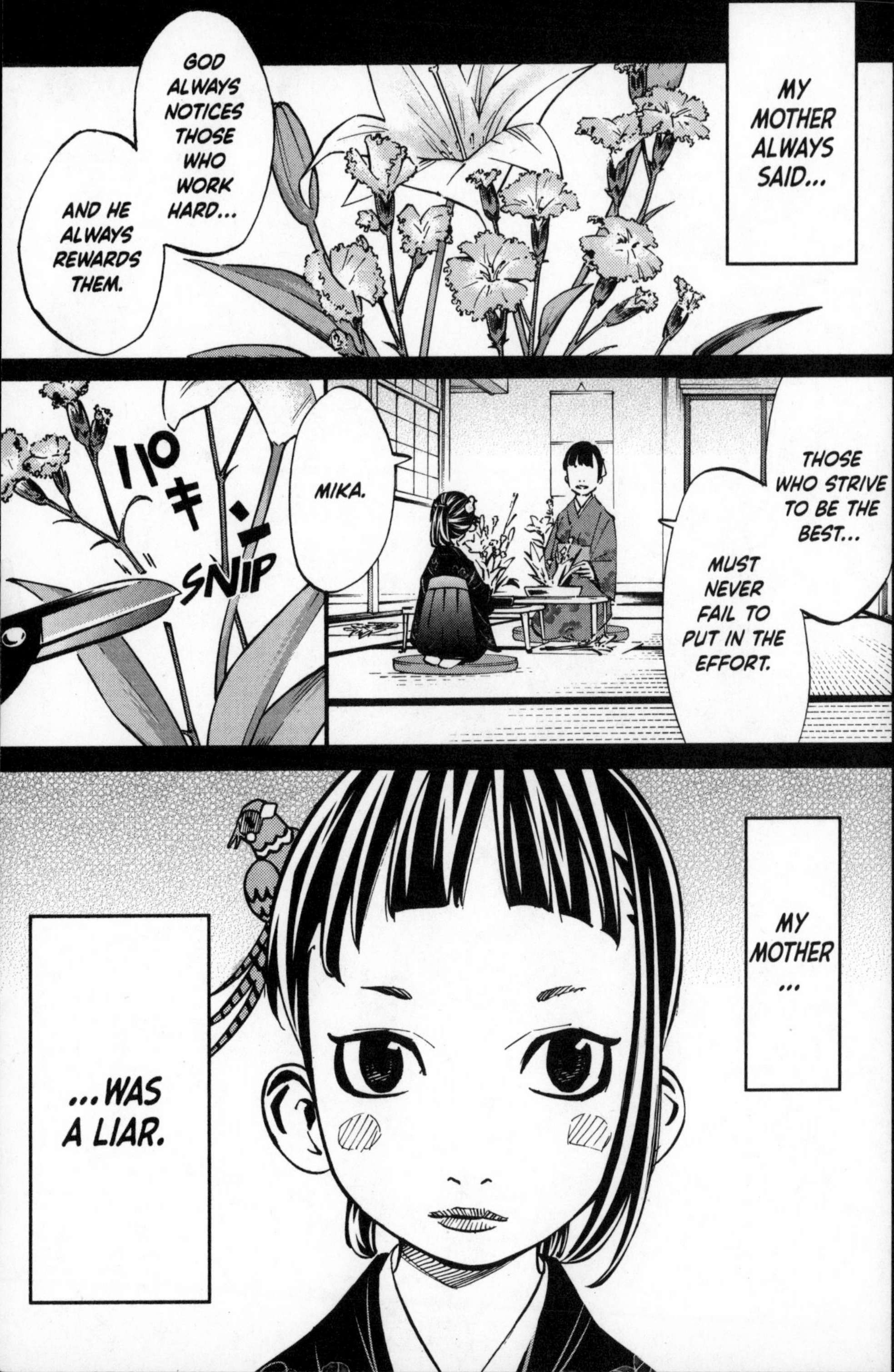
MY MOTHER ALWAYS SAID...
GOD ALWAYS NOTICES THOSE WHO WORK HARD...
AND HE ALWAYS REWARDS THEM.
THOSE WHO STRIVE TO BE THE BEST...
MUST NEVER FAIL TO PUT IN THE EFFORT.
MIKA.
パキン
SNIP
MY MOTHER...
...WAS A LIAR.

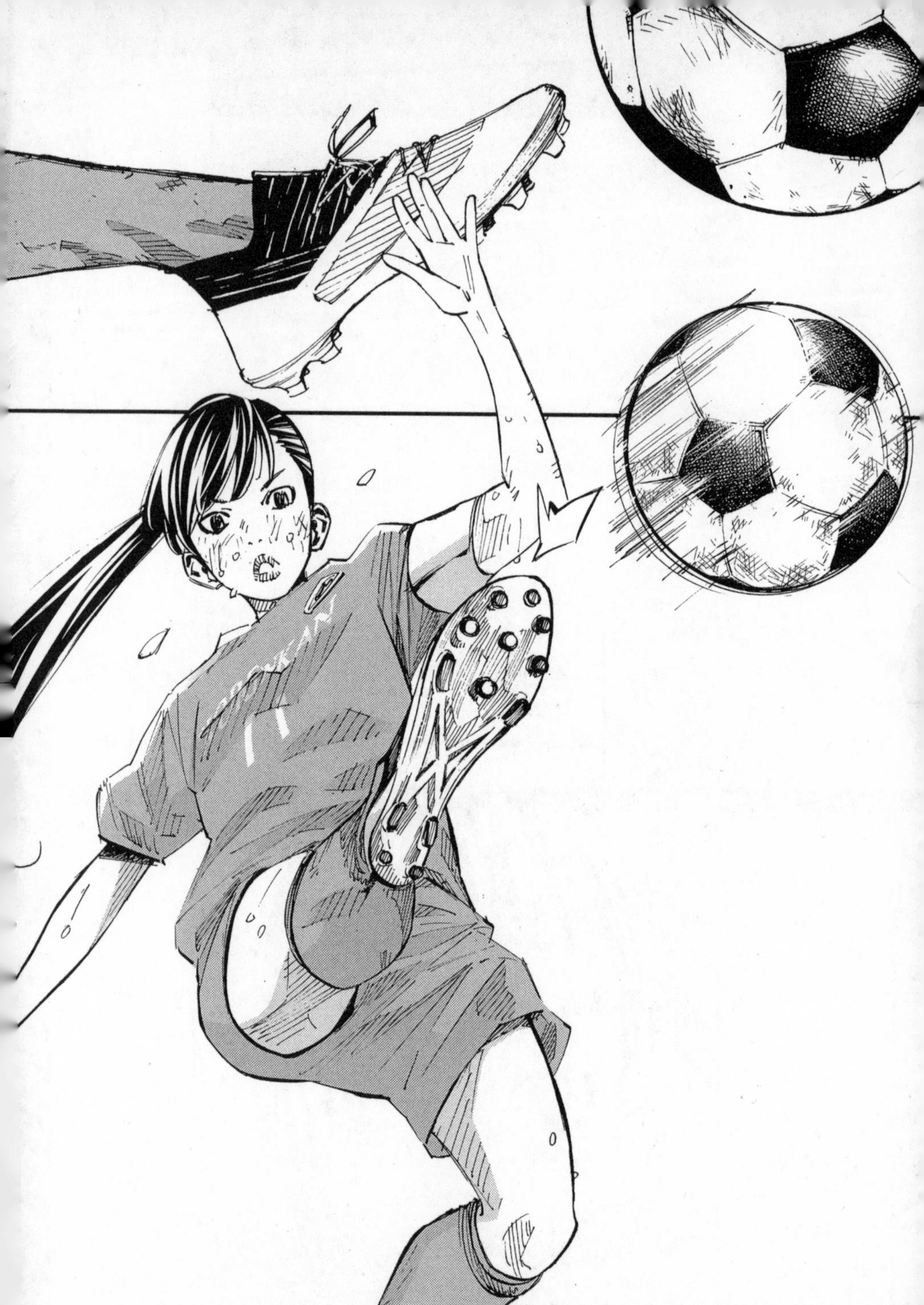

48. A FLOWER TAKING ROOT

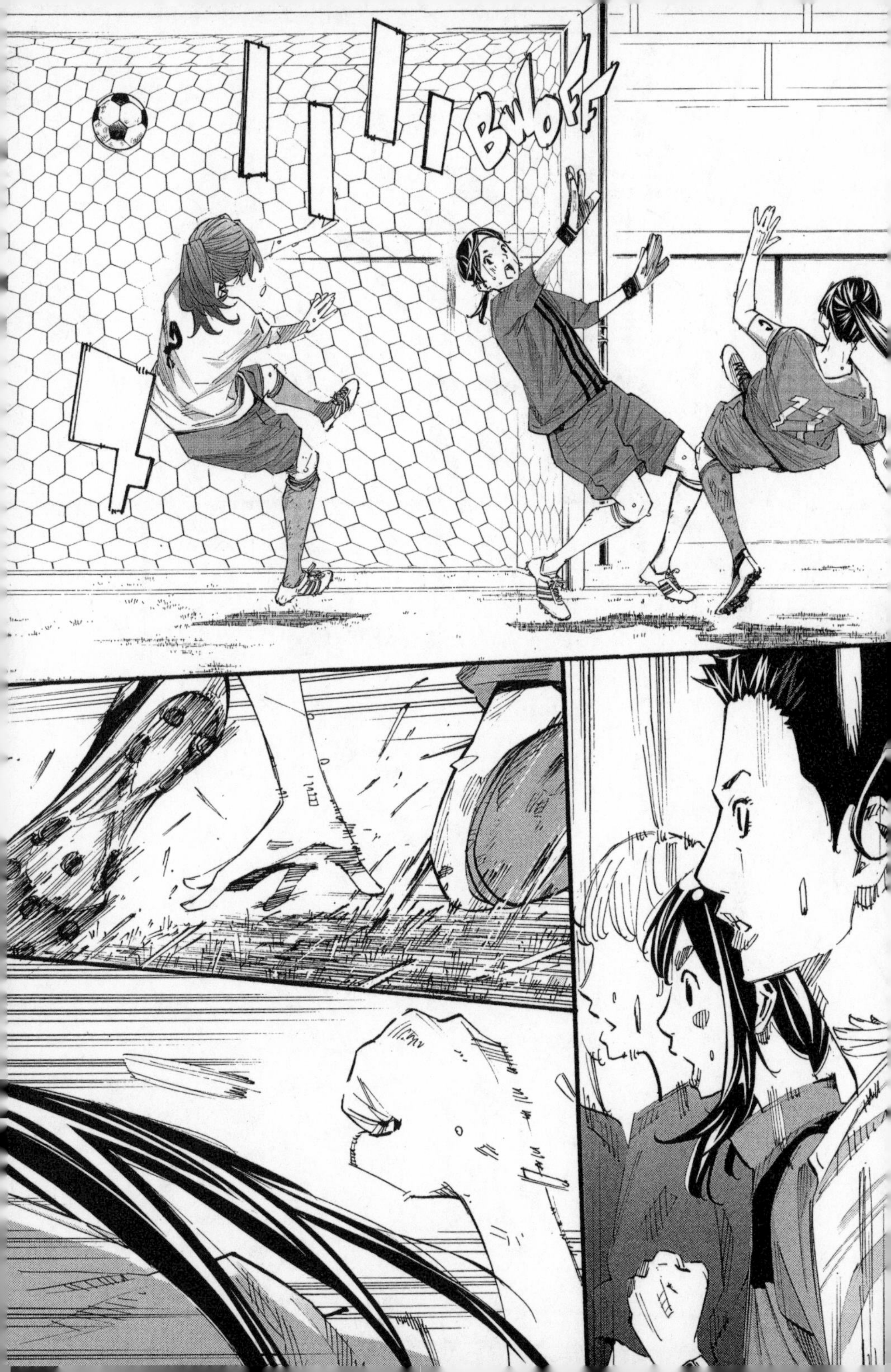
BWOFF

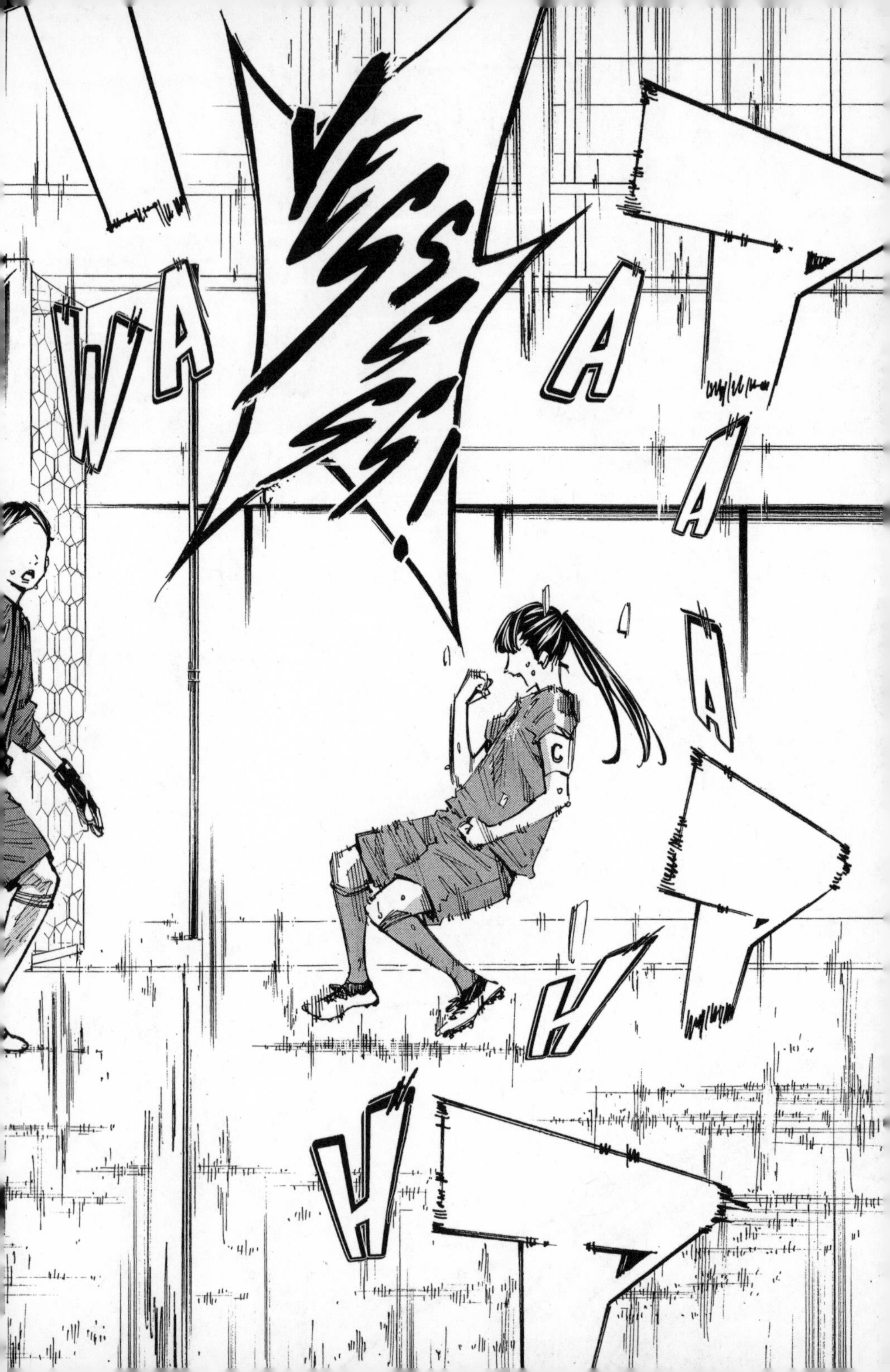
YESSSSSS!
WAAAAAHH

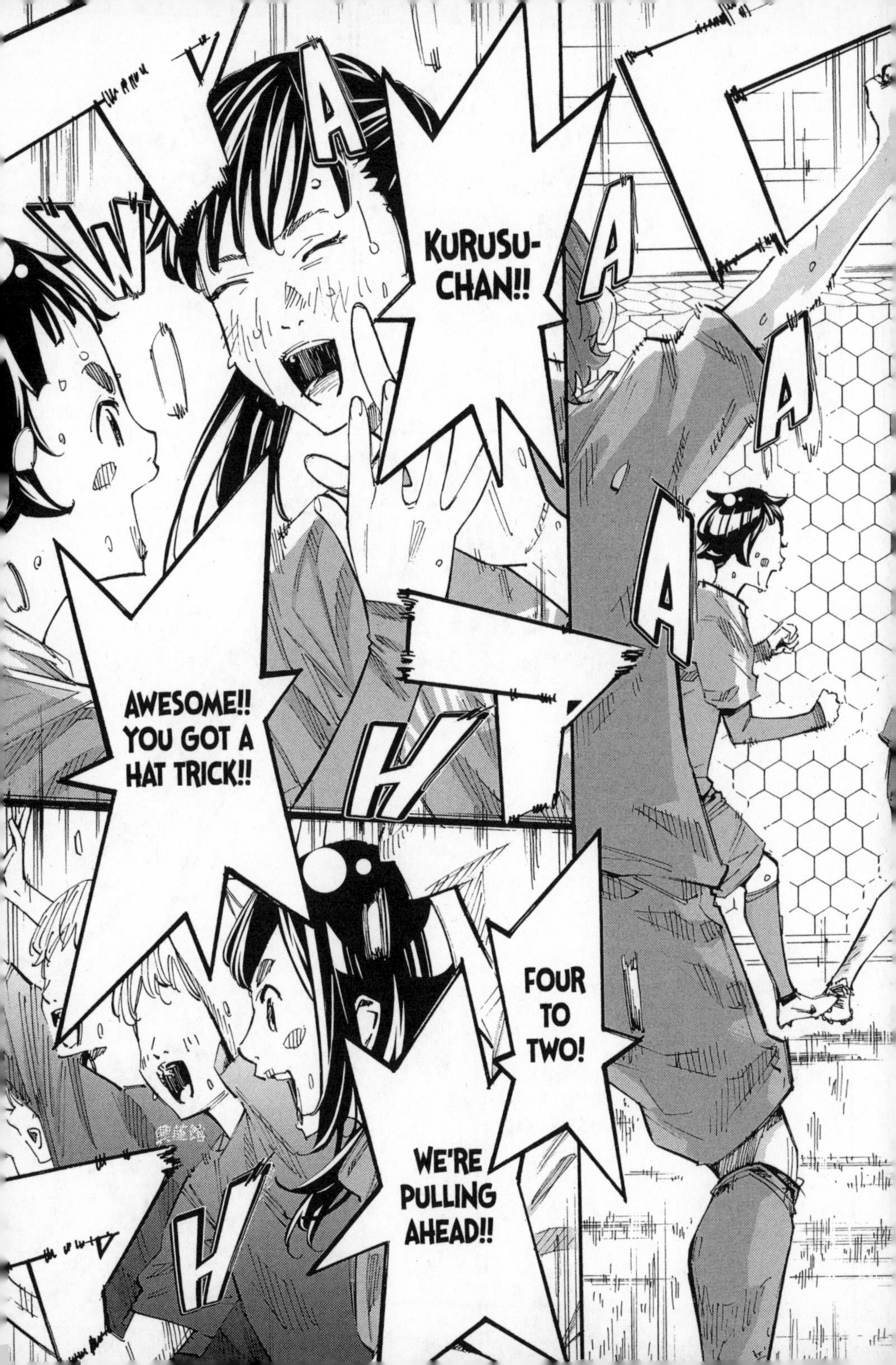
KURUSU-CHAN!!
AWESOME!! YOU GOT A HAT TRICK!!
FOUR TO TWO!
WE'RE PULLING AHEAD!!

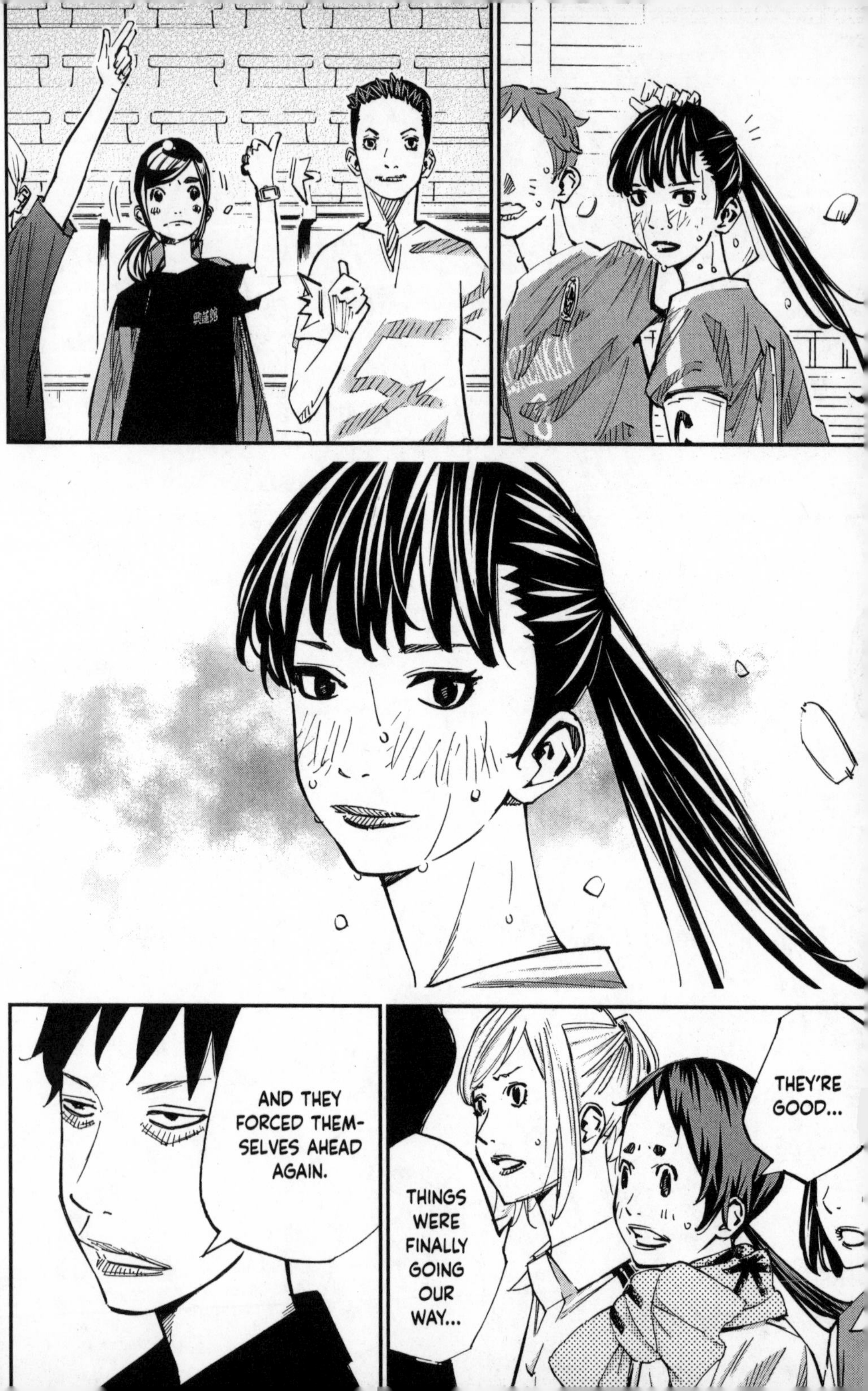
THEY'RE GOOD...
THINGS WERE FINALLY GOING OUR WAY...
AND THEY FORCED THEM-SELVES AHEAD AGAIN.

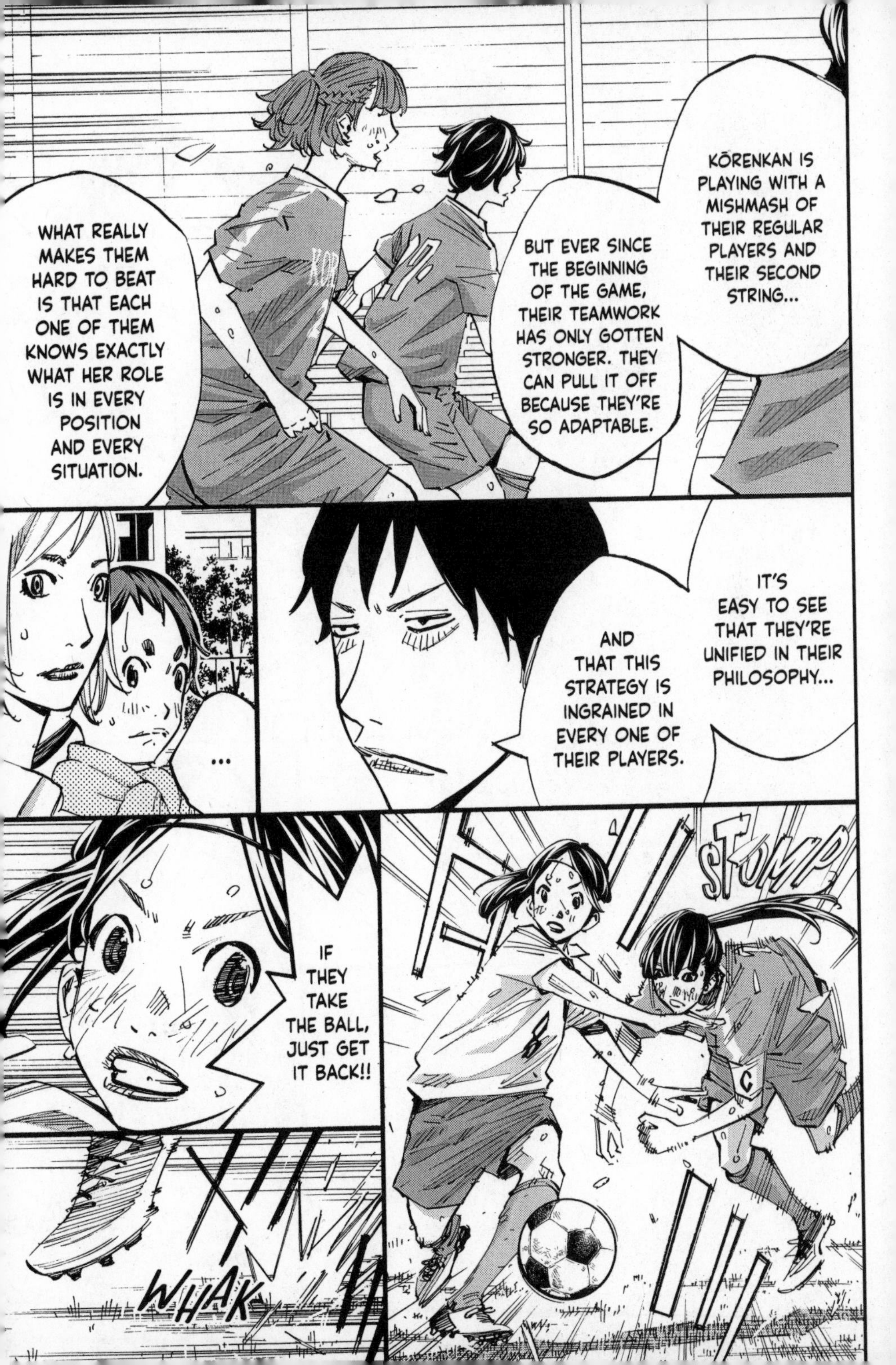
KŌRENKAN IS PLAYING WITH A MISHMASH OF THEIR REGULAR PLAYERS AND THEIR SECOND STRING...
BUT EVER SINCE THE BEGINNING OF THE GAME, THEIR TEAMWORK HAS ONLY GOTTEN STRONGER. THEY CAN PULL IT OFF BECAUSE THEY'RE SO ADAPTABLE.
WHAT REALLY MAKES THEM HARD TO BEAT IS THAT EACH ONE OF THEM KNOWS EXACTLY WHAT HER ROLE IS IN EVERY POSITION AND EVERY SITUATION.
IT'S EASY TO SEE THAT THEY'RE UNIFIED IN THEIR PHILOSOPHY...
AND THAT THIS STRATEGY IS INGRAINED IN EVERY ONE OF THEIR PLAYERS.
...
STOMP
IF THEY TAKE THE BALL, JUST GET IT BACK!!
WHAK

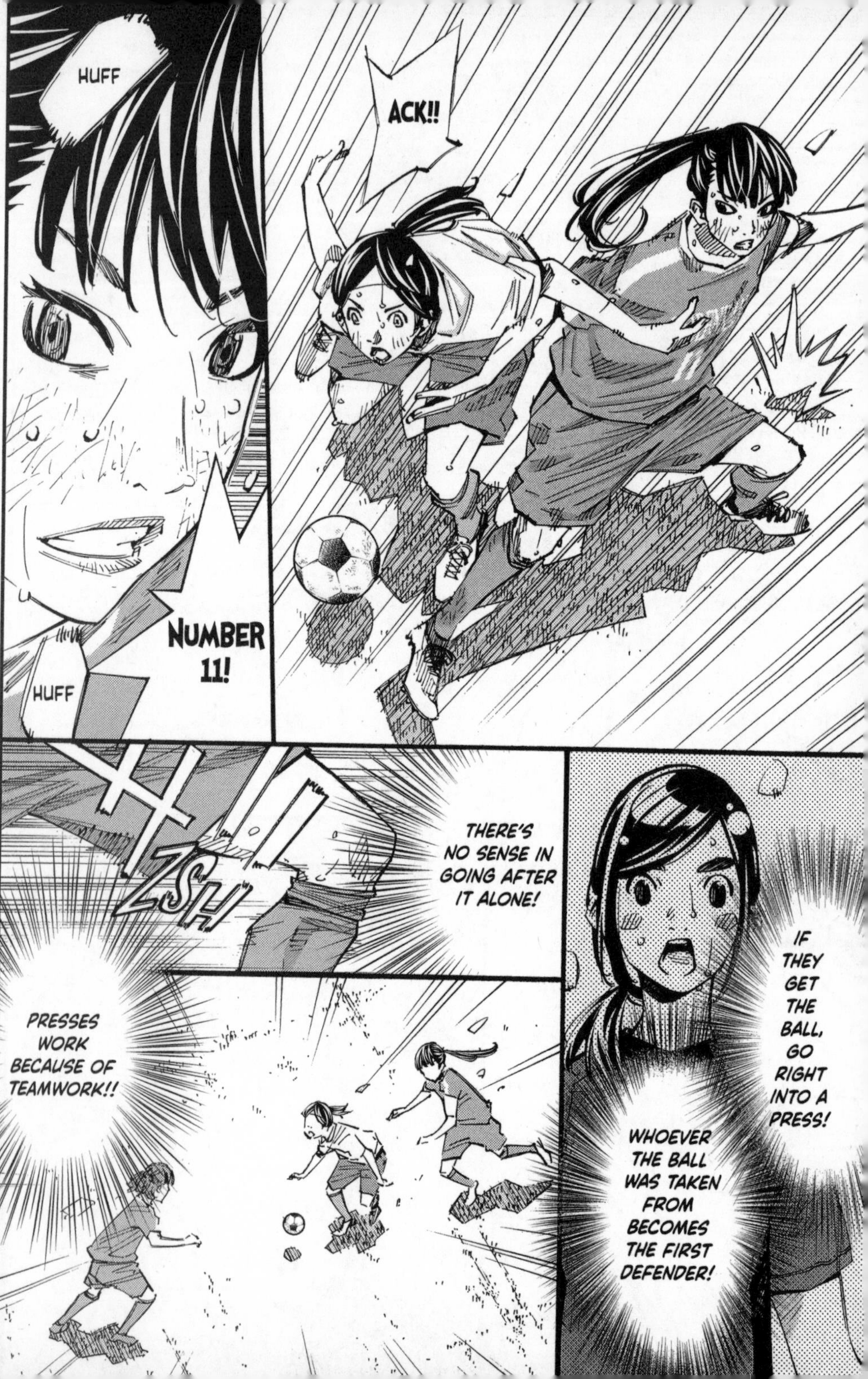
ACK!!
HUFF
NUMBER 11!
HUFF
IF THEY GET THE BALL, GO RIGHT INTO A PRESS!
WHOEVER THE BALL WAS TAKEN FROM BECOMES THE FIRST DEFENDER!
ZSH
THERE'S NO SENSE IN GOING AFTER IT ALONE!
PRESSES WORK BECAUSE OF TEAMWORK!!

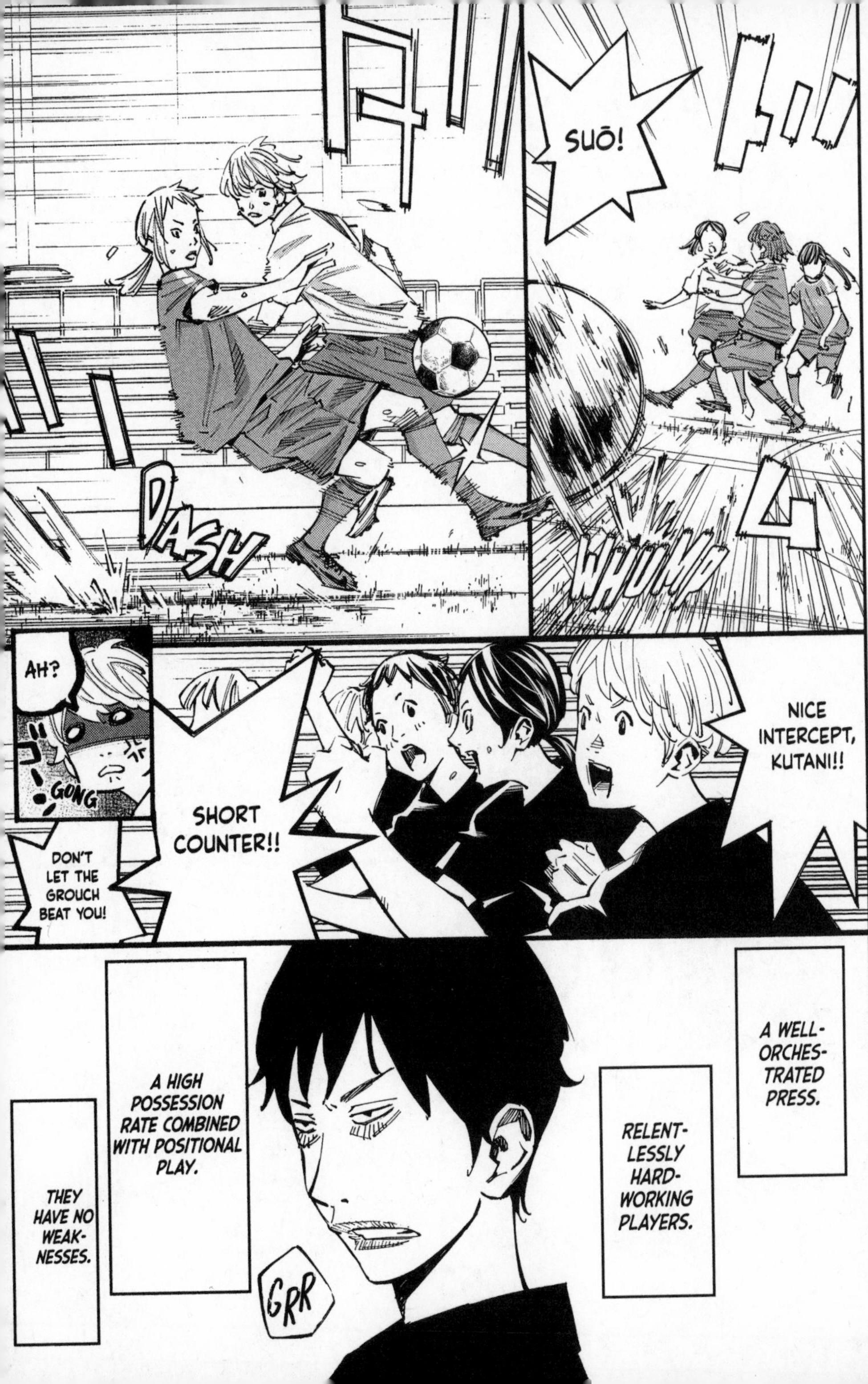
SUŌ!
WHUMP
DASH
NICE INTERCEPT, KUTANI!!
SHORT COUNTER!!
DON'T LET THE GROUCH BEAT YOU!
AH?
GONG
A WELL-ORCHESTRATED PRESS.
RELENTLESSLY HARD-WORKING PLAYERS.
A HIGH POSSESSION RATE COMBINED WITH POSITIONAL PLAY.
THEY HAVE NO WEAKNESSES.
GRR

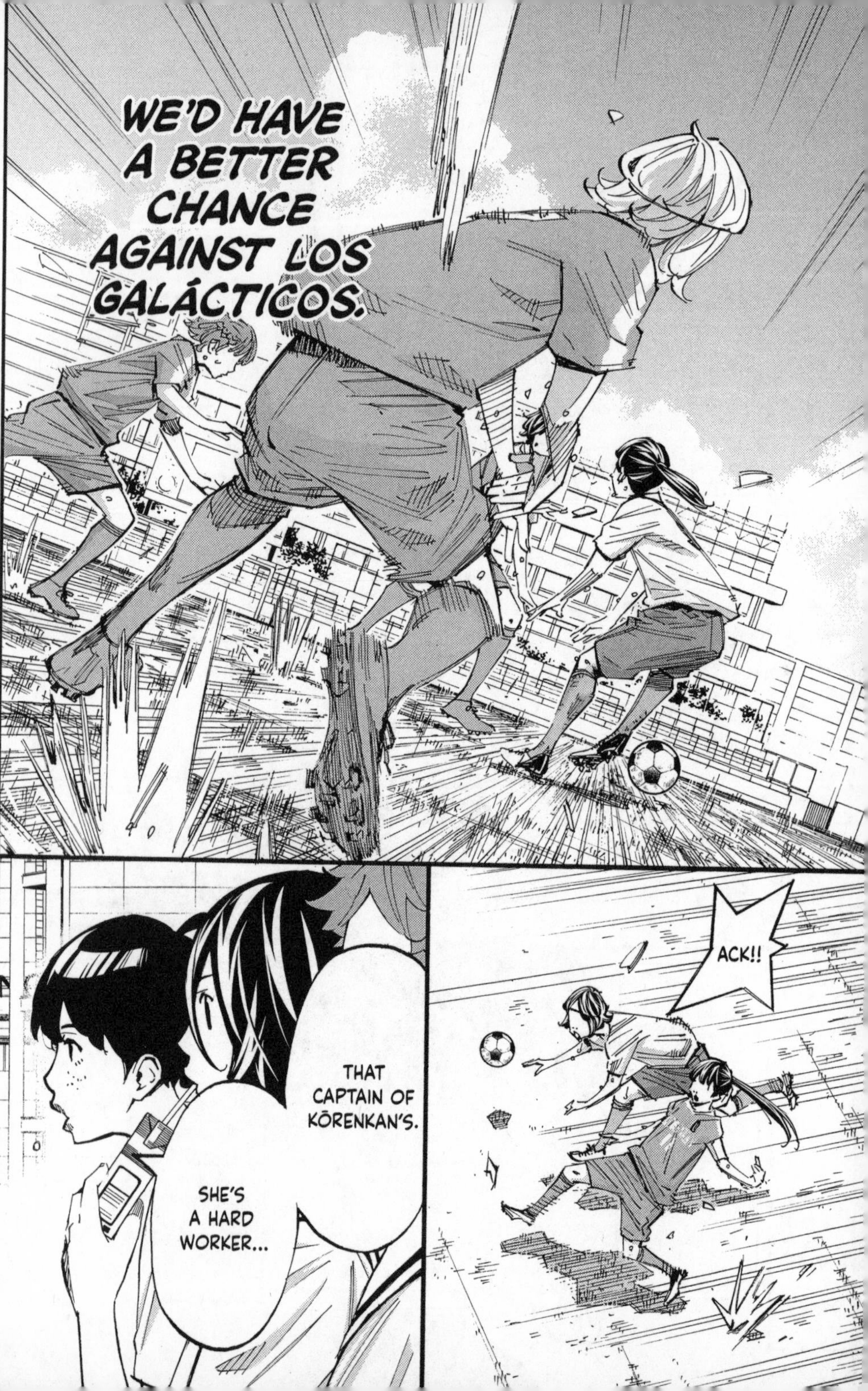

WE'D HAVE A BETTER CHANCE AGAINST LOS GALÁCTICOS.
ACK!!
THAT CAPTAIN OF KŌRENKAN'S.
SHE'S A HARD WORKER...

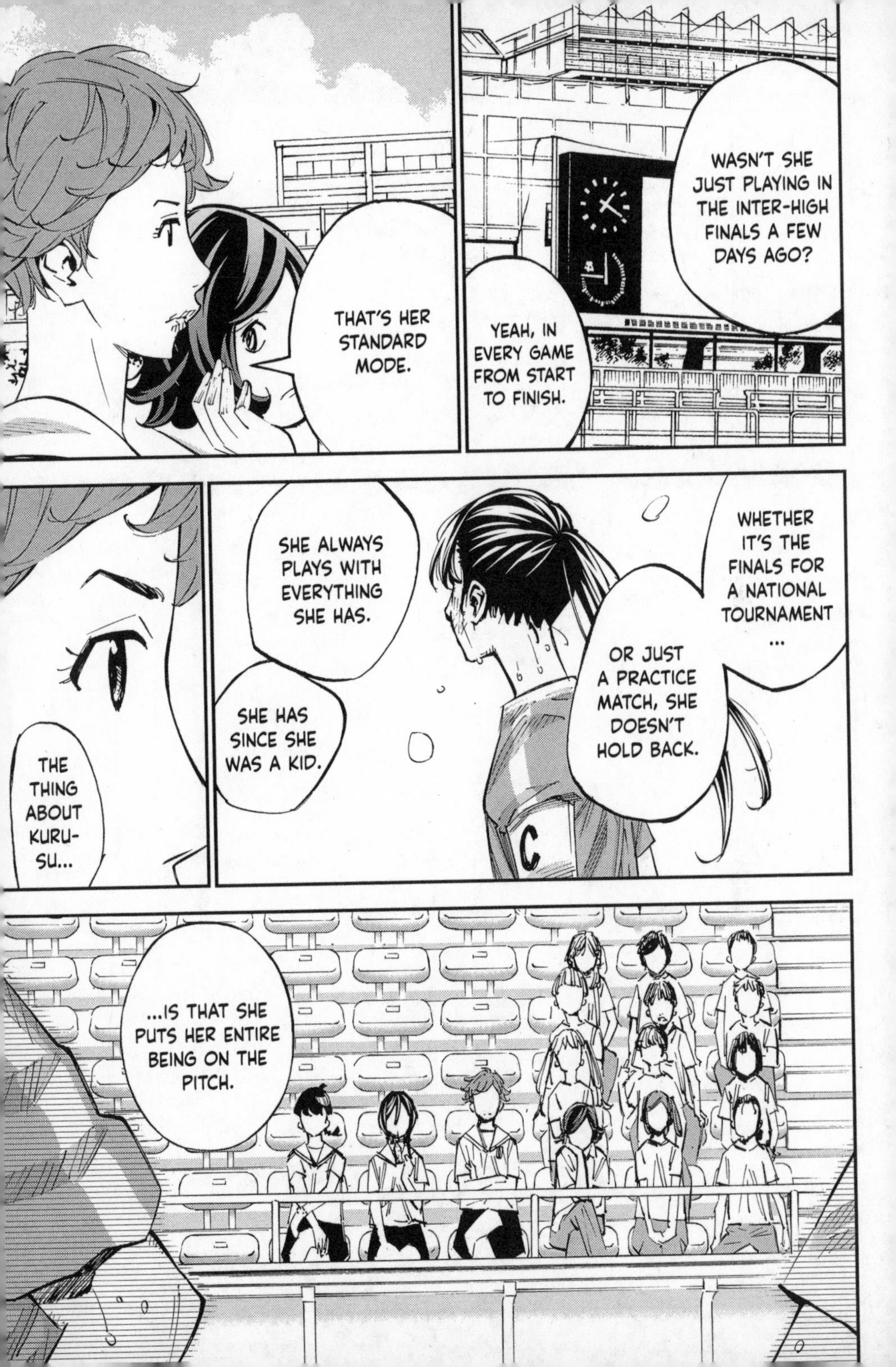
WASN'T SHE JUST PLAYING IN THE INTER-HIGH FINALS A FEW DAYS AGO?
YEAH, IN EVERY GAME FROM START TO FINISH.
THAT'S HER STANDARD MODE.
WHETHER IT'S THE FINALS FOR A NATIONAL TOURNAMENT...
OR JUST A PRACTICE MATCH, SHE DOESN'T HOLD BACK.
SHE ALWAYS PLAYS WITH EVERYTHING SHE HAS.
SHE HAS SINCE SHE WAS A KID.
THE THING ABOUT KURUSU...
...IS THAT SHE PUTS HER ENTIRE BEING ON THE PITCH.

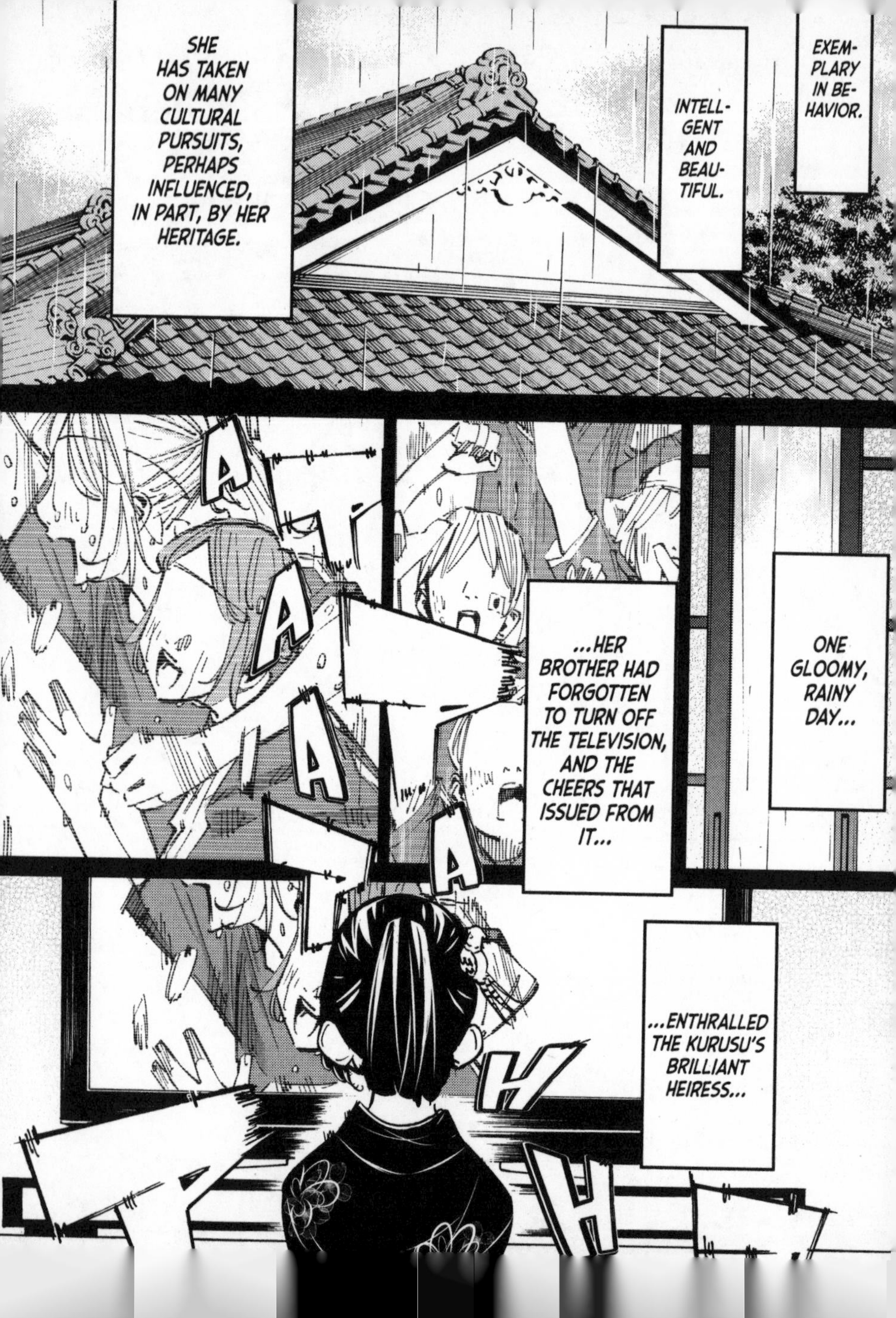
EXEM-PLARY IN BE-HAVIOR.
INTELL-GENT AND BEAU-TIFUL.
SHE HAS TAKEN ON MANY CULTURAL PURSUITS, PERHAPS INFLUENCED, IN PART, BY HER HERITAGE.
ONE GLOOMY, RAINY DAY...
...HER BROTHER HAD FORGOTTEN TO TURN OFF THE TELEVISION, AND THE CHEERS THAT ISSUED FROM IT...
AAAAHH
...ENTHRALLED THE KURUSU'S BRILLIANT HEIRESS...

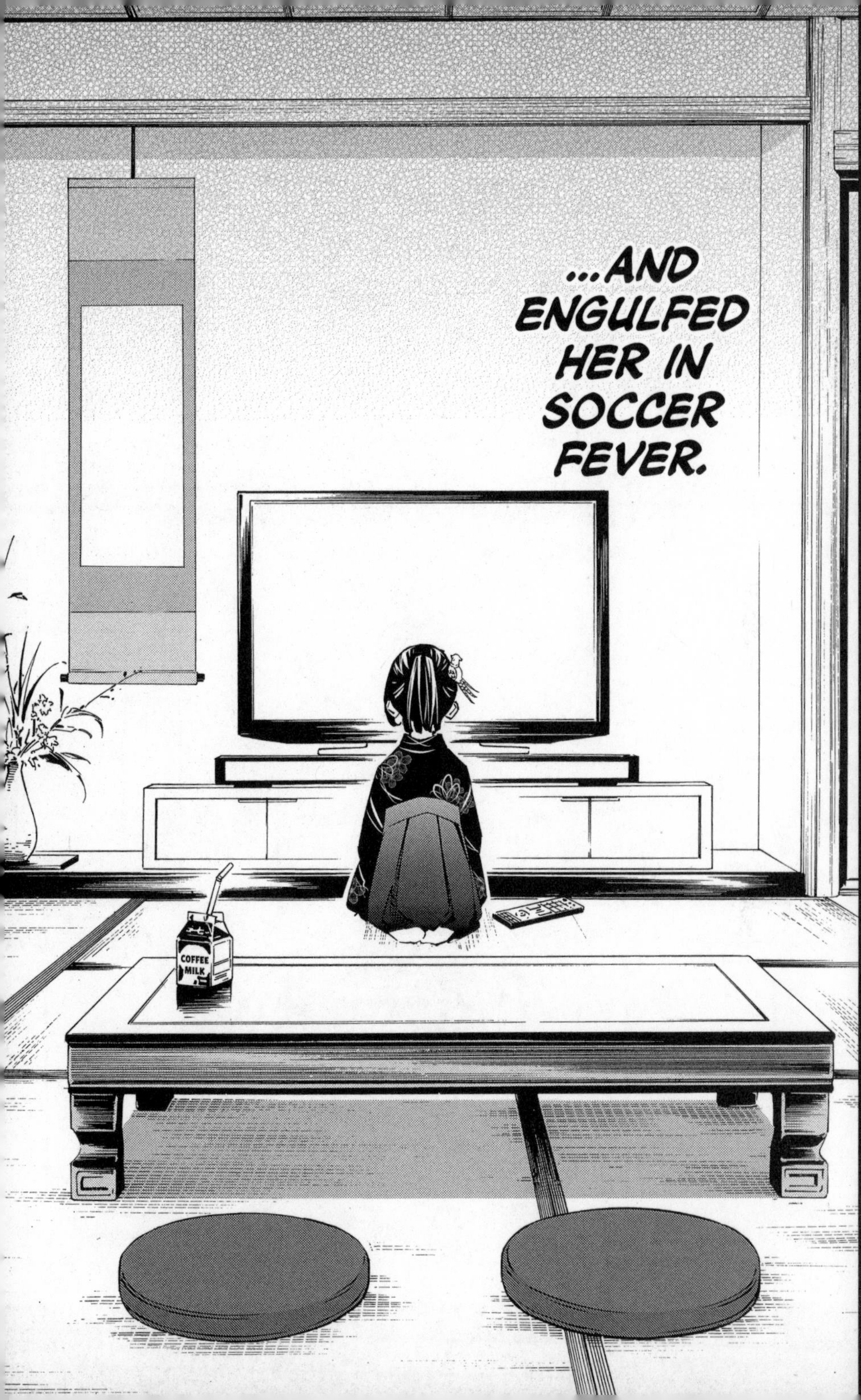
...AND ENGULFED HER IN SOCCER FEVER.
COFFEE MILK

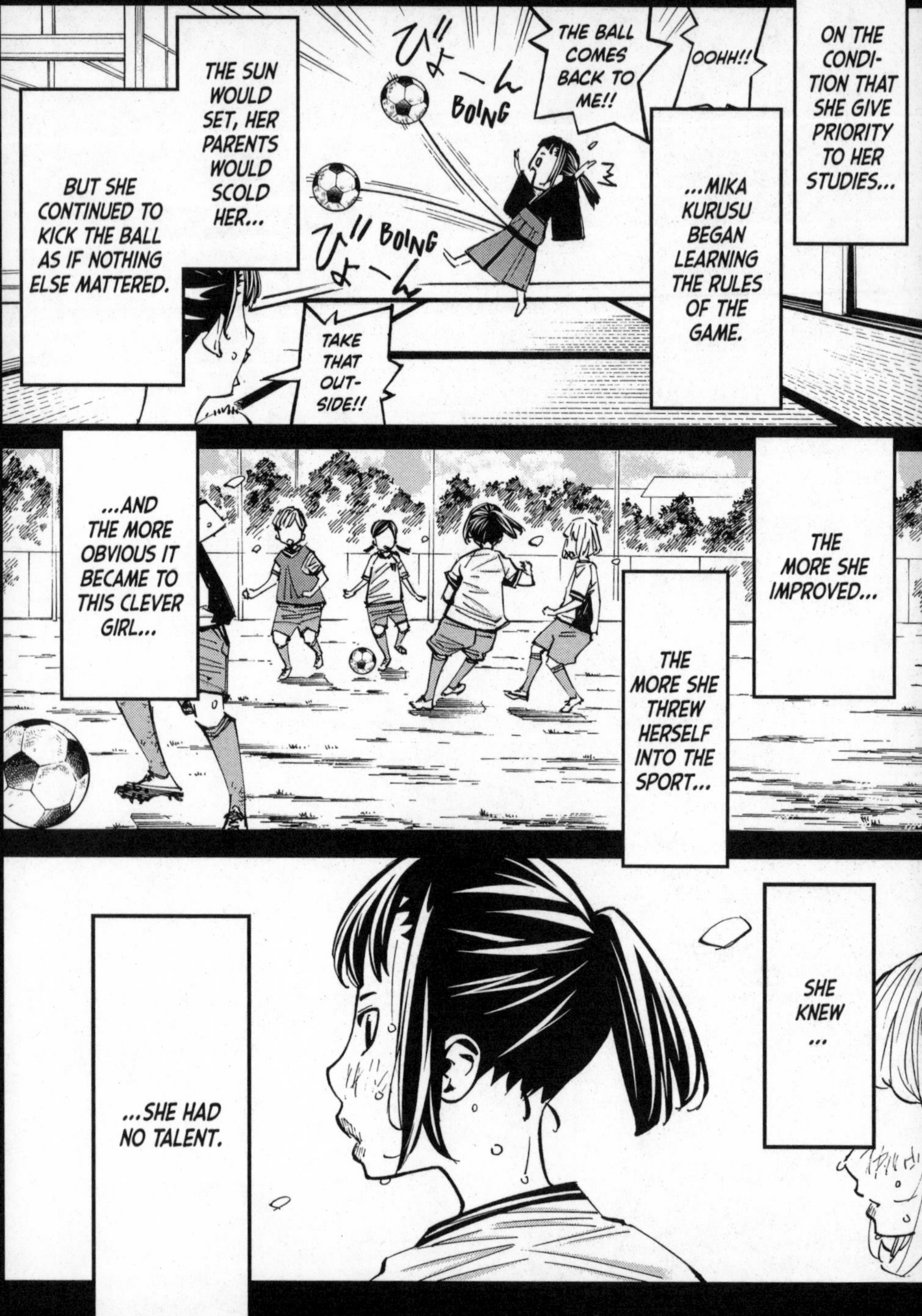
ON THE CONDITION THAT SHE GIVE PRIORITY TO HER STUDIES...
...MIKA KURUSU BEGAN LEARNING THE RULES OF THE GAME.
OOHH!!
THE BALL COMES BACK TO ME!!
びよーん
BOING
びよーん
BOING
THE SUN WOULD SET, HER PARENTS WOULD SCOLD HER...
BUT SHE CONTINUED TO KICK THE BALL AS IF NOTHING ELSE MATTERED.
TAKE THAT OUT-SIDE!!
THE MORE SHE IMPROVED...
THE MORE SHE THREW HERSELF INTO THE SPORT...
...AND THE MORE OBVIOUS IT BECAME TO THIS CLEVER GIRL...
SHE KNEW...
...SHE HAD NO TALENT.

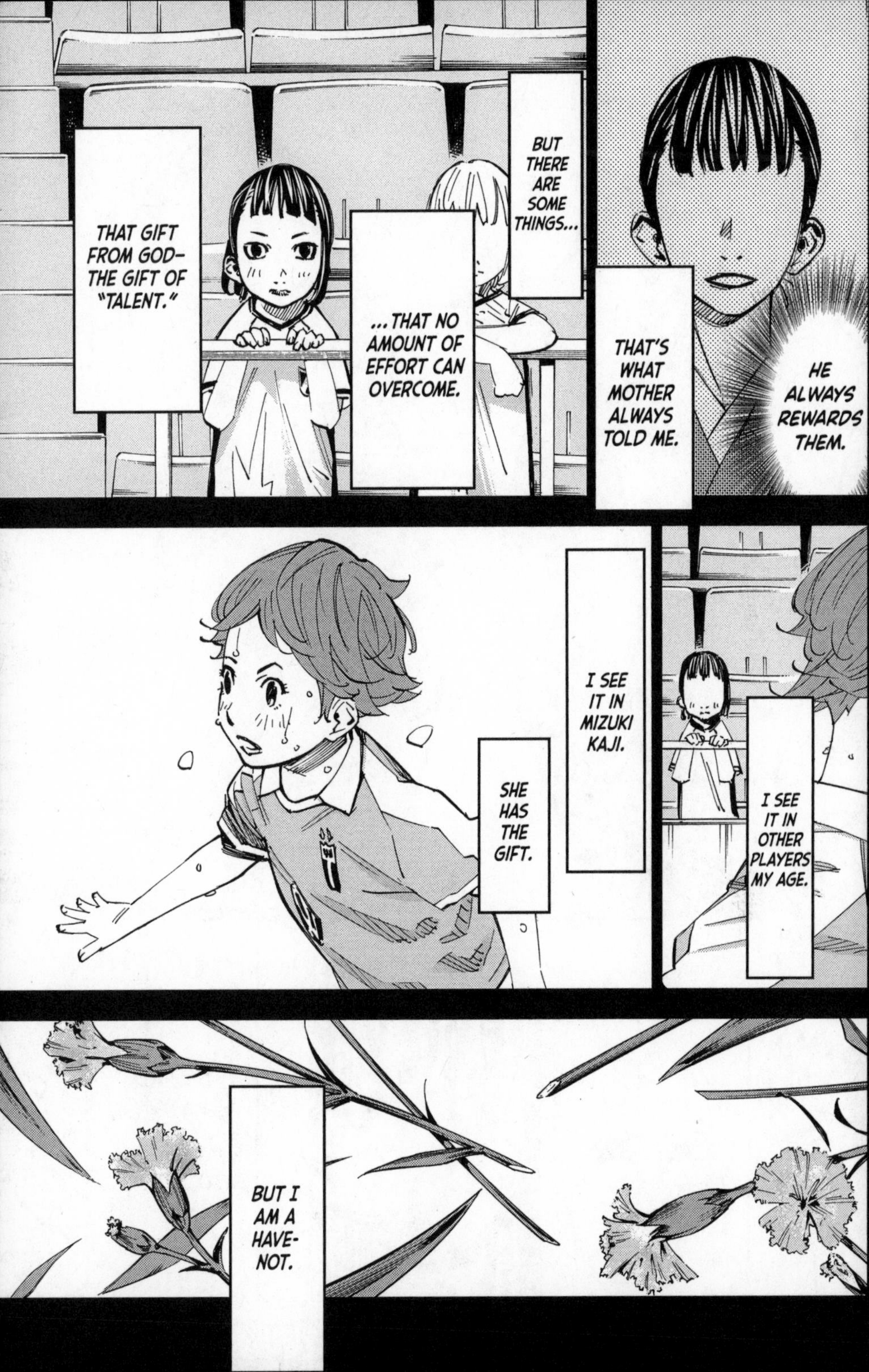
HE ALWAYS REWARDS THEM.
THAT'S WHAT MOTHER ALWAYS TOLD ME.
BUT THERE ARE SOME THINGS...
...THAT NO AMOUNT OF EFFORT CAN OVERCOME.
THAT GIFT FROM GOD—THE GIFT OF "TALENT."
I SEE IT IN OTHER PLAYERS MY AGE.
I SEE IT IN MIZUKI KAJI.
SHE HAS THE GIFT.
BUT I AM A HAVE-NOT.

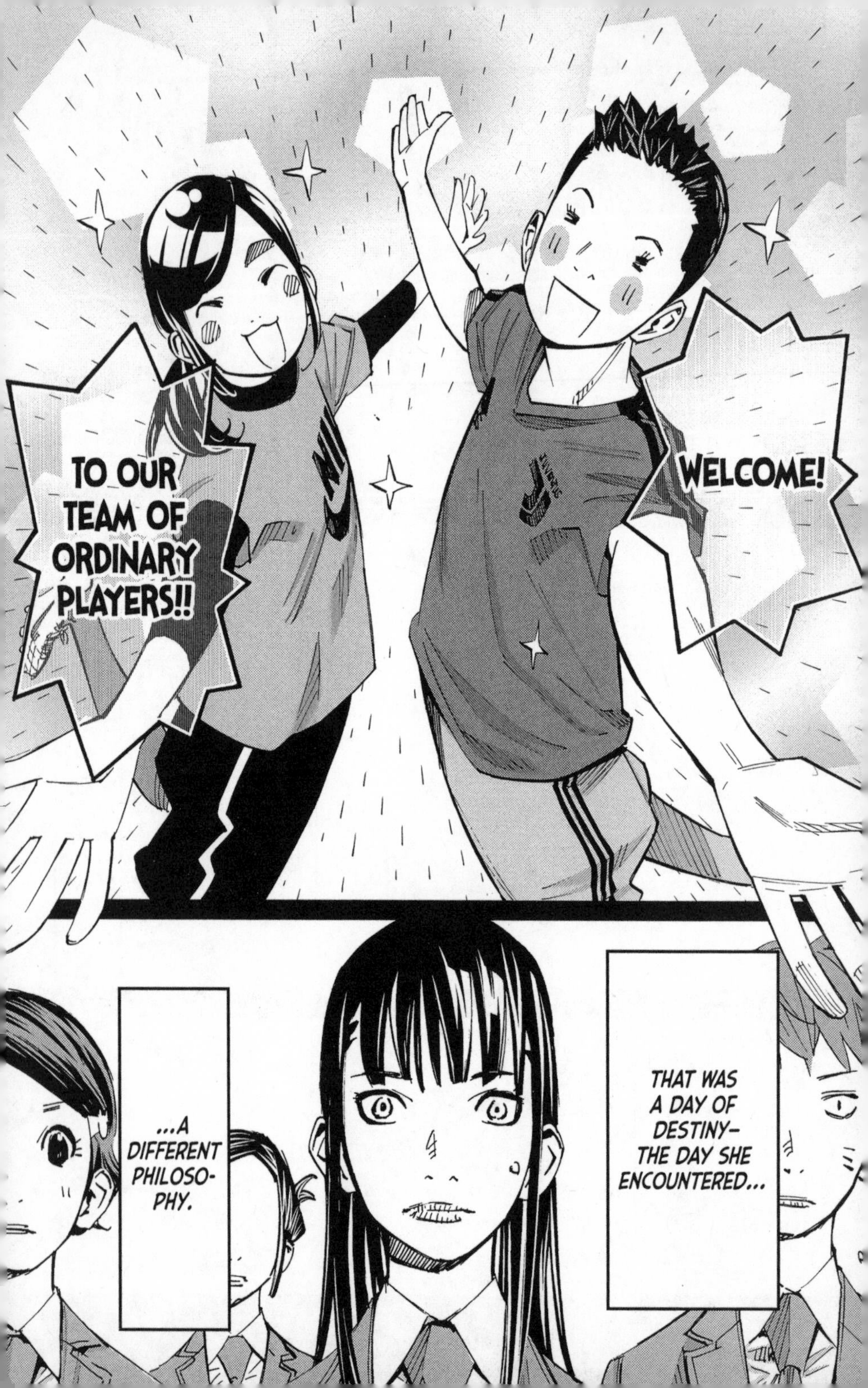
WELCOME!
TO OUR TEAM OF ORDINARY PLAYERS!!
THAT WAS A DAY OF DESTINY— THE DAY SHE ENCOUNTERED...
...A DIFFERENT PHILOSO-PHY.

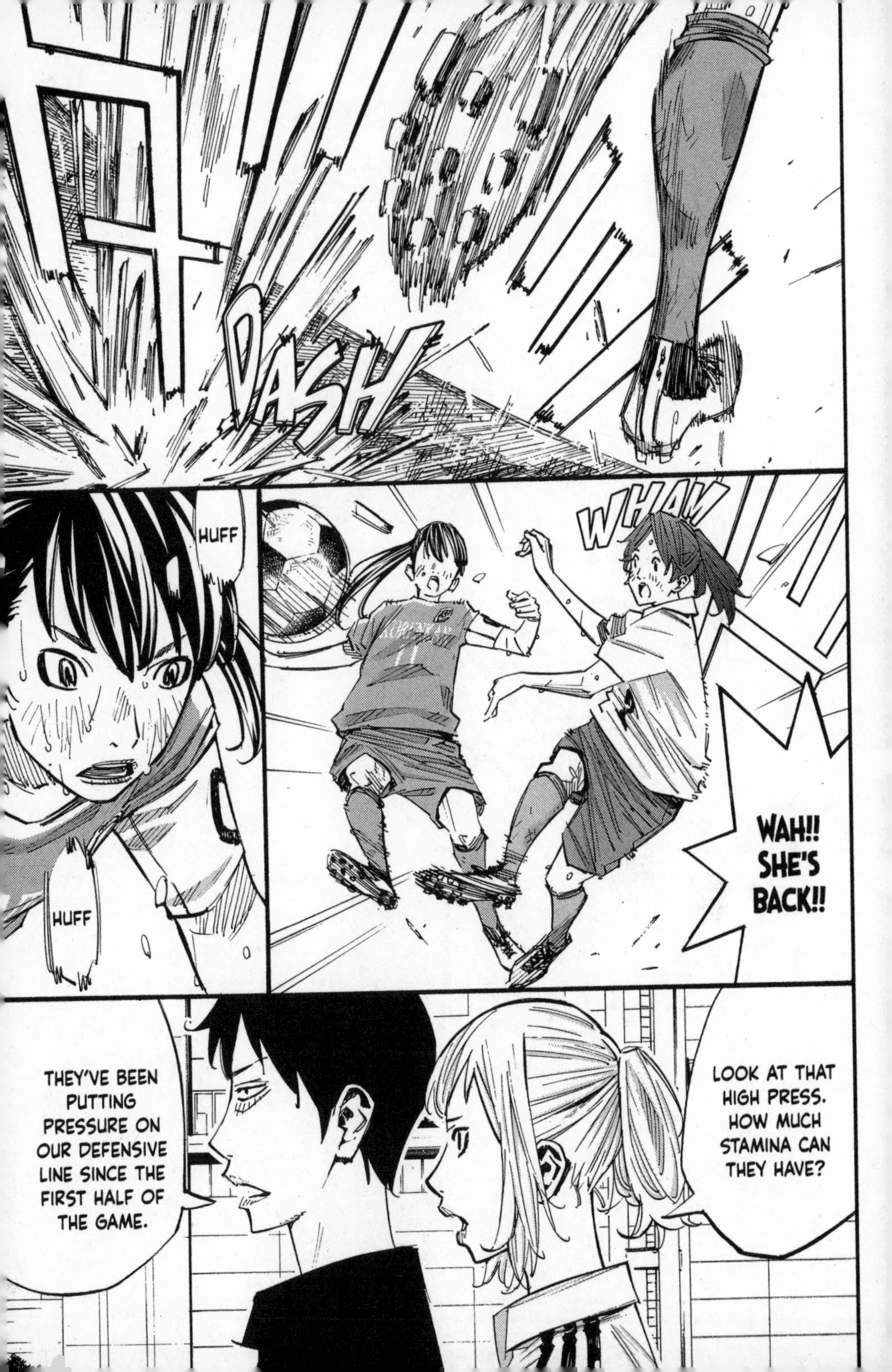
DASH
WHAM
WAH!! SHE'S BACK!!
HUFF
HUFF
LOOK AT THAT HIGH PRESS. HOW MUCH STAMINA CAN THEY HAVE?
THEY'VE BEEN PUTTING PRESSURE ON OUR DEFENSIVE LINE SINCE THE FIRST HALF OF THE GAME.

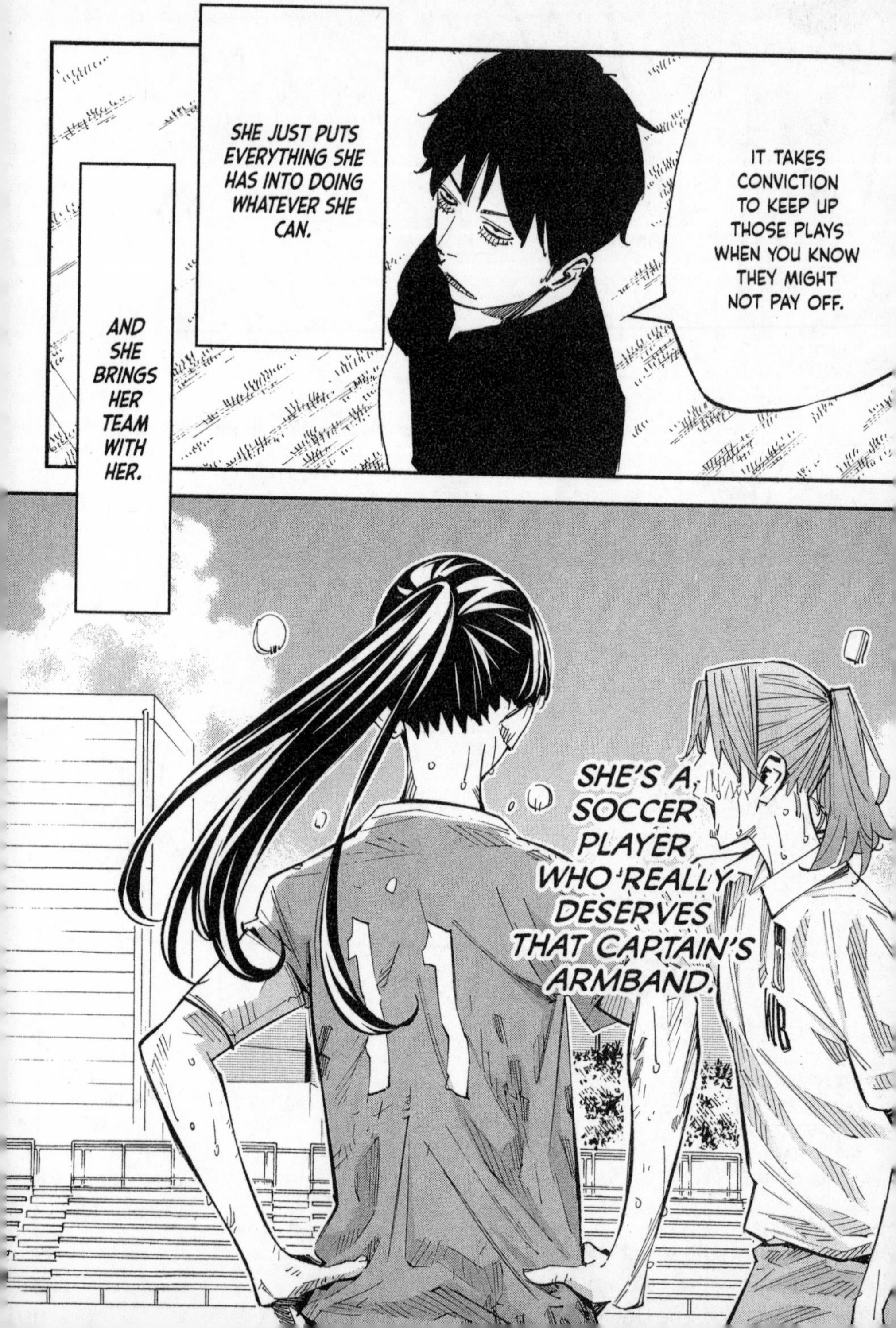
IT TAKES CONVICTION TO KEEP UP THOSE PLAYS WHEN YOU KNOW THEY MIGHT NOT PAY OFF.
SHE JUST PUTS EVERYTHING SHE HAS INTO DOING WHATEVER SHE CAN.
AND SHE BRINGS HER TEAM WITH HER.
SHE'S A SOCCER PLAYER WHO REALLY DESERVES THAT CAPTAIN'S ARMBAND.

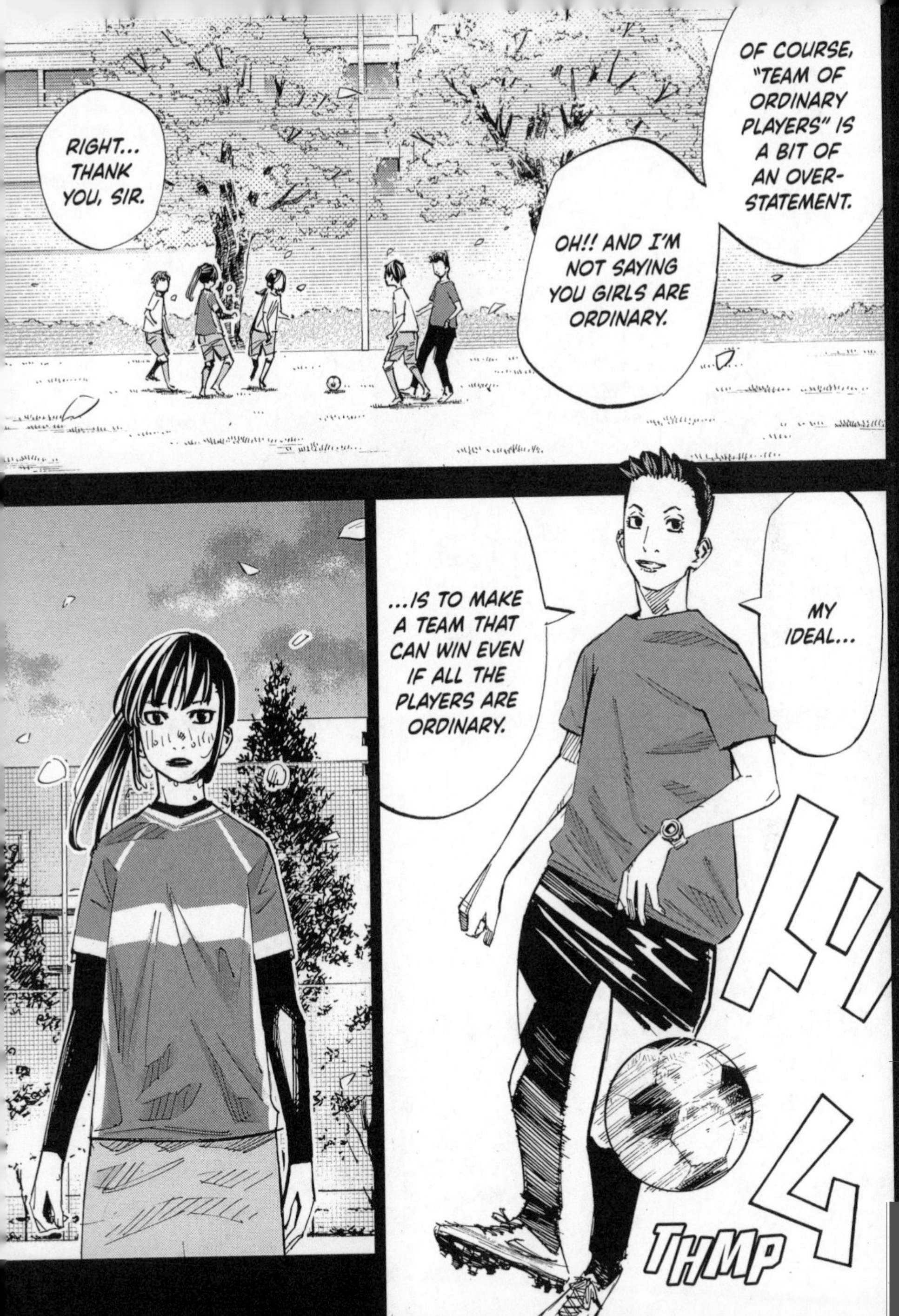
OF COURSE, "TEAM OF ORDINARY PLAYERS" IS A BIT OF AN OVER-STATEMENT.
OH!! AND I'M NOT SAYING YOU GIRLS ARE ORDINARY.
RIGHT... THANK YOU, SIR.
MY IDEAL...
...IS TO MAKE A TEAM THAT CAN WIN EVEN IF ALL THE PLAYERS ARE ORDINARY.
THMP

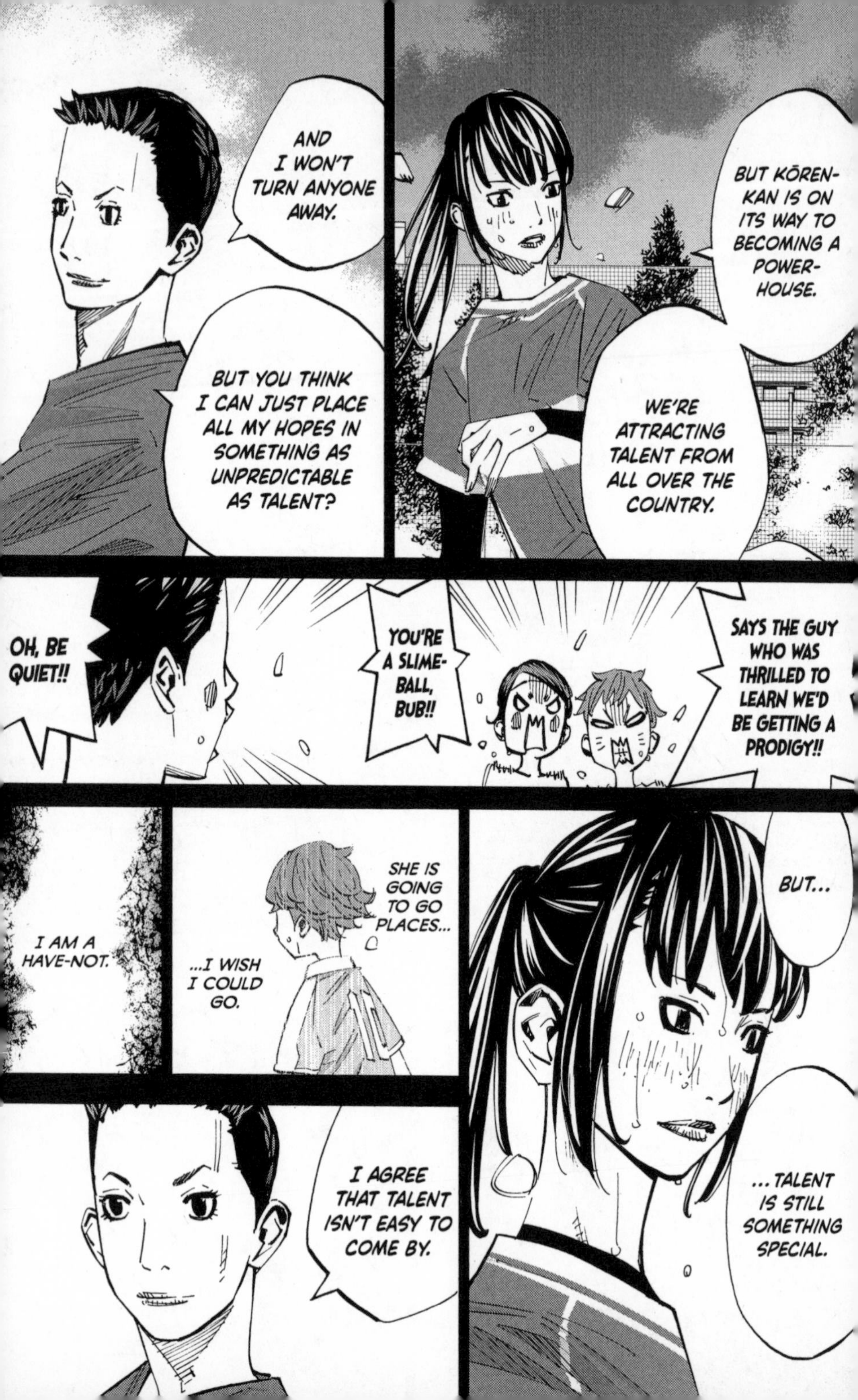
BUT KŌREN-KAN IS ON ITS WAY TO BECOMING A POWER-HOUSE.
WE'RE ATTRACTING TALENT FROM ALL OVER THE COUNTRY.
AND I WON'T TURN ANYONE AWAY.
BUT YOU THINK I CAN JUST PLACE ALL MY HOPES IN SOMETHING AS UNPREDICTABLE AS TALENT?
SAYS THE GUY WHO WAS THRILLED TO LEARN WE'D BE GETTING A PRODIGY!!
YOU'RE A SLIME-BALL, BUB!!
OH, BE QUIET!!
BUT...
...TALENT IS STILL SOMETHING SPECIAL.
SHE IS GOING TO GO PLACES...
...I WISH I COULD GO.
I AM A HAVE-NOT.
I AGREE THAT TALENT ISN'T EASY TO COME BY.

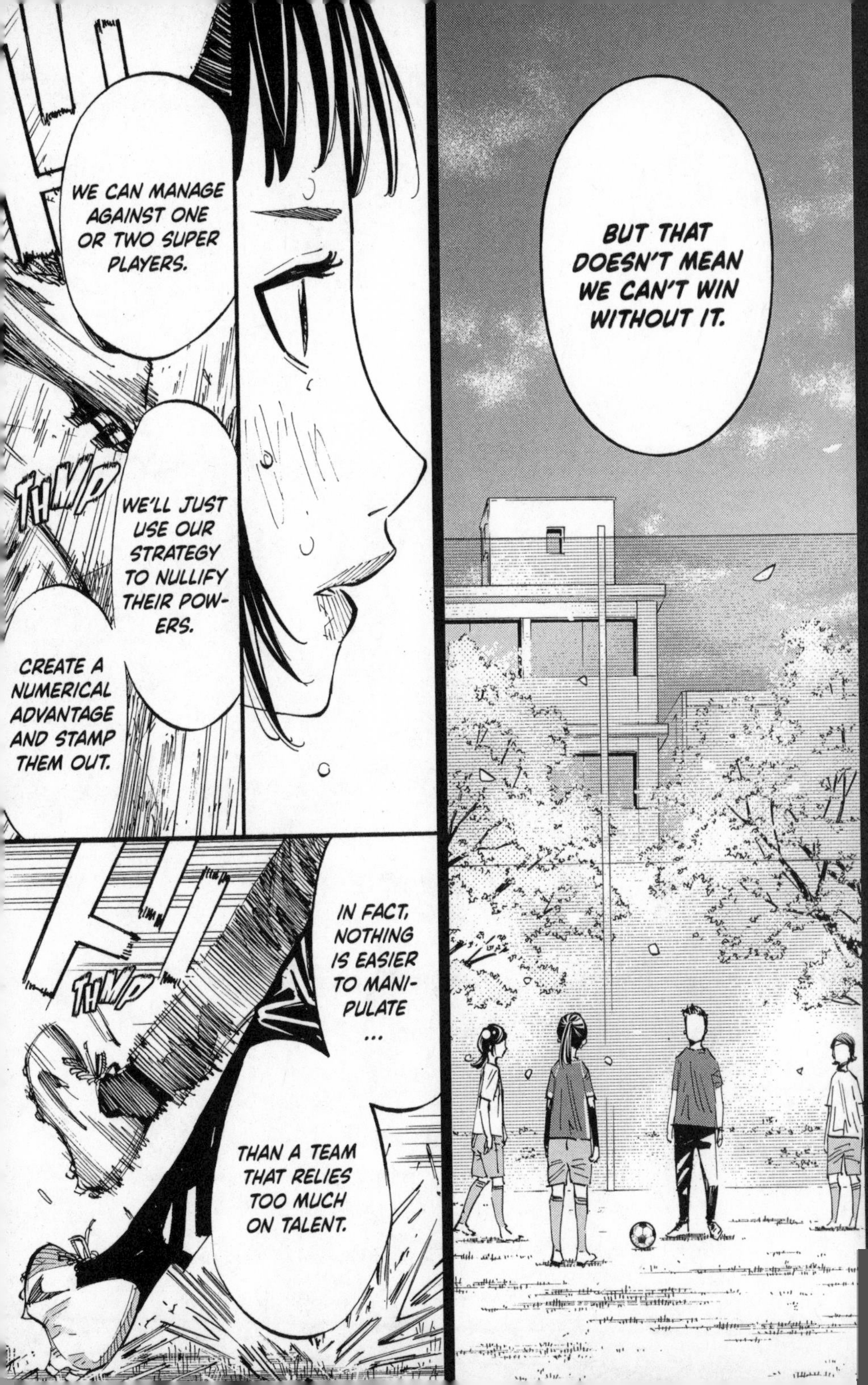
BUT THAT DOESN'T MEAN WE CAN'T WIN WITHOUT IT.
WE CAN MANAGE AGAINST ONE OR TWO SUPER PLAYERS.
WE'LL JUST USE OUR STRATEGY TO NULLIFY THEIR POW-ERS.
THMP
CREATE A NUMERICAL ADVANTAGE AND STAMP THEM OUT.
IN FACT, NOTHING IS EASIER TO MANI-PULATE ...
THMP
THAN A TEAM THAT RELIES TOO MUCH ON TALENT.

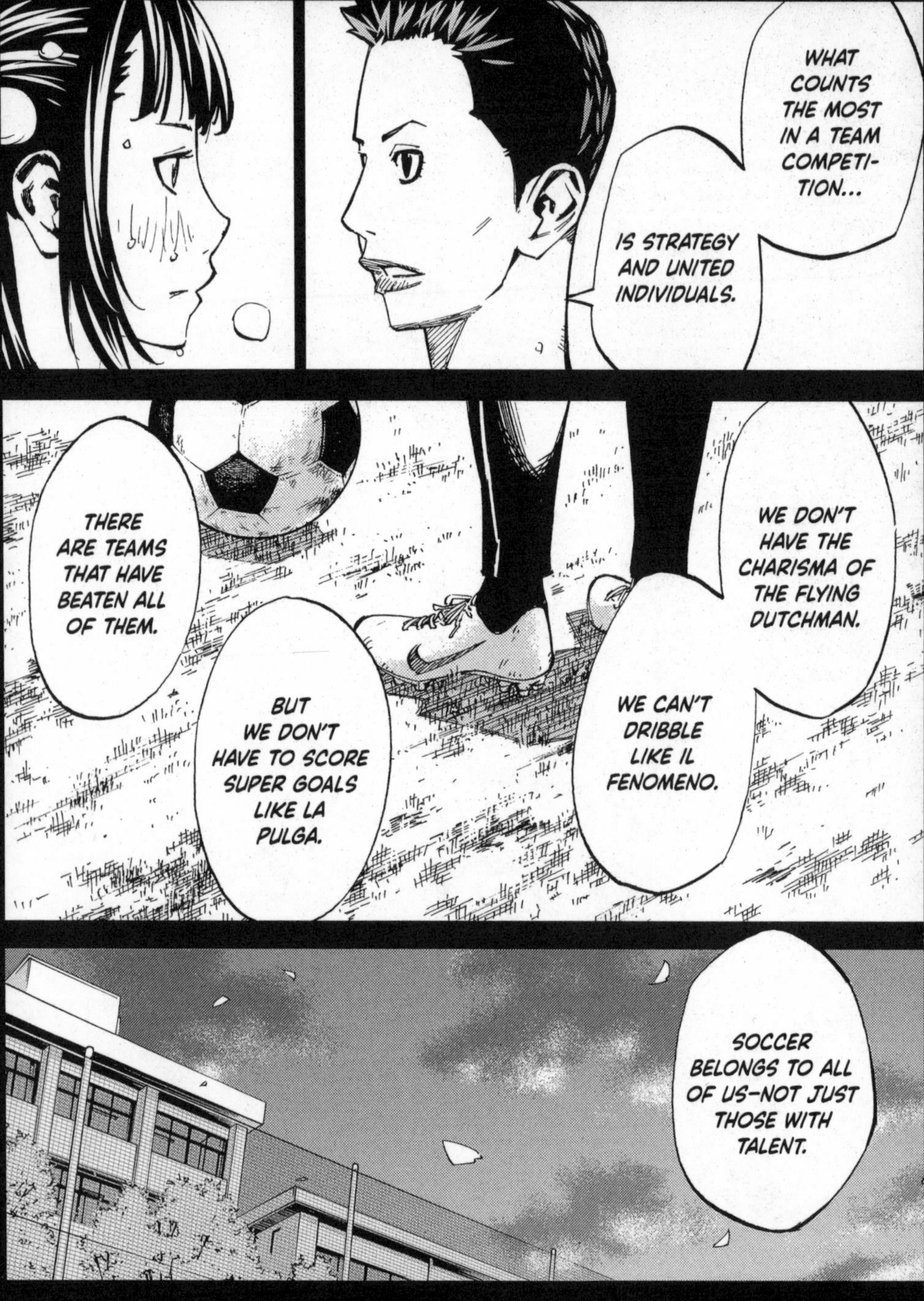
WHAT COUNTS THE MOST IN A TEAM COMPETITION...
IS STRATEGY AND UNITED INDIVIDUALS.
WE DON'T HAVE THE CHARISMA OF THE FLYING DUTCHMAN.
WE CAN'T DRIBBLE LIKE IL FENOMENO.
BUT WE DON'T HAVE TO SCORE SUPER GOALS LIKE LA PULGA.
THERE ARE TEAMS THAT HAVE BEATEN ALL OF THEM.
SOCCER BELONGS TO ALL OF US—NOT JUST THOSE WITH TALENT.

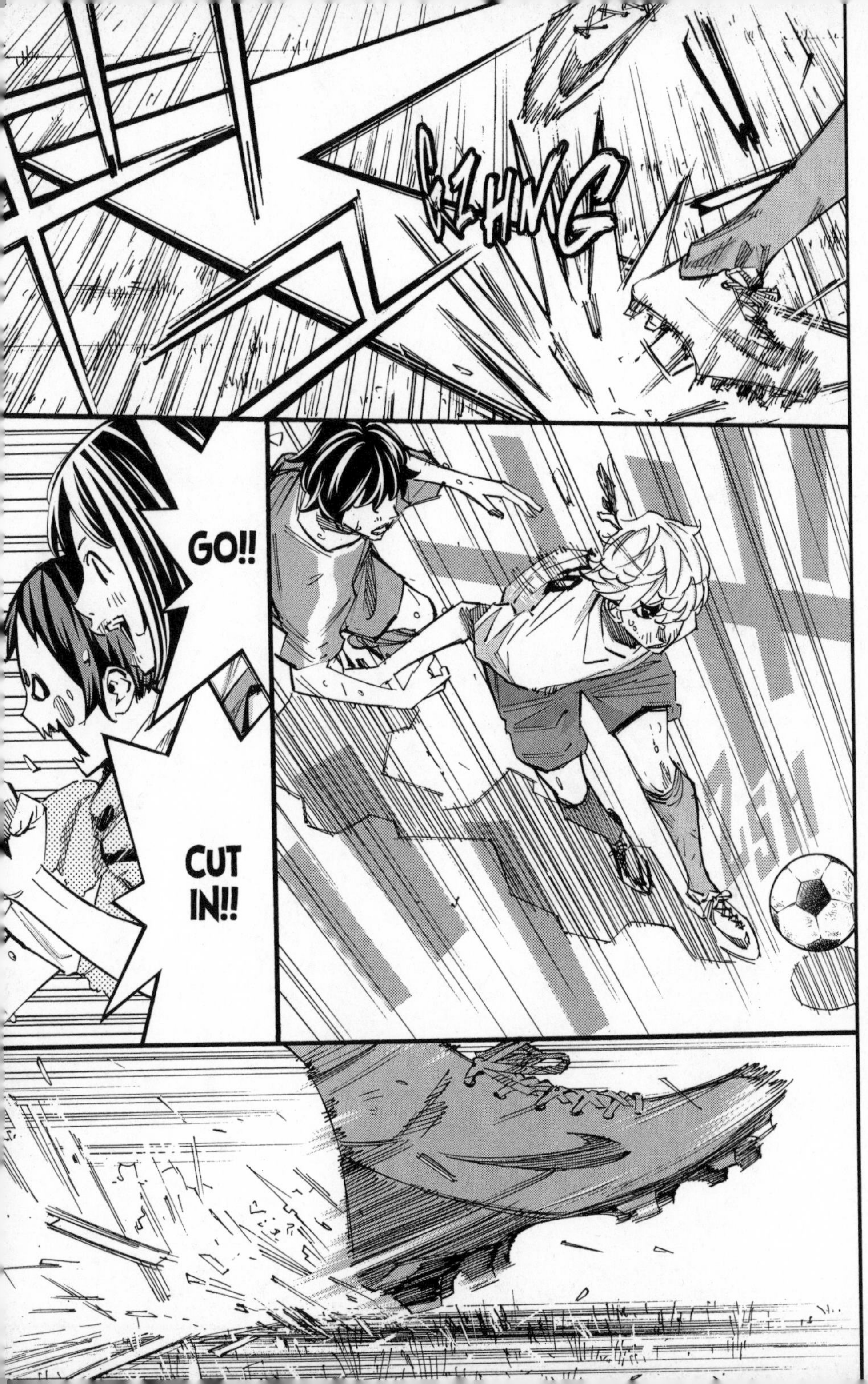
GO!!
CUT IN!!

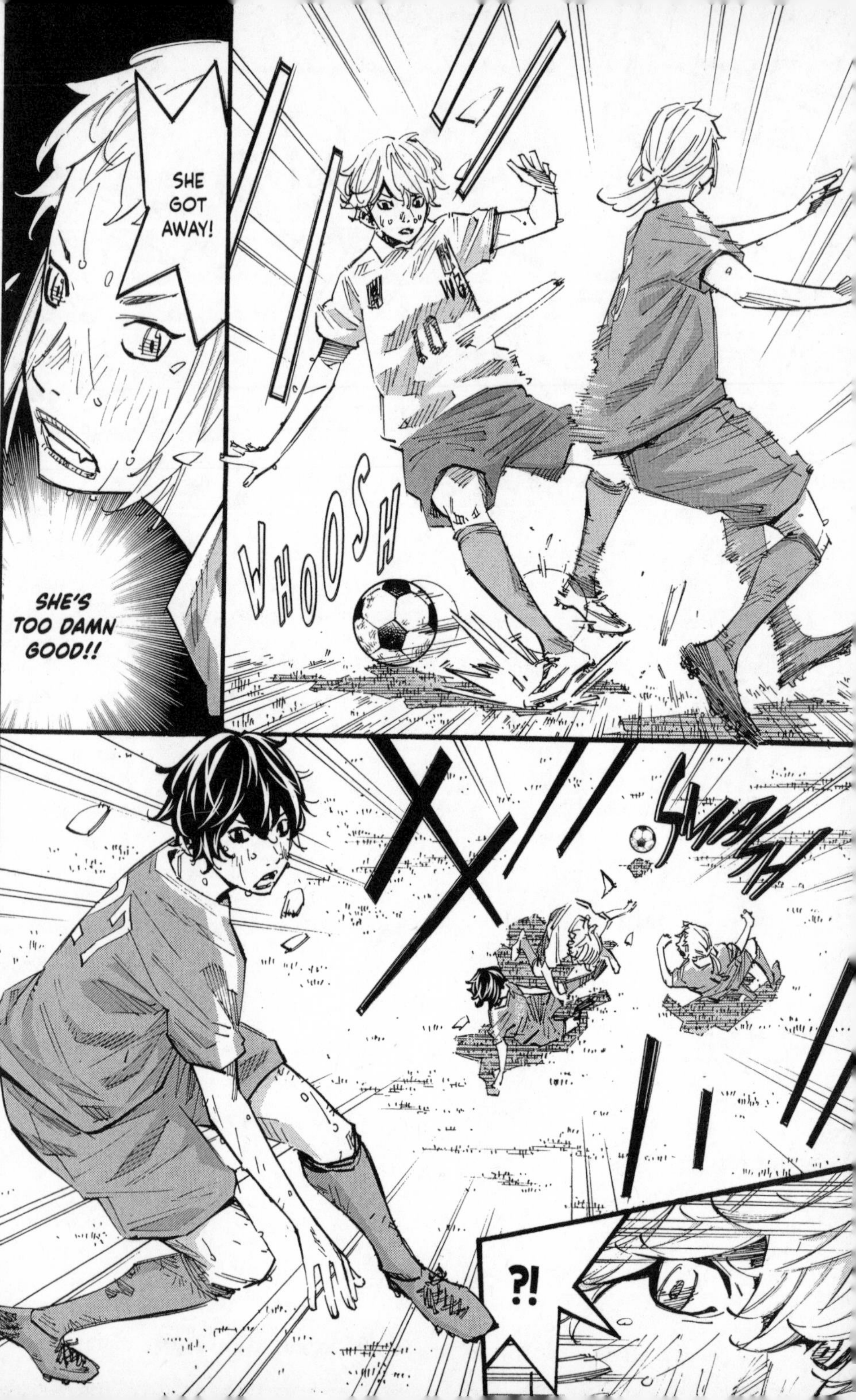
WHOOSH
SHE GOT AWAY!
SHE'S TOO DAMN GOOD!!
SMASH
?!

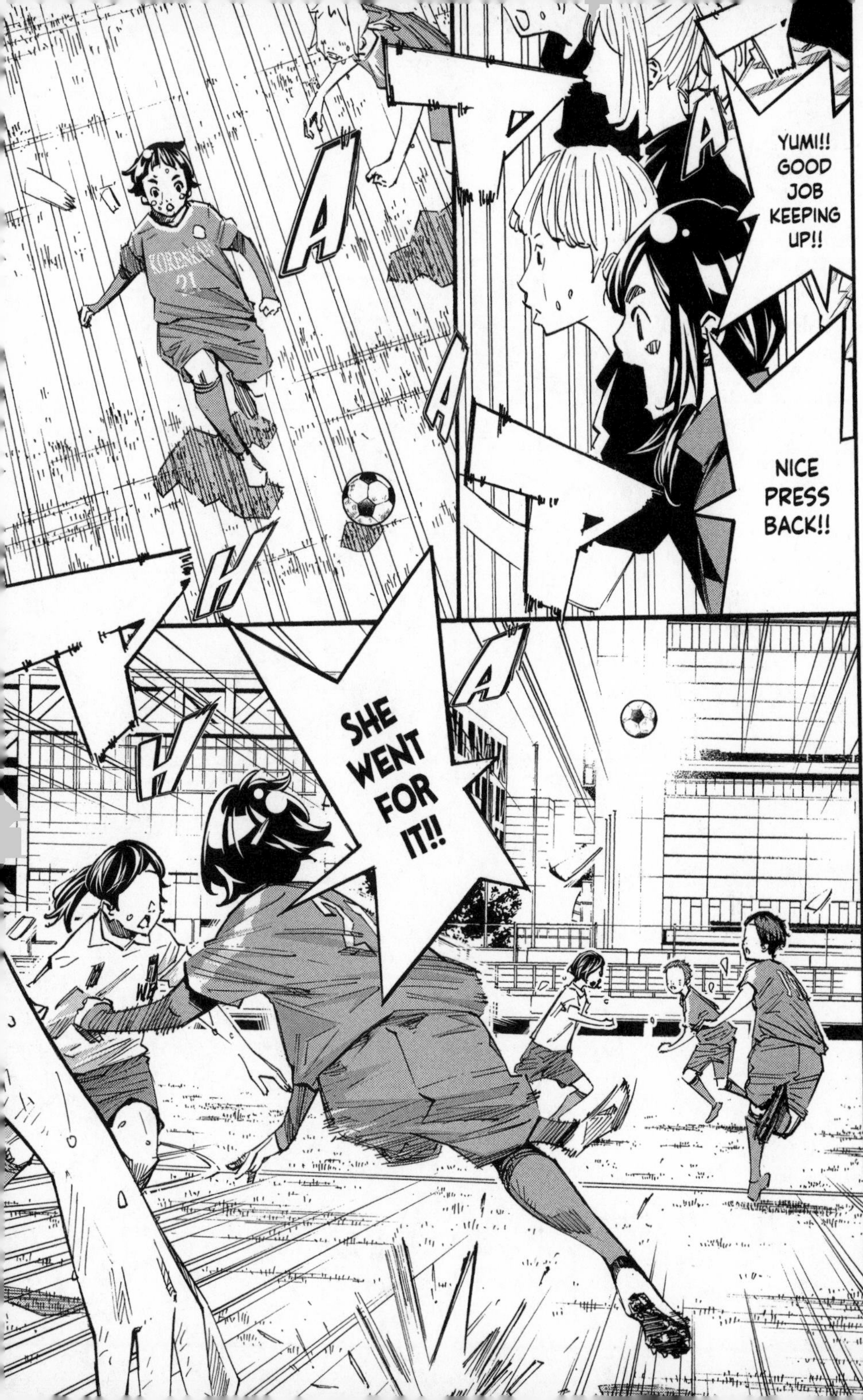
YUMI!! GOOD JOB KEEPING UP!!
NICE PRESS BACK!!
SHE WENT FOR IT!!

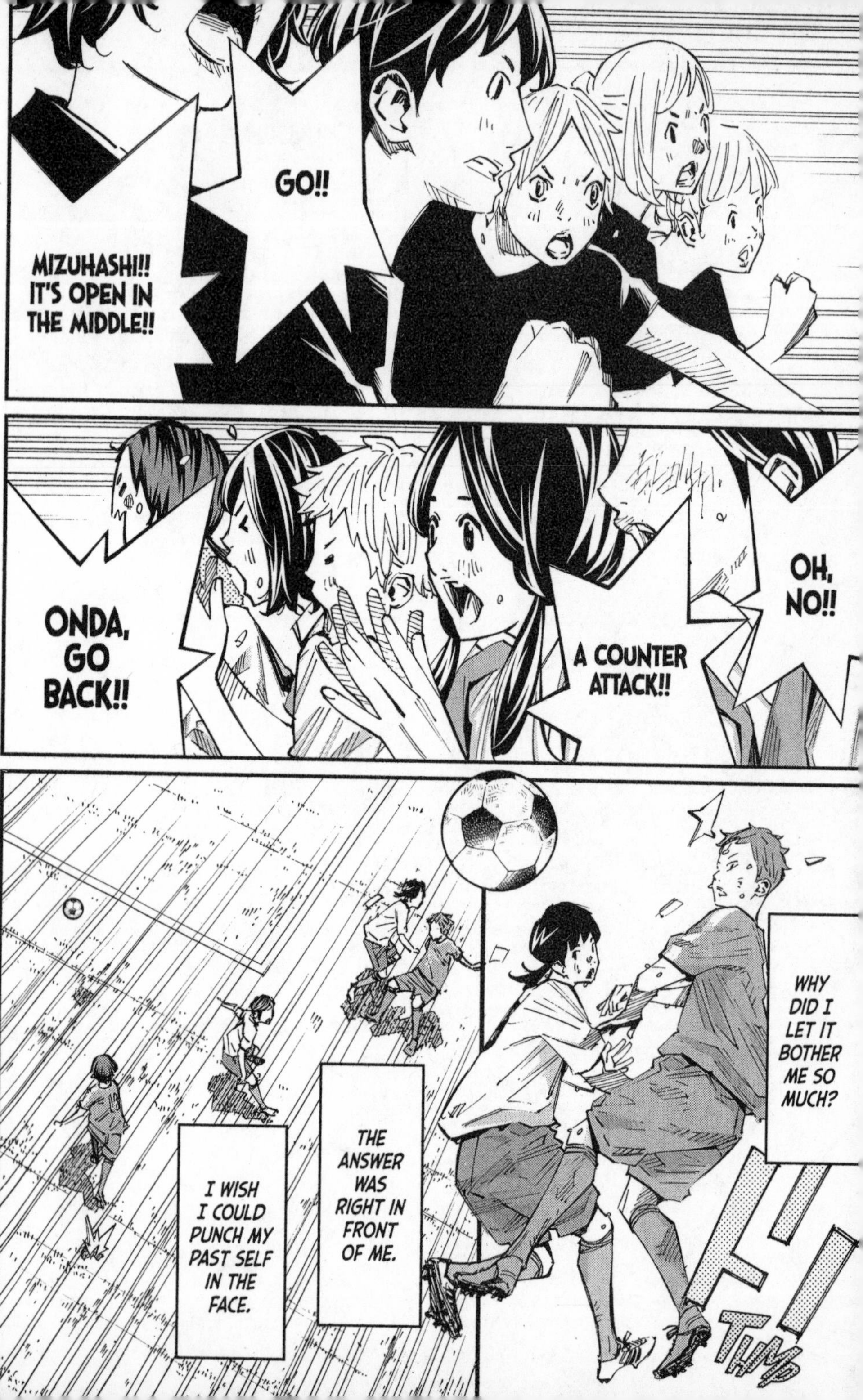
GO!!
MIZUHASHI!! IT'S OPEN IN THE MIDDLE!!
OH, NO!!
A COUNTER ATTACK!!
ONDA, GO BACK!!
WHY DID I LET IT BOTHER ME SO MUCH?
THMP
THE ANSWER WAS RIGHT IN FRONT OF ME.
I WISH I COULD PUNCH MY PAST SELF IN THE FACE.

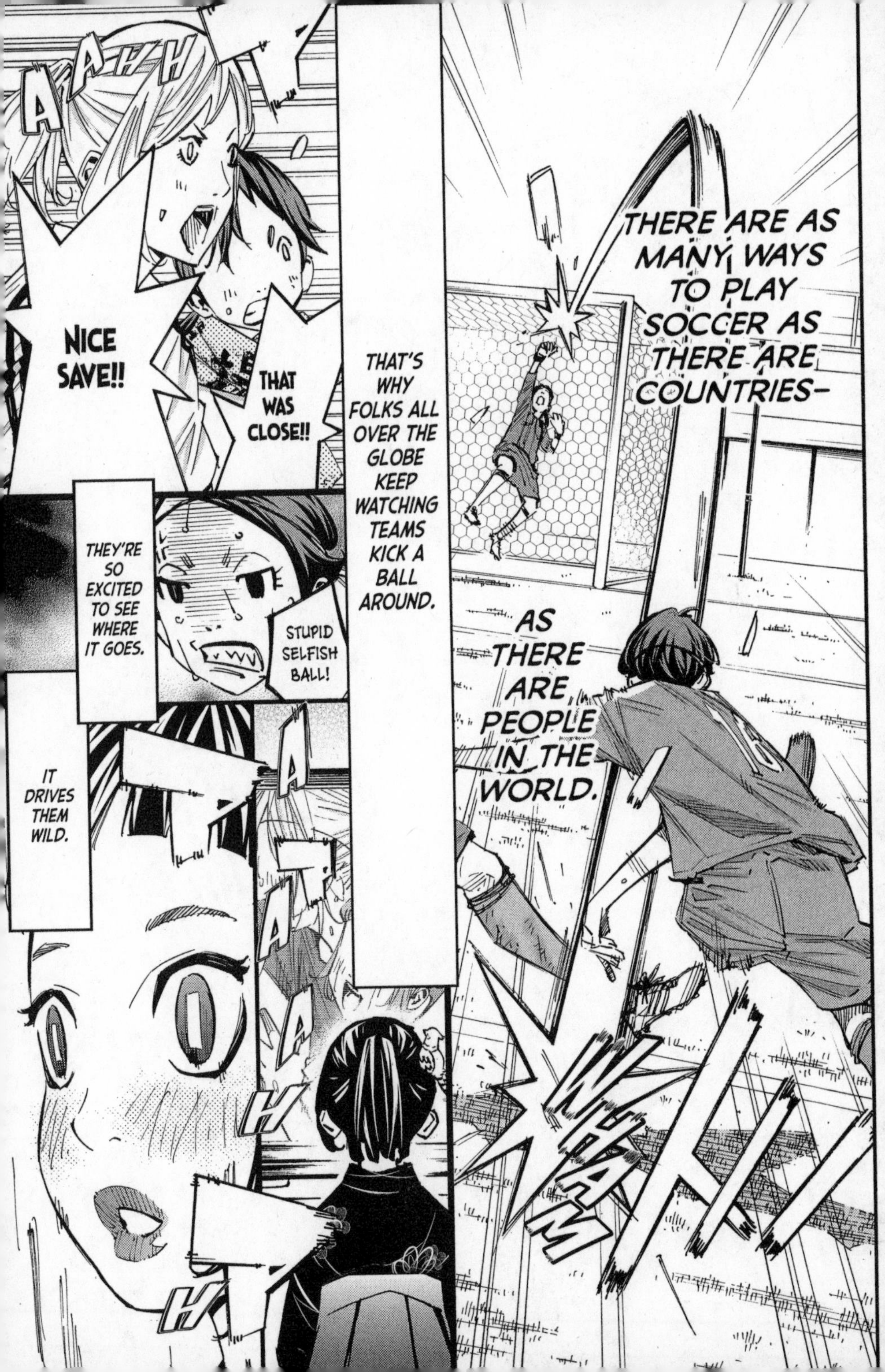
THERE ARE AS MANY WAYS TO PLAY SOCCER AS THERE ARE COUNTRIES–
AS THERE ARE PEOPLE IN THE WORLD.
WHAM
THAT'S WHY FOLKS ALL OVER THE GLOBE KEEP WATCHING TEAMS KICK A BALL AROUND.
AAHH
THAT WAS CLOSE!!
NICE SAVE!!
STUPID SELFISH BALL!
THEY'RE SO EXCITED TO SEE WHERE IT GOES.
IT DRIVES THEM WILD.
AAAAHH

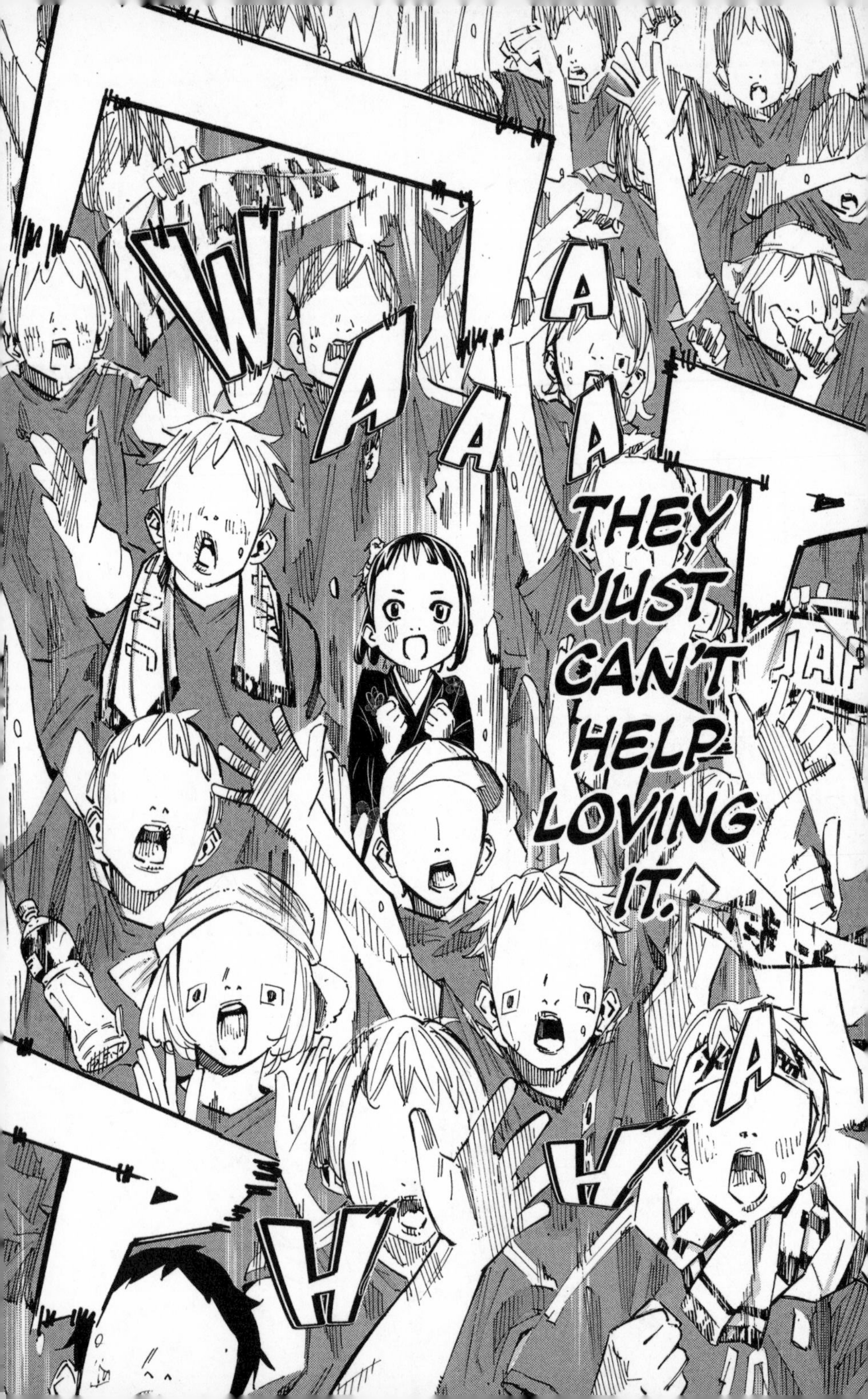
WAAAA
THEY JUST CAN'T HELP LOVING IT.
AHH

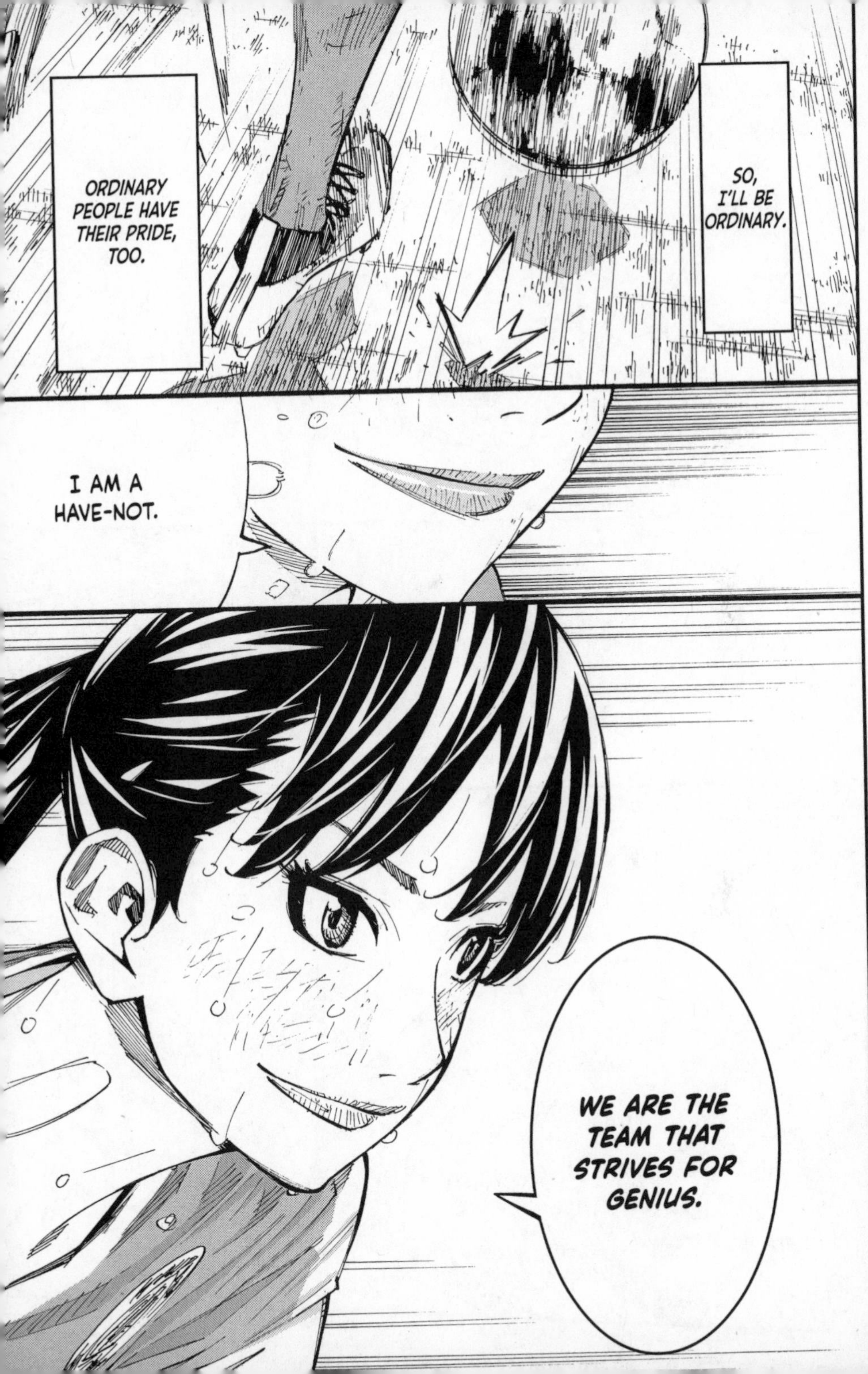
SO, I'LL BE ORDINARY.
ORDINARY PEOPLE HAVE THEIR PRIDE, TOO.
I AM A HAVE-NOT.
WE ARE THE TEAM THAT STRIVES FOR GENIUS.

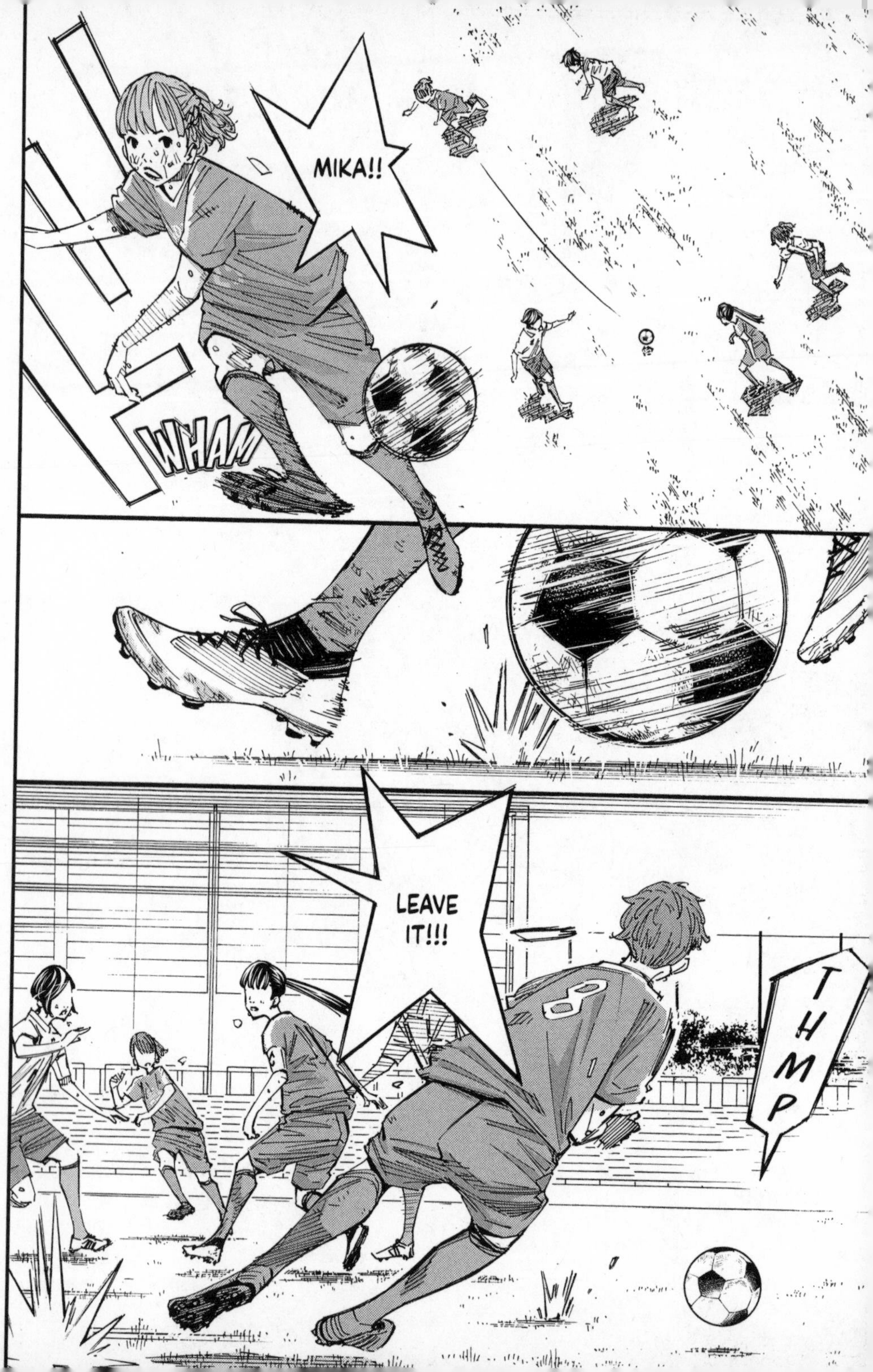
MIKA!!
WHAM
LEAVE IT!!!
THMP

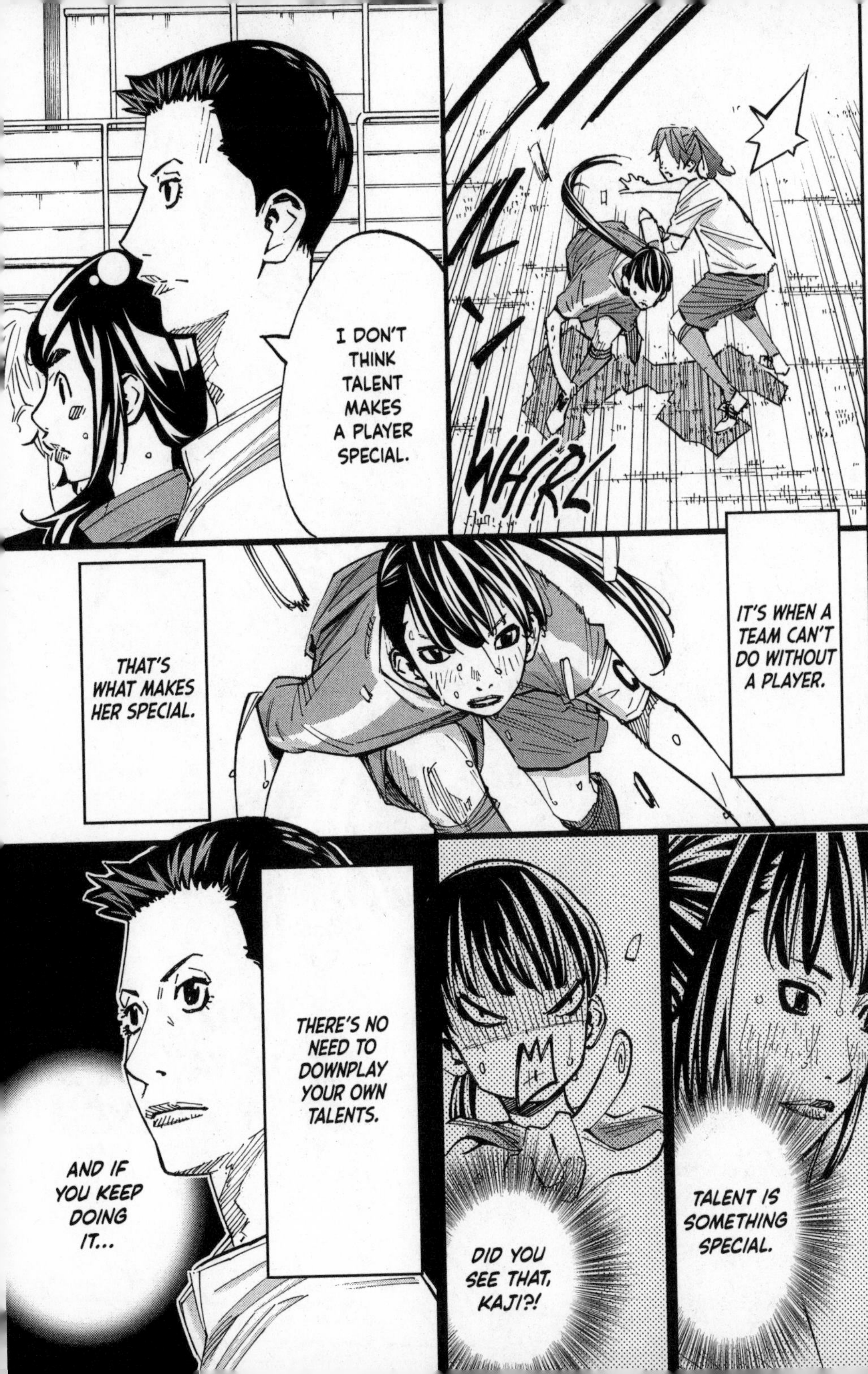
WHIRL
I DON'T THINK TALENT MAKES A PLAYER SPECIAL.
IT'S WHEN A TEAM CAN'T DO WITHOUT A PLAYER.
THAT'S WHAT MAKES HER SPECIAL.
TALENT IS SOMETHING SPECIAL.
DID YOU SEE THAT, KAJI?!
THERE'S NO NEED TO DOWNPLAY YOUR OWN TALENTS.
AND IF YOU KEEP DOING IT...

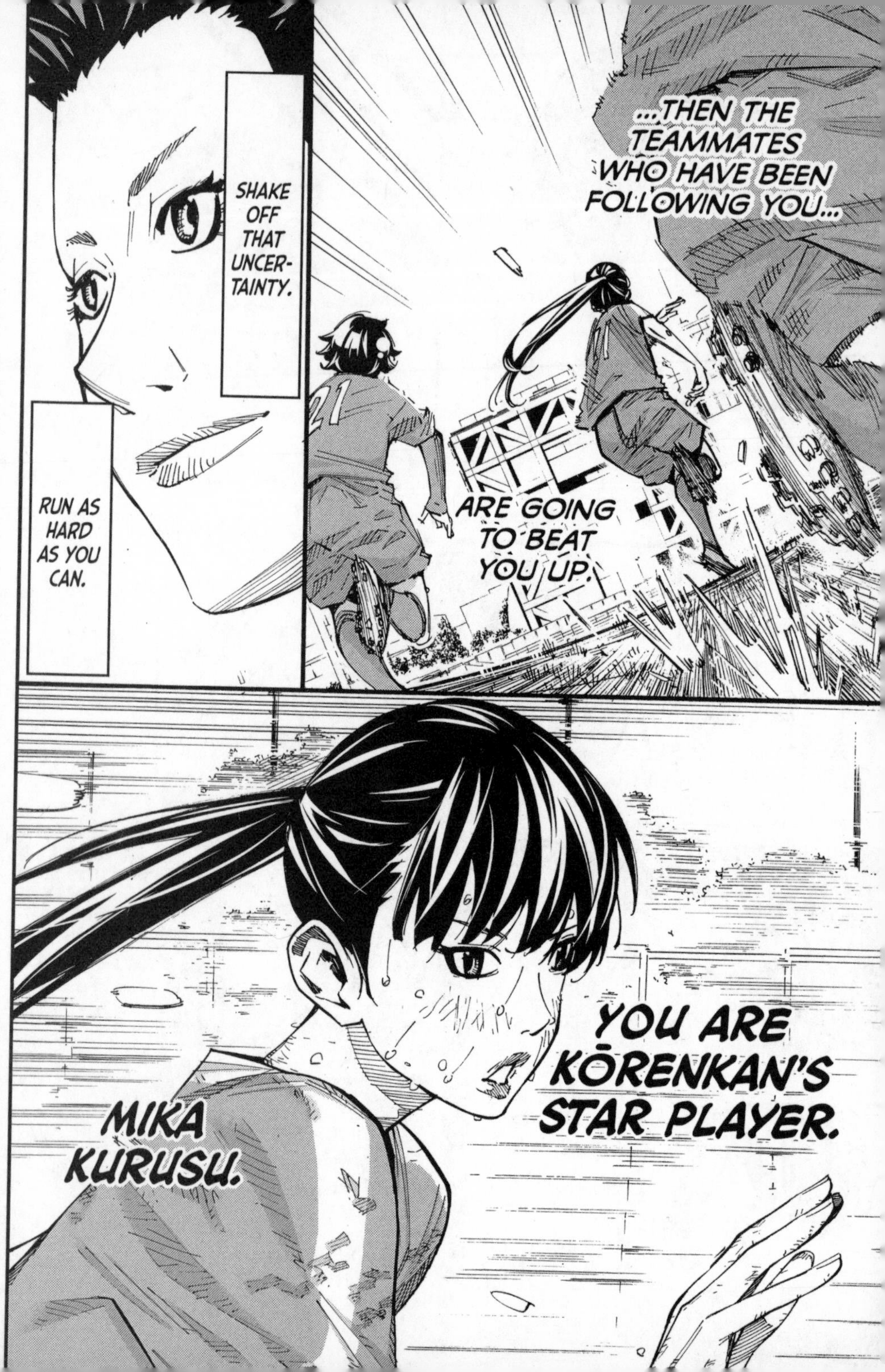
...THEN THE TEAMMATES WHO HAVE BEEN FOLLOWING YOU...
ARE GOING TO BEAT YOU UP.
SHAKE OFF THAT UNCER-TAINTY.
RUN AS HARD AS YOU CAN.
YOU ARE KŌRENKAN'S STAR PLAYER.
MIKA KURUSU.

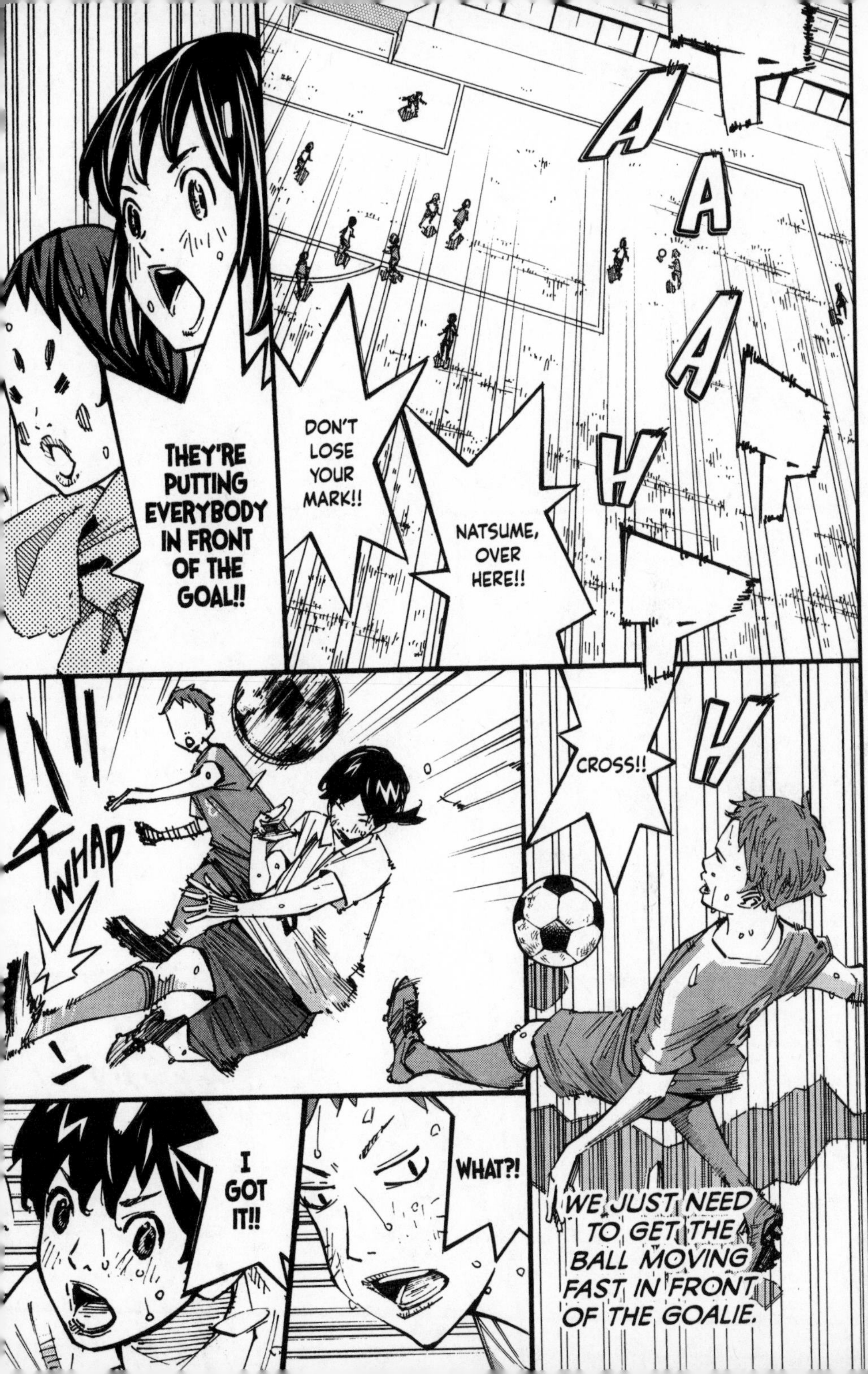

AAAAHH
NATSUME, OVER HERE!!
DON'T LOSE YOUR MARK!!
THEY'RE PUTTING EVERYBODY IN FRONT OF THE GOAL!!
H
CROSS!!
WHAP
WE JUST NEED TO GET THE BALL MOVING FAST IN FRONT OF THE GOALIE.
WHAT?!
I GOT IT!!

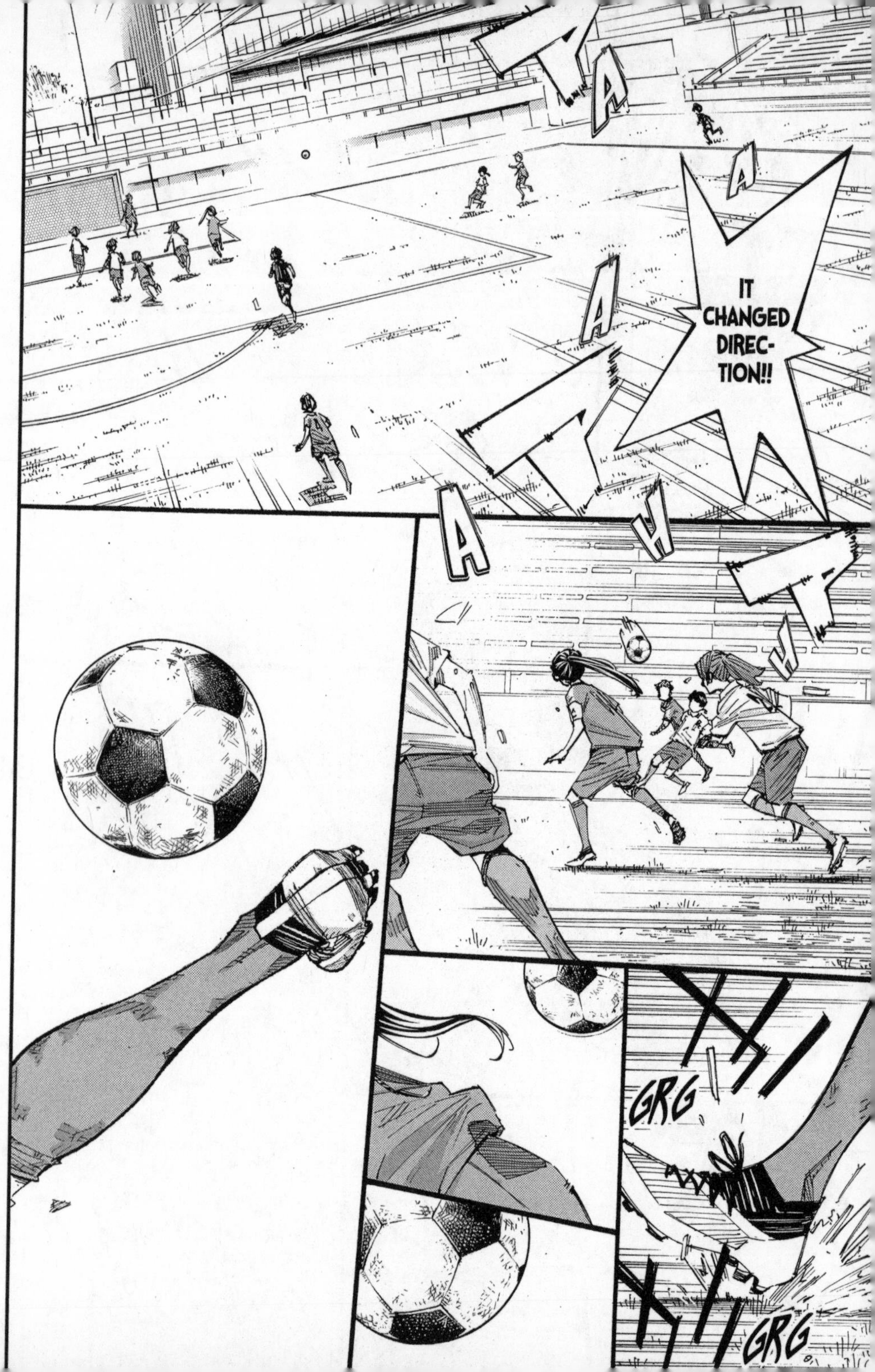
IT CHANGED DIREC-TION!!
GRG
GRG

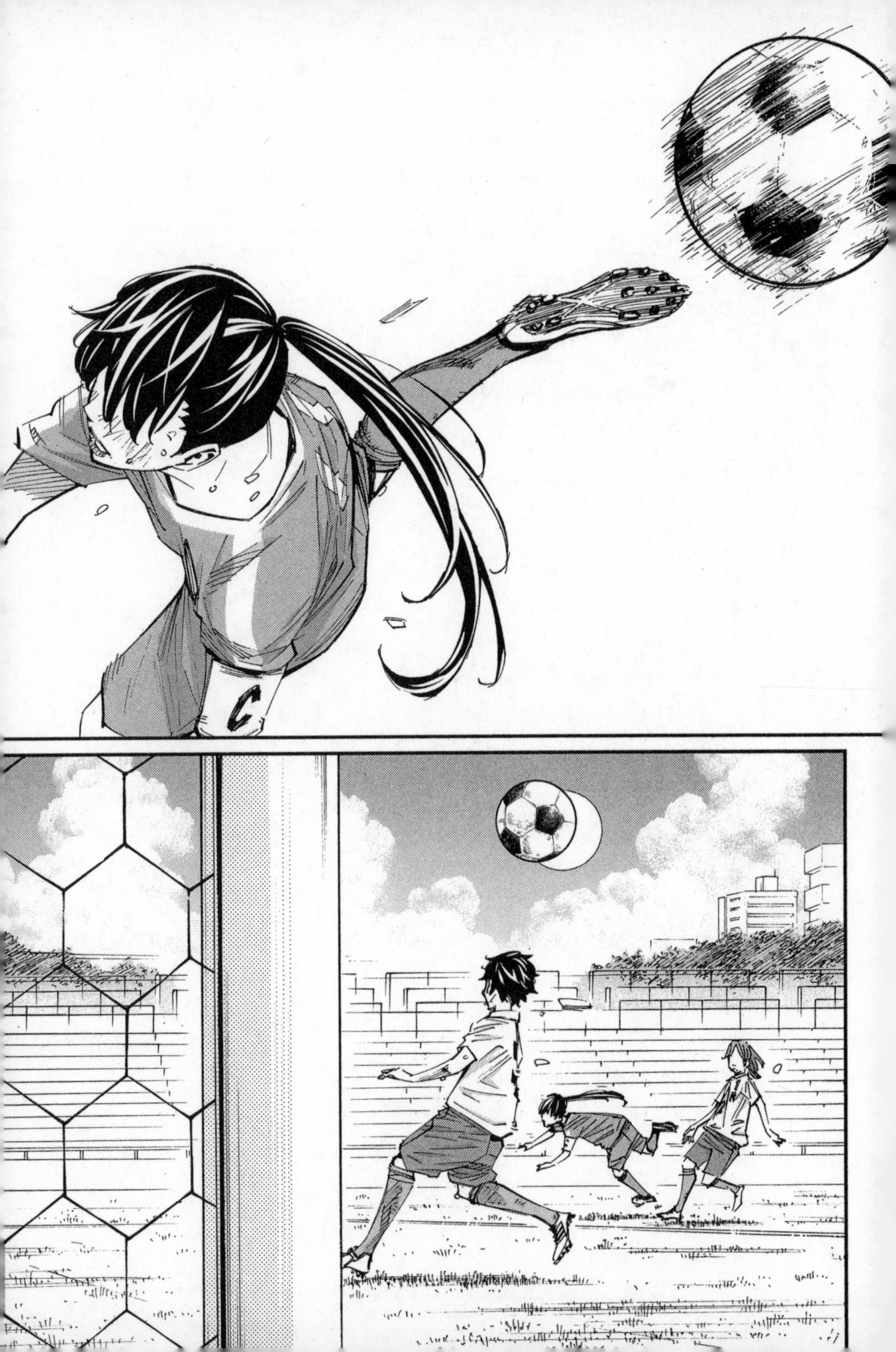
C

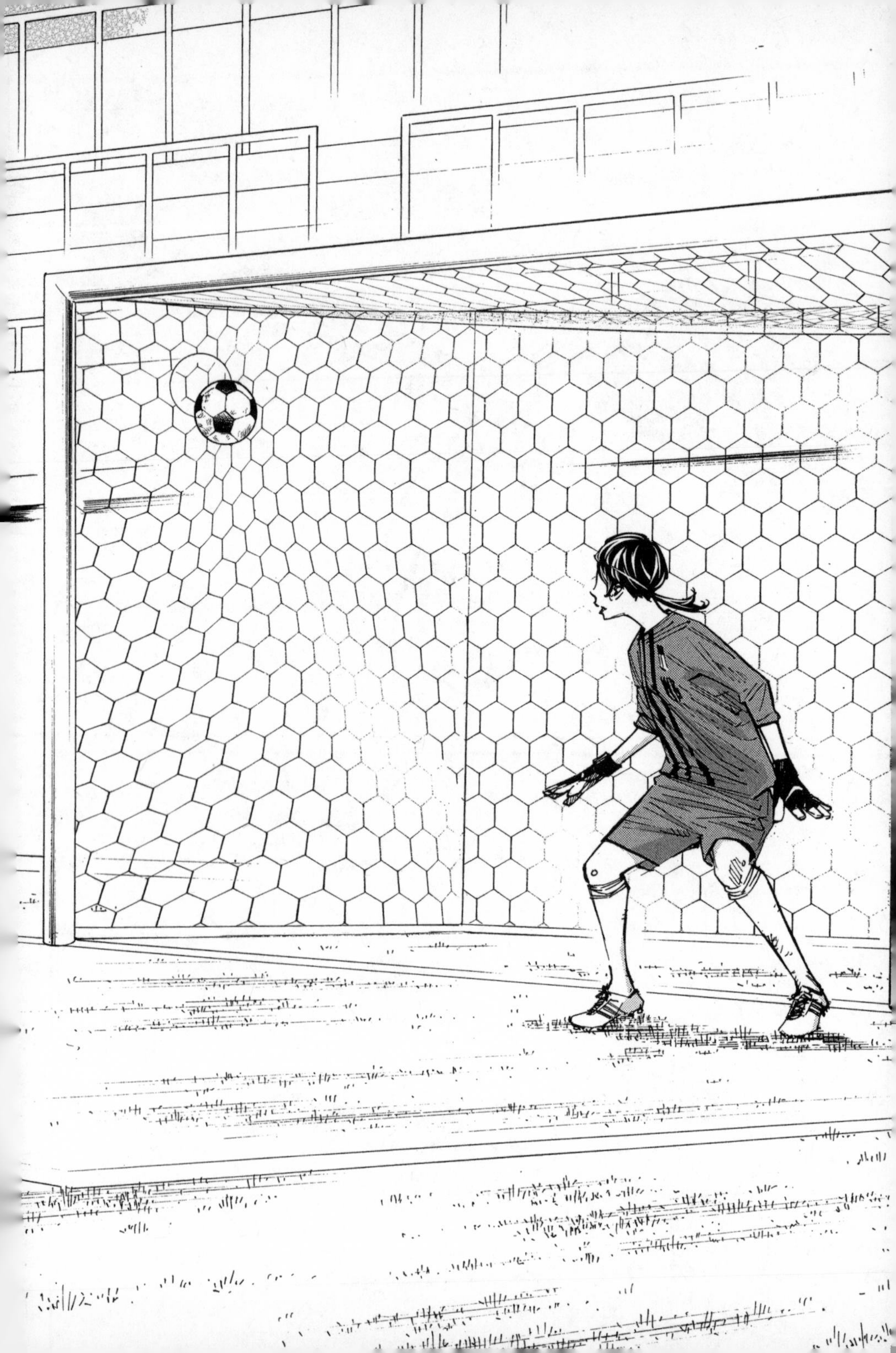

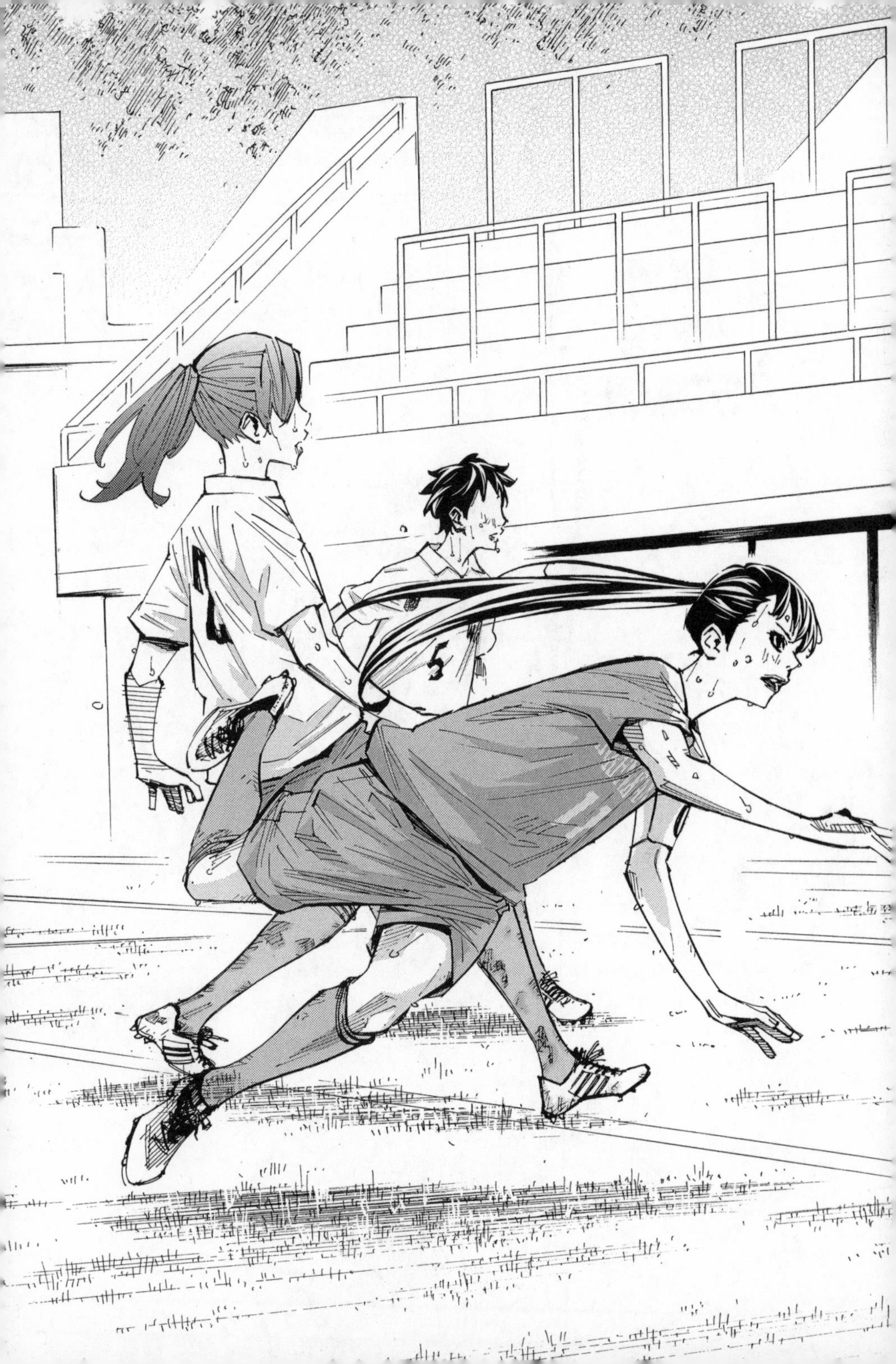

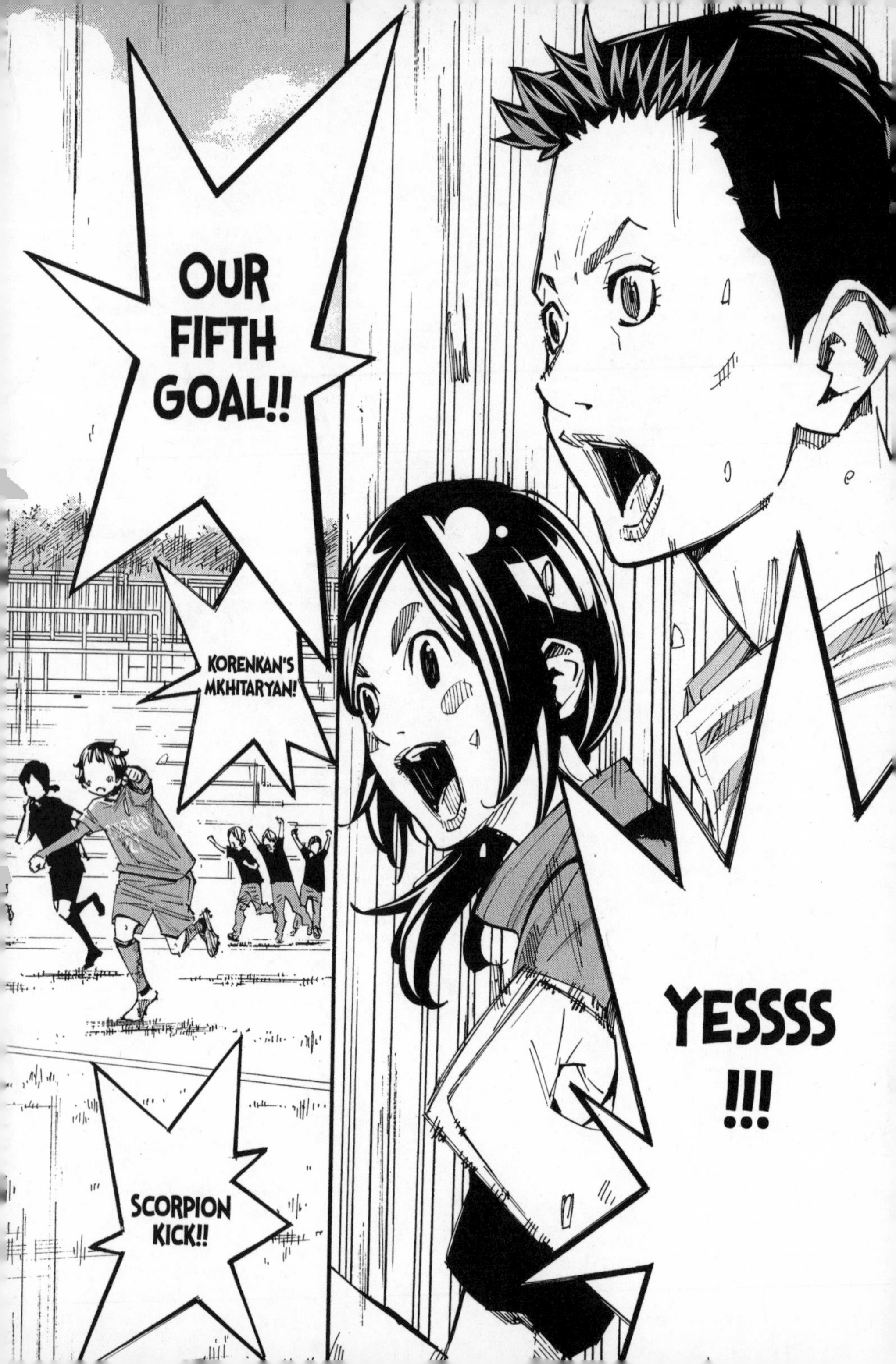
OUR FIFTH GOAL!!
KORENKAN'S MKHITARYAN!
SCORPION KICK!!
YESSSS!!!

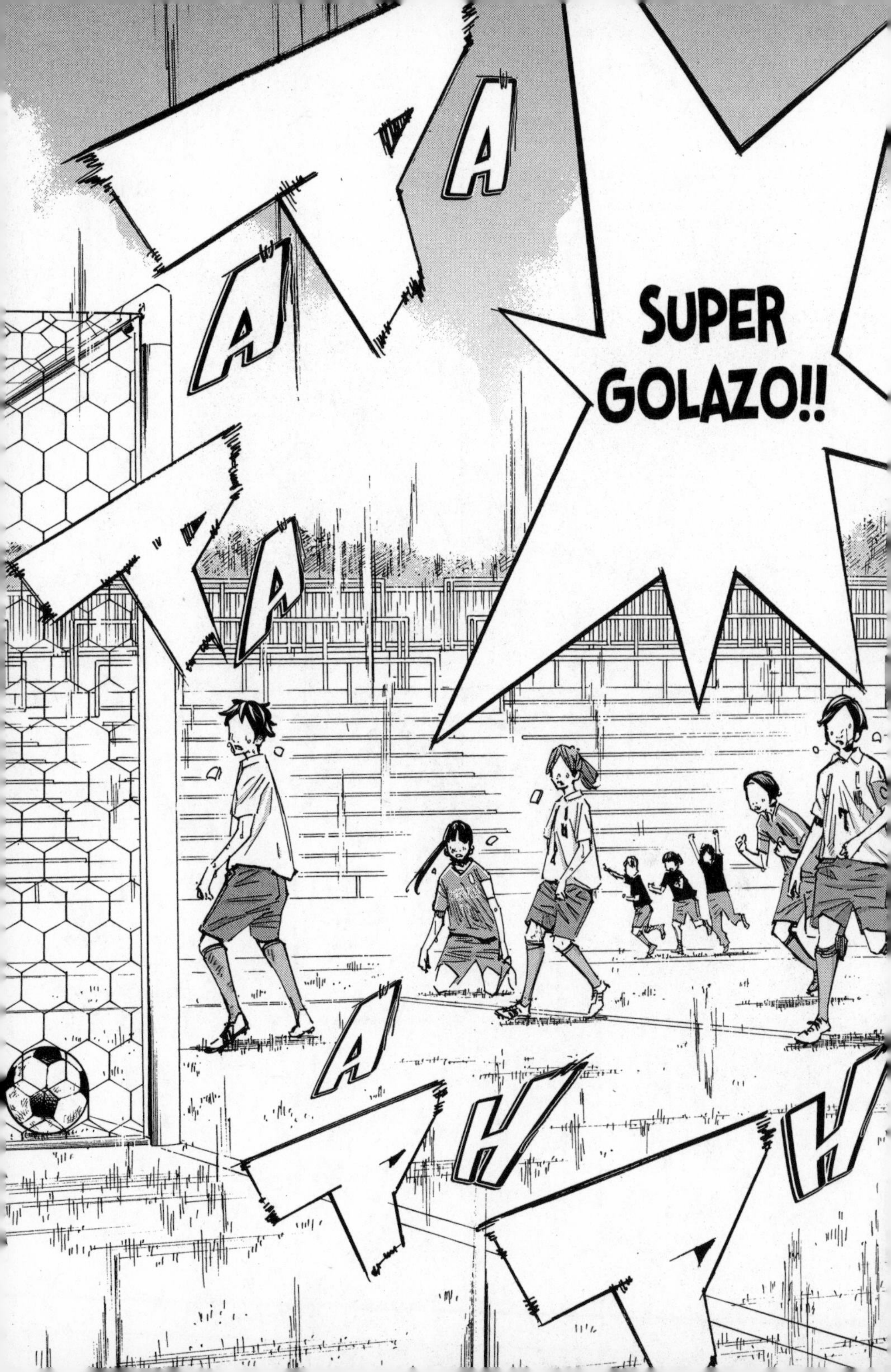
SUPER GOLAZO!!
AAAAHH

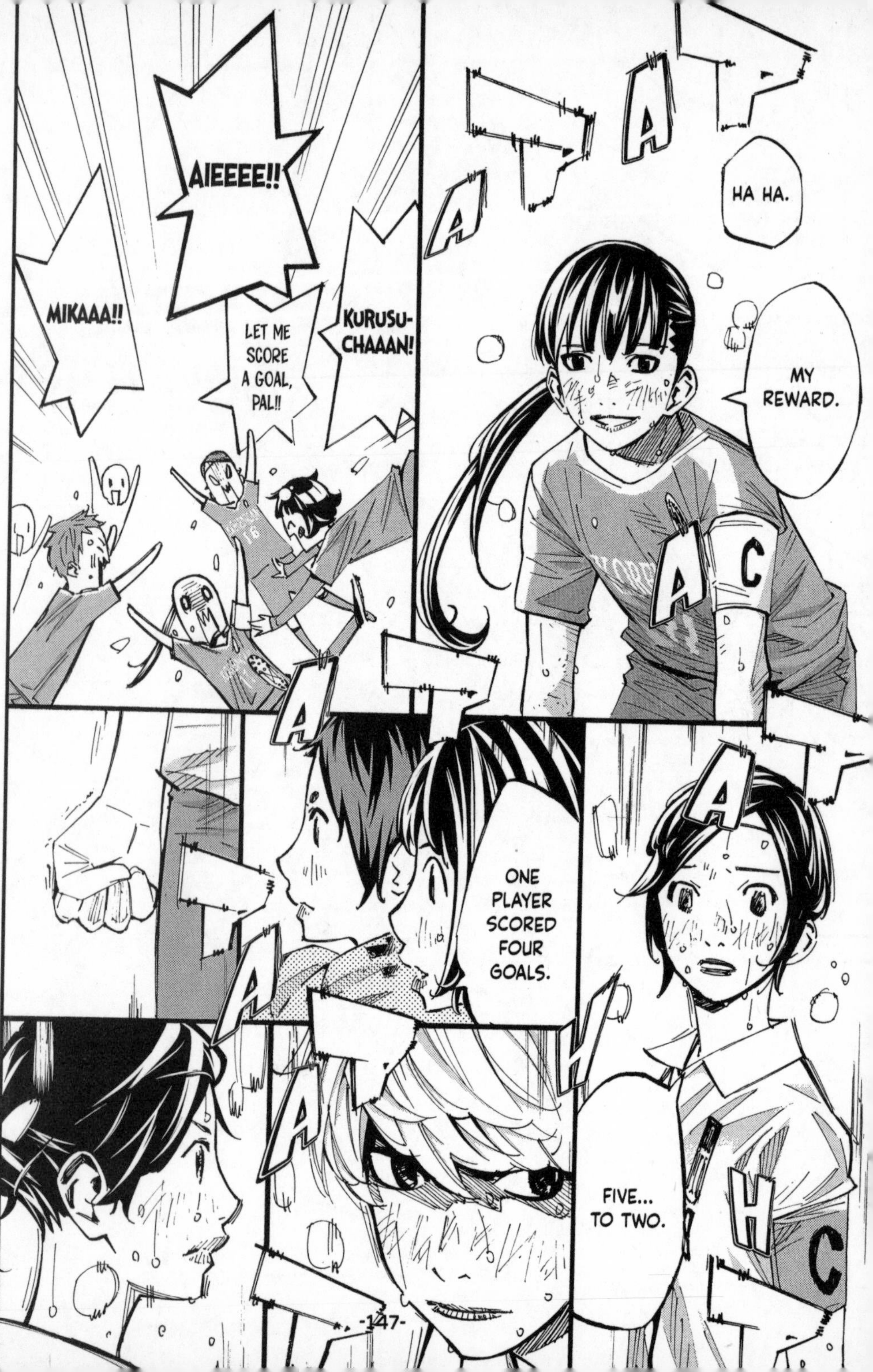
HA HA.
MY REWARD.
AIEEEE!!
KURUSU-CHAAAN!
LET ME SCORE A GOAL, PAL!!
MIKAAA!!
ONE PLAYER SCORED FOUR GOALS.
FIVE... TO TWO.

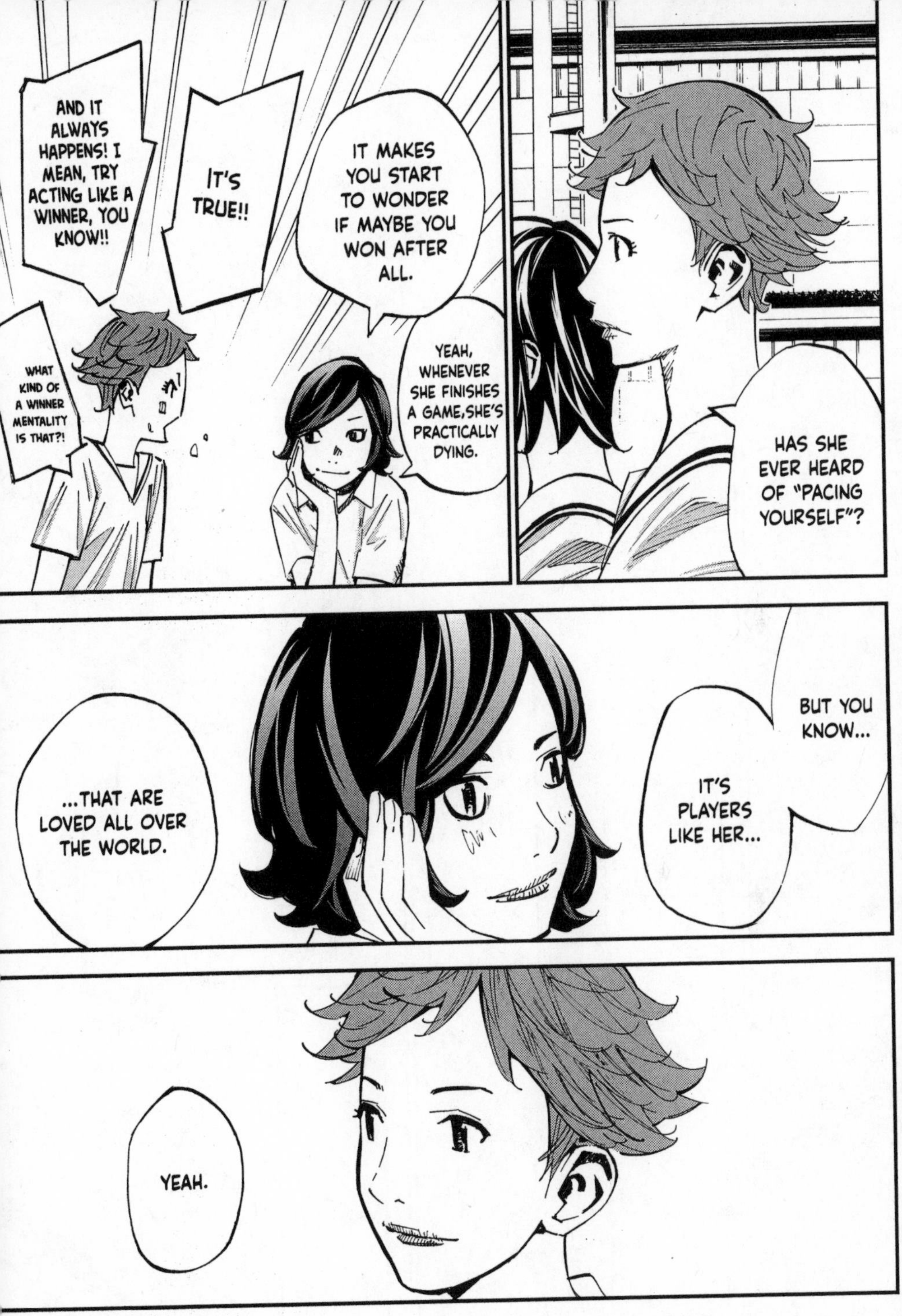
HAS SHE EVER HEARD OF "PACING YOURSELF"?
YEAH, WHENEVER SHE FINISHES A GAME, SHE'S PRACTICALLY DYING.
IT MAKES YOU START TO WONDER IF MAYBE YOU WON AFTER ALL.
IT'S TRUE!!
AND IT ALWAYS HAPPENS! I MEAN, TRY ACTING LIKE A WINNER, YOU KNOW!!
WHAT KIND OF A WINNER MENTALITY IS THAT?!
BUT YOU KNOW...
IT'S PLAYERS LIKE HER...
...THAT ARE LOVED ALL OVER THE WORLD.
YEAH.

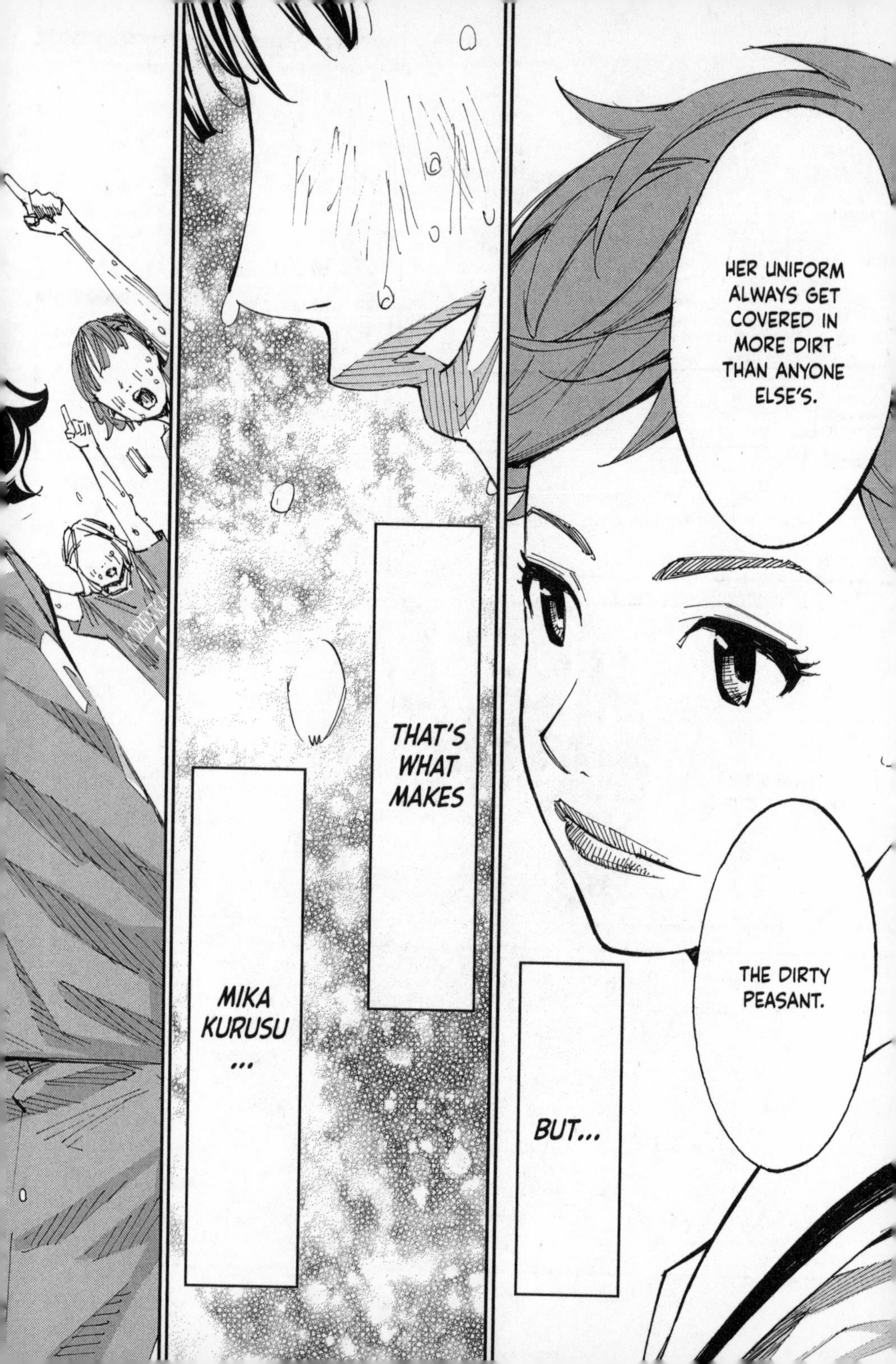
HER UNIFORM ALWAYS GET COVERED IN MORE DIRT THAN ANYONE ELSE'S.
THE DIRTY PEASANT.
BUT...
THAT'S WHAT MAKES
MIKA KURUSU ...

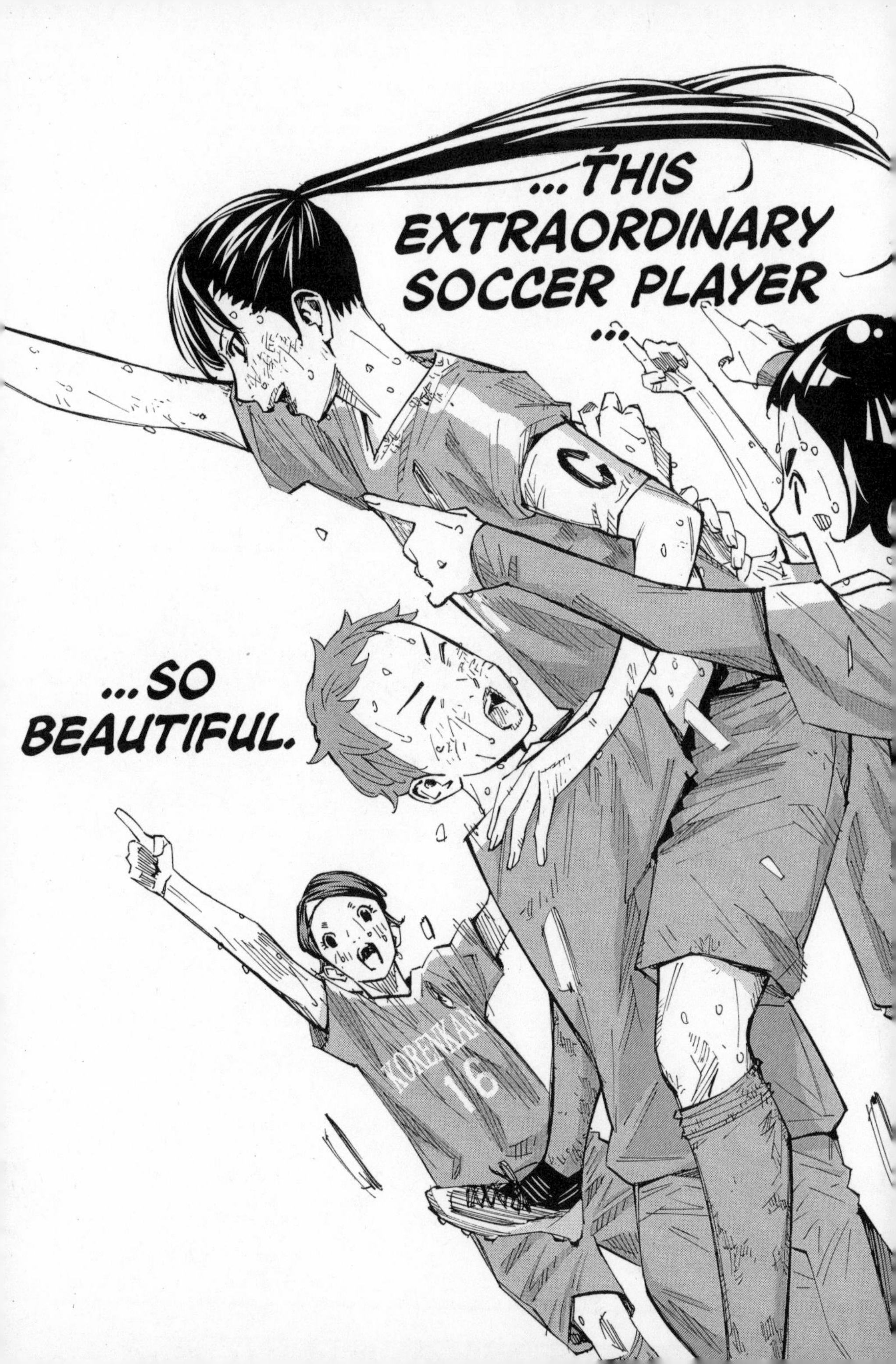
...THIS EXTRAORDINARY SOCCER PLAYER ...
...SO BEAUTIFUL.
KORENKAN 16

Farewell, My Dear Cramer

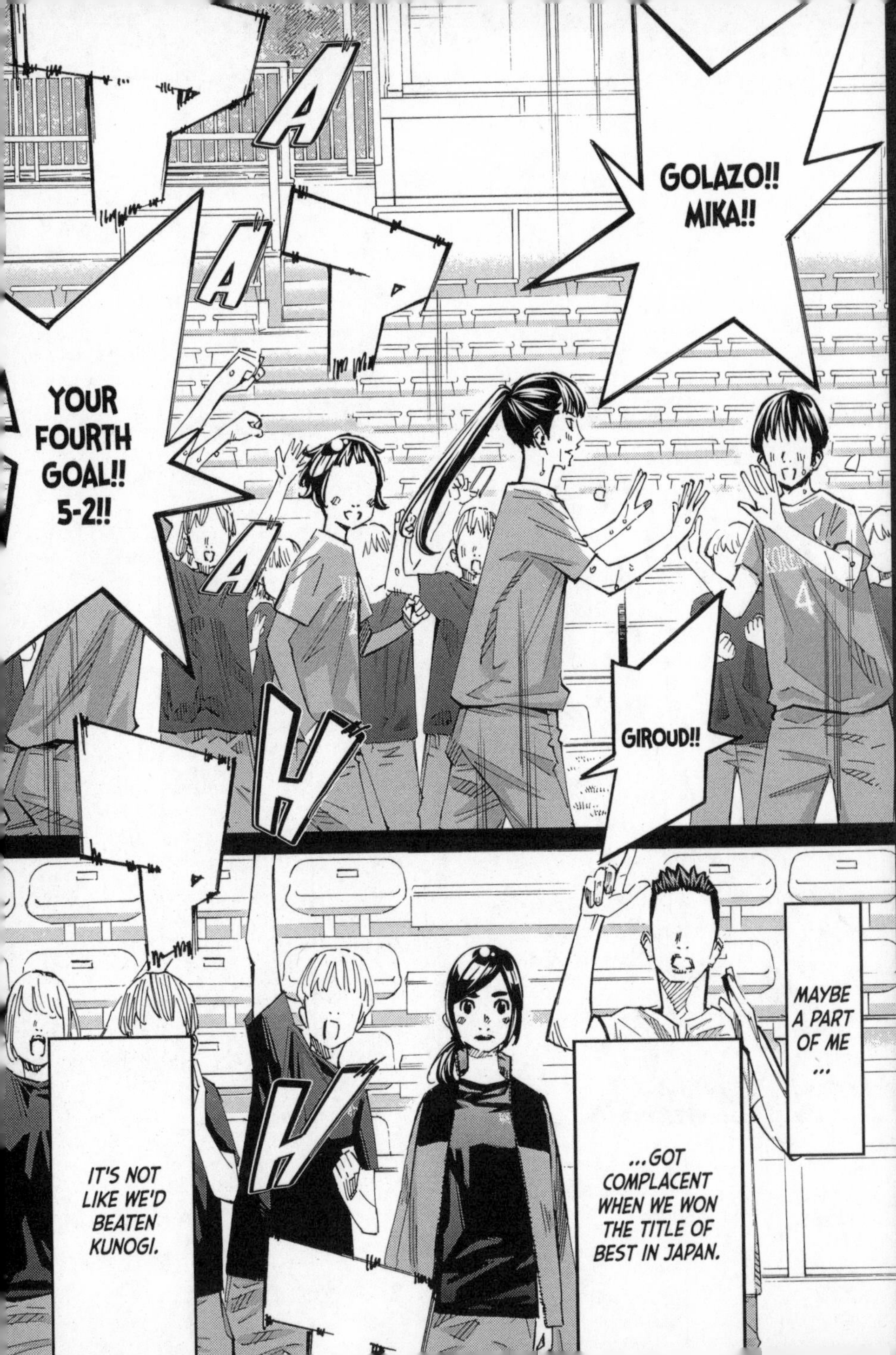
GOLAZO!! MIKA!!
AAAAHH
YOUR FOURTH GOAL!! 5-2!!
GIROUD!!
MAYBE A PART OF ME ...
...GOT COMPLACENT WHEN WE WON THE TITLE OF BEST IN JAPAN.
IT'S NOT LIKE WE'D BEATEN KUNOGI.

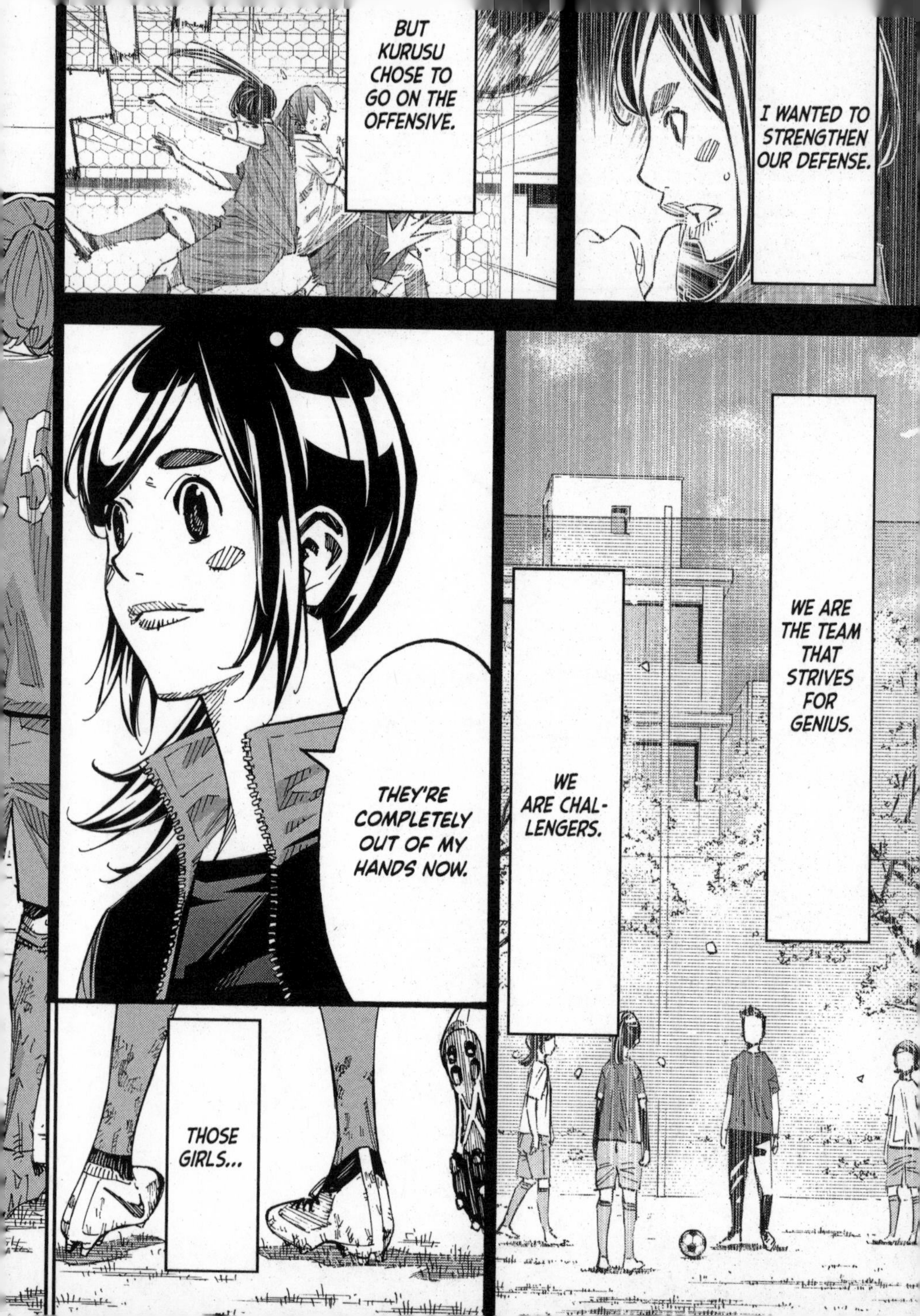
I WANTED TO STRENGTHEN OUR DEFENSE.
BUT KURUSU CHOSE TO GO ON THE OFFENSIVE.
WE ARE THE TEAM THAT STRIVES FOR GENIUS.
WE ARE CHAL-LENGERS.
THEY'RE COMPLETELY OUT OF MY HANDS NOW.
THOSE GIRLS...

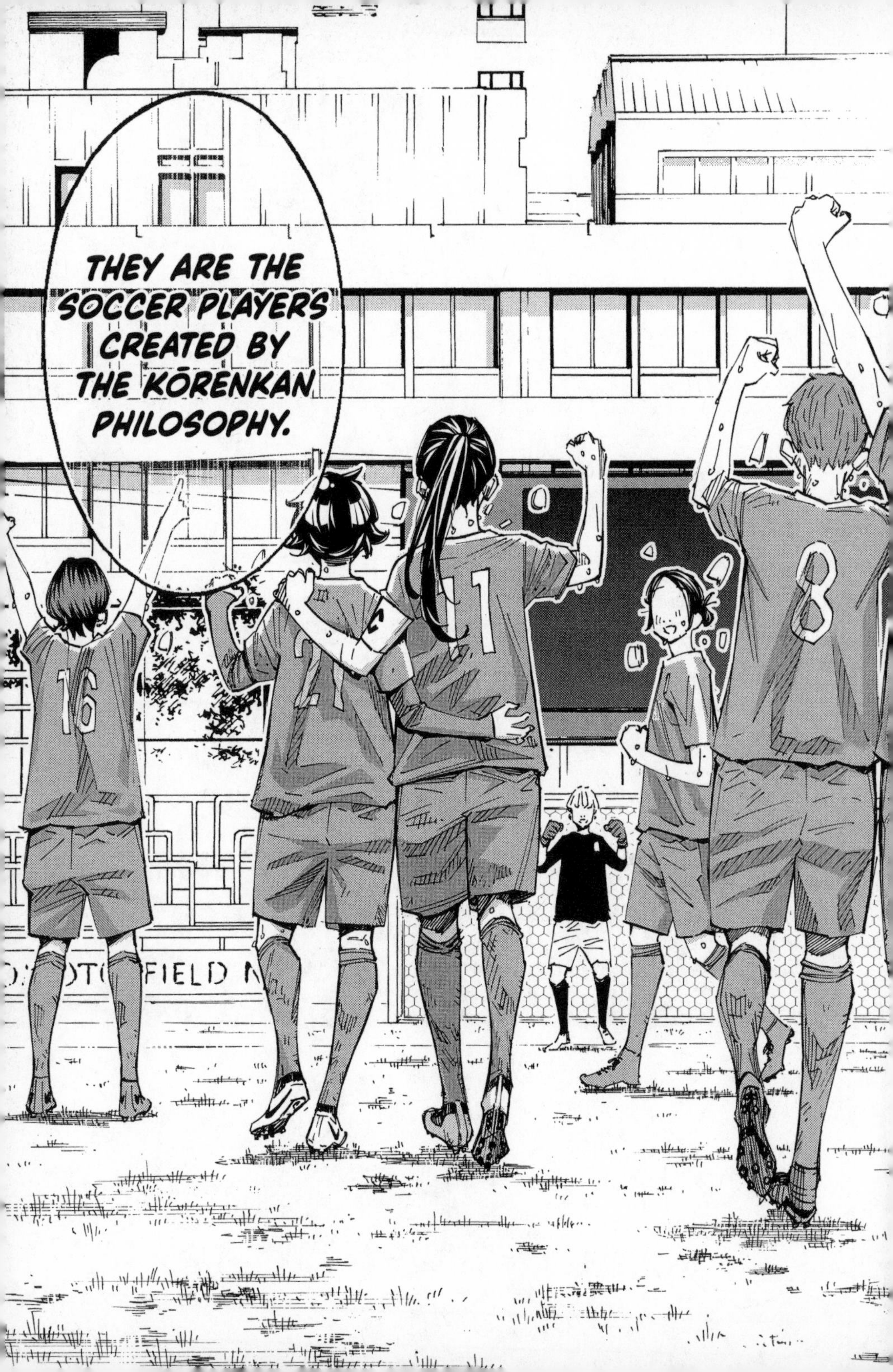
THEY ARE THE SOCCER PLAYERS CREATED BY THE KŌRENKAN PHILOSOPHY.
FIELD

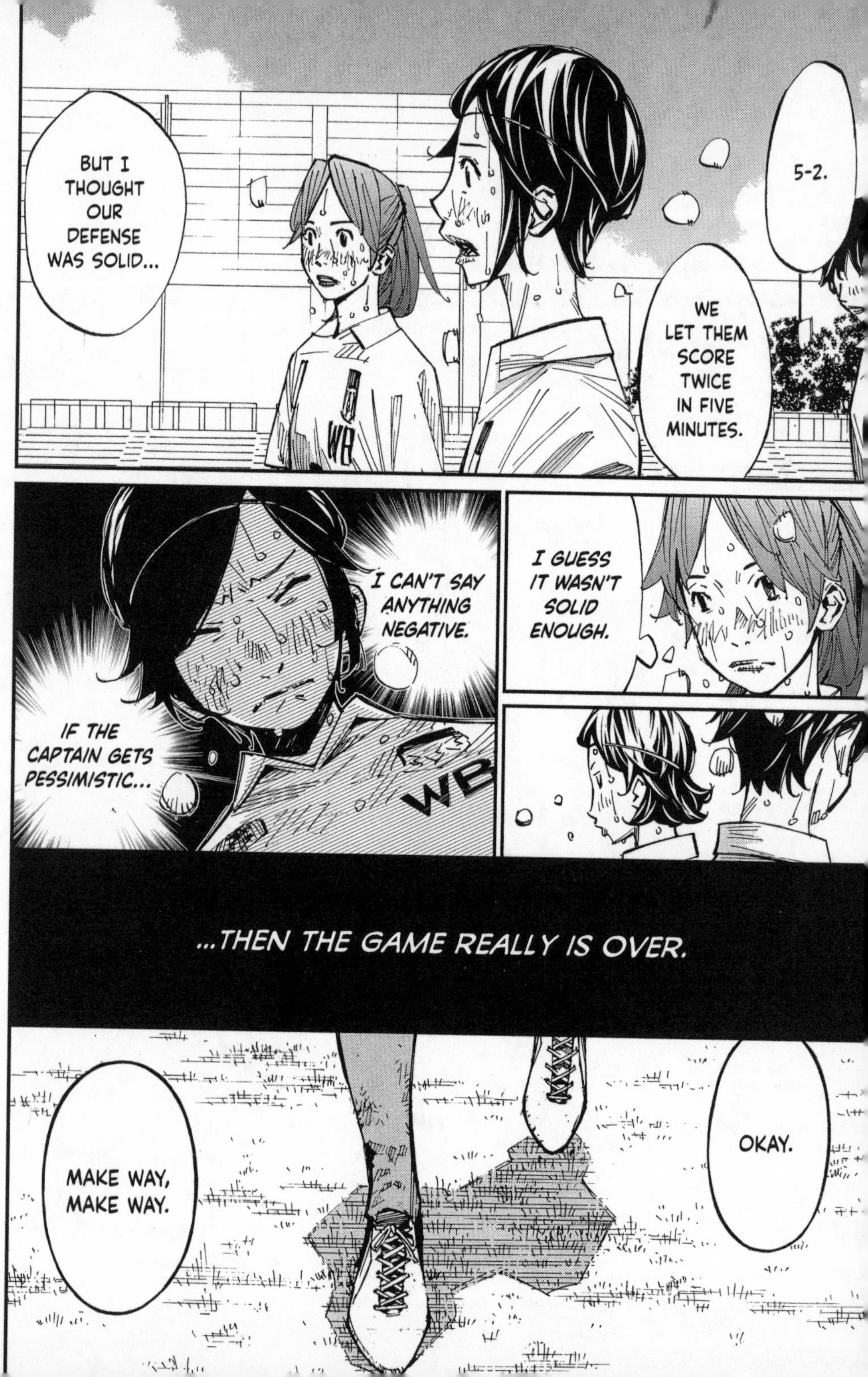
5-2.
WE LET THEM SCORE TWICE IN FIVE MINUTES.
BUT I THOUGHT OUR DEFENSE WAS SOLID...
I GUESS IT WASN'T SOLID ENOUGH.
I CAN'T SAY ANYTHING NEGATIVE.
IF THE CAPTAIN GETS PESSIMISTIC...
...THEN THE GAME REALLY IS OVER.
OKAY.
MAKE WAY, MAKE WAY.

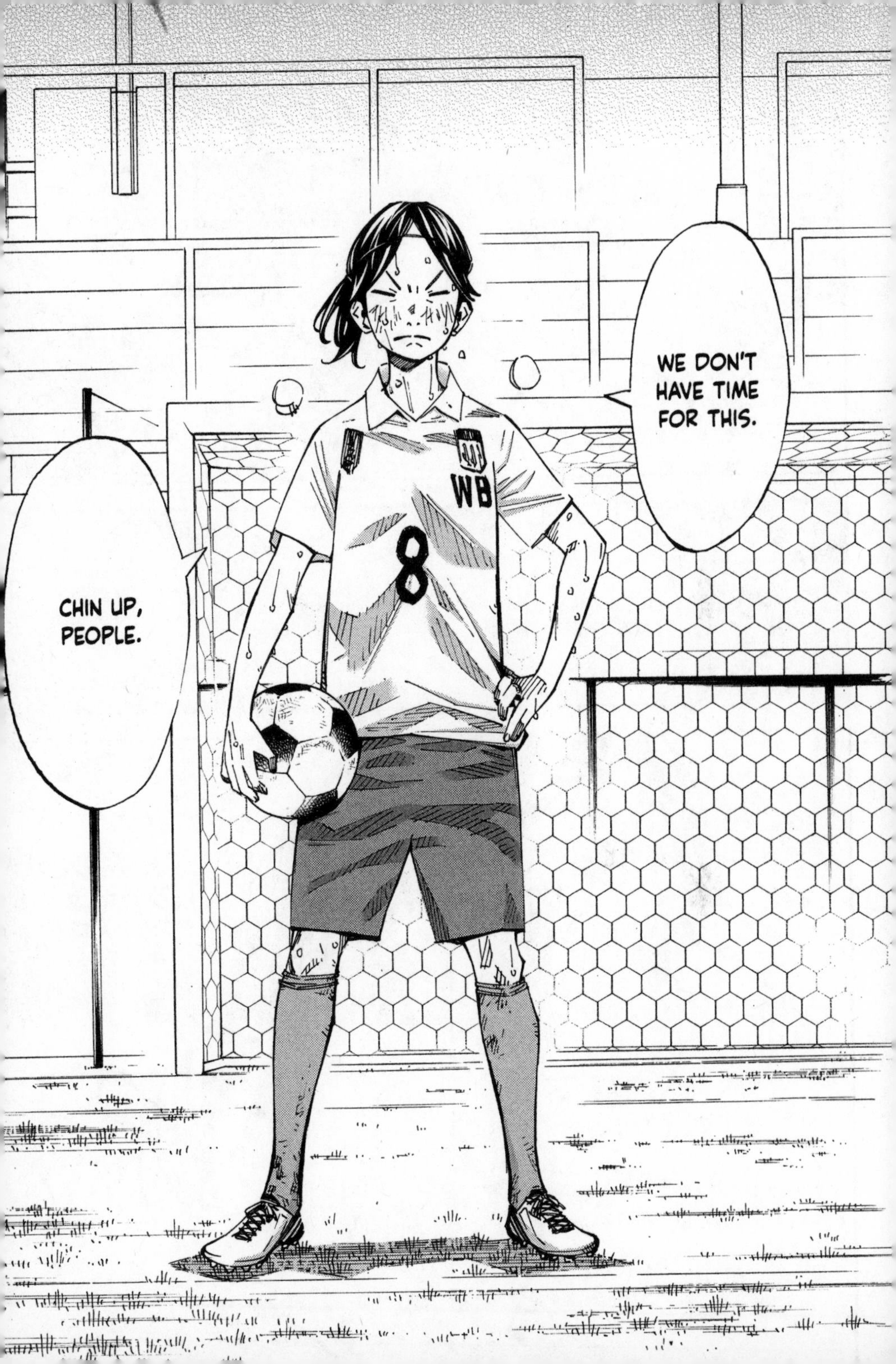
WE DON'T HAVE TIME FOR THIS.
CHIN UP, PEOPLE.

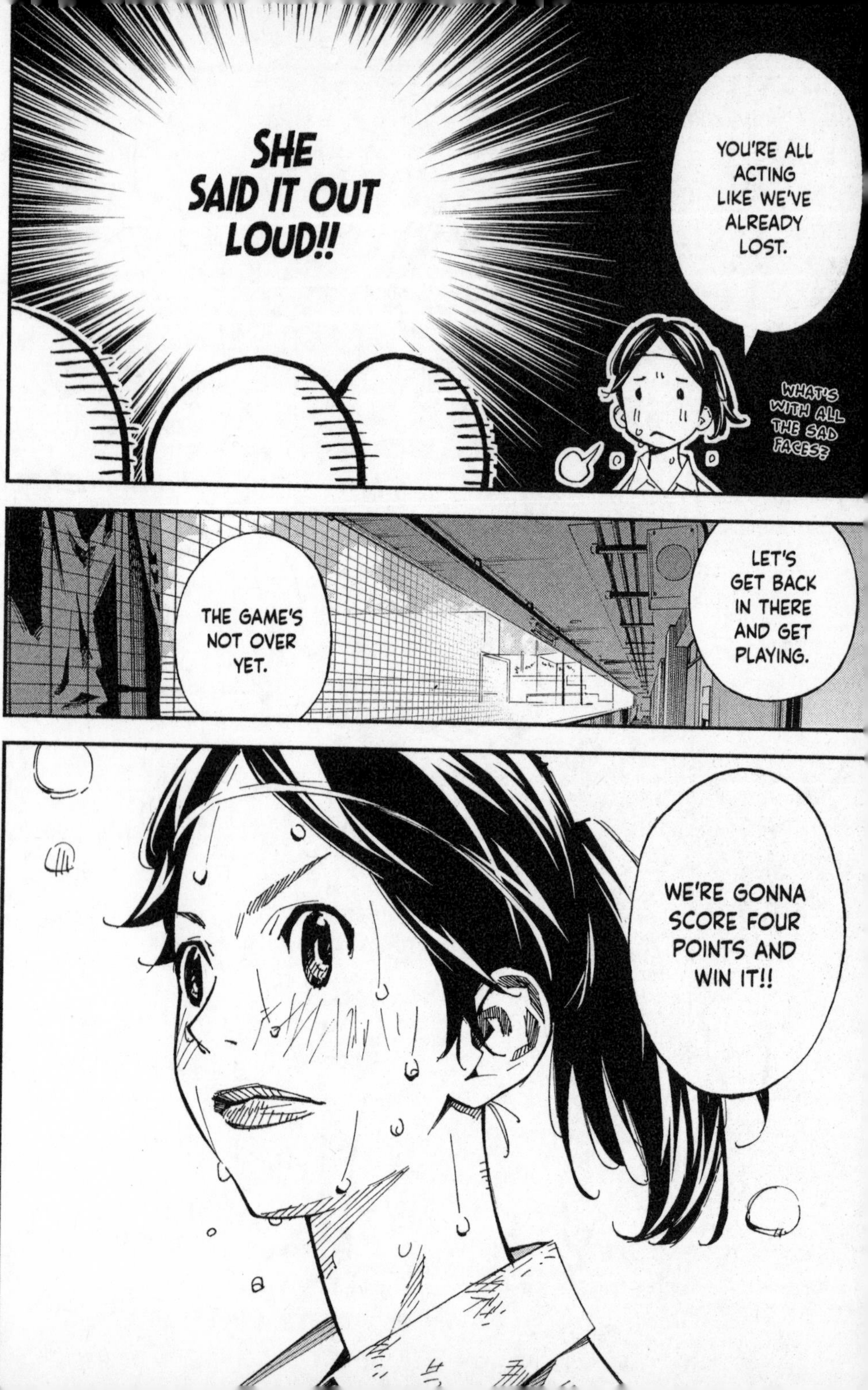
YOU'RE ALL ACTING LIKE WE'VE ALREADY LOST.
WHAT'S WITH ALL THE SAD FACES?
SHE SAID IT OUT LOUD!!
LET'S GET BACK IN THERE AND GET PLAYING.
THE GAME'S NOT OVER YET.
WE'RE GONNA SCORE FOUR POINTS AND WIN IT!!

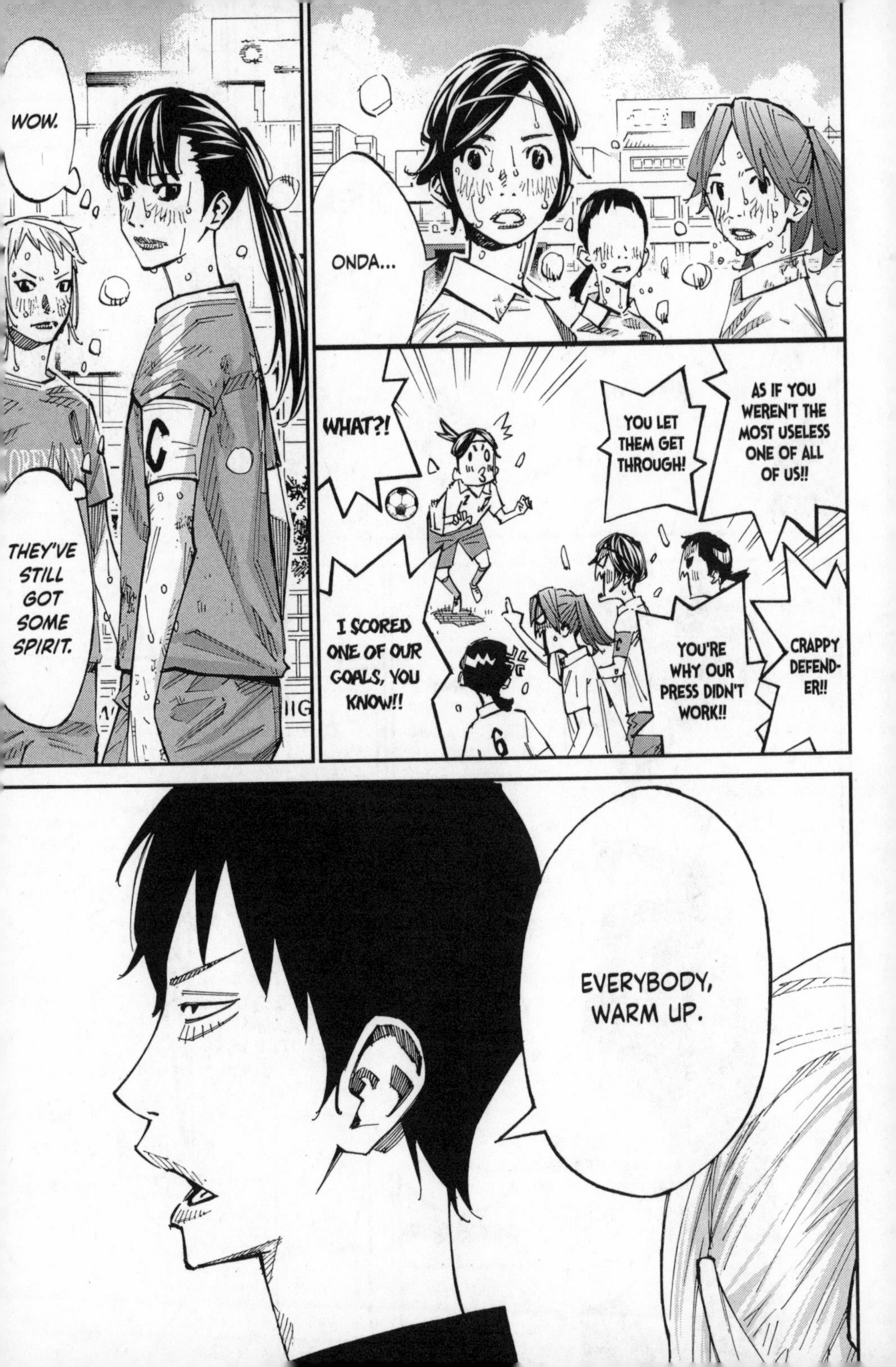
ONDA...
AS IF YOU WEREN'T THE MOST USELESS ONE OF ALL OF US!!
YOU LET THEM GET THROUGH!
WHAT?!
CRAPPY DEFENDER!!
YOU'RE WHY OUR PRESS DIDN'T WORK!!
I SCORED ONE OF OUR GOALS, YOU KNOW!!
WOW.
THEY'VE STILL GOT SOME SPIRIT.
EVERYBODY, WARM UP.

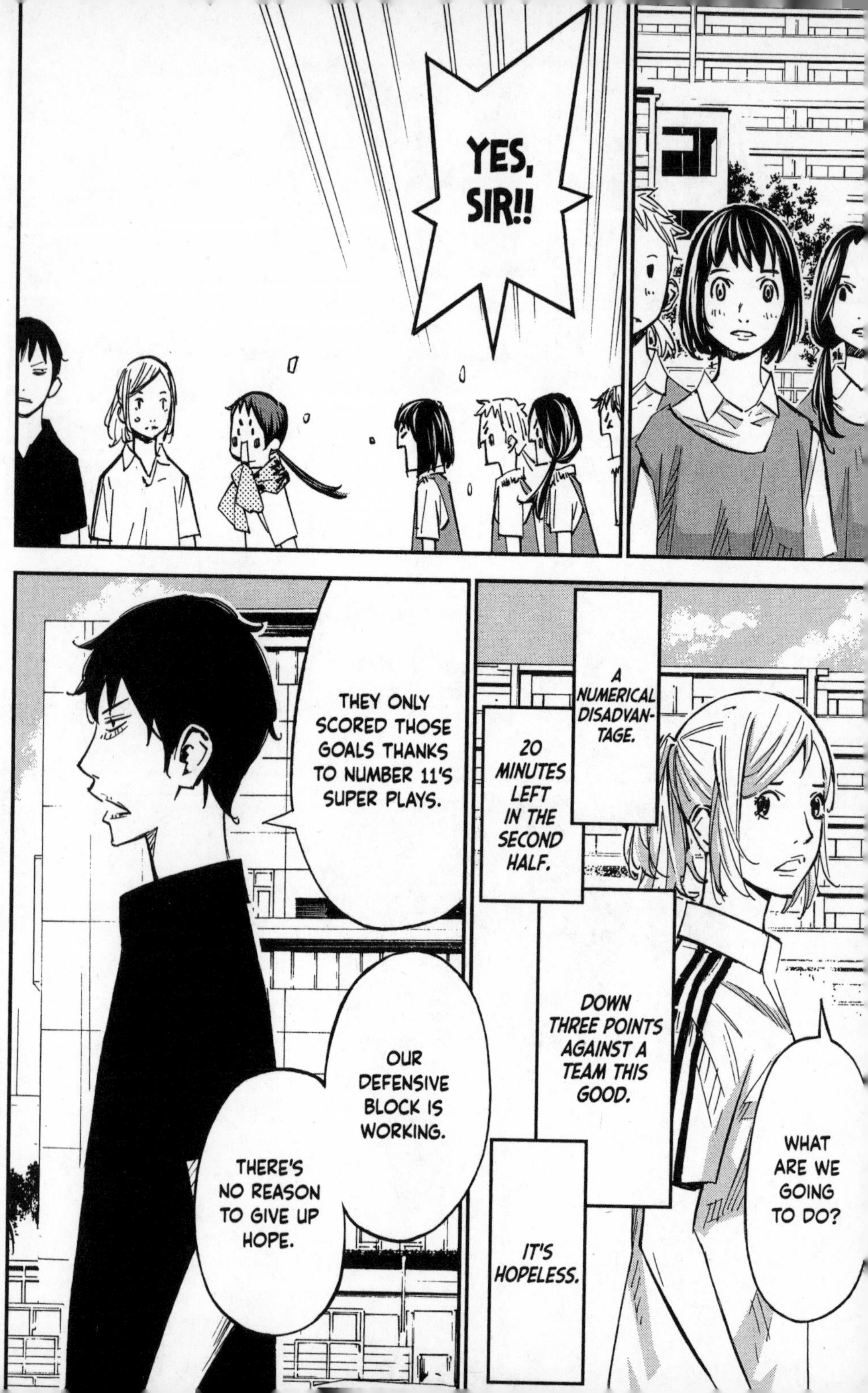
YES, SIR!!
A NUMERICAL DISADVAN-TAGE.
20 MINUTES LEFT IN THE SECOND HALF.
DOWN THREE POINTS AGAINST A TEAM THIS GOOD.
WHAT ARE WE GOING TO DO?
IT'S HOPELESS.
THEY ONLY SCORED THOSE GOALS THANKS TO NUMBER 11'S SUPER PLAYS.
OUR DEFENSIVE BLOCK IS WORKING.
THERE'S NO REASON TO GIVE UP HOPE.

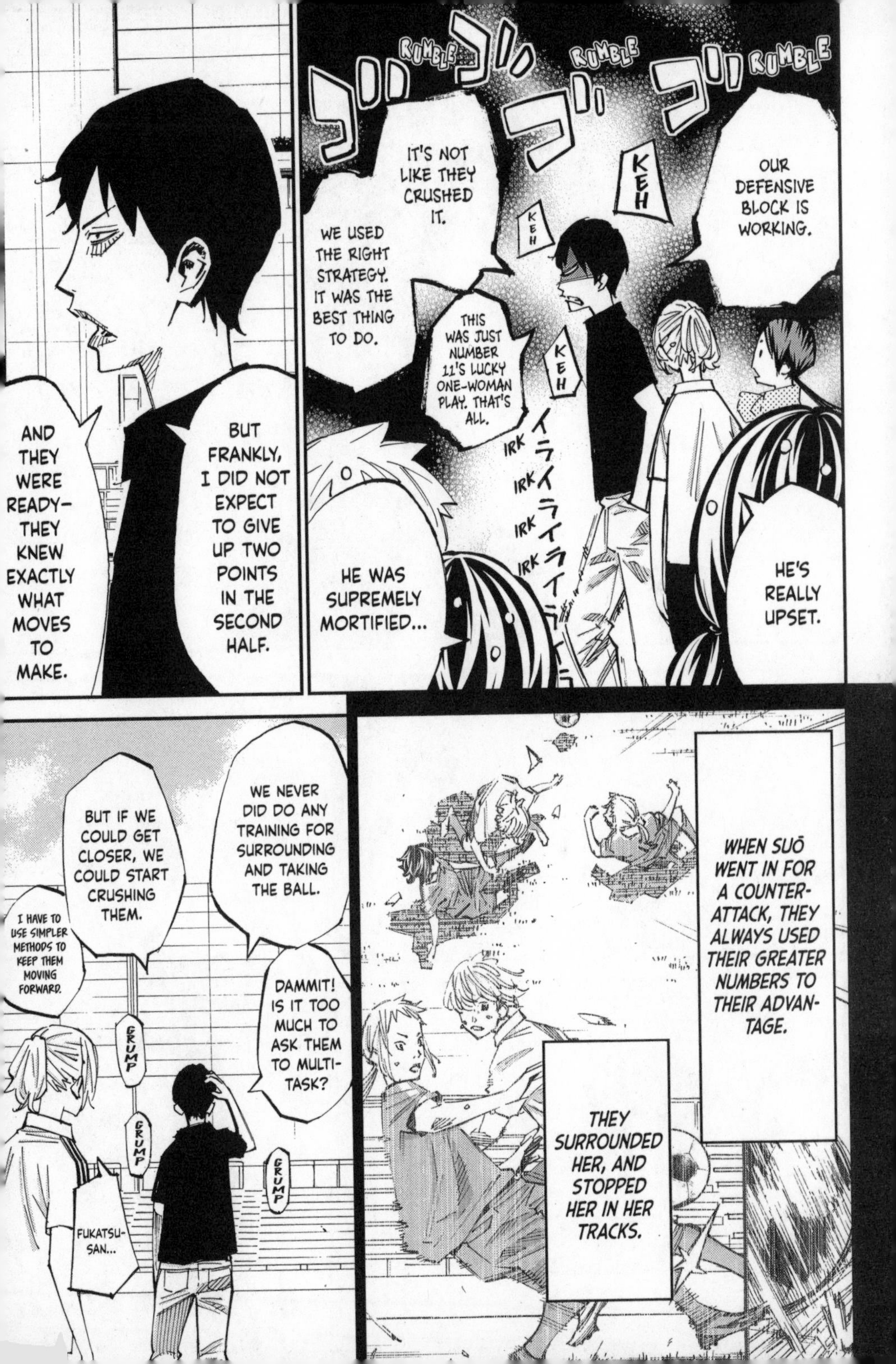
RUMBLE
RUMBLE
RUMBLE
OUR DEFENSIVE BLOCK IS WORKING.
KEH
KEH
IT'S NOT LIKE THEY CRUSHED IT.
WE USED THE RIGHT STRATEGY. IT WAS THE BEST THING TO DO.
KEH
THIS WAS JUST NUMBER 11'S LUCKY ONE-WOMAN PLAY. THAT'S ALL.
IRK IRK IRK IRK
HE'S REALLY UPSET.
HE WAS SUPREMELY MORTIFIED...
BUT FRANKLY, I DID NOT EXPECT TO GIVE UP TWO POINTS IN THE SECOND HALF.
AND THEY WERE READY— THEY KNEW EXACTLY WHAT MOVES TO MAKE.
WHEN SUŌ WENT IN FOR A COUNTER-ATTACK, THEY ALWAYS USED THEIR GREATER NUMBERS TO THEIR ADVANTAGE.
THEY SURROUNDED HER, AND STOPPED HER IN HER TRACKS.
WE NEVER DID DO ANY TRAINING FOR SURROUNDING AND TAKING THE BALL.
BUT IF WE COULD GET CLOSER, WE COULD START CRUSHING THEM.
I HAVE TO USE SIMPLER METHODS TO KEEP THEM MOVING FORWARD.
DAMMIT! IS IT TOO MUCH TO ASK THEM TO MULTI-TASK?
GRUMP
GRUMP
GRUMP
FUKATSU-SAN...

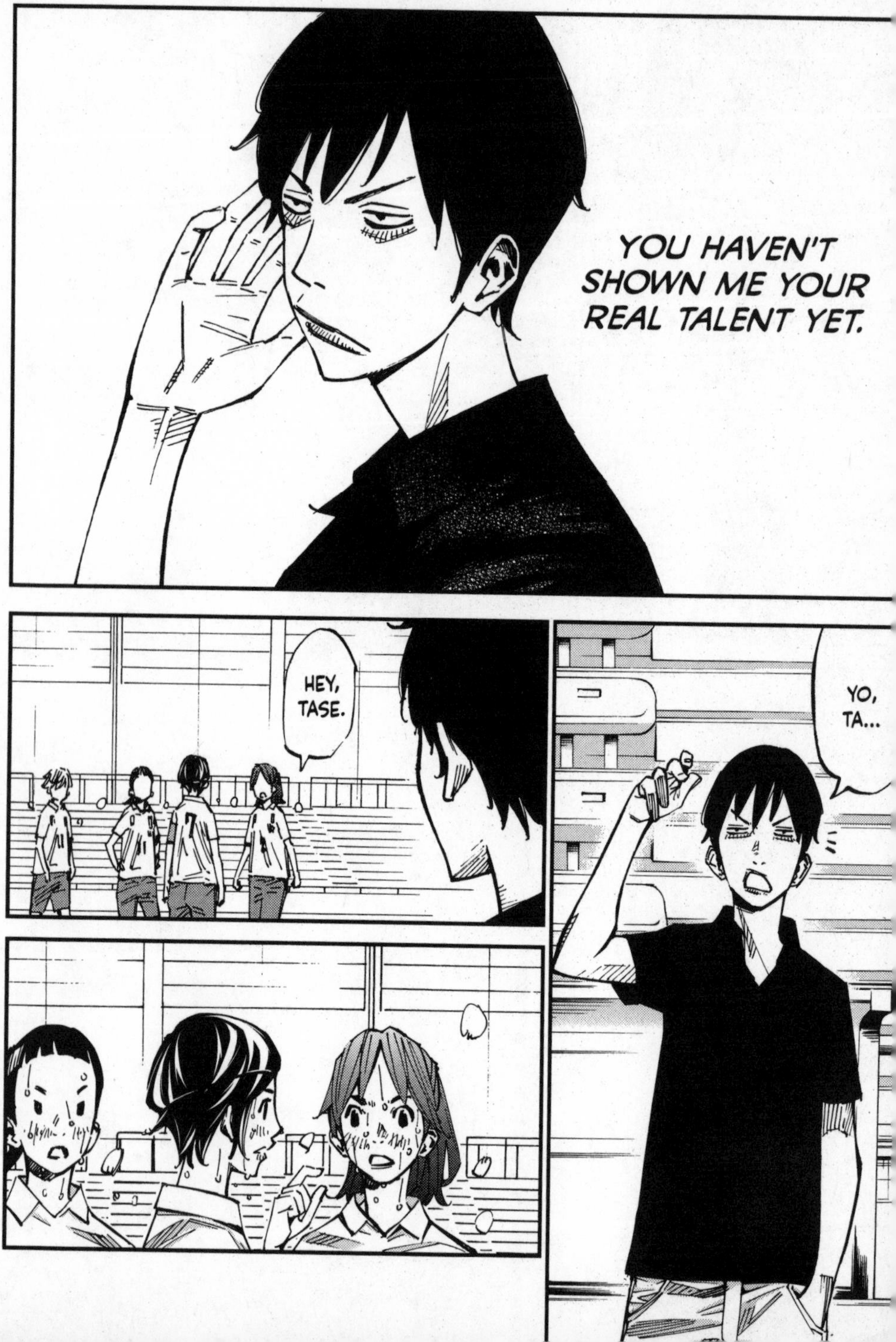
YOU HAVEN'T SHOWN ME YOUR REAL TALENT YET.
YO, TA...
HEY, TASE.

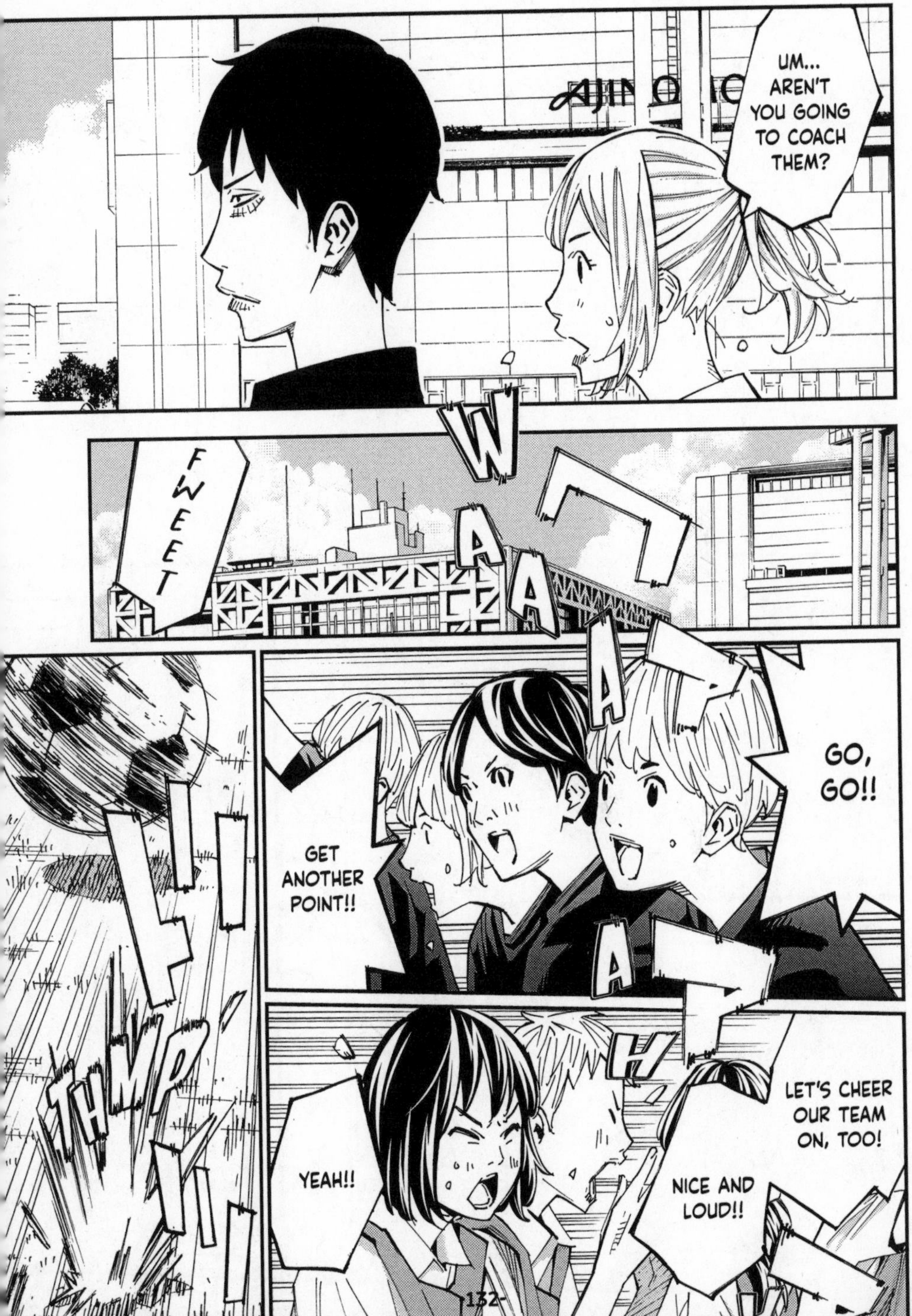
UM... AREN'T YOU GOING TO COACH THEM?
FWEET
WAAAAHH
GO, GO!!
GET ANOTHER POINT!!
LET'S CHEER OUR TEAM ON, TOO!
NICE AND LOUD!!
YEAH!!
THMP

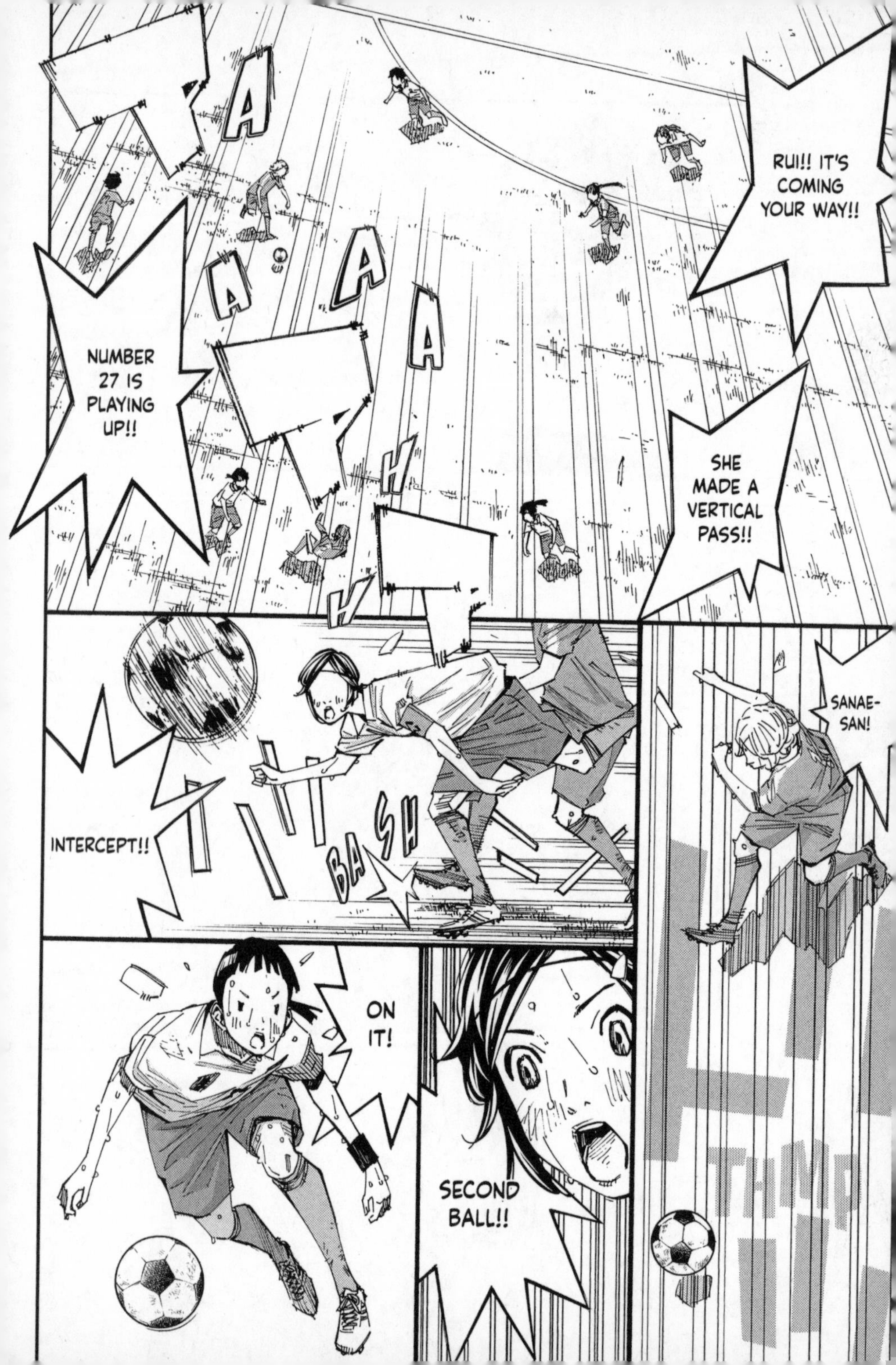
RUI!! IT'S COMING YOUR WAY!!
SHE MADE A VERTICAL PASS!!
AAAAAHH
NUMBER 27 IS PLAYING UP!!
SANAE-SAN!
THMP
INTERCEPT!!
BASH
SECOND BALL!!
ON IT!

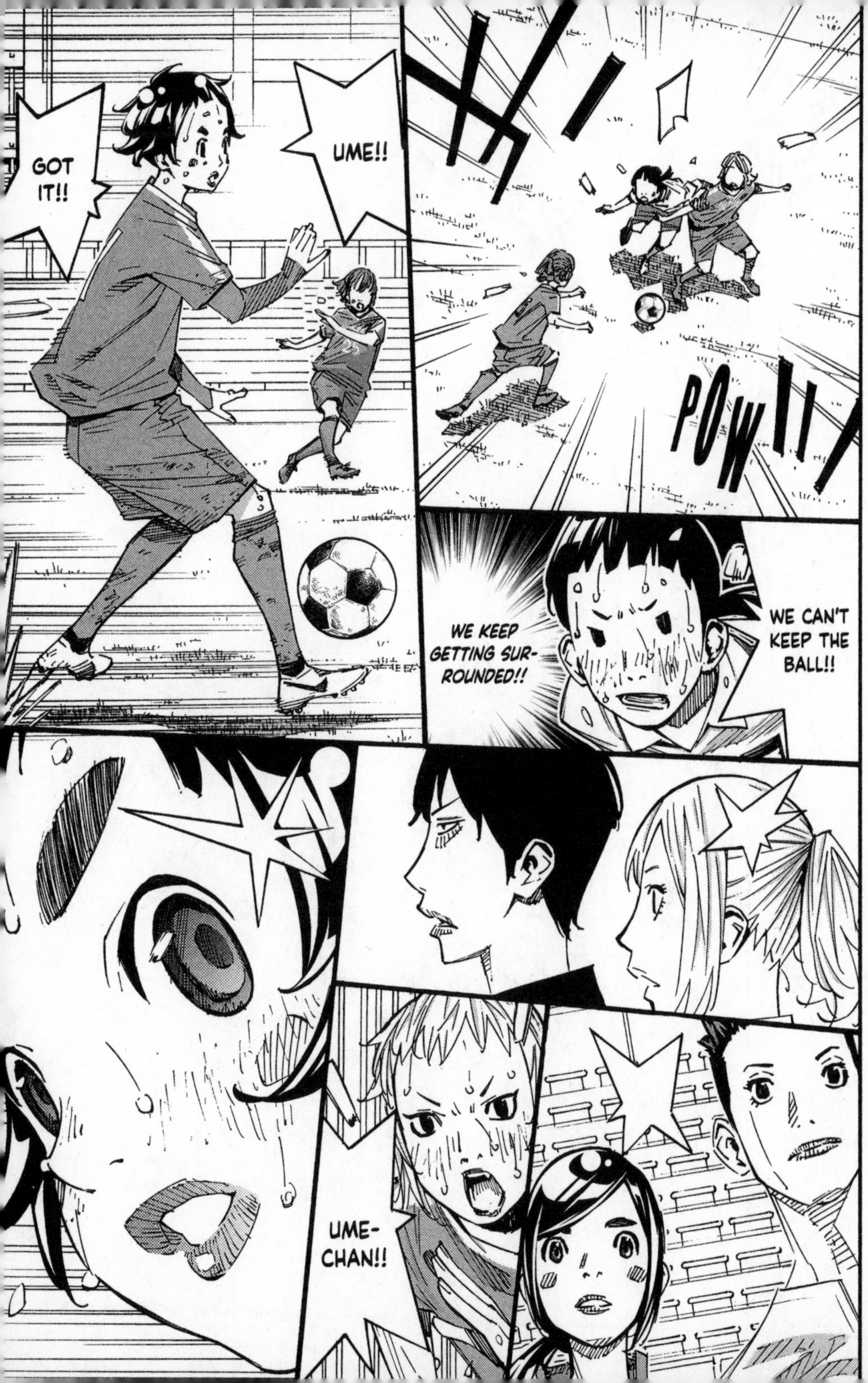
POW!!
WE CAN'T KEEP THE BALL!!
WE KEEP GETTING SUR-ROUNDED!!
UME!!
GOT IT!!
UME-CHAN!!

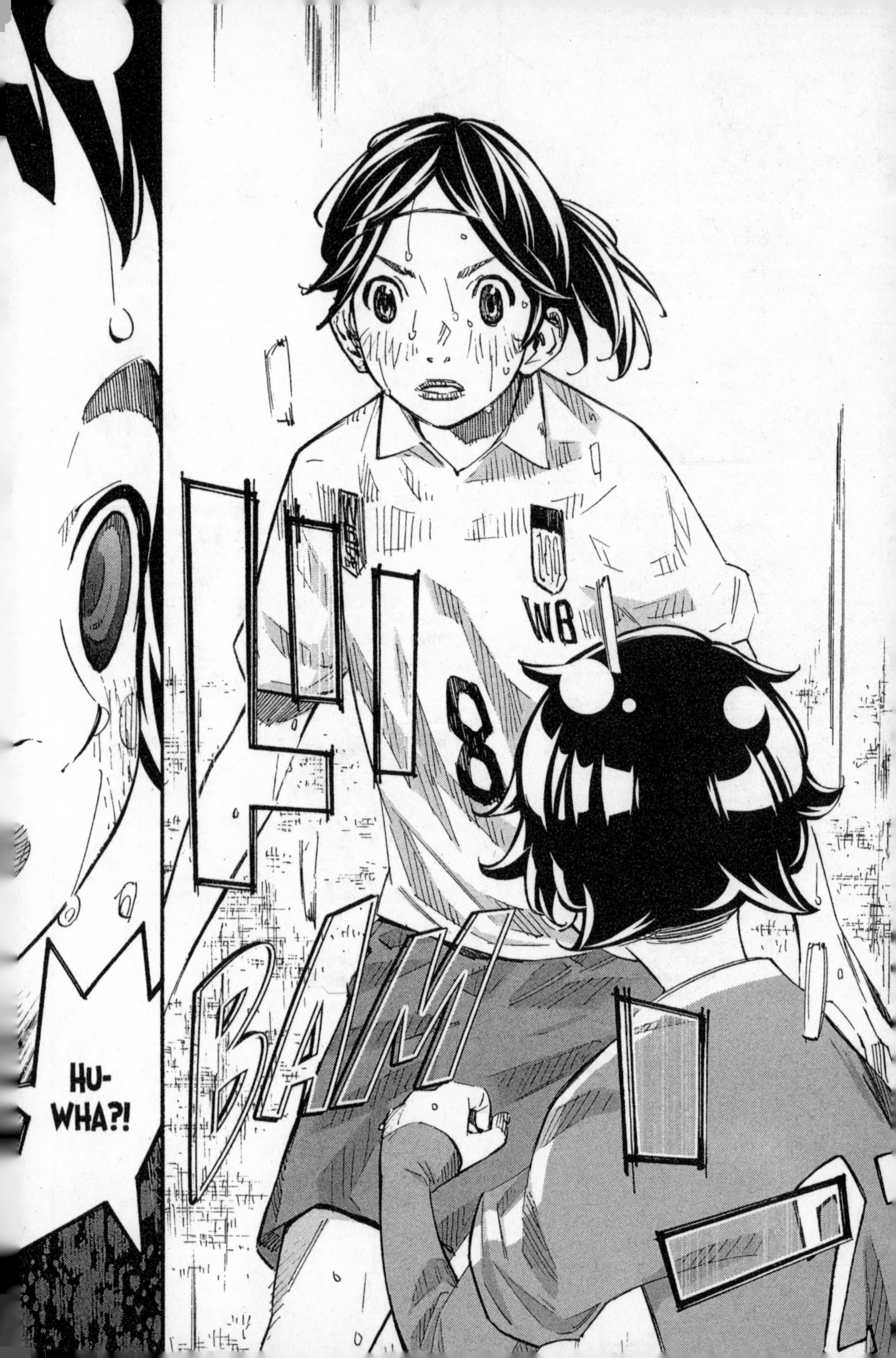
BAM
HU-
WHA?!

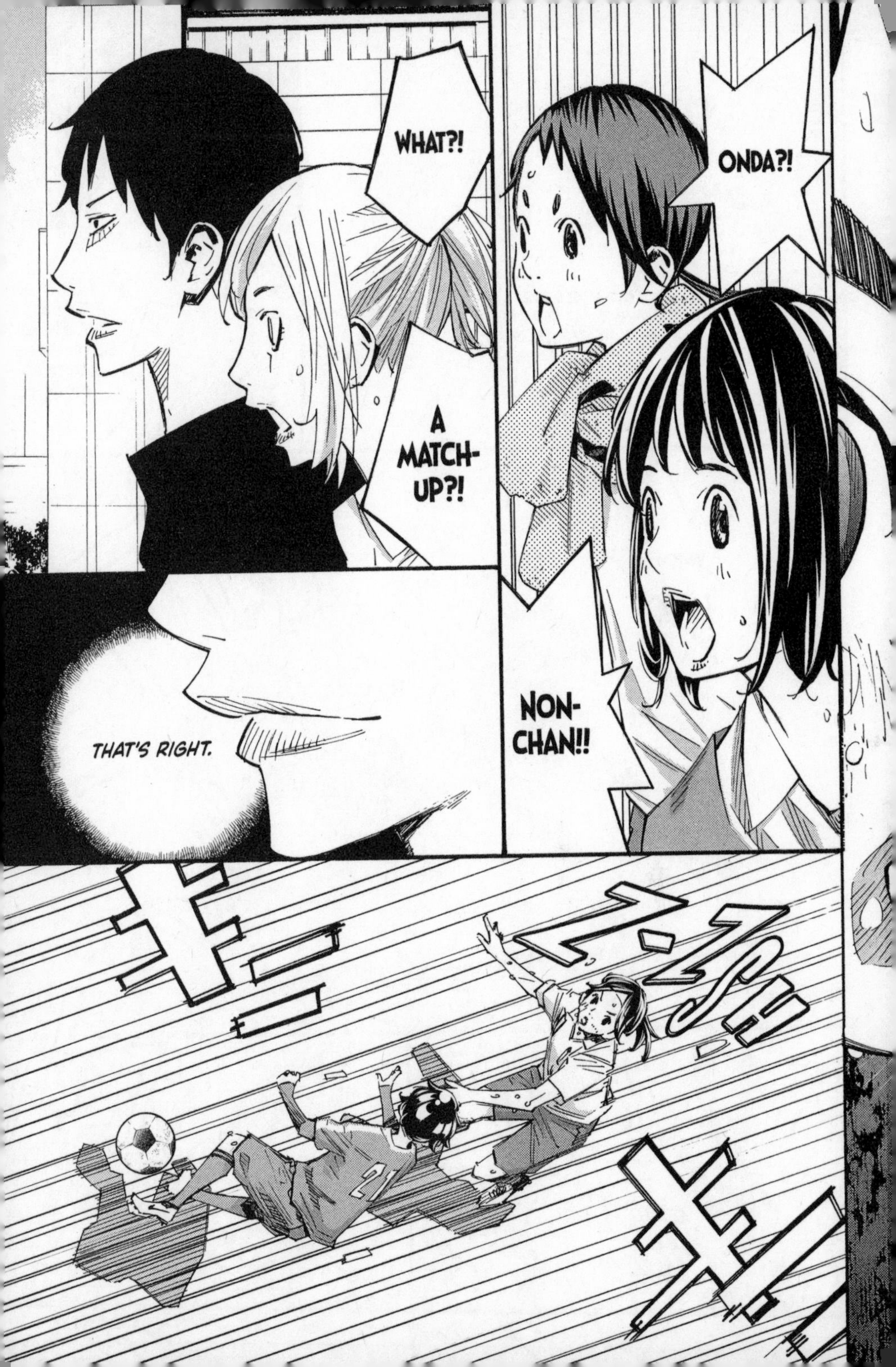
ONDA?!
NON-CHAN!!
WHAT?!
A MATCH-UP?!
THAT'S RIGHT.

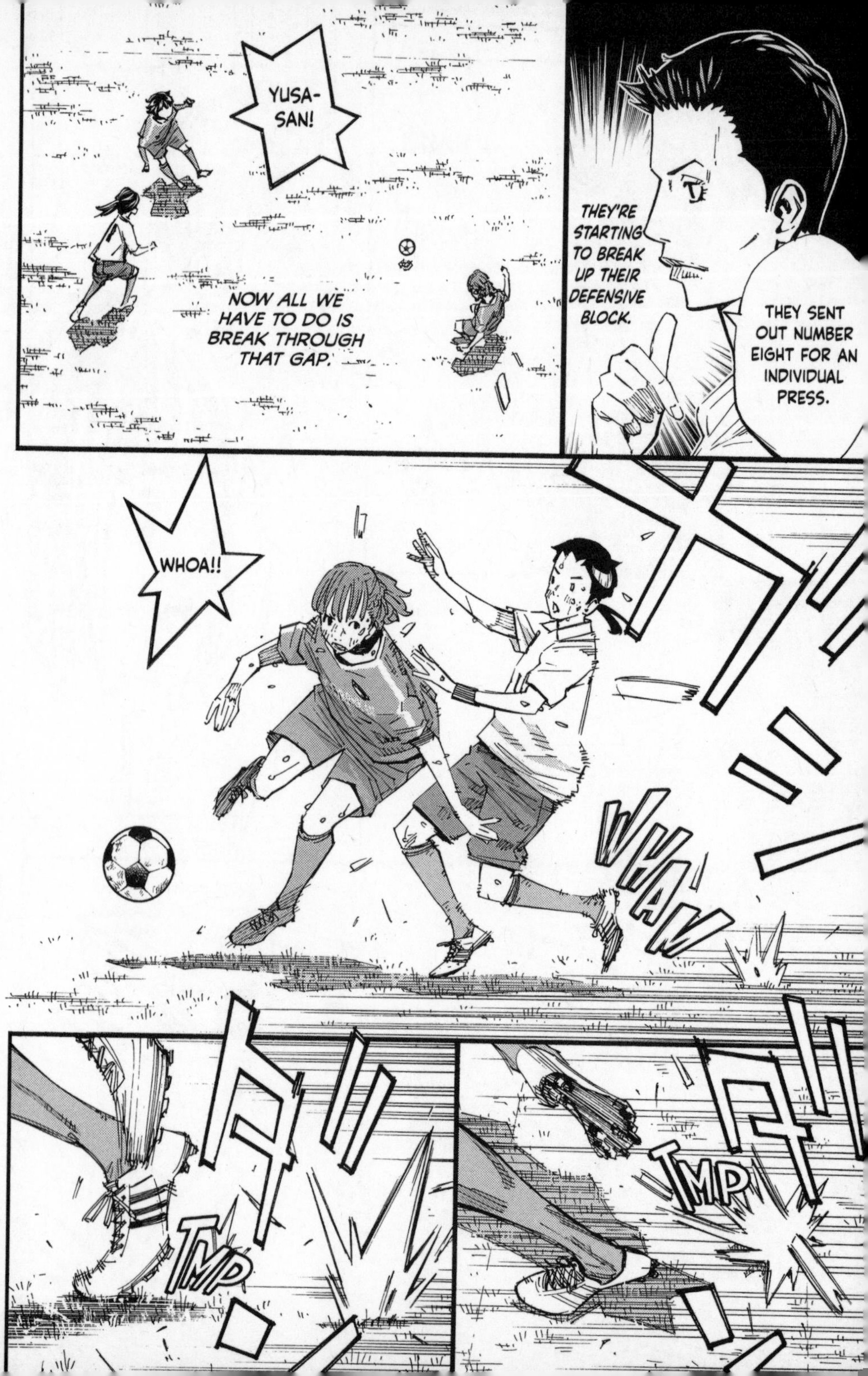
THEY SENT OUT NUMBER EIGHT FOR AN INDIVIDUAL PRESS.
THEY'RE STARTING TO BREAK UP THEIR DEFENSIVE BLOCK.
YUSA-SAN!
NOW ALL WE HAVE TO DO IS BREAK THROUGH THAT GAP.
WHOA!!
WHAM
TMP
TMP

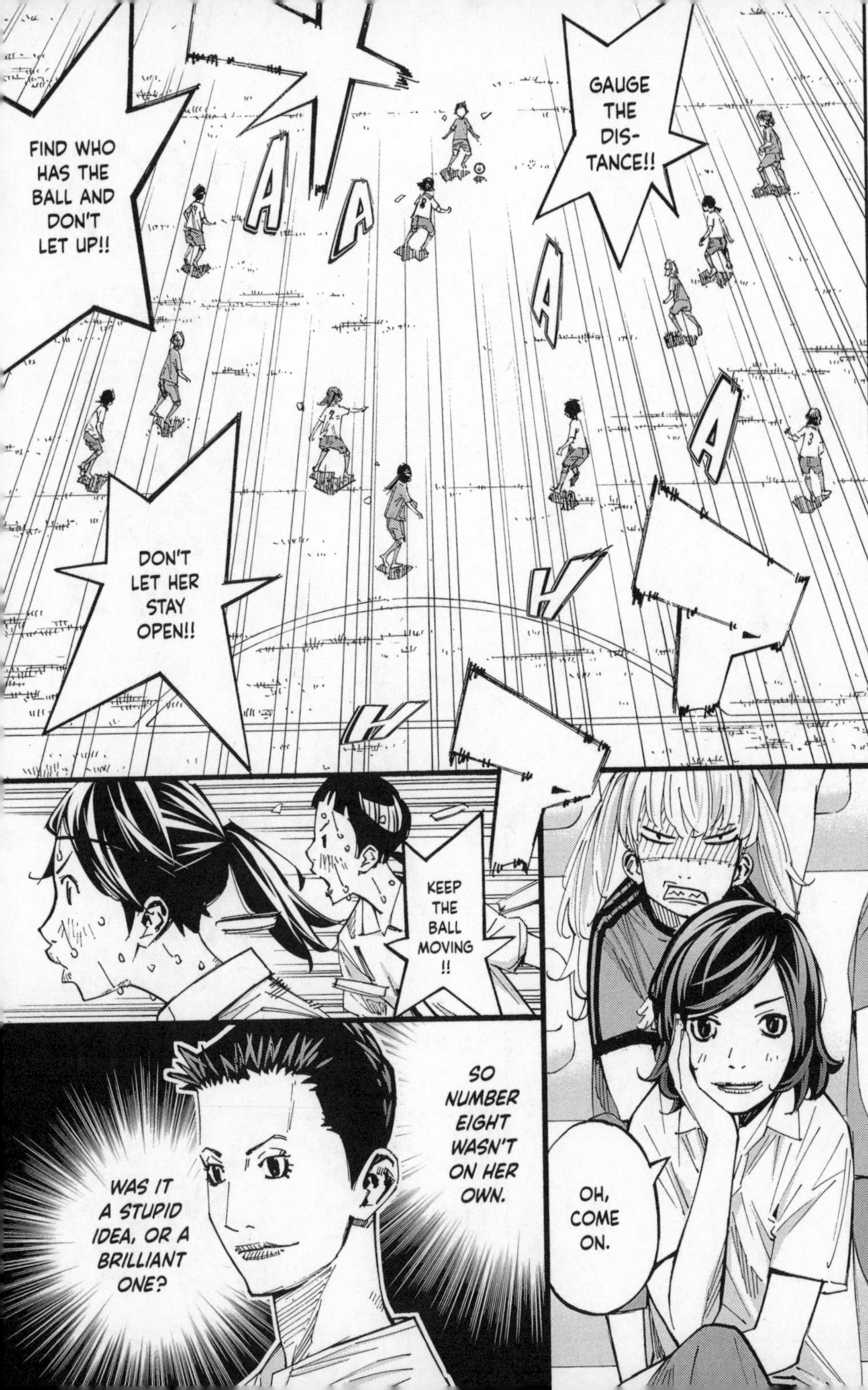
GAUGE THE DIS-TANCE!!
FIND WHO HAS THE BALL AND DON'T LET UP!!
AAAA
HH
DON'T LET HER STAY OPEN!!
OH, COME ON.
KEEP THE BALL MOVING!!
SO NUMBER EIGHT WASN'T ON HER OWN.
WAS IT A STUPID IDEA, OR A BRILLIANT ONE?

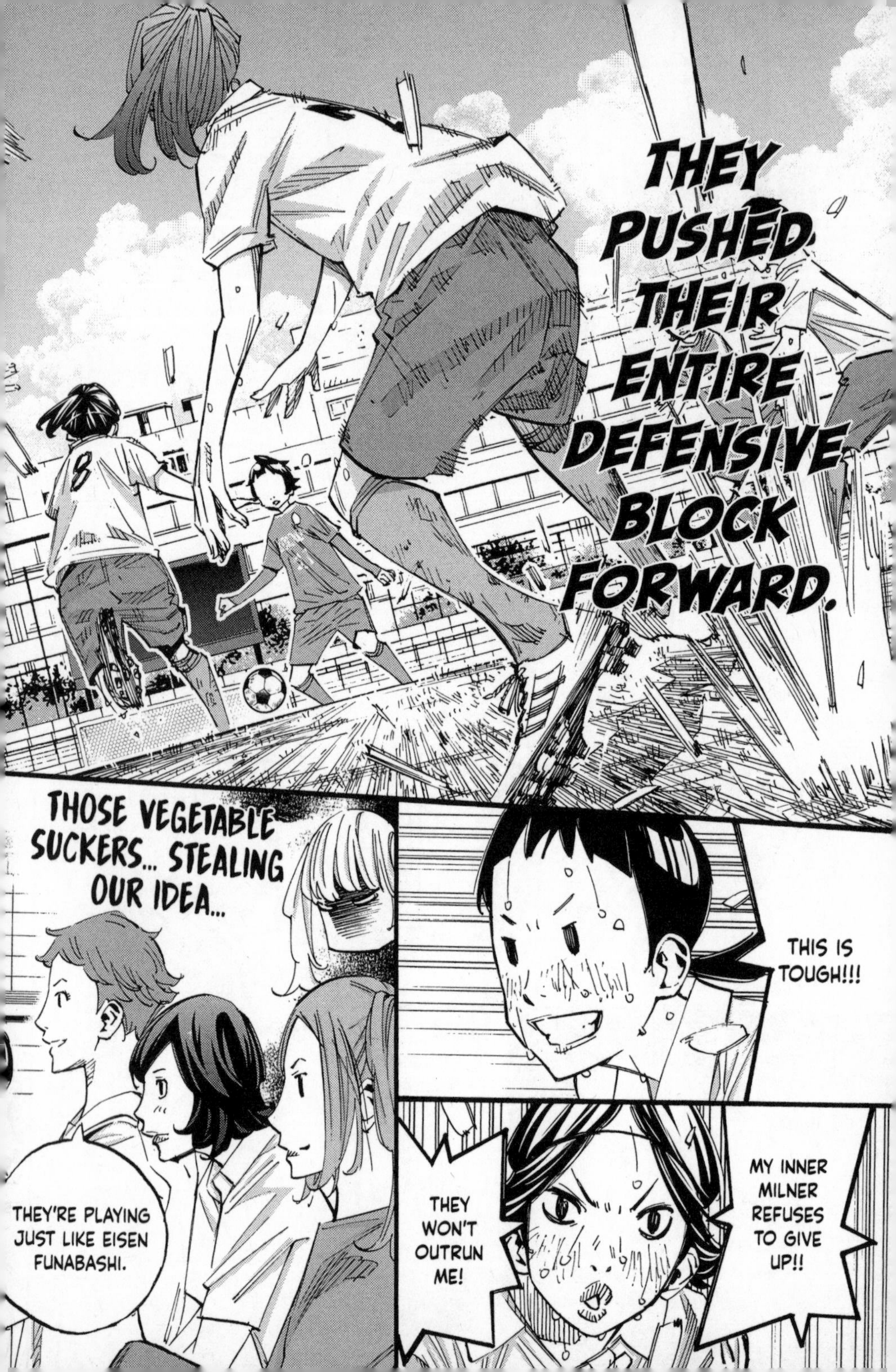
THEY PUSHED THEIR ENTIRE DEFENSIVE BLOCK FORWARD.
THIS IS TOUGH!!!
MY INNER MILNER REFUSES TO GIVE UP!!
THEY WON'T OUTRUN ME!
THOSE VEGETABLE SUCKERS... STEALING OUR IDEA...
THEY'RE PLAYING JUST LIKE EISEN FUNABASHI.

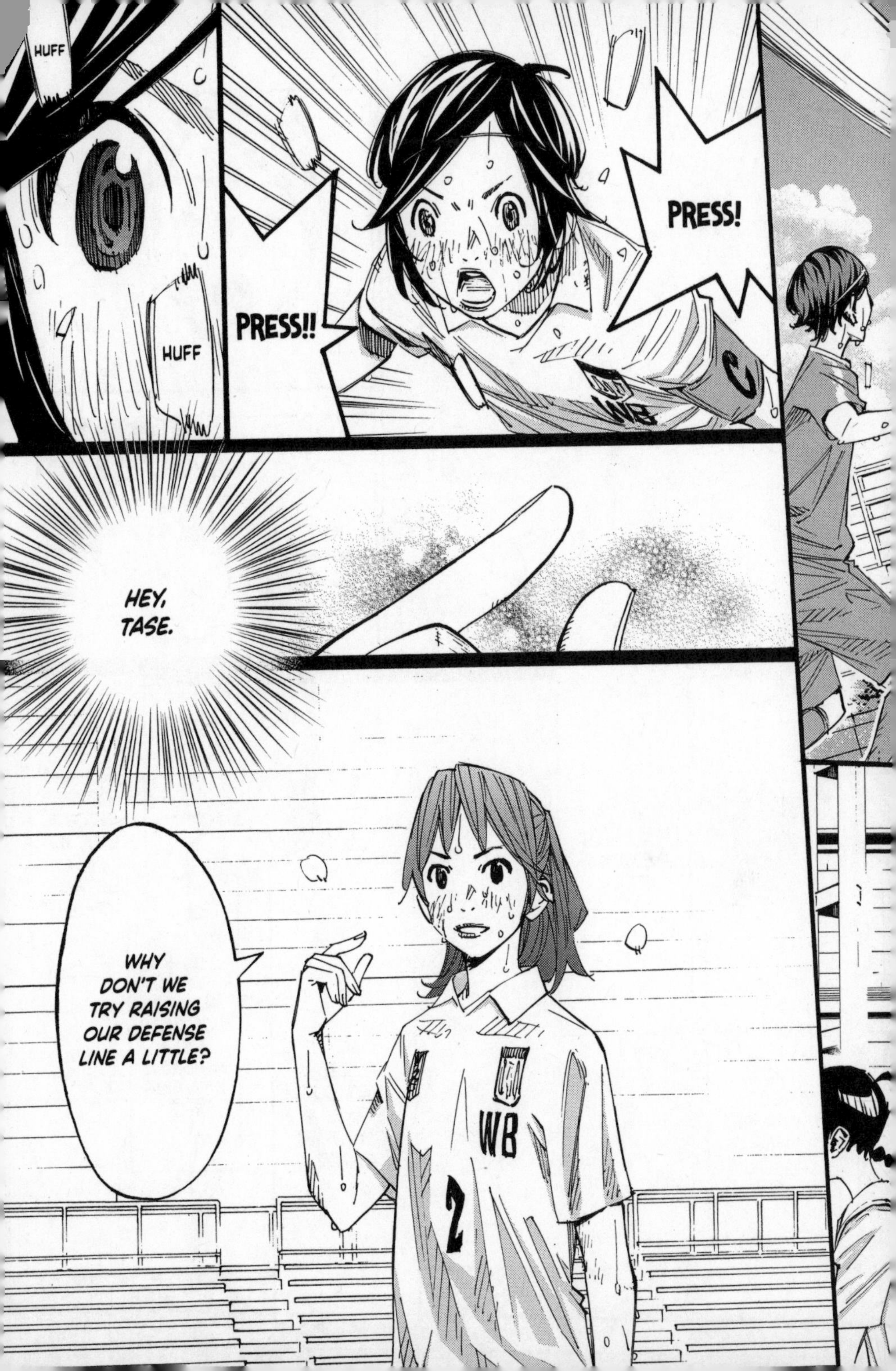
PRESS!
PRESS!!
HUFF
HUFF
HEY, TASE.
WHY DON'T WE TRY RAISING OUR DEFENSE LINE A LITTLE?

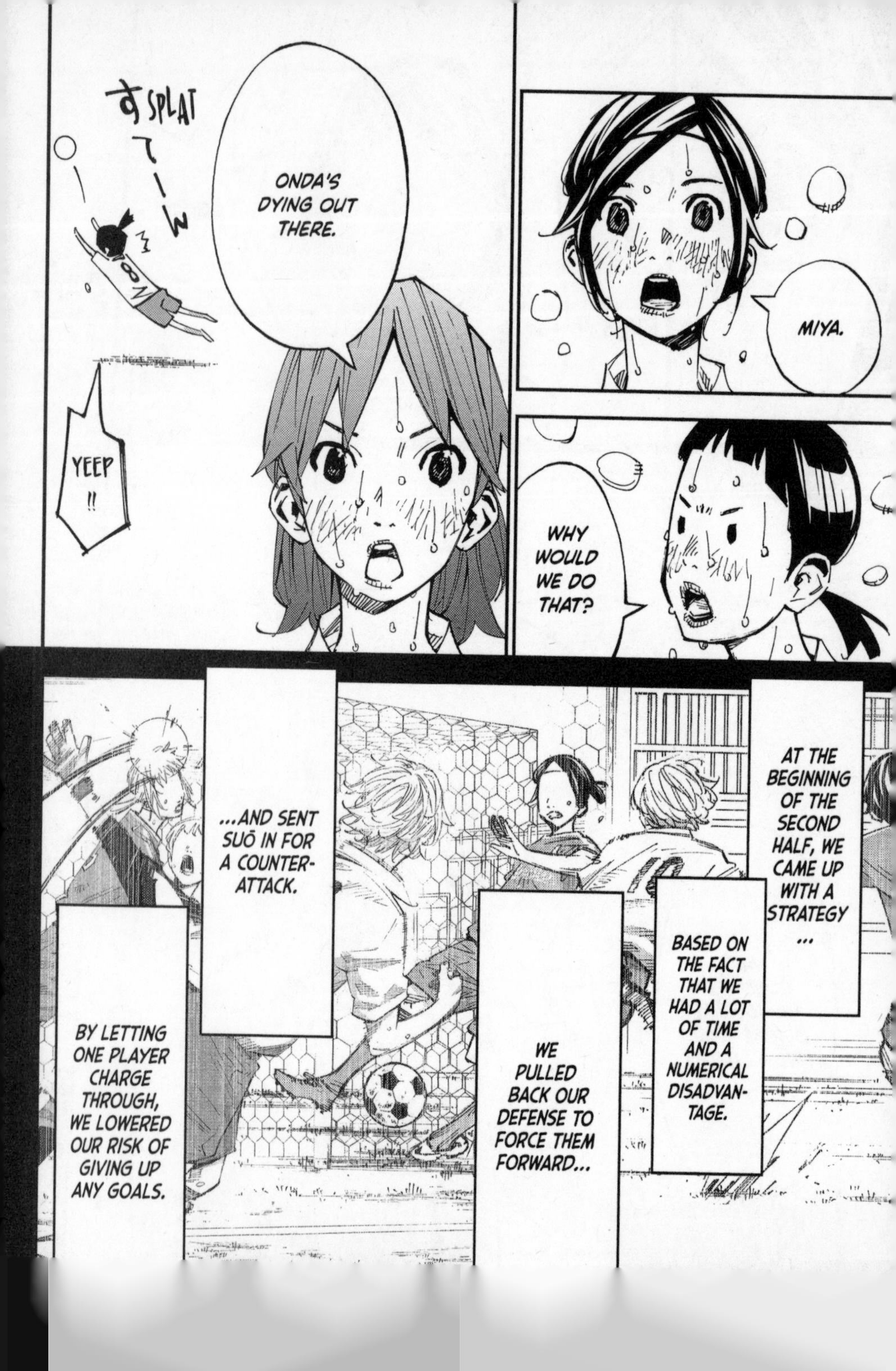
MIYA.
WHY WOULD WE DO THAT?
ONDA'S DYING OUT THERE.
す SPLAT
YEEP !!
AT THE BEGINNING OF THE SECOND HALF, WE CAME UP WITH A STRATEGY ...
BASED ON THE FACT THAT WE HAD A LOT OF TIME AND A NUMERICAL DISADVANTAGE.
WE PULLED BACK OUR DEFENSE TO FORCE THEM FORWARD...
...AND SENT SUŌ IN FOR A COUNTER-ATTACK.
BY LETTING ONE PLAYER CHARGE THROUGH, WE LOWERED OUR RISK OF GIVING UP ANY GOALS.

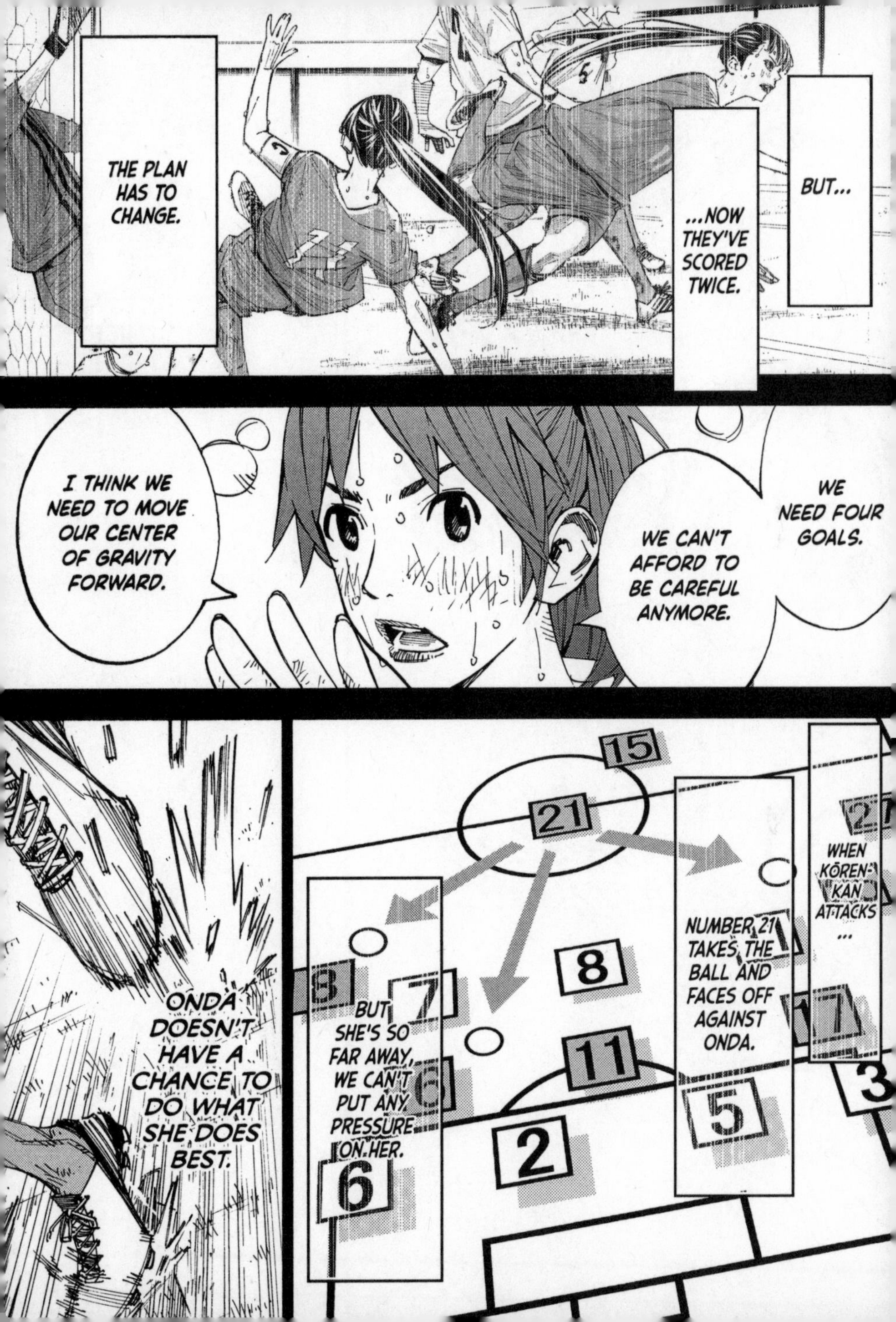
BUT...
...NOW THEY'VE SCORED TWICE.
THE PLAN HAS TO CHANGE.
WE NEED FOUR GOALS.
WE CAN'T AFFORD TO BE CAREFUL ANYMORE.
I THINK WE NEED TO MOVE OUR CENTER OF GRAVITY FORWARD.
WHEN KŌREN-KAN ATTACKS...
NUMBER 21 TAKES THE BALL AND FACES OFF AGAINST ONDA.
BUT SHE'S SO FAR AWAY, WE CAN'T PUT ANY PRESSURE ON HER.
ONDA DOESN'T HAVE A CHANCE TO DO WHAT SHE DOES BEST.

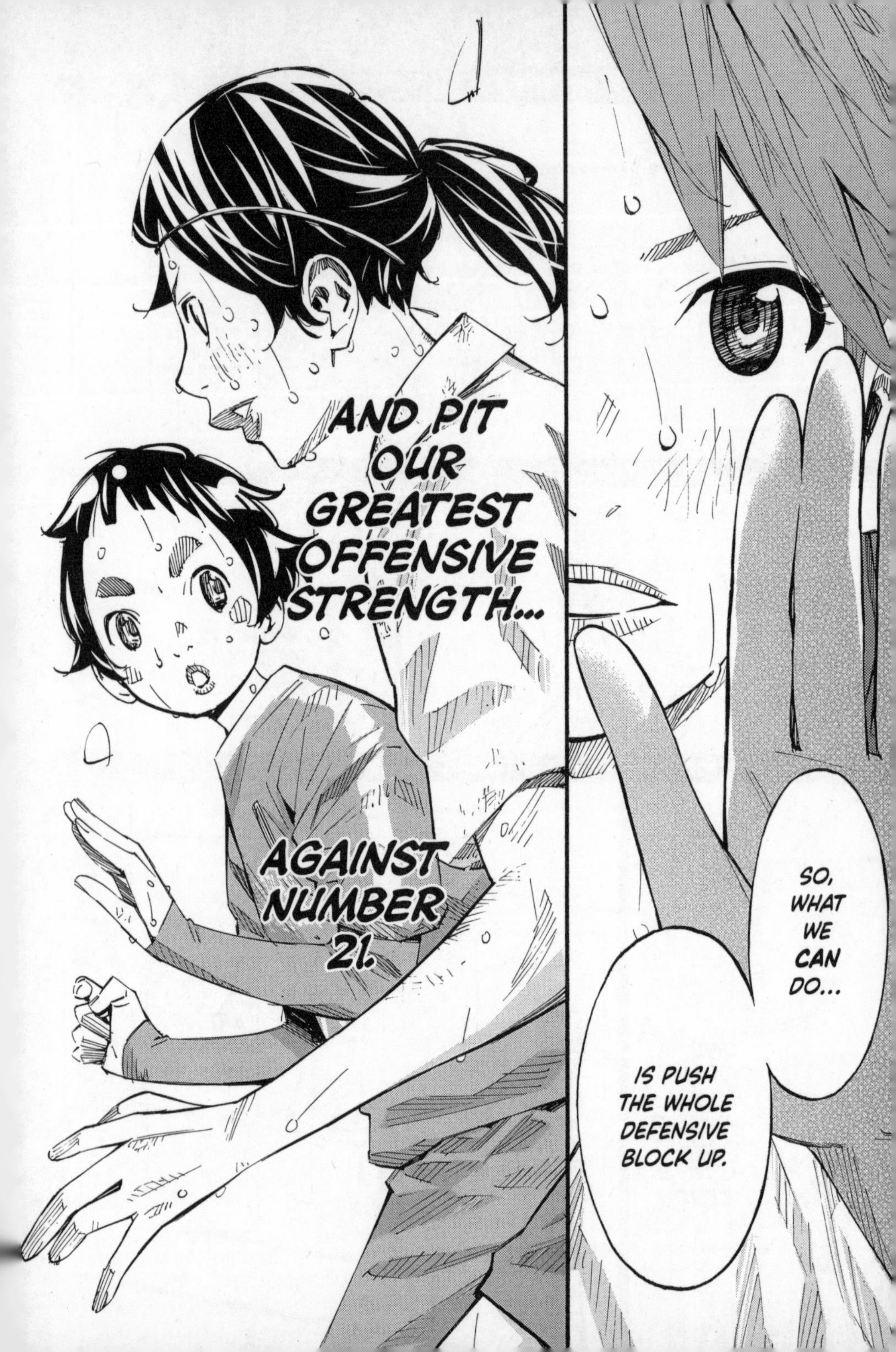
SO, WHAT WE CAN DO...
IS PUSH THE WHOLE DEFENSIVE BLOCK UP.
AND PIT OUR GREATEST OFFENSIVE STRENGTH...
AGAINST NUMBER 21.

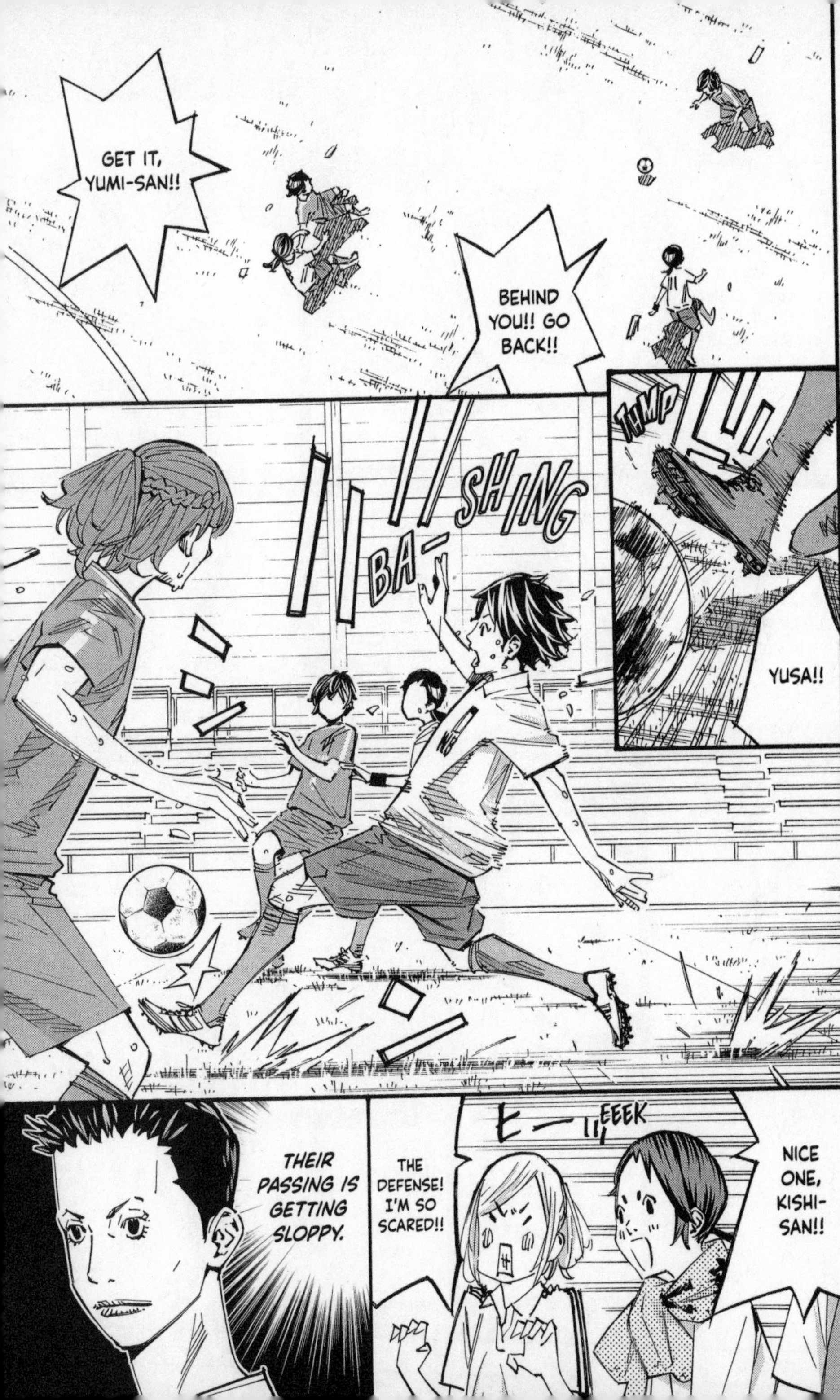
BEHIND YOU!! GO BACK!!
GET IT, YUMI-SAN!!
TUMP
YUSA!!
BA-SHING
ヒー EEEK
NICE ONE, KISHI-SAN!!
THE DEFENSE! I'M SO SCARED!!
THEIR PASSING IS GETTING SLOPPY.

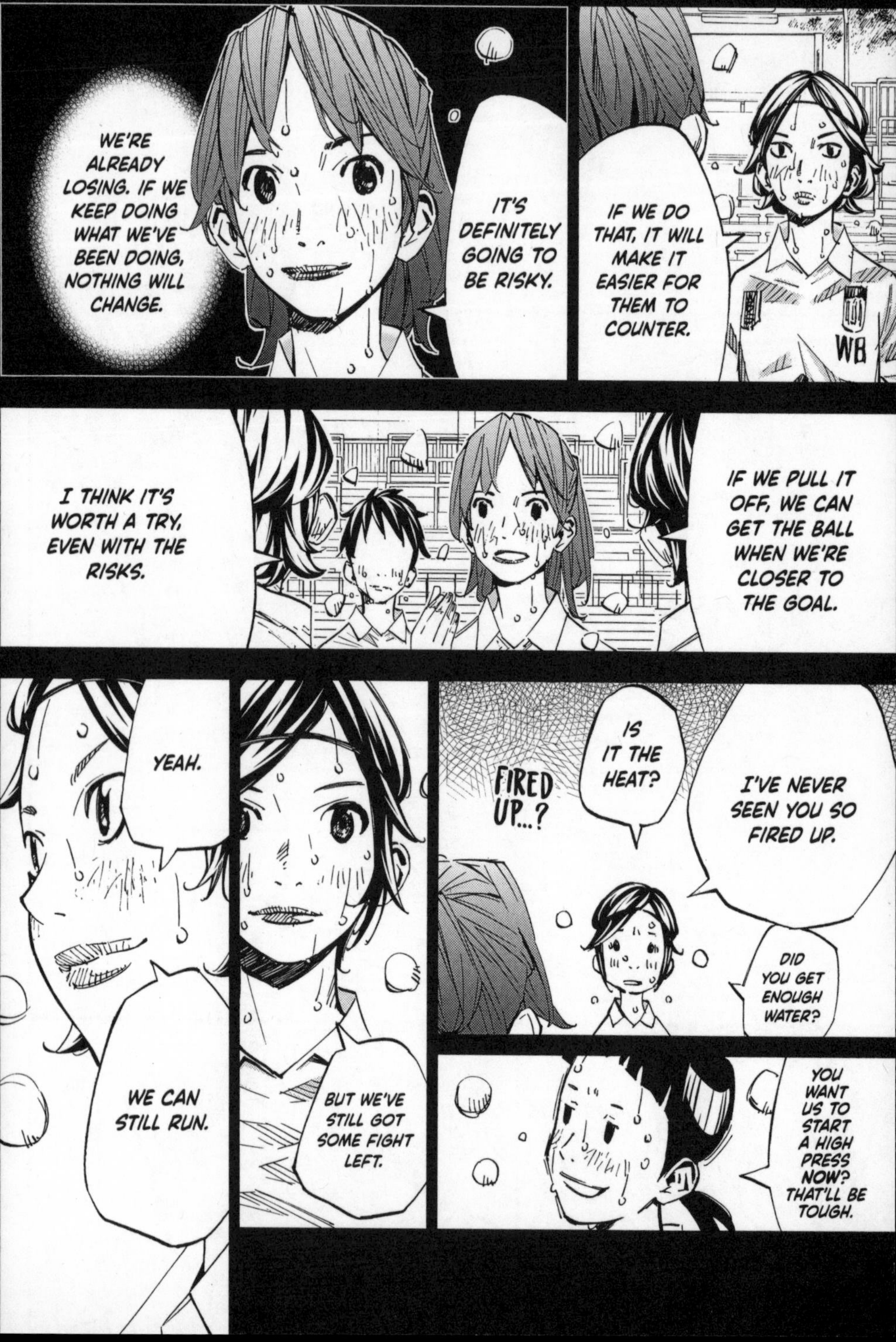
IF WE DO THAT, IT WILL MAKE IT EASIER FOR THEM TO COUNTER.
IT'S DEFINITELY GOING TO BE RISKY.
WE'RE ALREADY LOSING. IF WE KEEP DOING WHAT WE'VE BEEN DOING, NOTHING WILL CHANGE.
IF WE PULL IT OFF, WE CAN GET THE BALL WHEN WE'RE CLOSER TO THE GOAL.
I THINK IT'S WORTH A TRY, EVEN WITH THE RISKS.
I'VE NEVER SEEN YOU SO FIRED UP.
IS IT THE HEAT?
FIRED UP...?
DID YOU GET ENOUGH WATER?
YOU WANT US TO START A HIGH PRESS NOW? THAT'LL BE TOUGH.
BUT WE'VE STILL GOT SOME FIGHT LEFT.
YEAH.
WE CAN STILL RUN.

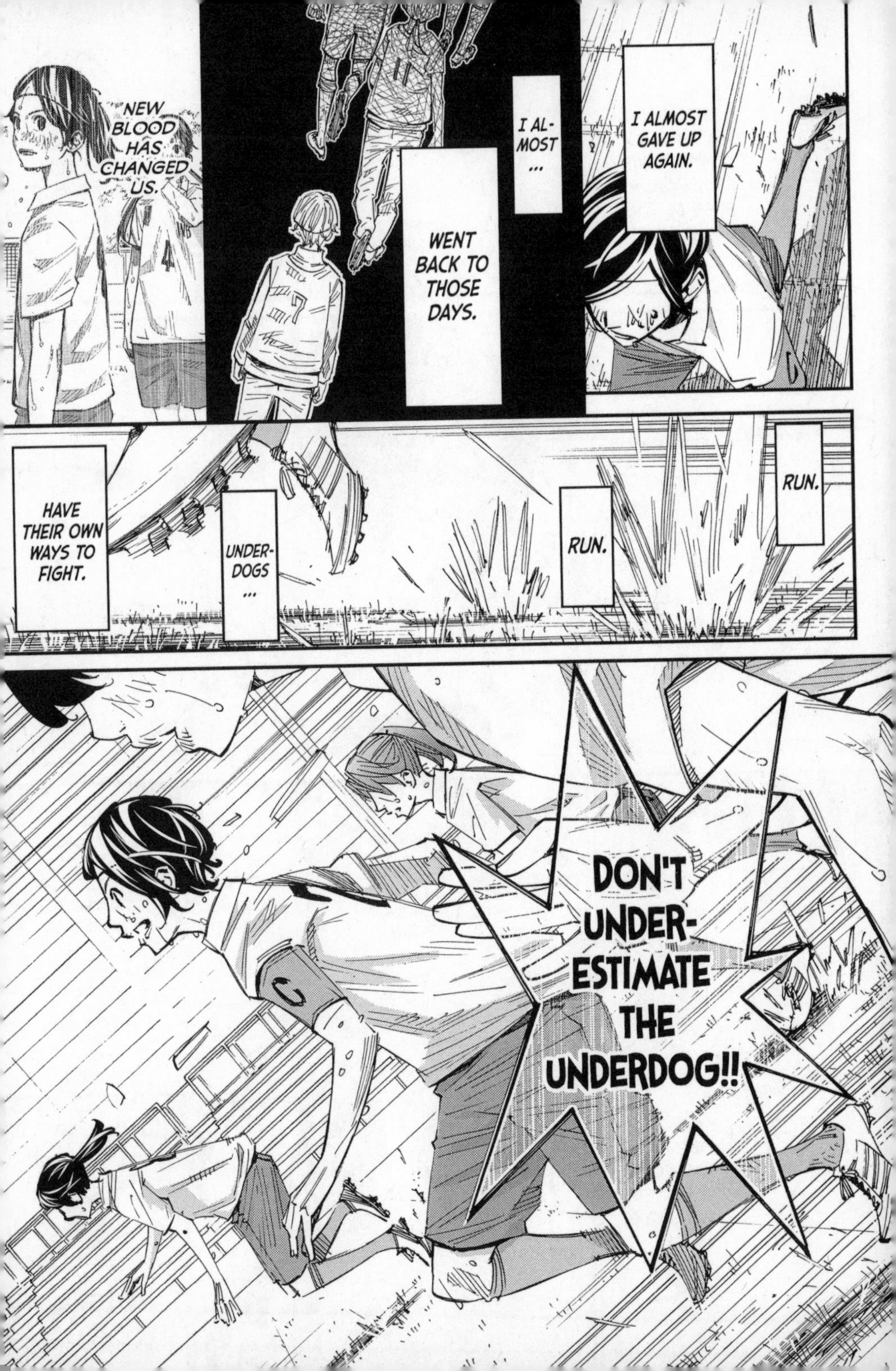
I ALMOST GAVE UP AGAIN.
I AL-MOST ...
WENT BACK TO THOSE DAYS.
NEW BLOOD HAS CHANGED US.
RUN.
RUN.
UNDER-DOGS ...
HAVE THEIR OWN WAYS TO FIGHT.
DON'T UNDER-ESTIMATE THE UNDERDOG!!

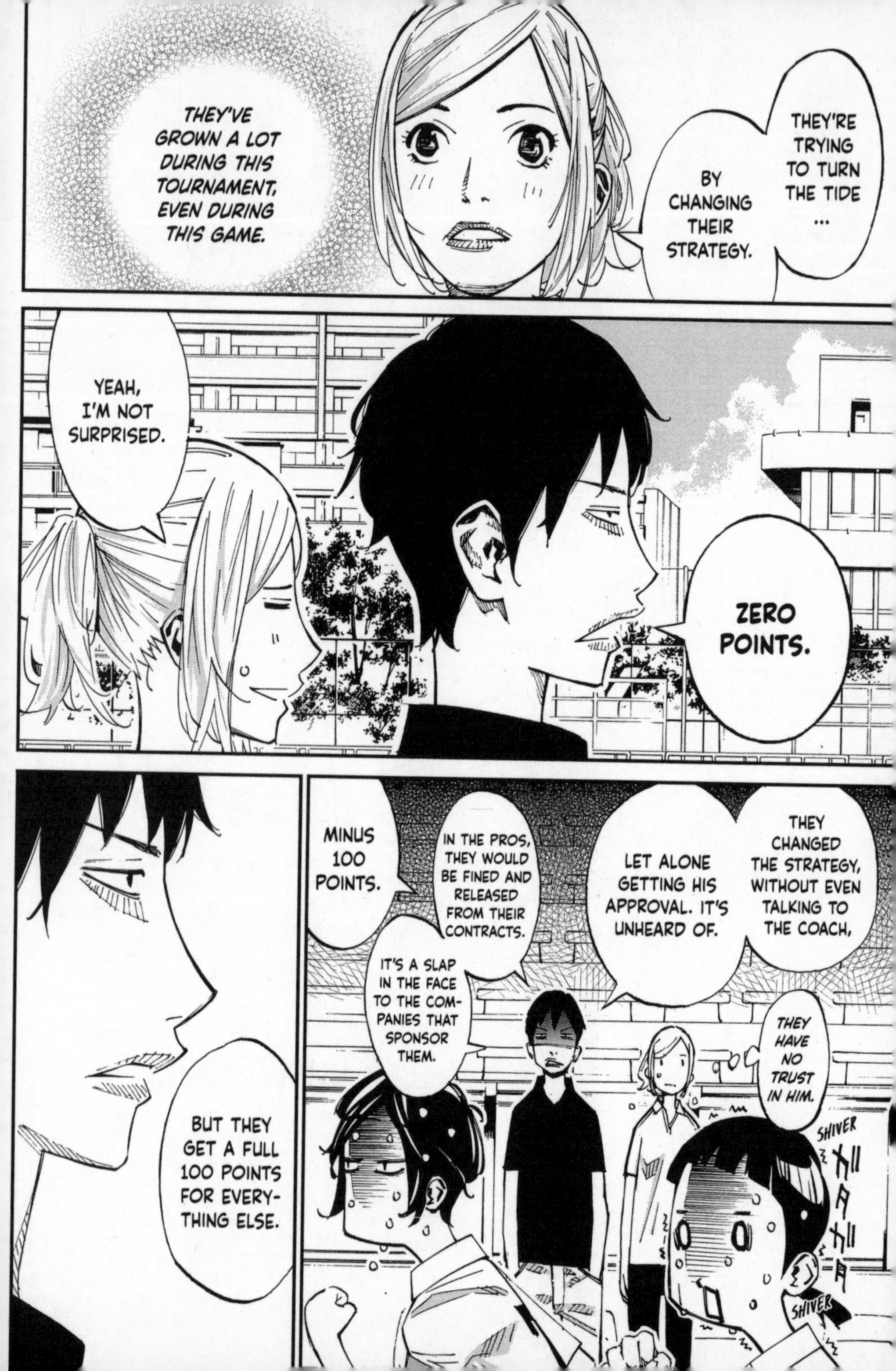
THEY'RE TRYING TO TURN THE TIDE ...
BY CHANGING THEIR STRATEGY.
THEY'VE GROWN A LOT DURING THIS TOURNAMENT, EVEN DURING THIS GAME.
YEAH, I'M NOT SURPRISED.
ZERO POINTS.
THEY CHANGED THE STRATEGY, WITHOUT EVEN TALKING TO THE COACH,
LET ALONE GETTING HIS APPROVAL. IT'S UNHEARD OF.
IN THE PROS, THEY WOULD BE FINED AND RELEASED FROM THEIR CONTRACTS.
MINUS 100 POINTS.
THEY HAVE NO TRUST IN HIM.
IT'S A SLAP IN THE FACE TO THE COMPANIES THAT SPONSOR THEM.
SHIVER
SHIVER
BUT THEY GET A FULL 100 POINTS FOR EVERYTHING ELSE.

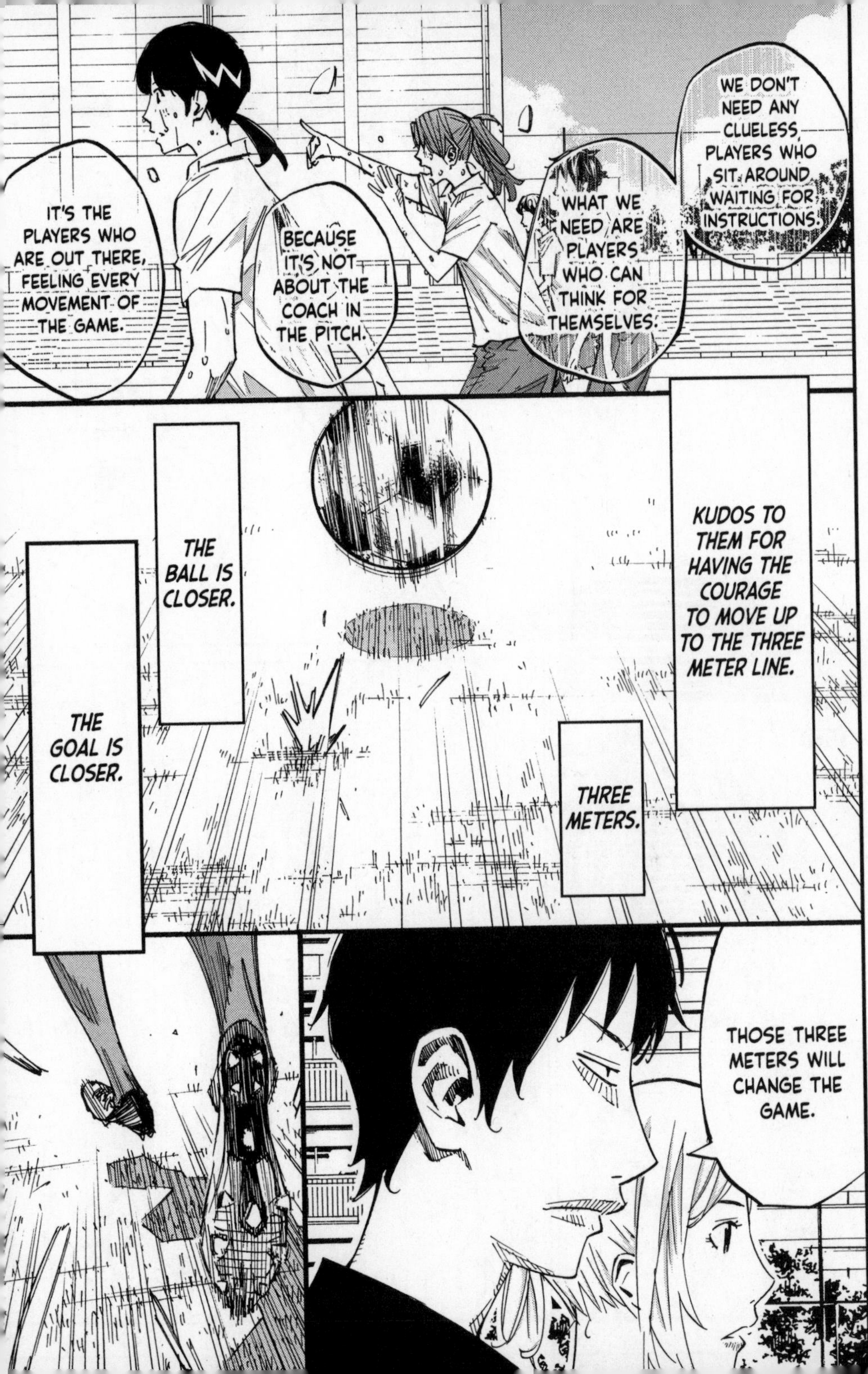
WE DON'T NEED ANY CLUELESS PLAYERS WHO SIT AROUND WAITING FOR INSTRUCTIONS.
WHAT WE NEED ARE PLAYERS WHO CAN THINK FOR THEMSELVES.
BECAUSE IT'S NOT ABOUT THE COACH IN THE PITCH.
IT'S THE PLAYERS WHO ARE OUT THERE, FEELING EVERY MOVEMENT OF THE GAME.
KUDOS TO THEM FOR HAVING THE COURAGE TO MOVE UP TO THE THREE METER LINE.
THREE METERS.
THE BALL IS CLOSER.
THE GOAL IS CLOSER.
THOSE THREE METERS WILL CHANGE THE GAME.

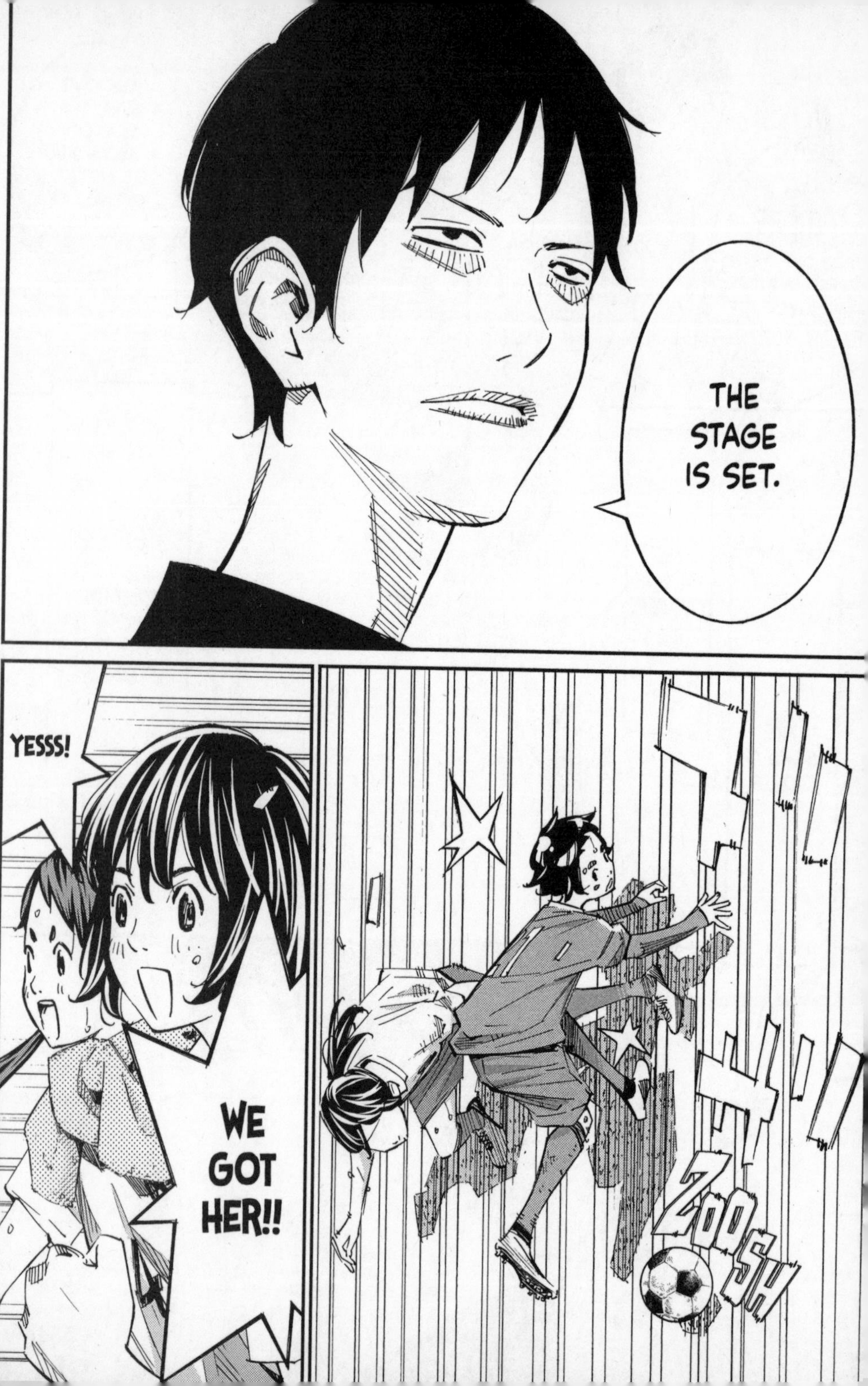
THE STAGE IS SET.
ZOOSH
YESSS!
WE GOT HER!!

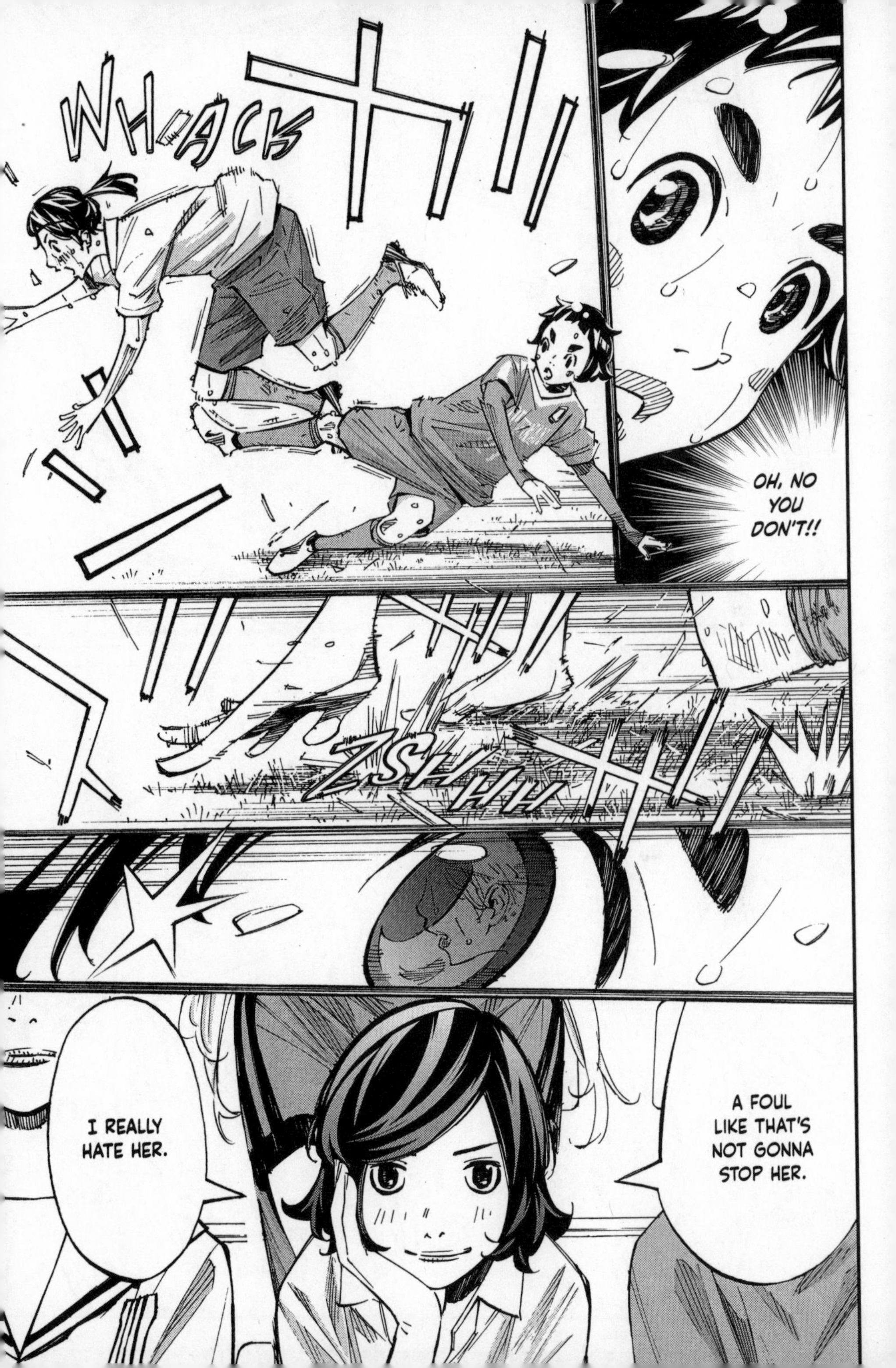
OH, NO YOU DON'T!!
WHACK
ZSHHH
A FOUL LIKE THAT'S NOT GONNA STOP HER.
I REALLY HATE HER.

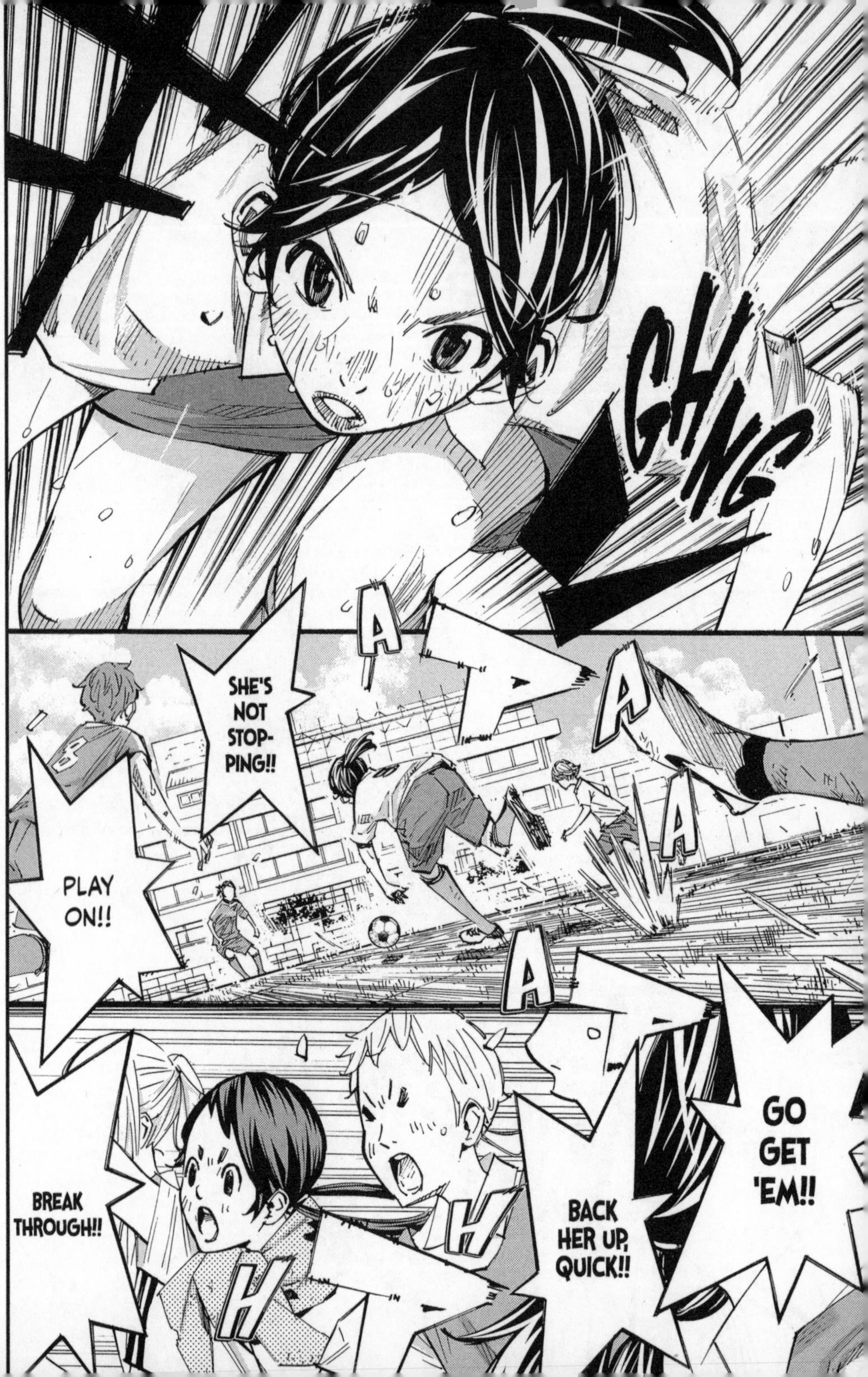
GHNG
A
A
A
A
SHE'S NOT STOPPING!!
PLAY ON!!
GO GET 'EM!!
BACK HER UP, QUICK!!
H
H
BREAK THROUGH!!

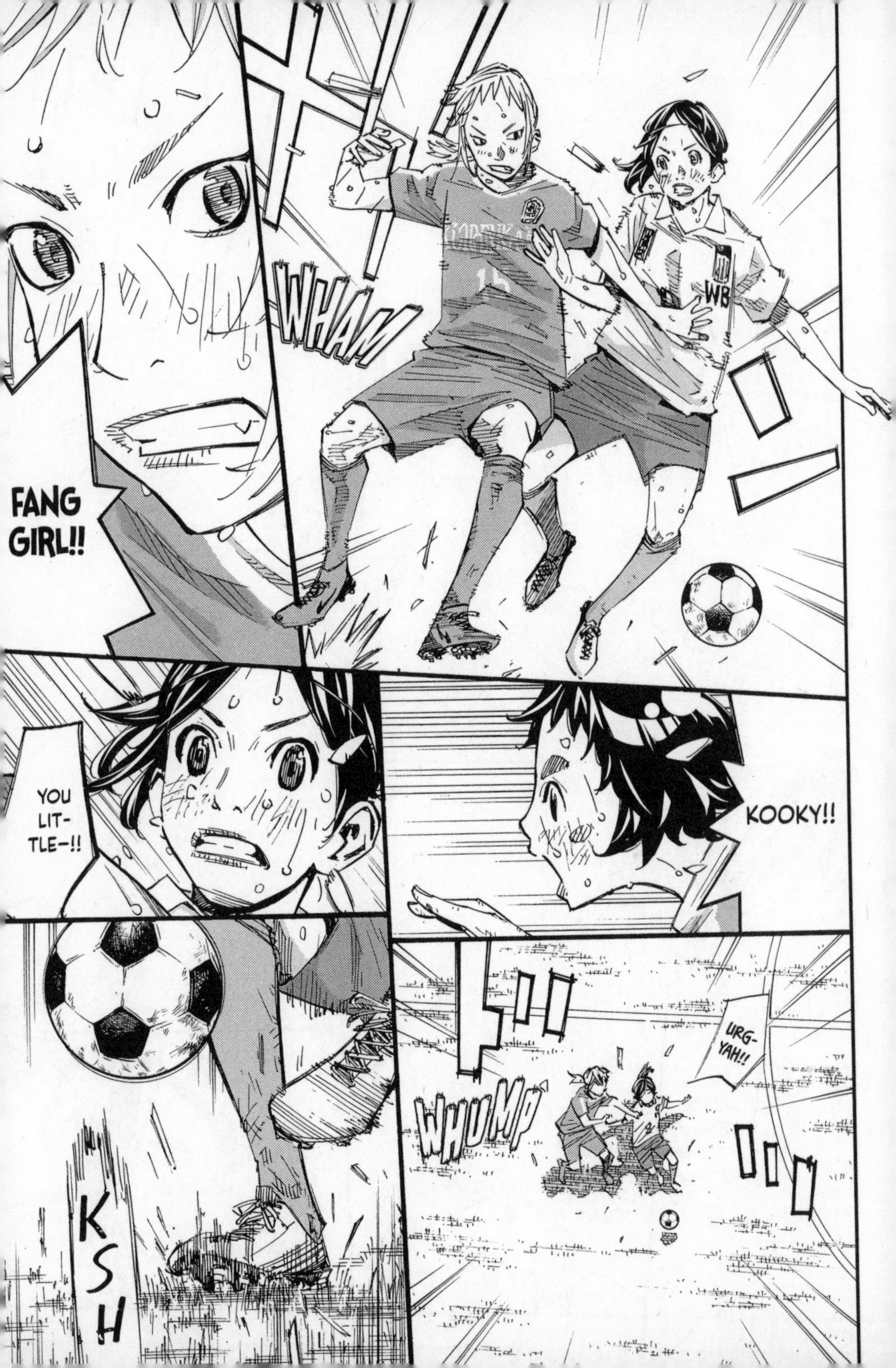

WHAM
FANG GIRL!!
KOOKY!!
YOU LIT-TLE—!!
URG-YAH!!
WHUMP
KSH

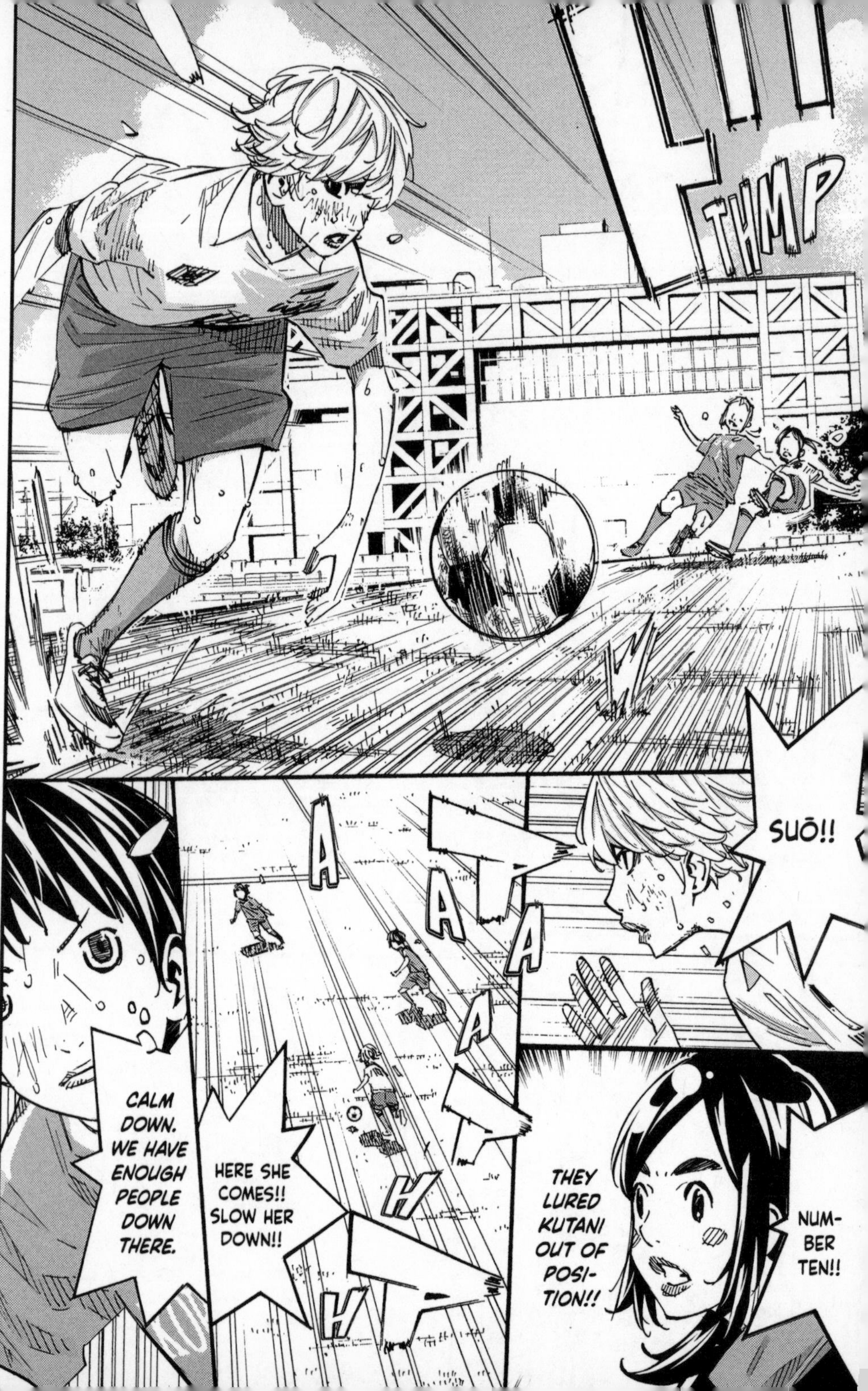
THMP
SUŌ!!
NUM-BER TEN!!
THEY LURED KUTANI OUT OF POSI-TION!!
AAAAAHH
HERE SHE COMES!! SLOW HER DOWN!!
CALM DOWN. WE HAVE ENOUGH PEOPLE DOWN THERE.

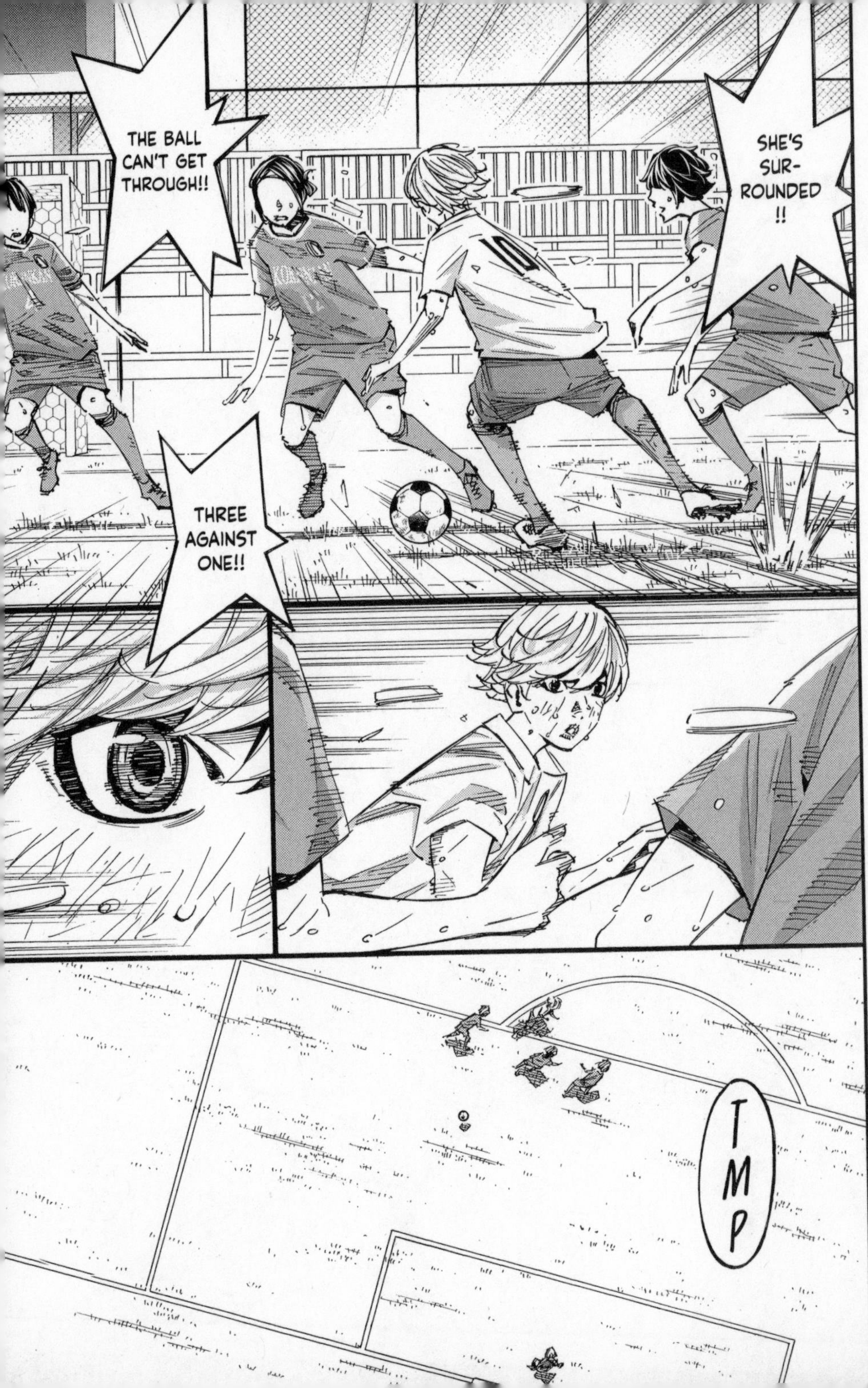
SHE'S SUR-ROUNDED !!
THE BALL CAN'T GET THROUGH!!
THREE AGAINST ONE!!
TMP

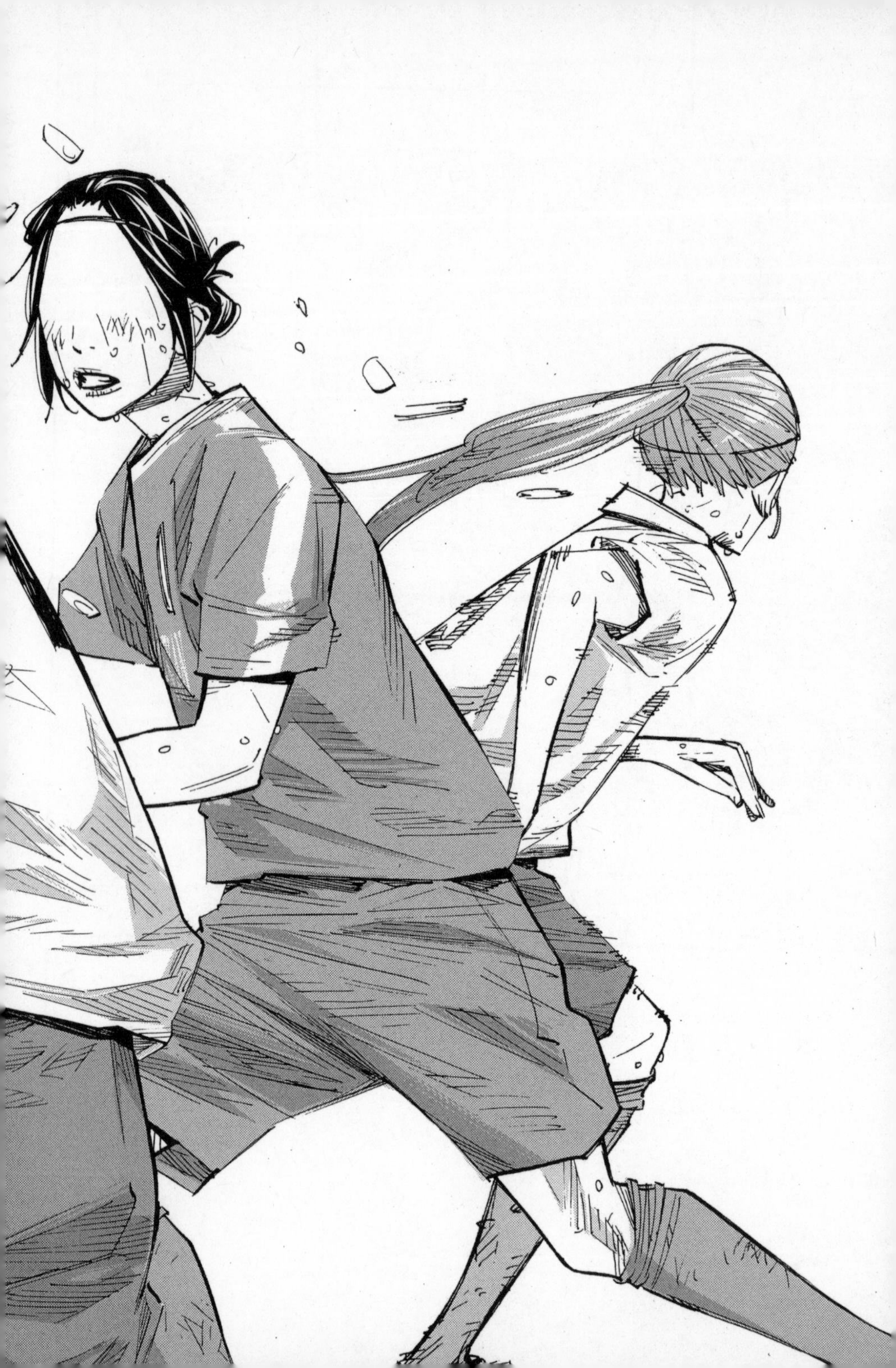

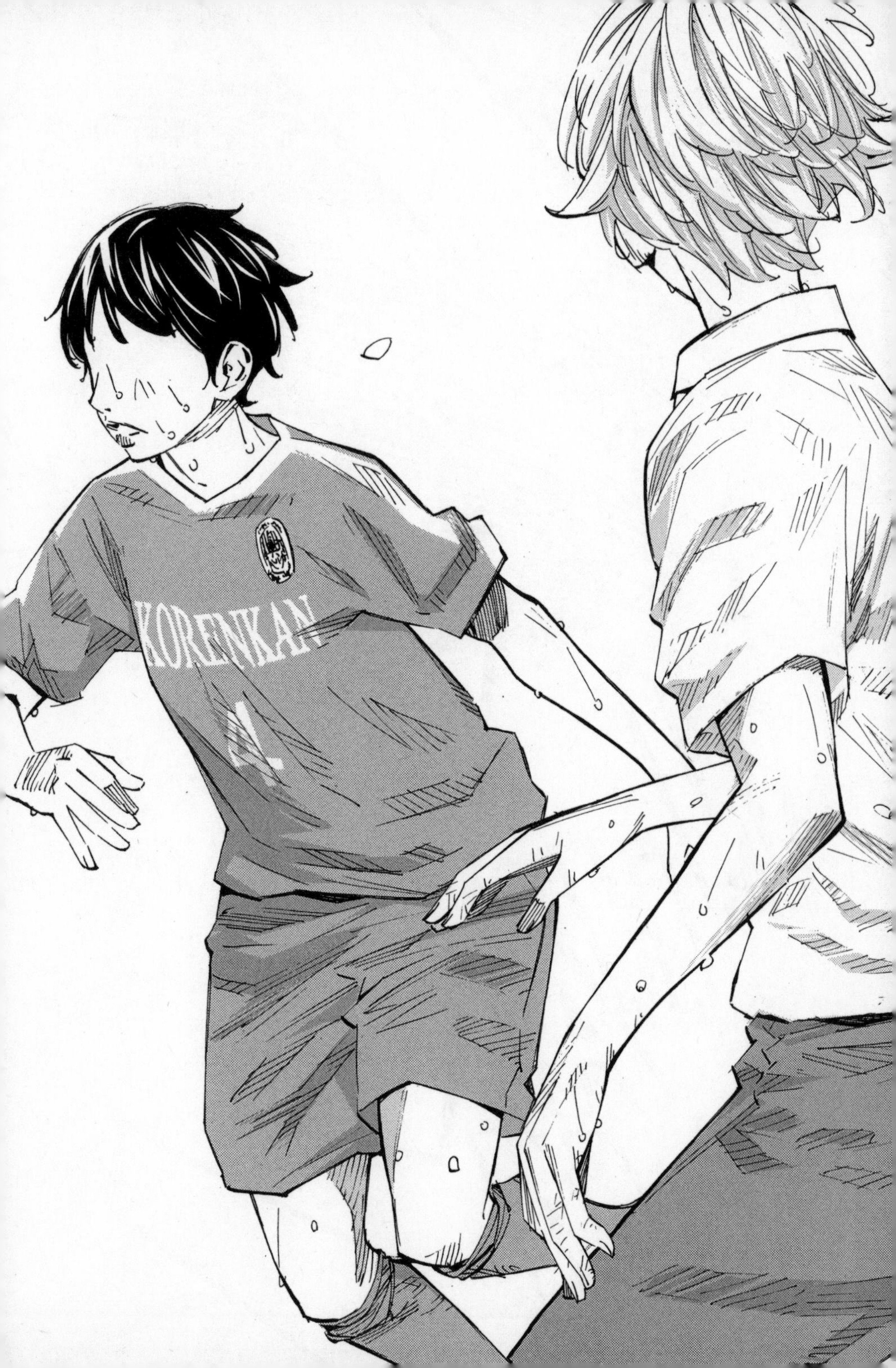
KORENKAN

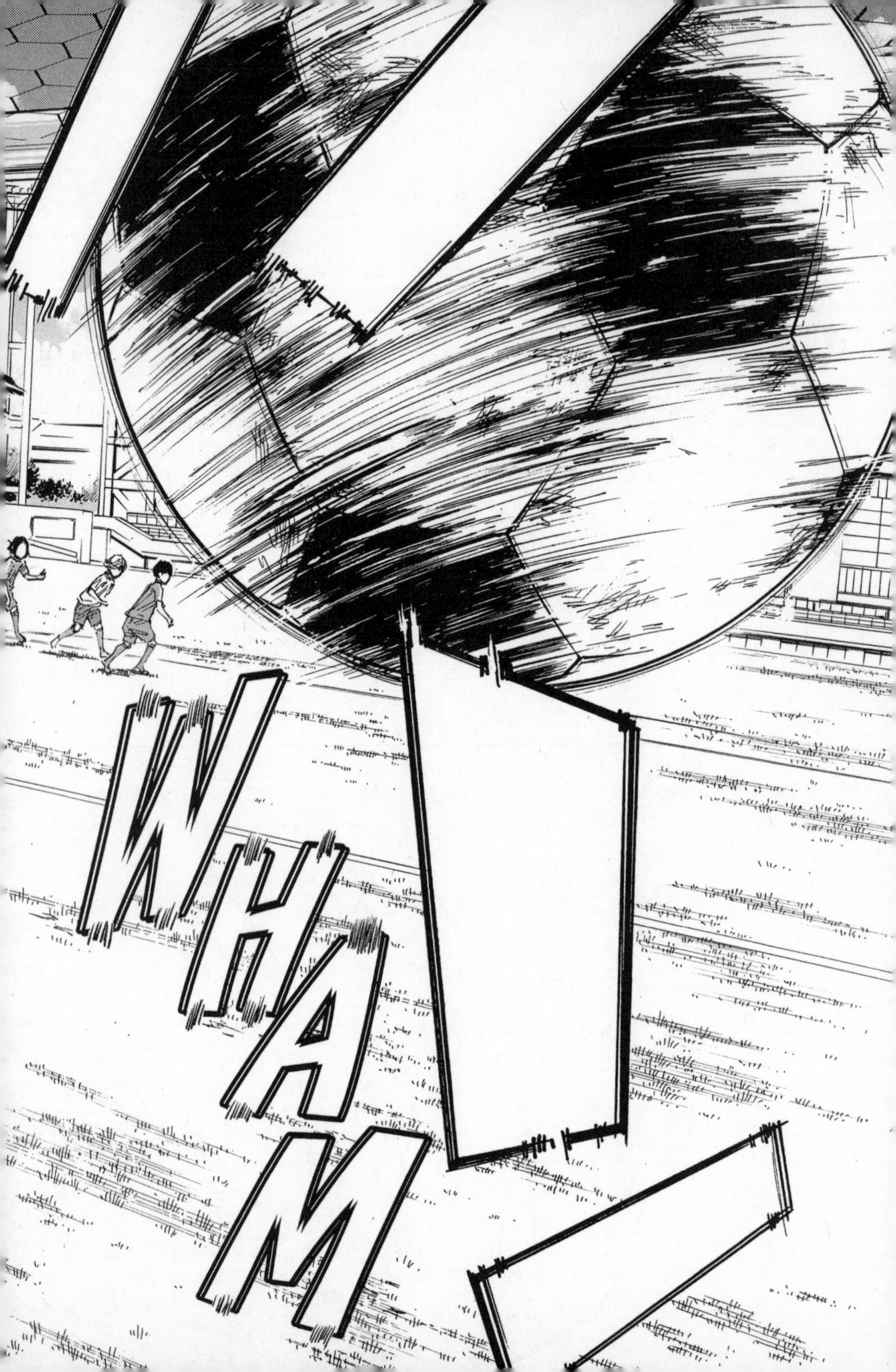
WHAM

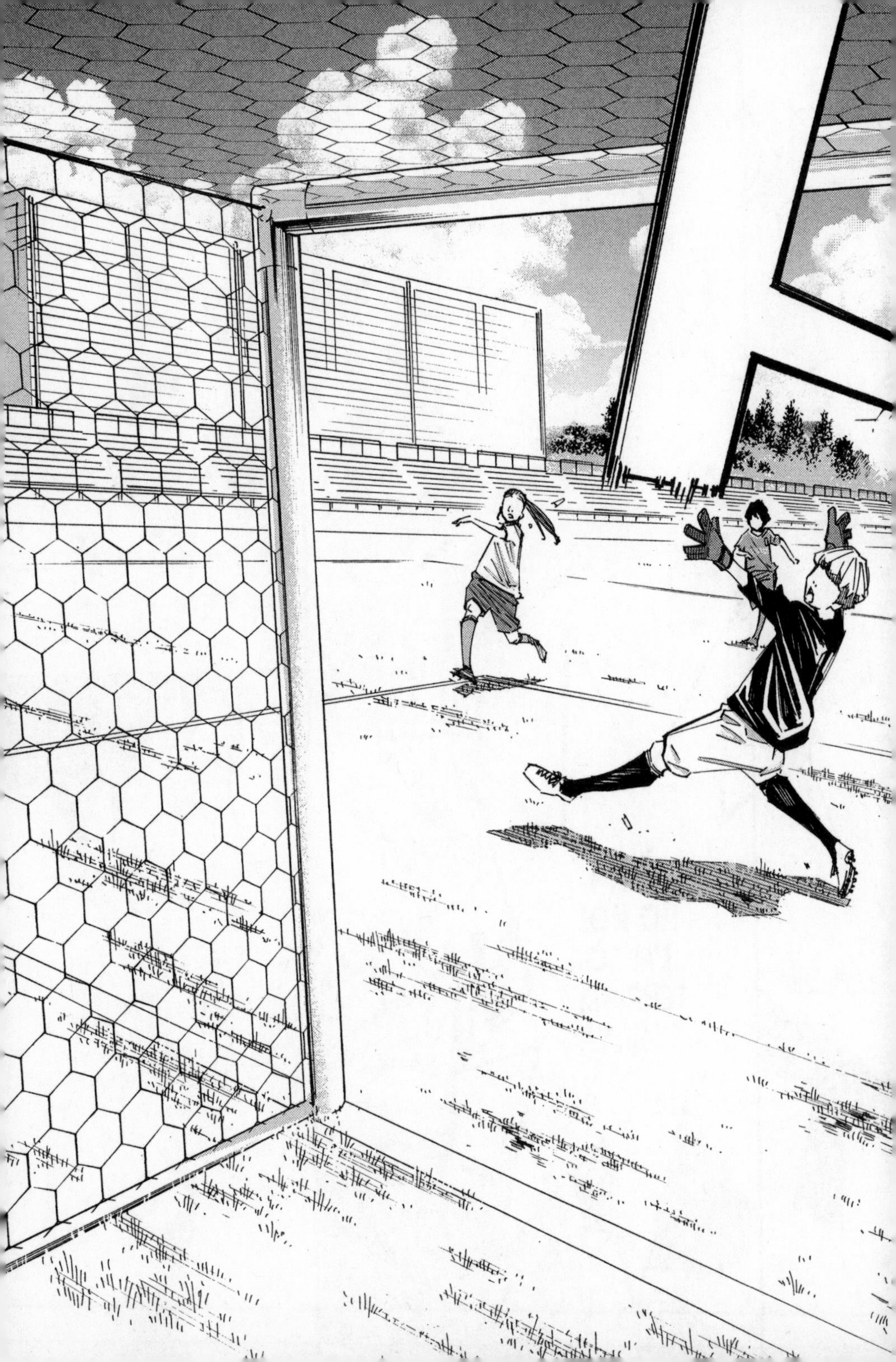

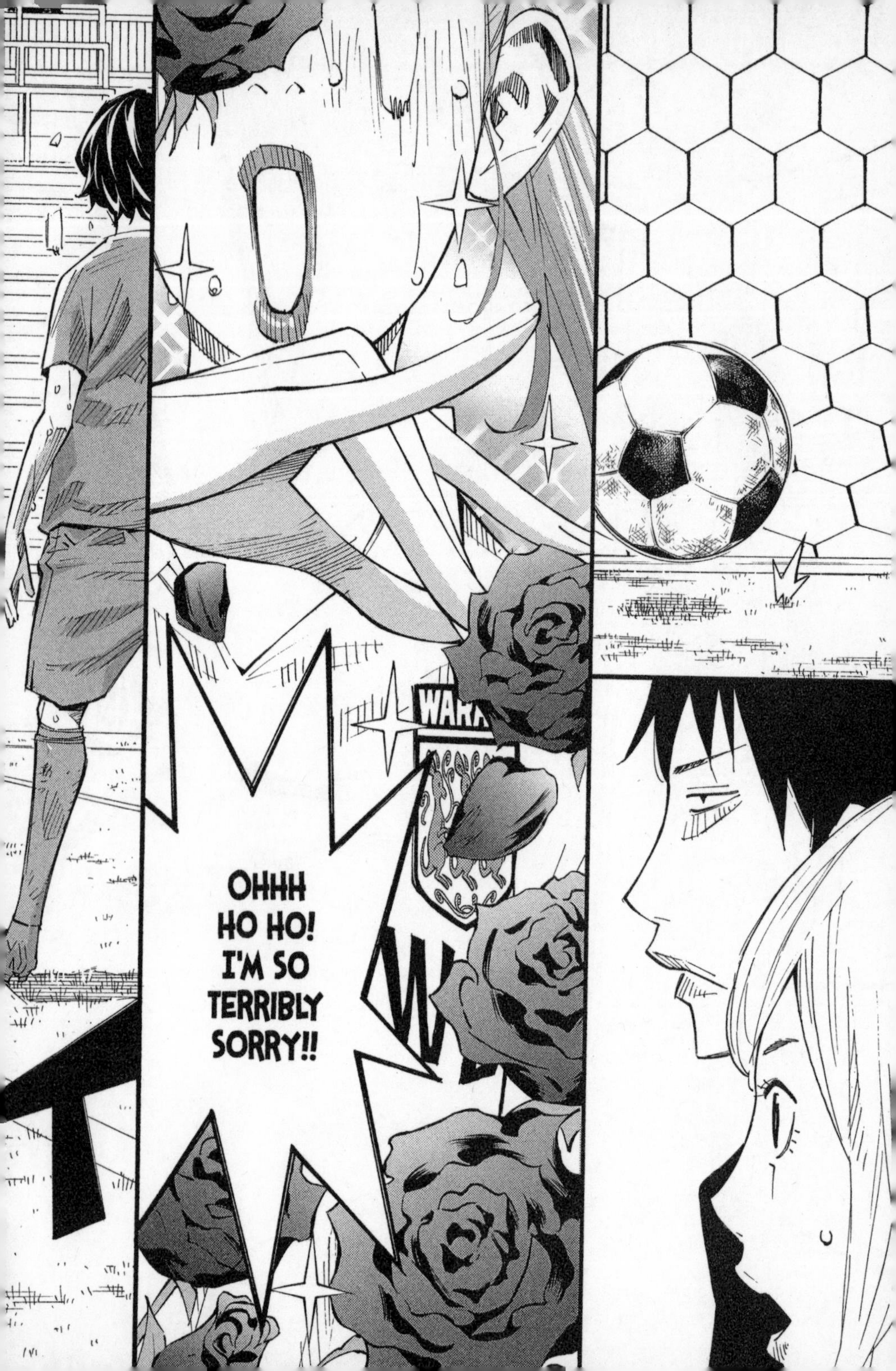
OHHH HO HO! I'M SO TERRIBLY SORRY!!

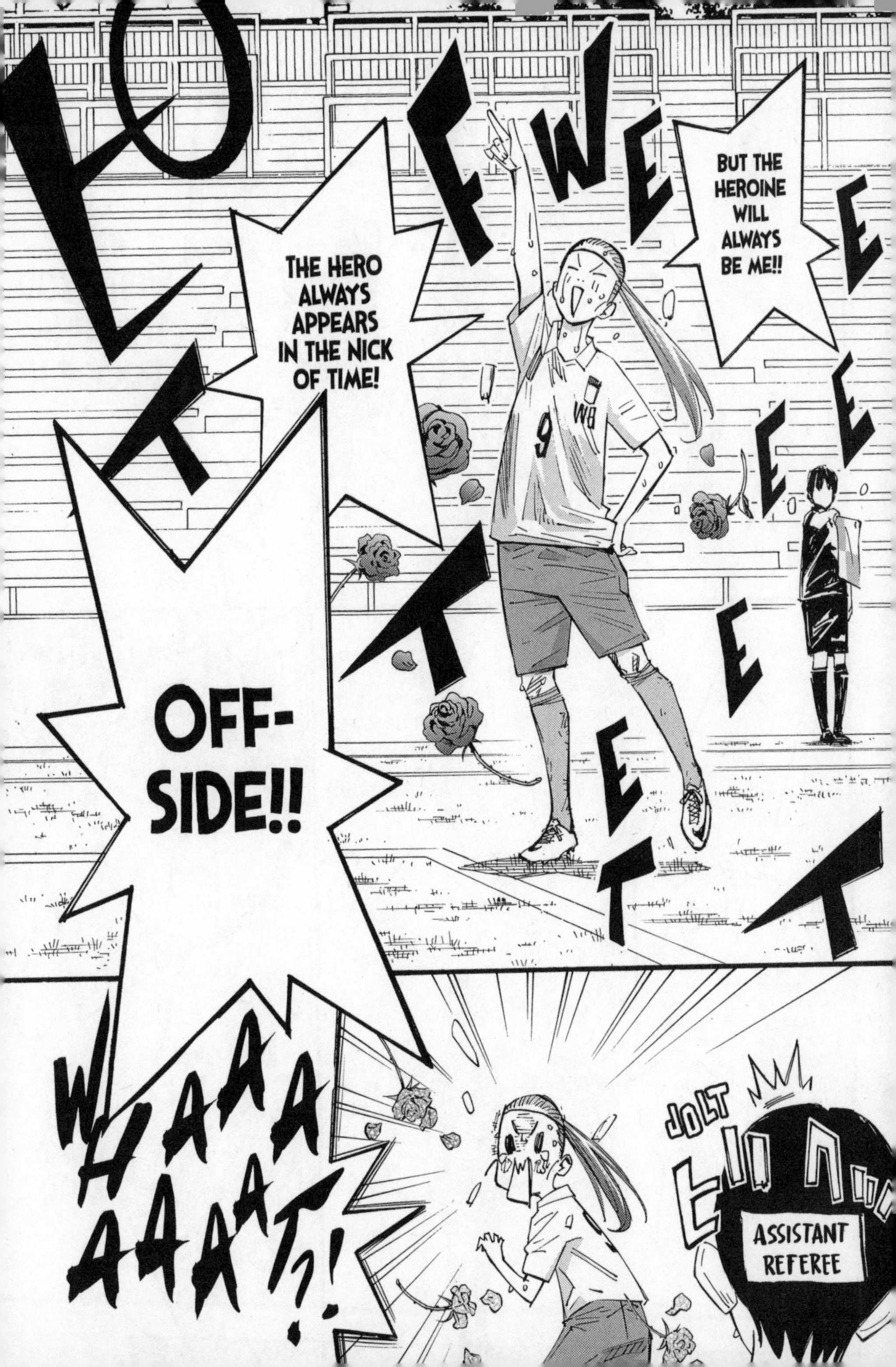
THE HERO ALWAYS APPEARS IN THE NICK OF TIME!
BUT THE HEROINE WILL ALWAYS BE ME!!
OFF-SIDE!!
JOLT
ASSISTANT REFEREE
WHAAAAAAAT?!

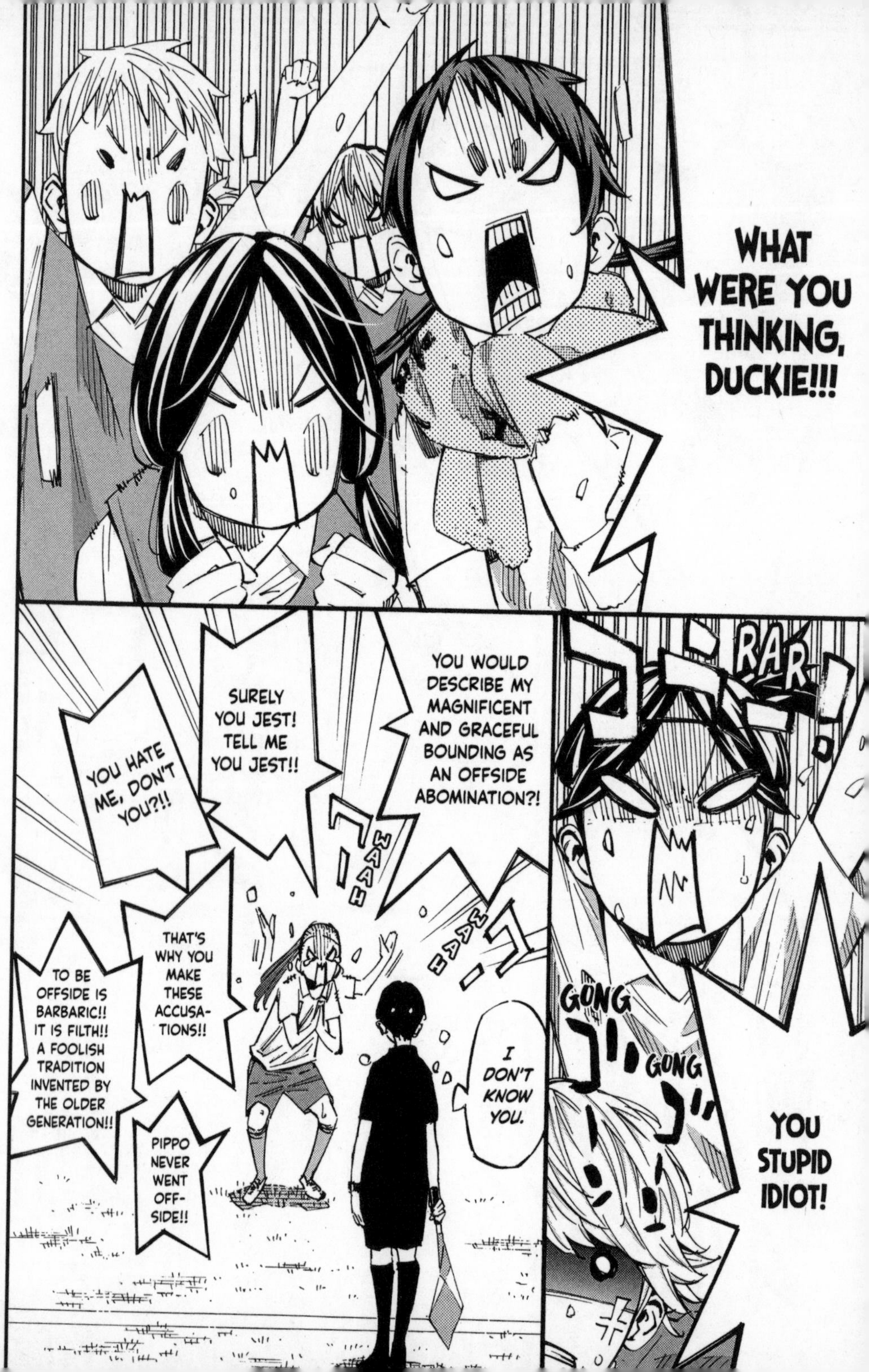
WHAT WERE YOU THINKING, DUCKIE!!!
RAR
GONG
GONG
YOU STUPID IDIOT!
YOU WOULD DESCRIBE MY MAGNIFICENT AND GRACEFUL BOUNDING AS AN OFFSIDE ABOMINATION?!
SURELY YOU JEST! TELL ME YOU JEST!!
YOU HATE ME, DON'T YOU?!!
WAAAH
WAAAH
I DON'T KNOW YOU.
THAT'S WHY YOU MAKE THESE ACCUSATIONS!!
TO BE OFFSIDE IS BARBARIC!! IT IS FILTH!! A FOOLISH TRADITION INVENTED BY THE OLDER GENERATION!!
PIPPO NEVER WENT OFFSIDE!!

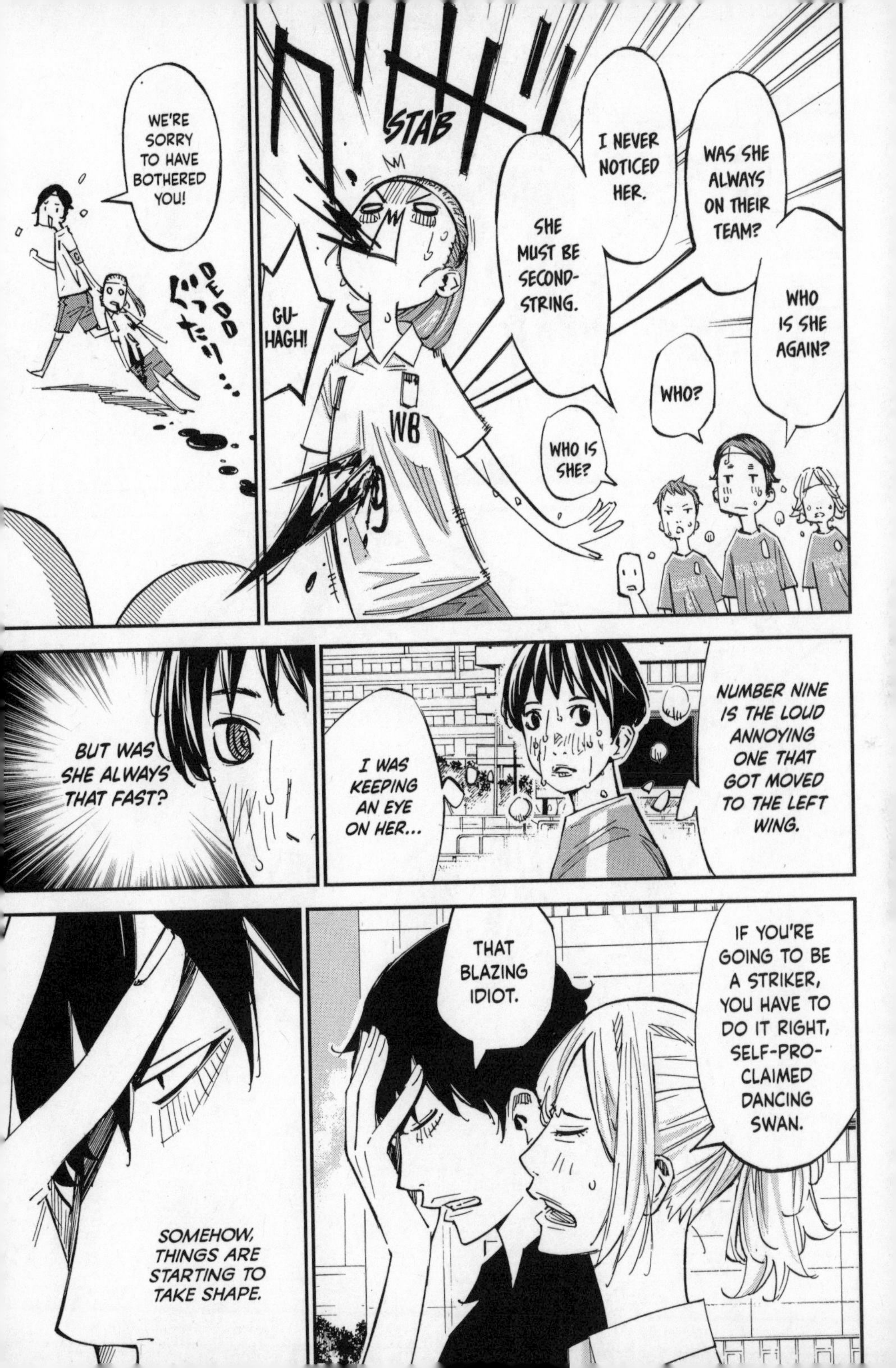
WAS SHE ALWAYS ON THEIR TEAM?
I NEVER NOTICED HER.
STAB
SHE MUST BE SECOND-STRING.
WHO IS SHE AGAIN?
WHO?
WHO IS SHE?
GU-HAGH!
WE'RE SORRY TO HAVE BOTHERED YOU!
NUMBER NINE IS THE LOUD ANNOYING ONE THAT GOT MOVED TO THE LEFT WING.
I WAS KEEPING AN EYE ON HER...
BUT WAS SHE ALWAYS THAT FAST?
IF YOU'RE GOING TO BE A STRIKER, YOU HAVE TO DO IT RIGHT, SELF-PRO-CLAIMED DANCING SWAN.
THAT BLAZING IDIOT.
SOMEHOW, THINGS ARE STARTING TO TAKE SHAPE.

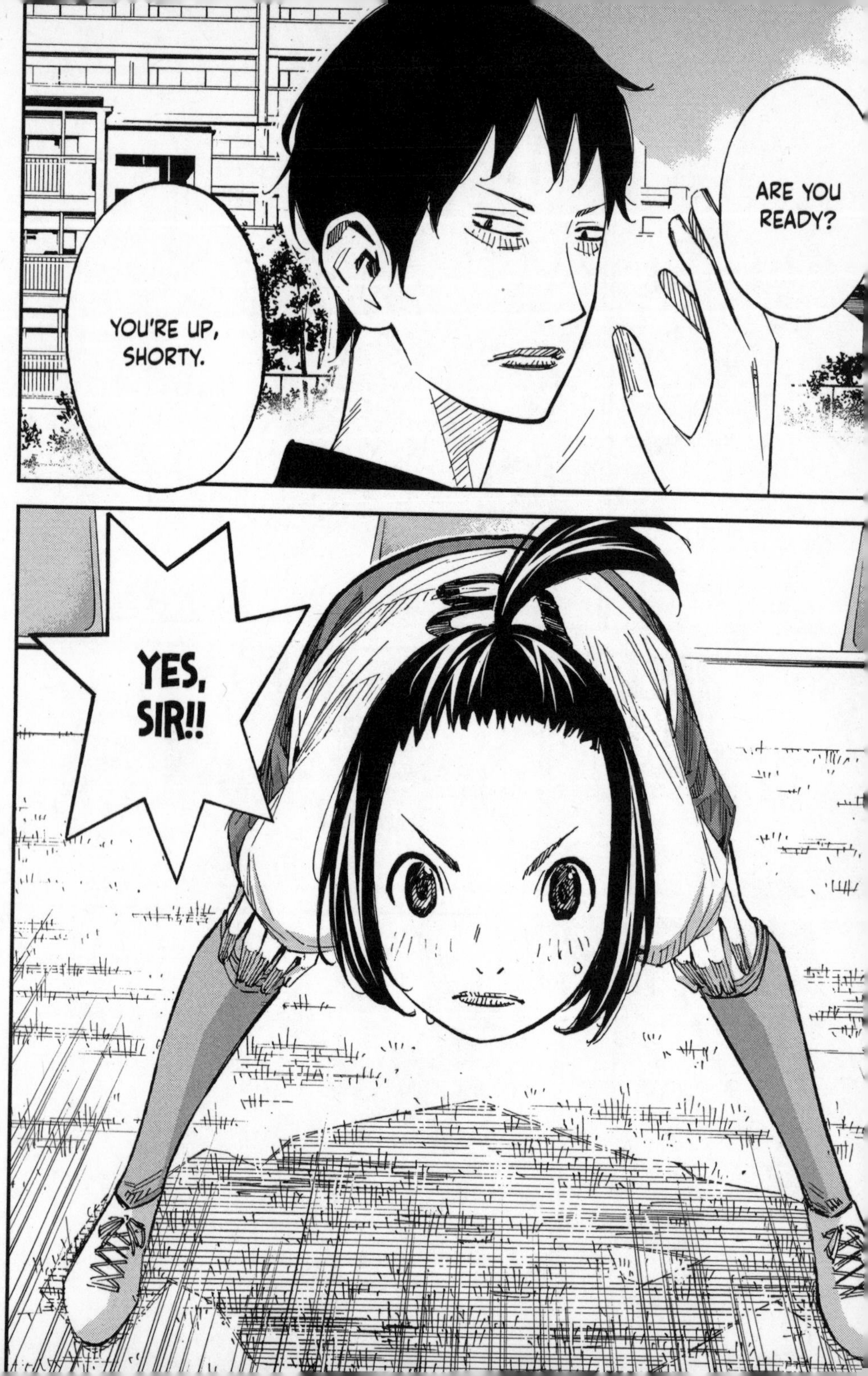
ARE YOU READY?
YOU'RE UP, SHORTY.
YES, SIR!!

Farewell, My Dear Cramer

Farewell,
My Dear
Cramer

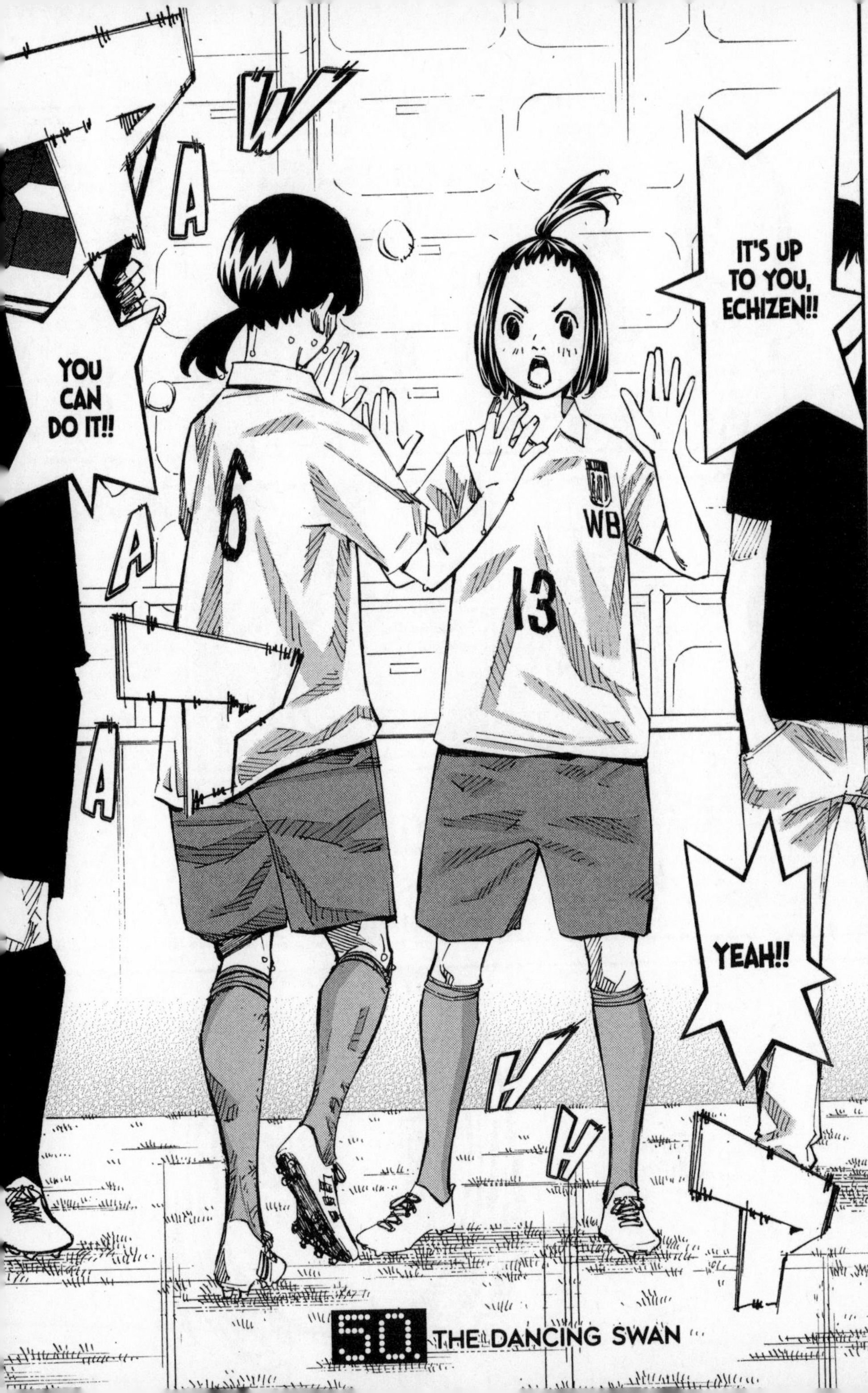
IT'S UP TO YOU, ECHIZEN!!
WAAAA
YOU CAN DO IT!!
YEAH!!
HH

50. THE DANCING SWAN

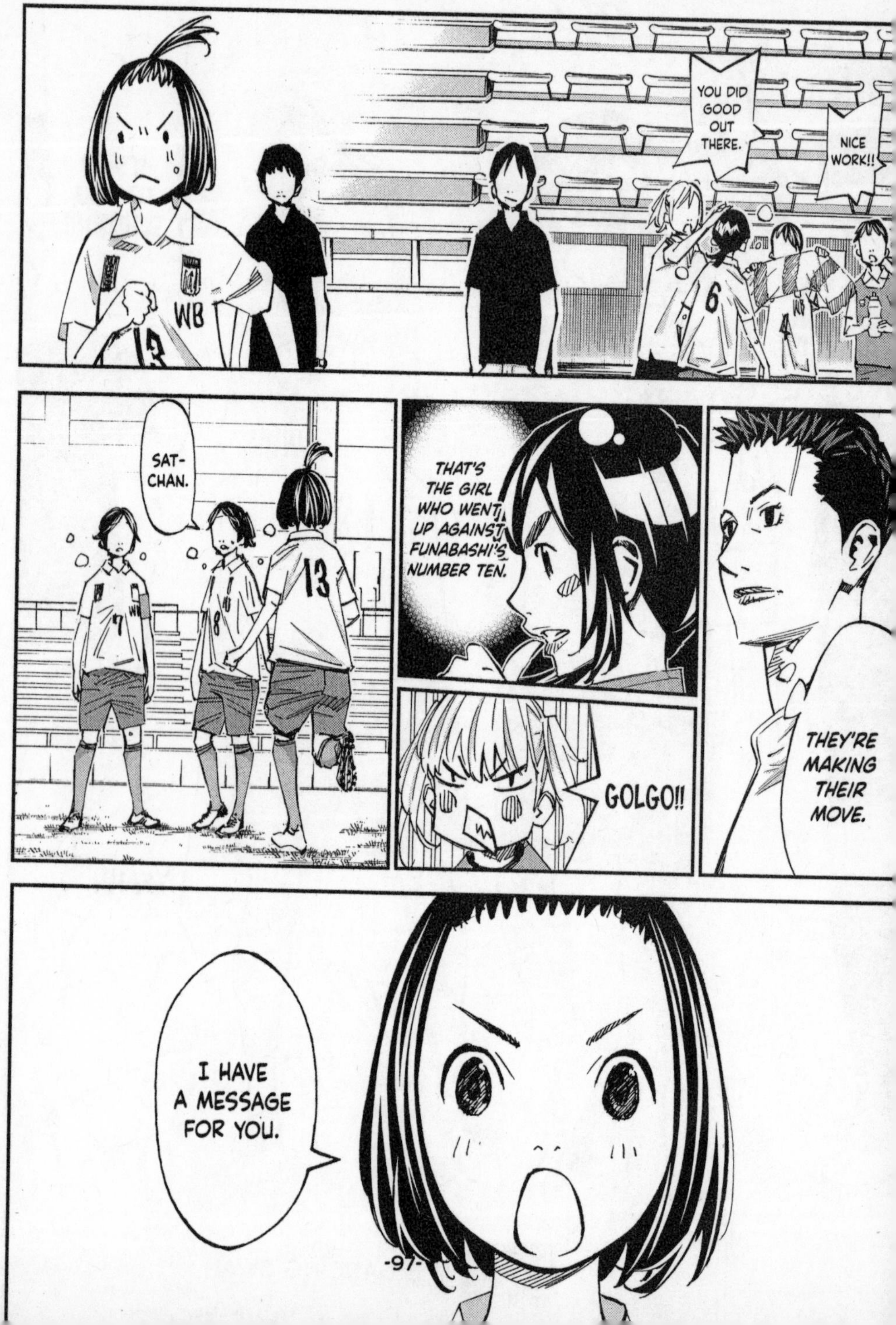
NICE WORK!!
YOU DID GOOD OUT THERE.
THEY'RE MAKING THEIR MOVE.
THAT'S THE GIRL WHO WENT UP AGAINST FUNABASHI'S NUMBER TEN.
GOLGO!!
SAT-CHAN.
I HAVE A MESSAGE FOR YOU.

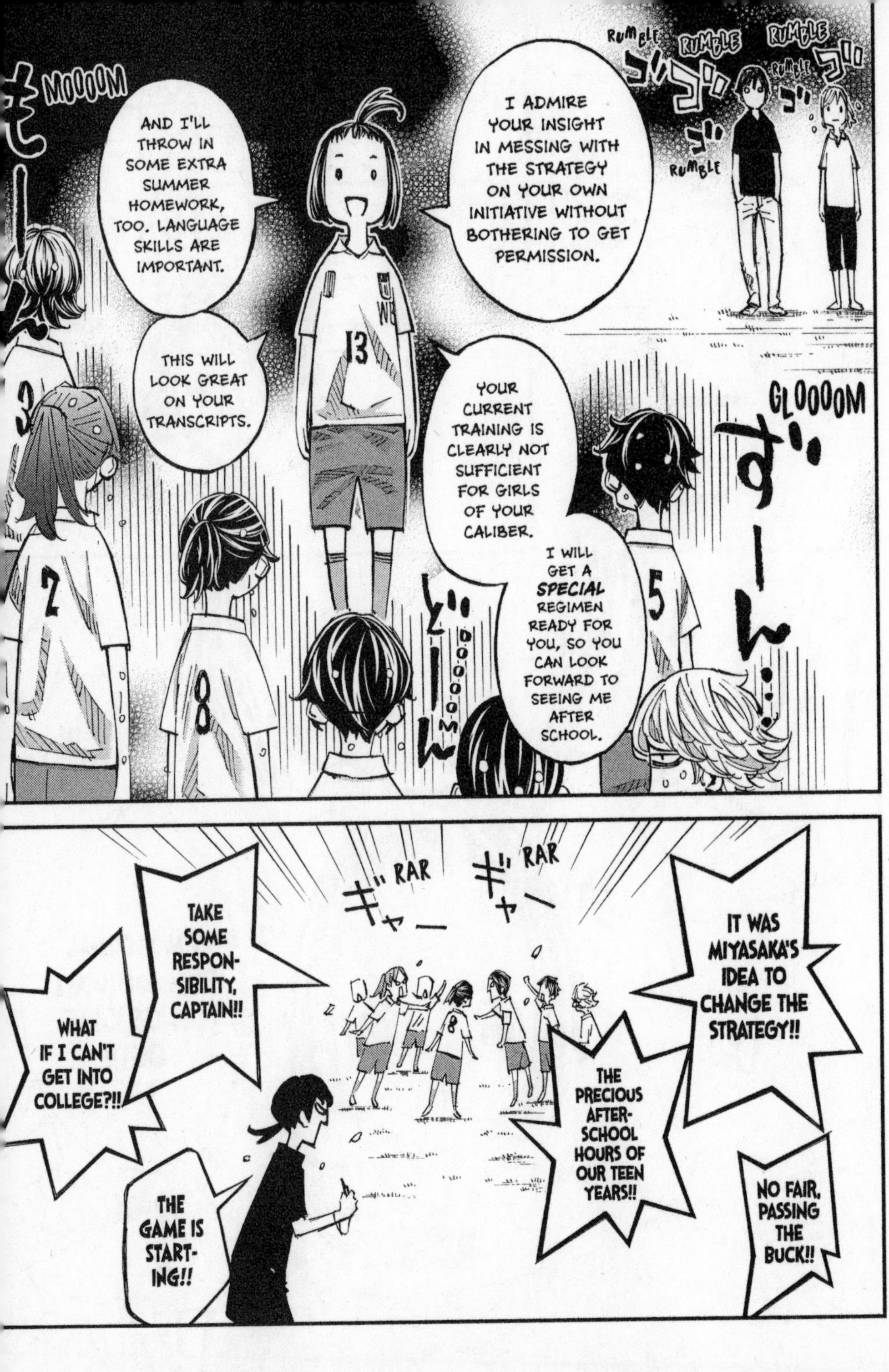
RUMBLE RUMBLE RUMBLE RUMBLE RUMBLE
I ADMIRE YOUR INSIGHT IN MESSING WITH THE STRATEGY ON YOUR OWN INITIATIVE WITHOUT BOTHERING TO GET PERMISSION.
AND I'LL THROW IN SOME EXTRA SUMMER HOMEWORK, TOO. LANGUAGE SKILLS ARE IMPORTANT.
MOOOOM
GLOOOOM
YOUR CURRENT TRAINING IS CLEARLY NOT SUFFICIENT FOR GIRLS OF YOUR CALIBER.
THIS WILL LOOK GREAT ON YOUR TRANSCRIPTS.
I WILL GET A ***SPECIAL*** REGIMEN READY FOR YOU, SO YOU CAN LOOK FORWARD TO SEEING ME AFTER SCHOOL.
DOOOOOM
IT WAS MIYASAKA'S IDEA TO CHANGE THE STRATEGY!!
RAR RAR
TAKE SOME RESPON-SIBILITY, CAPTAIN!!
NO FAIR, PASSING THE BUCK!!
THE PRECIOUS AFTER-SCHOOL HOURS OF OUR TEEN YEARS!!
WHAT IF I CAN'T GET INTO COLLEGE?!!
THE GAME IS START-ING!!

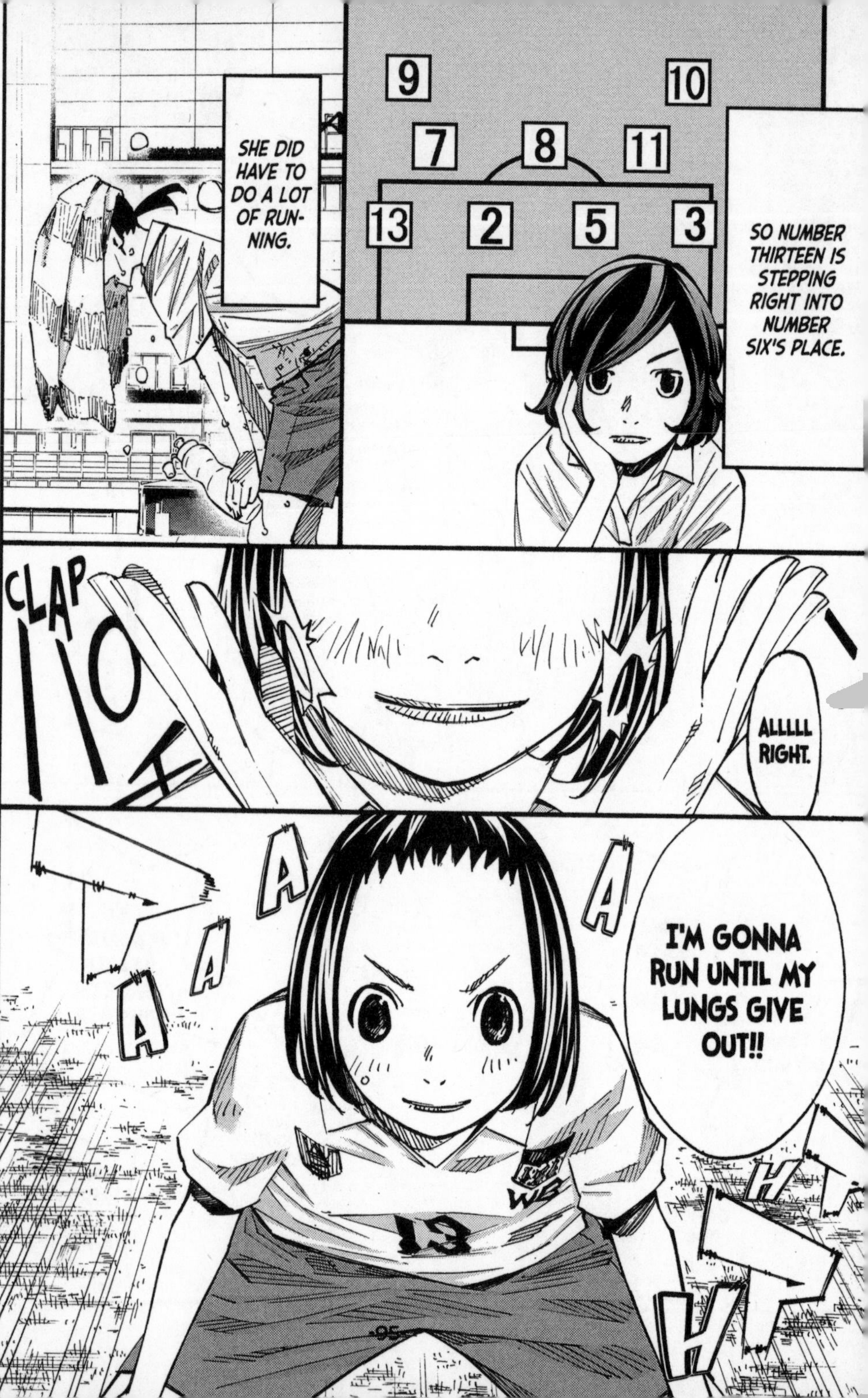

9
10
7
8
11
13
2
5
3
SO NUMBER THIRTEEN IS STEPPING RIGHT INTO NUMBER SIX'S PLACE.
SHE DID HAVE TO DO A LOT OF RUN-NING.
ALLLLL RIGHT.
CLAP
I'M GONNA RUN UNTIL MY LUNGS GIVE OUT!!

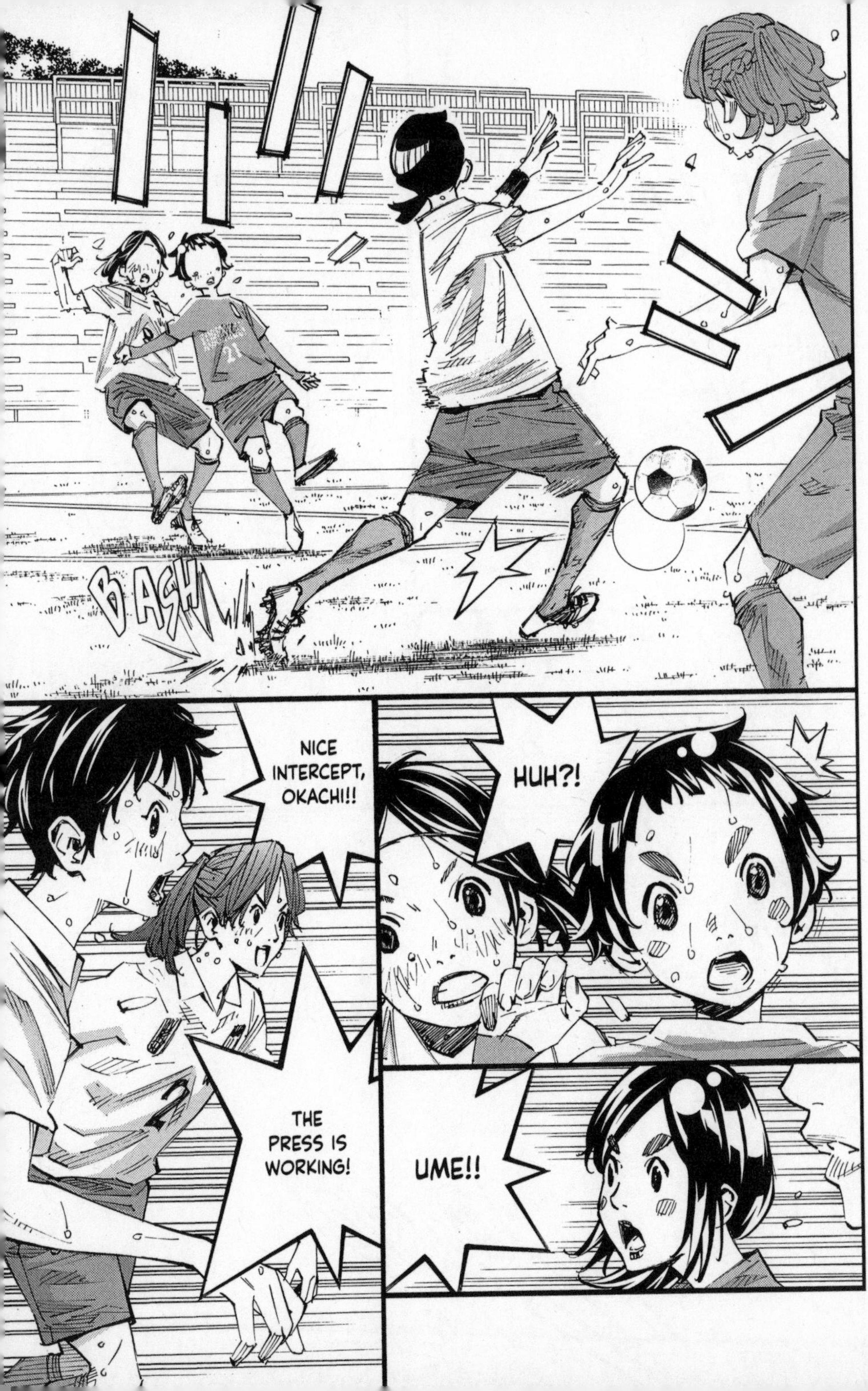
BASH
HUH?!
UME!!
NICE INTERCEPT, OKACHI!!
THE PRESS IS WORKING!

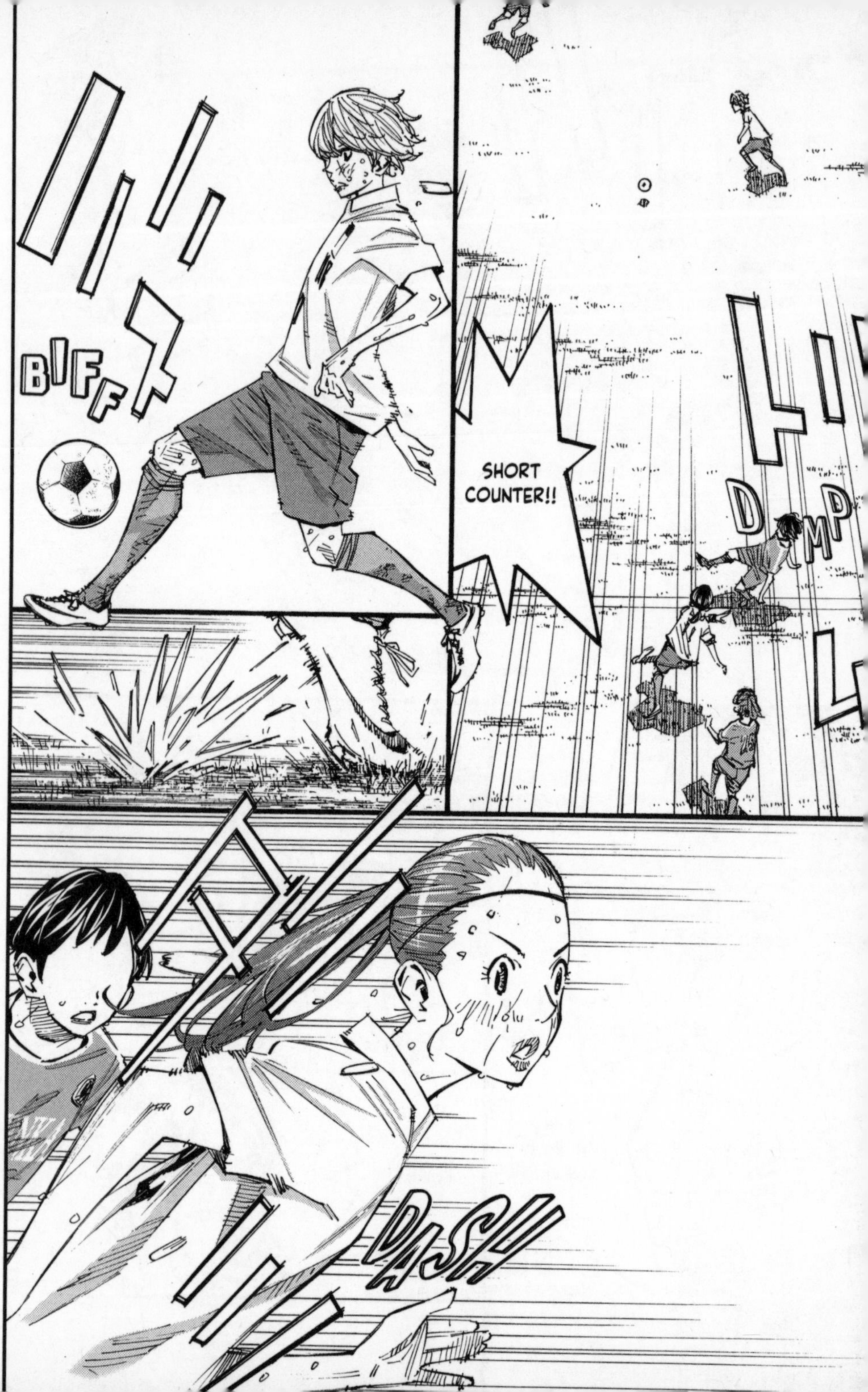
SHORT
COUNTER!!
BIFF
DASH

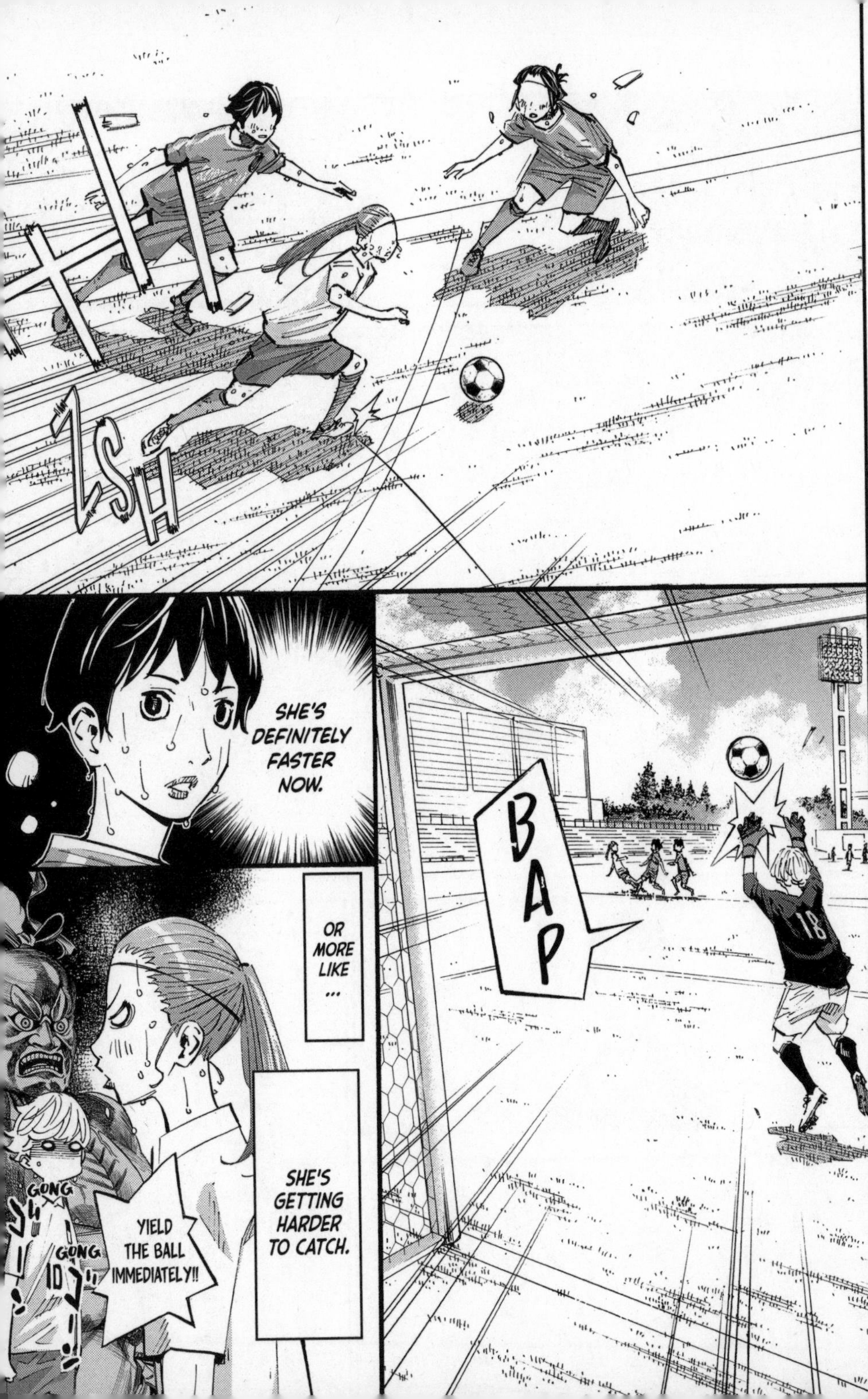
ZSH
BAP
SHE'S DEFINITELY FASTER NOW.
OR MORE LIKE ...
SHE'S GETTING HARDER TO CATCH.
GONG
GONG
YIELD THE BALL IMMEDIATELY!!

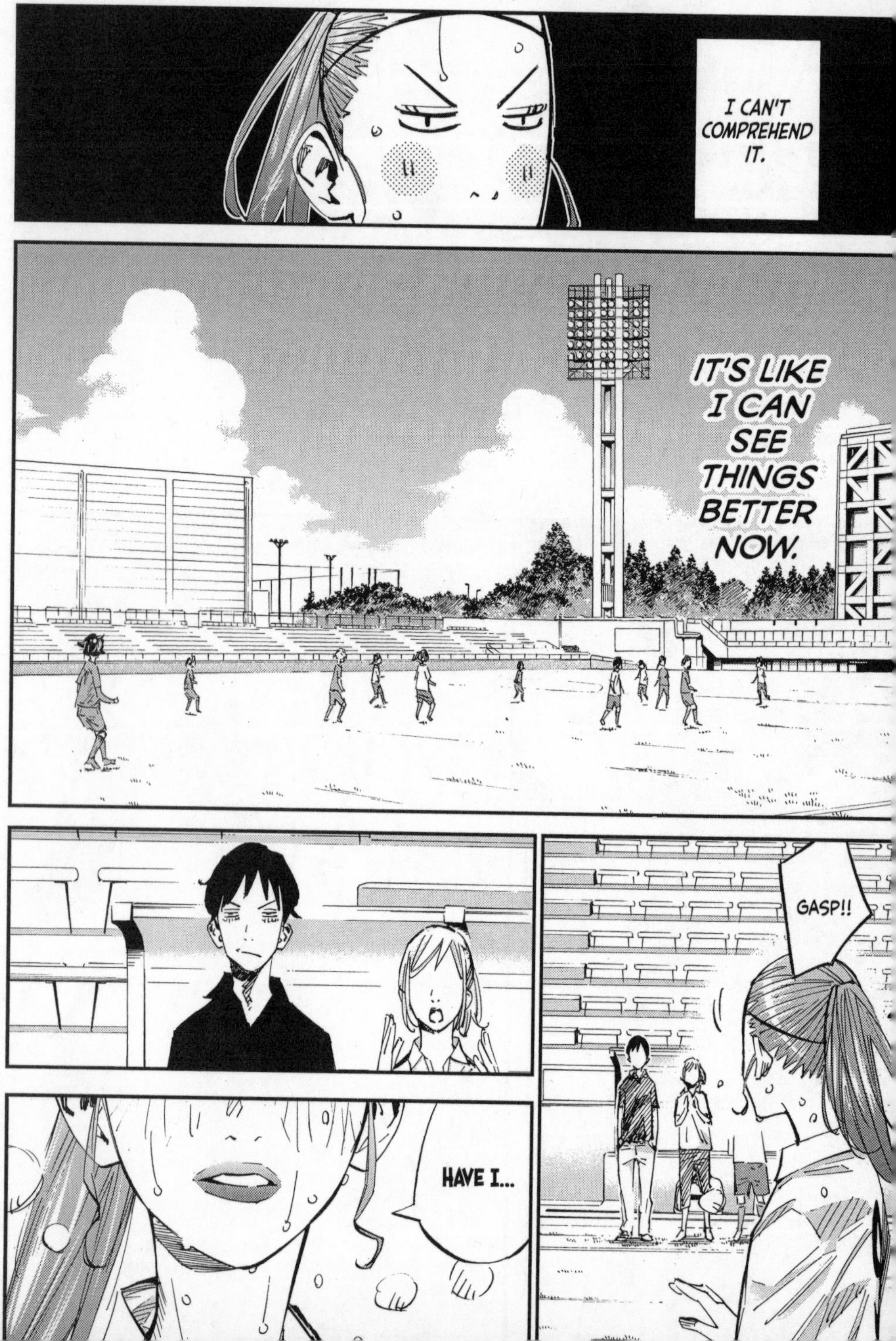
I CAN'T COMPREHEND IT.
IT'S LIKE I CAN SEE THINGS BETTER NOW.
GASP!!
HAVE I...

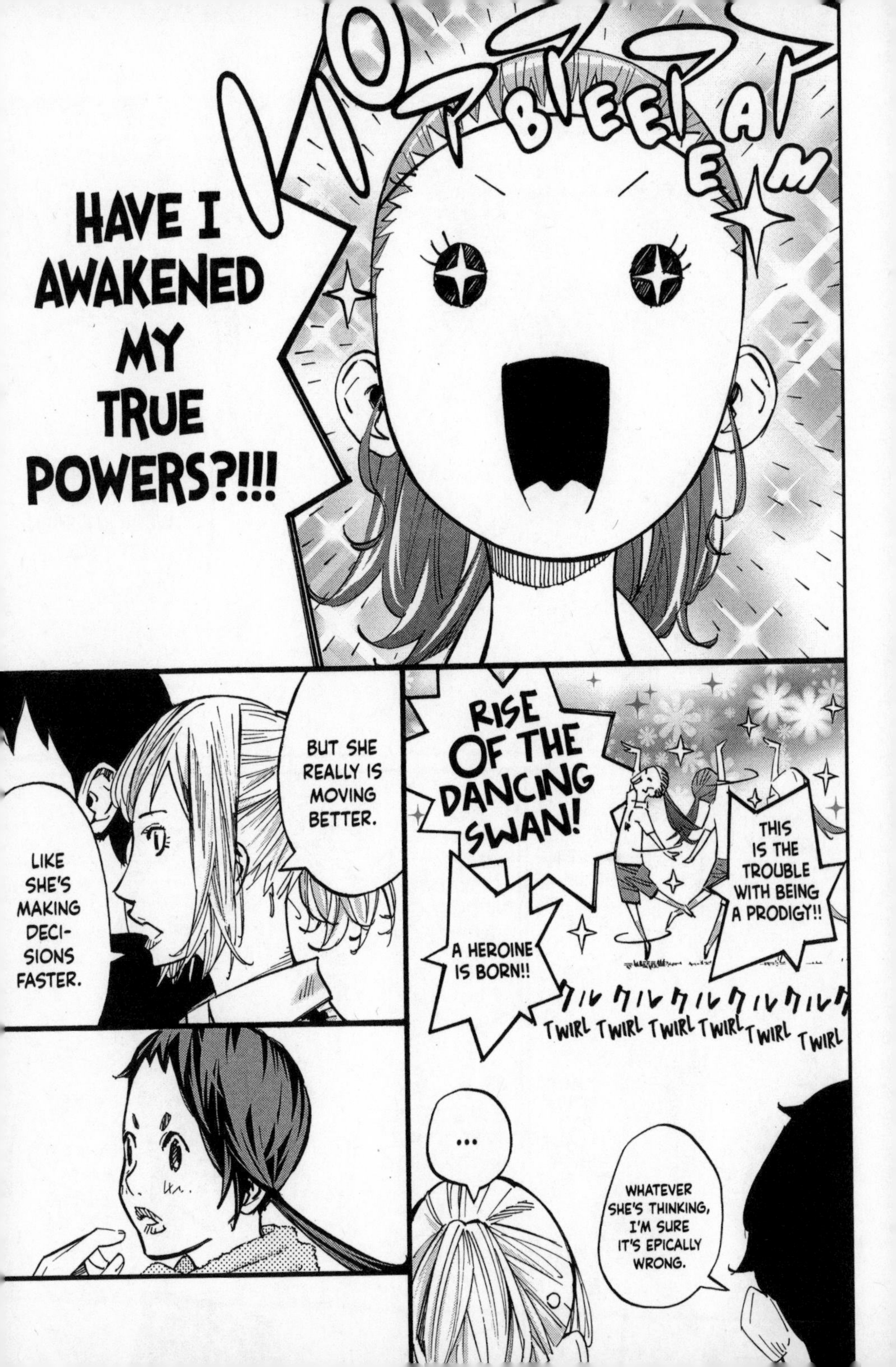
BEEEAM
HAVE I AWAKENED MY TRUE POWERS?!!!
RISE OF THE DANCING SWAN!
THIS IS THE TROUBLE WITH BEING A PRODIGY!!
A HEROINE IS BORN!!
クルクルクルクルクルクル
TWIRL TWIRL TWIRL TWIRL TWIRL TWIRL
BUT SHE REALLY IS MOVING BETTER.
LIKE SHE'S MAKING DECI-SIONS FASTER.
...
WHATEVER SHE'S THINKING, I'M SURE IT'S EPICALLY WRONG.

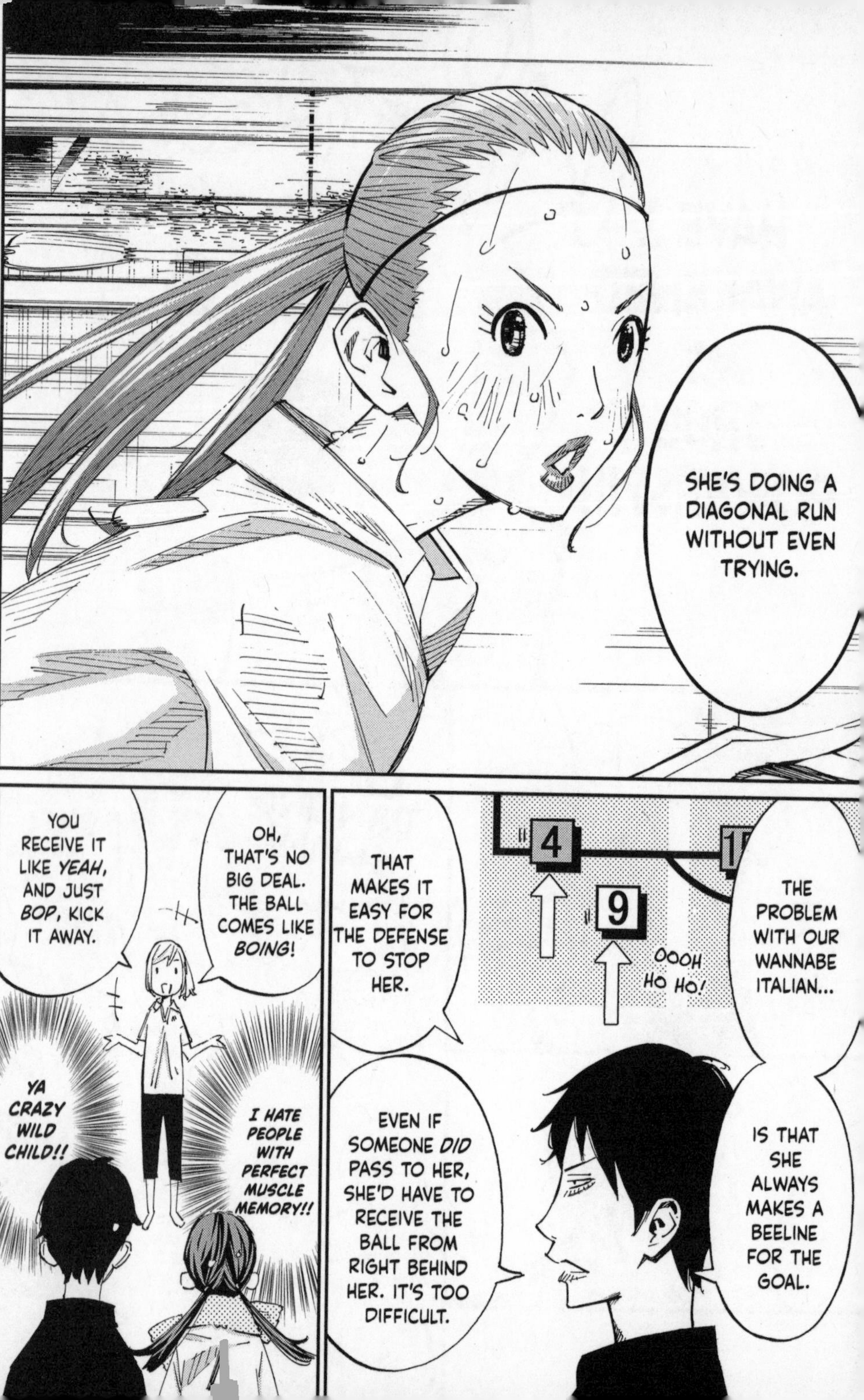

SHE'S DOING A DIAGONAL RUN WITHOUT EVEN TRYING.
4
9
THE PROBLEM WITH OUR WANNABE ITALIAN...
OOOH HO HO!
IS THAT SHE ALWAYS MAKES A BEELINE FOR THE GOAL.
THAT MAKES IT EASY FOR THE DEFENSE TO STOP HER.
EVEN IF SOMEONE *DID* PASS TO HER, SHE'D HAVE TO RECEIVE THE BALL FROM RIGHT BEHIND HER. IT'S TOO DIFFICULT.
OH, THAT'S NO BIG DEAL. THE BALL COMES LIKE *BOING*!
YOU RECEIVE IT LIKE *YEAH*, AND JUST *BOP*, KICK IT AWAY.
I HATE PEOPLE WITH PERFECT MUSCLE MEMORY!!
YA CRAZY WILD CHILD!!

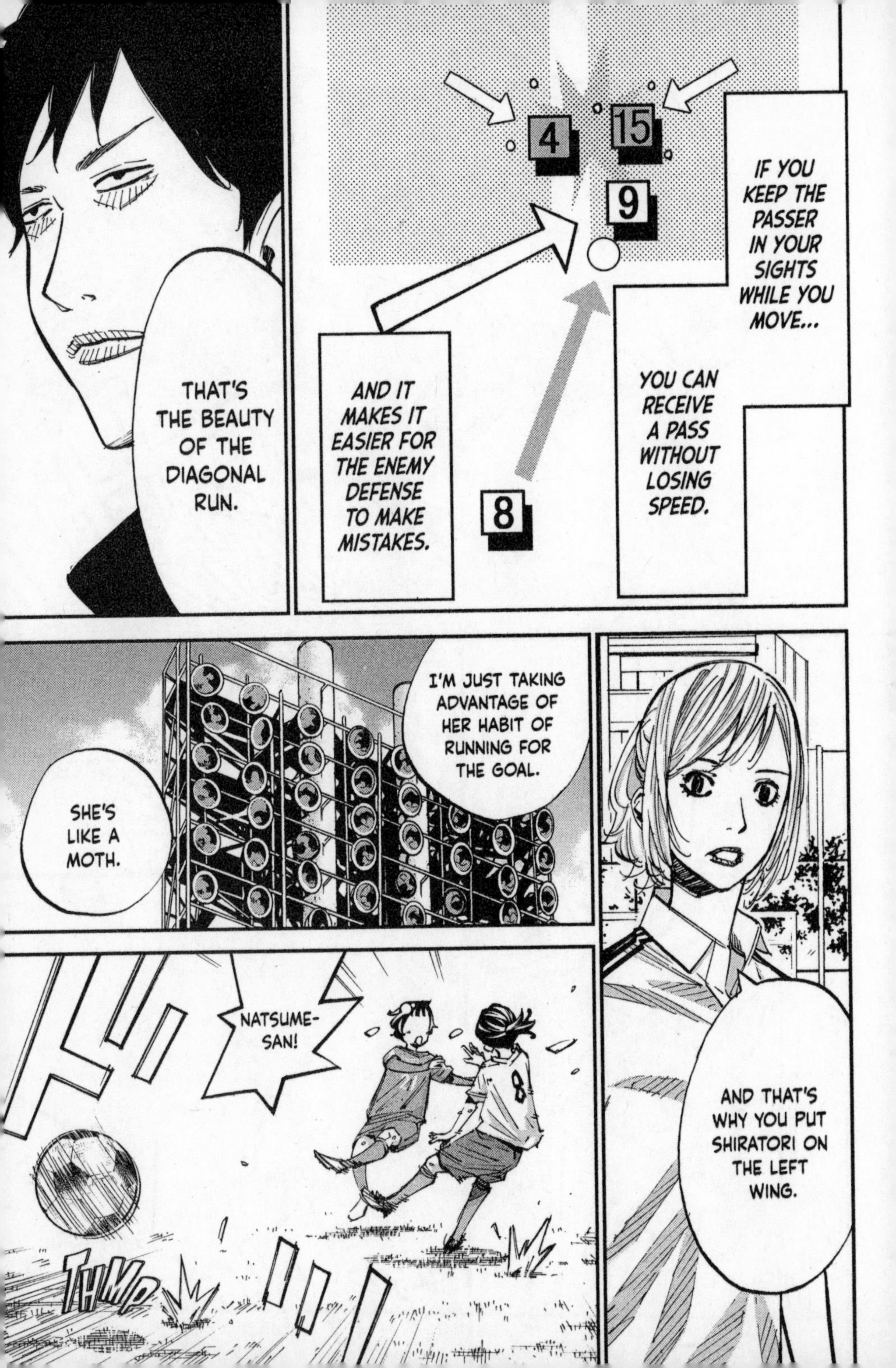
4
15
9
8
IF YOU KEEP THE PASSER IN YOUR SIGHTS WHILE YOU MOVE...
YOU CAN RECEIVE A PASS WITHOUT LOSING SPEED.
AND IT MAKES IT EASIER FOR THE ENEMY DEFENSE TO MAKE MISTAKES.
THAT'S THE BEAUTY OF THE DIAGONAL RUN.
AND THAT'S WHY YOU PUT SHIRATORI ON THE LEFT WING.
I'M JUST TAKING ADVANTAGE OF HER HABIT OF RUNNING FOR THE GOAL.
SHE'S LIKE A MOTH.
NATSUME-SAN!
THMP

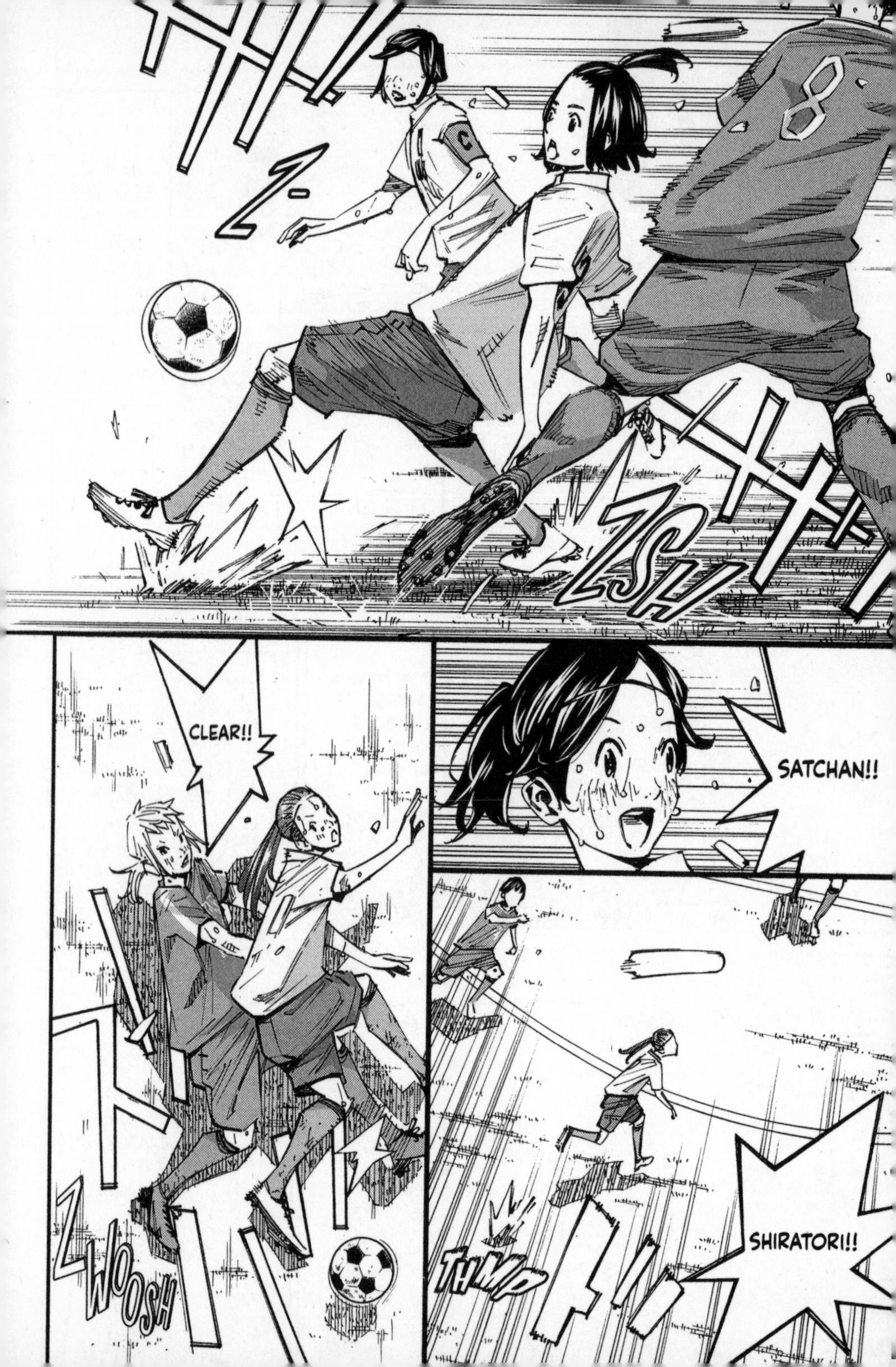
ZSH
SATCHAN!!
SHIRATORI!!
THMP
CLEAR!!
ZWOOSH

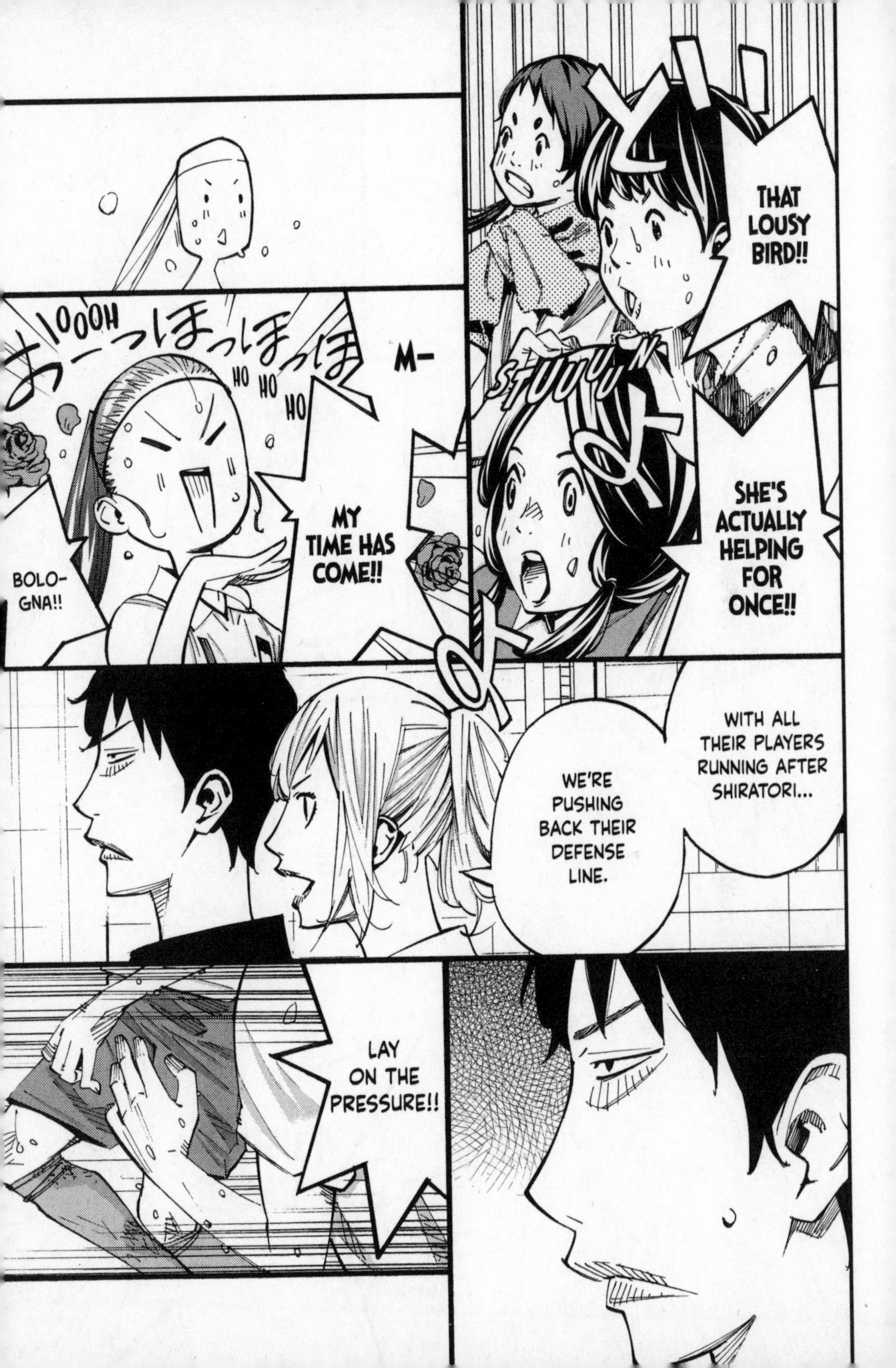
THAT LOUSY BIRD!!
SFUUUN
SHE'S ACTUALLY HELPING FOR ONCE!!
おーっほっほっほ
OOOOH HO HO HO
M- MY TIME HAS COME!!
BOLOGNA!!
WITH ALL THEIR PLAYERS RUNNING AFTER SHIRATORI...
WE'RE PUSHING BACK THEIR DEFENSE LINE.
LAY ON THE PRESSURE!!

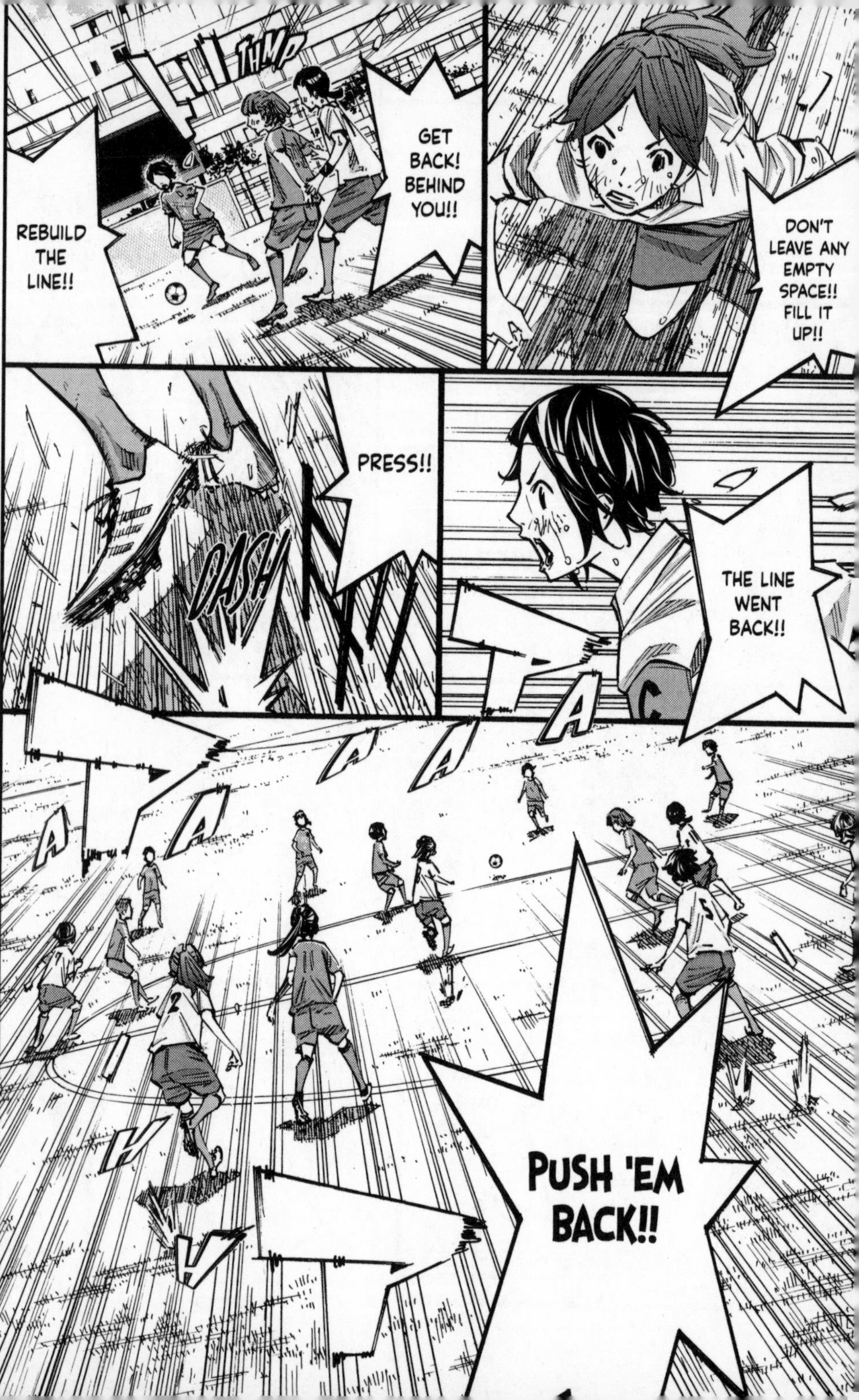
DON'T LEAVE ANY EMPTY SPACE!! FILL IT UP!!
THMP
GET BACK! BEHIND YOU!!
REBUILD THE LINE!!
THE LINE WENT BACK!!
PRESS!!
DASH
PUSH 'EM BACK!!

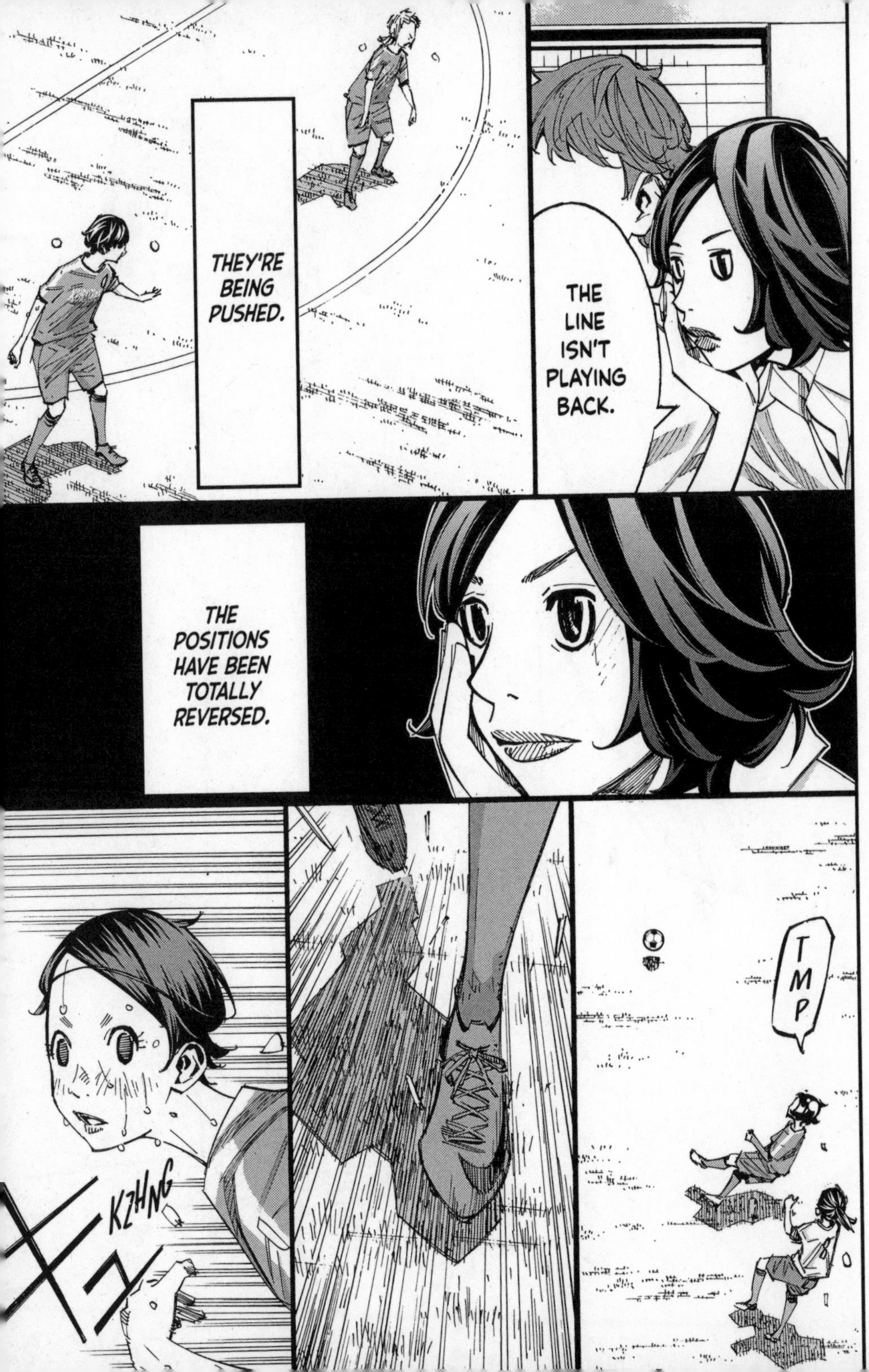
THE LINE ISN'T PLAYING BACK.
THEY'RE BEING PUSHED.
THE POSITIONS HAVE BEEN TOTALLY REVERSED.
TMP
KZHNG

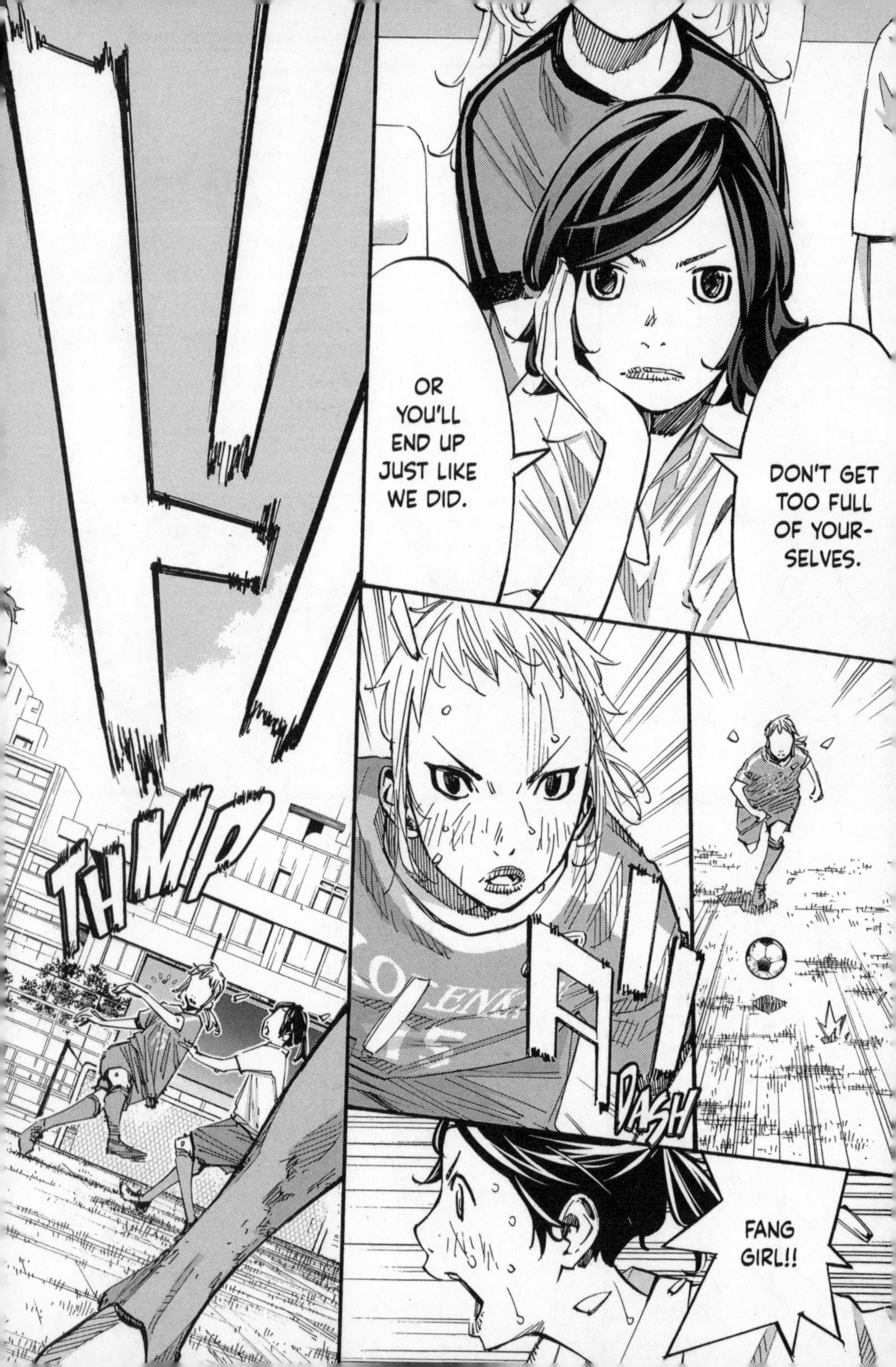
DON'T GET TOO FULL OF YOUR-SELVES.
OR YOU'LL END UP JUST LIKE WE DID.
DASH
FANG GIRL!!
THMP

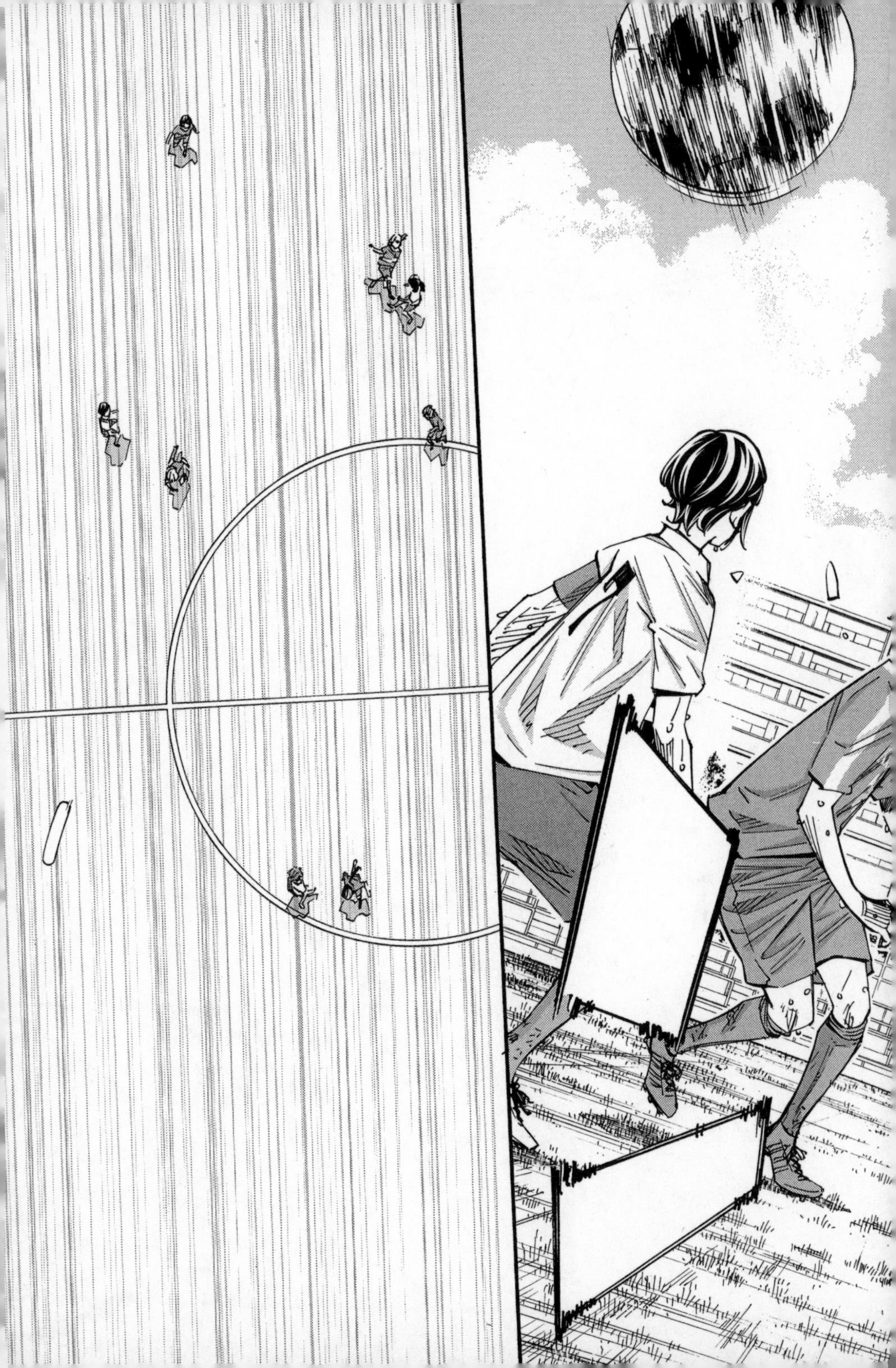

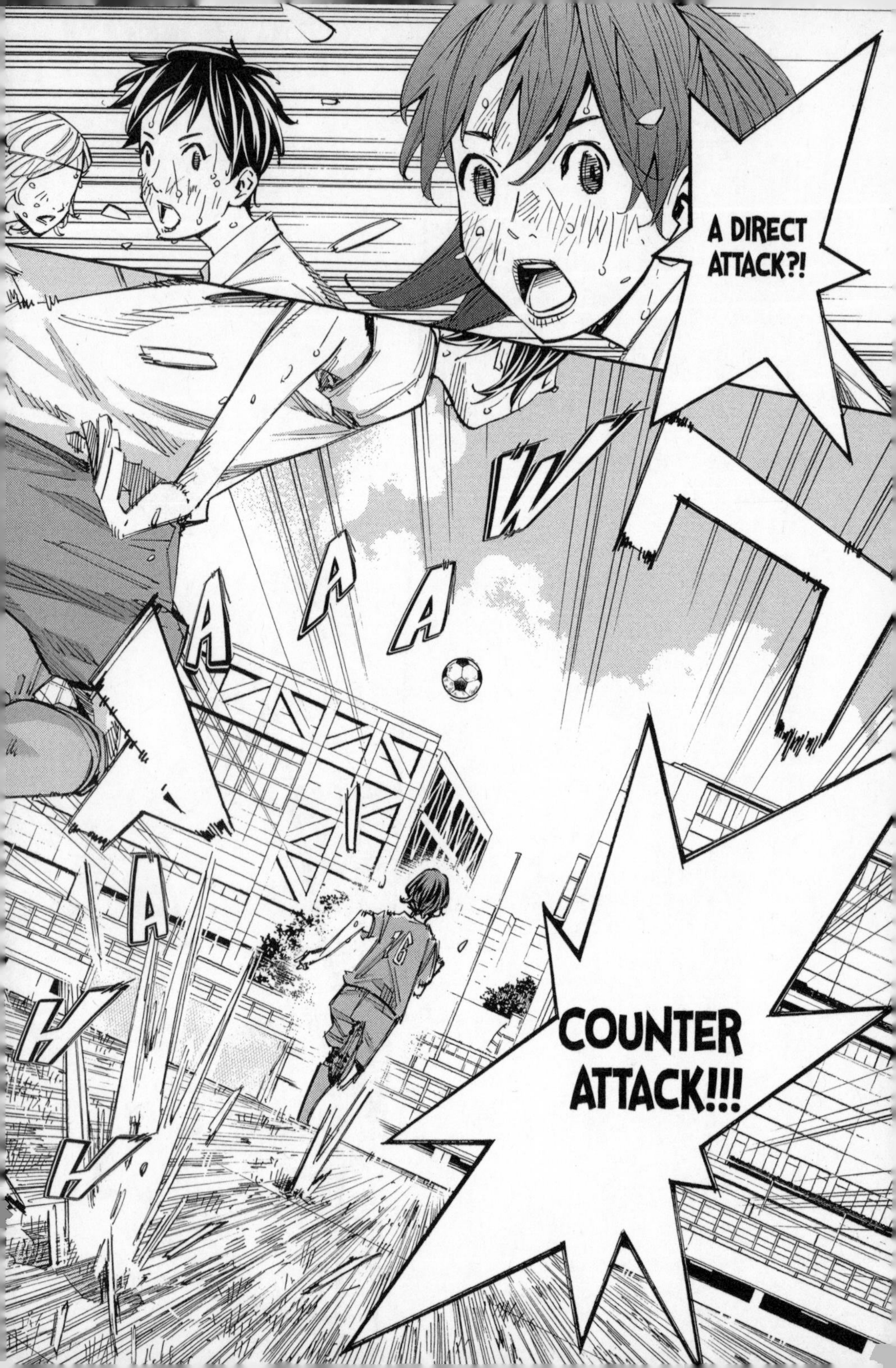
A DIRECT ATTACK?!
WAAAAHH
COUNTER ATTACK!!!

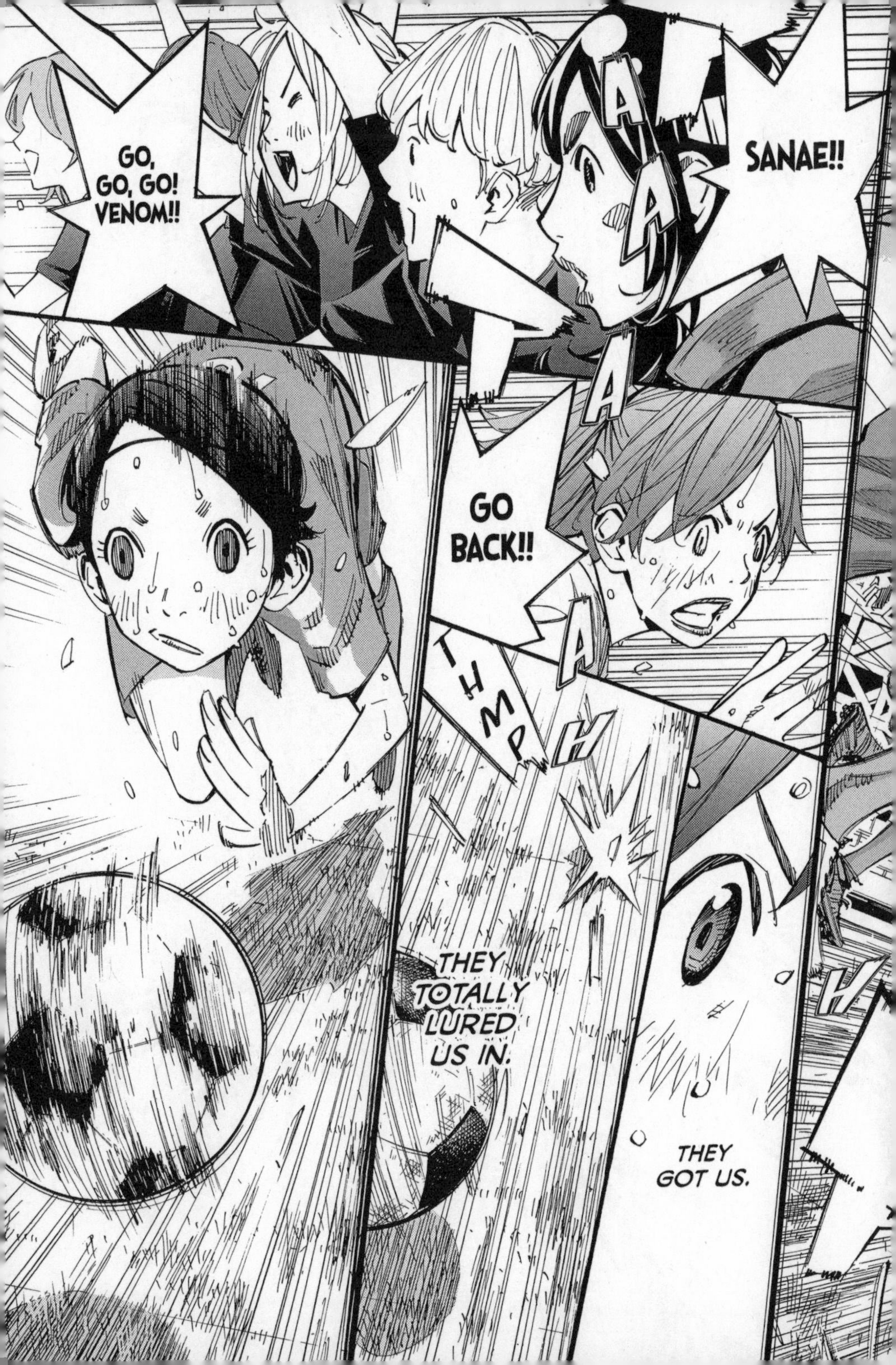
SANAE!!
AAAAAH
GO, GO, GO! VENOM!!
GO BACK!!
H
THEY GOT US.
THMP
THEY TOTALLY LURED US IN.

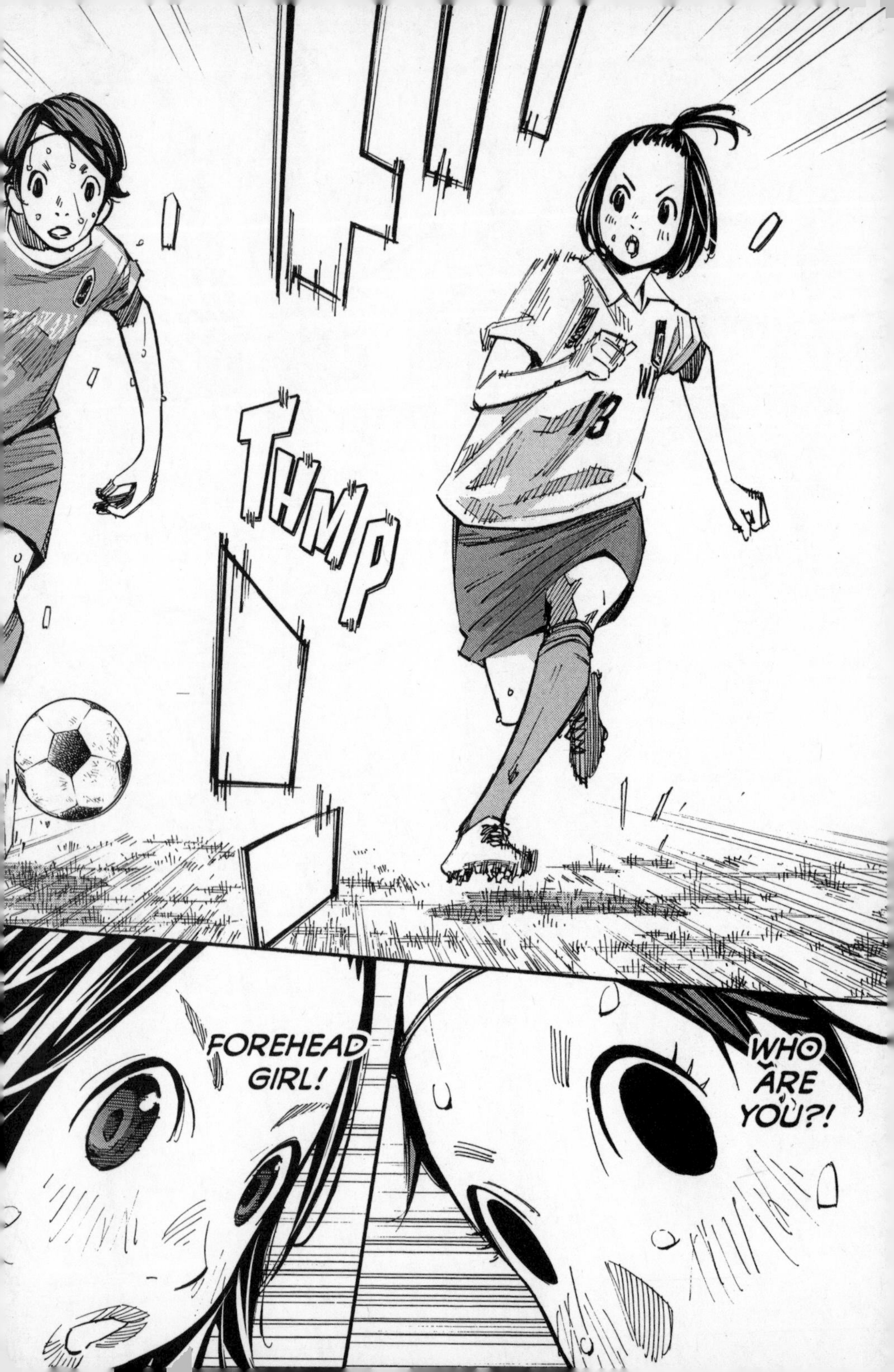
THMP
WHO ARE YOU?!
FOREHEAD GIRL!

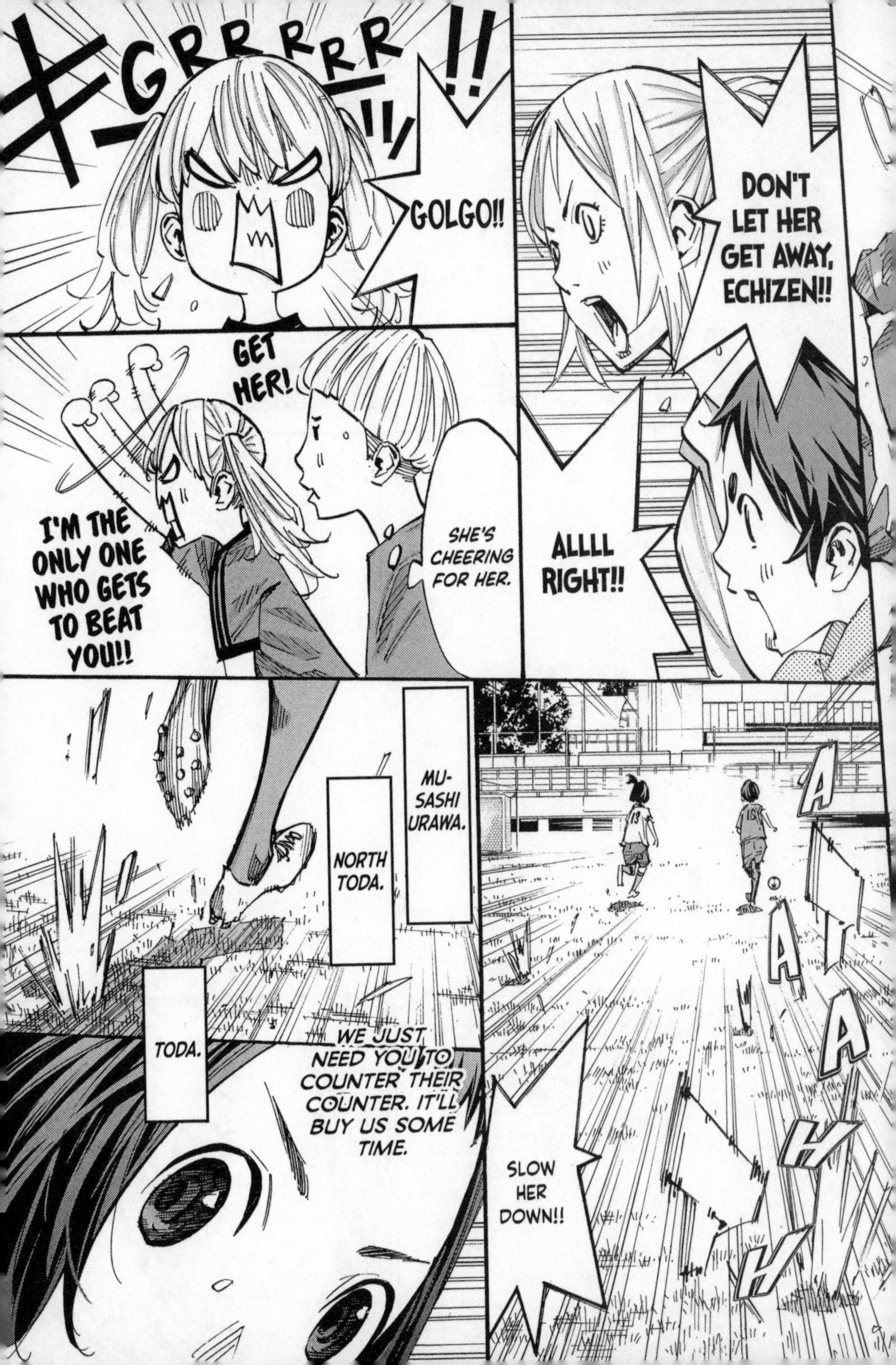
DON'T LET HER GET AWAY, ECHIZEN!!
GRRRRRR!!
GOLGO!!
ALLLL RIGHT!!
GET HER!
SHE'S CHEERING FOR HER.
I'M THE ONLY ONE WHO GETS TO BEAT YOU!!
AAAAHH
SLOW HER DOWN!!
MU-SASHI URAWA.
NORTH TODA.
TODA.
WE JUST NEED YOU TO COUNTER THEIR COUNTER. IT'LL BUY US SOME TIME.

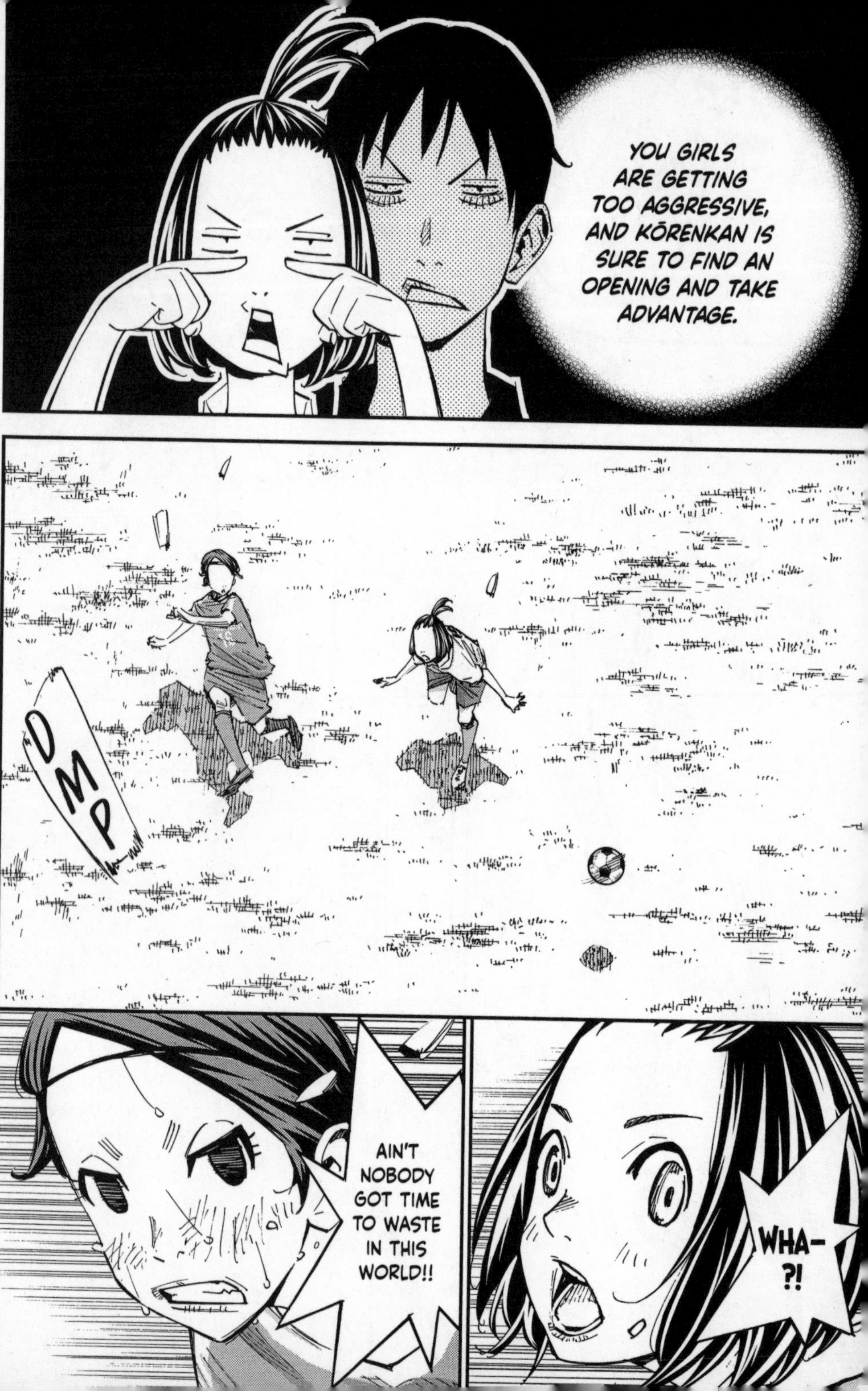
YOU GIRLS ARE GETTING TOO AGGRESSIVE, AND KŌRENKAN IS SURE TO FIND AN OPENING AND TAKE ADVANTAGE.
DMP
WHA- ?!
AIN'T NOBODY GOT TIME TO WASTE IN THIS WORLD!!

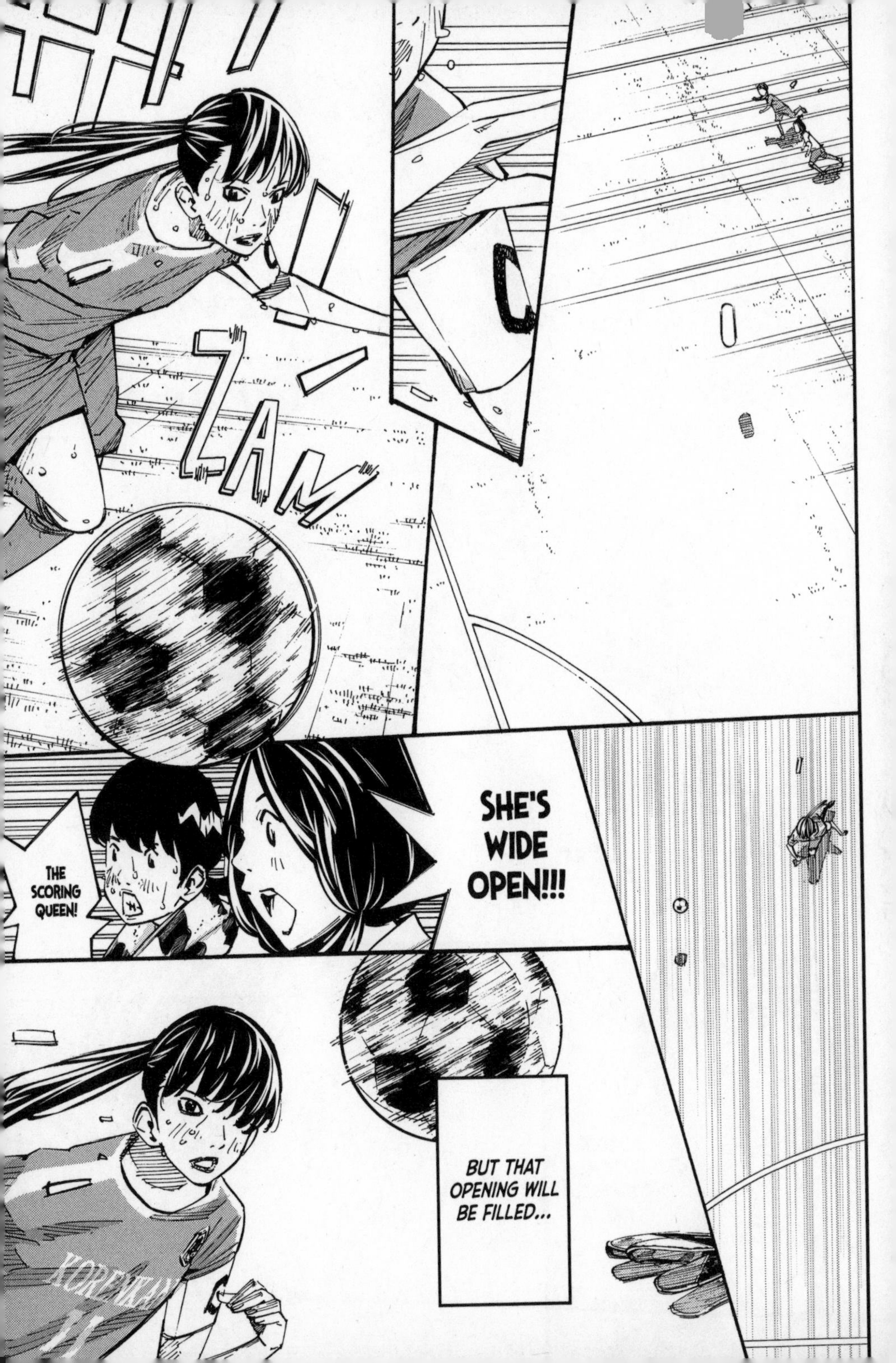
ZAM
SHE'S WIDE OPEN!!!
THE SCORING QUEEN!
BUT THAT OPENING WILL BE FILLED...

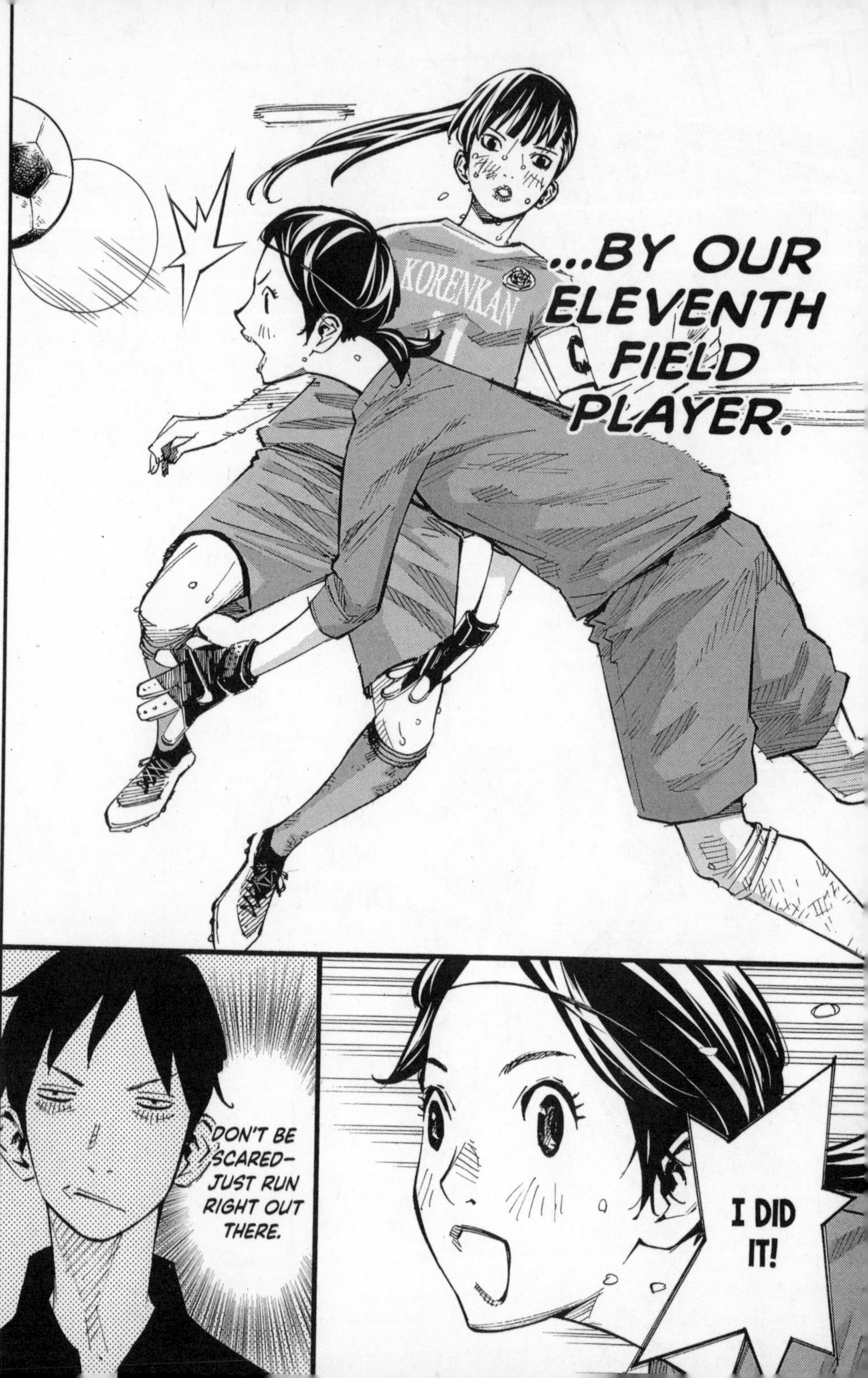
KORENKAN
...BY OUR ELEVENTH FIELD PLAYER.
I DID IT!
DON'T BE SCARED—JUST RUN RIGHT OUT THERE.

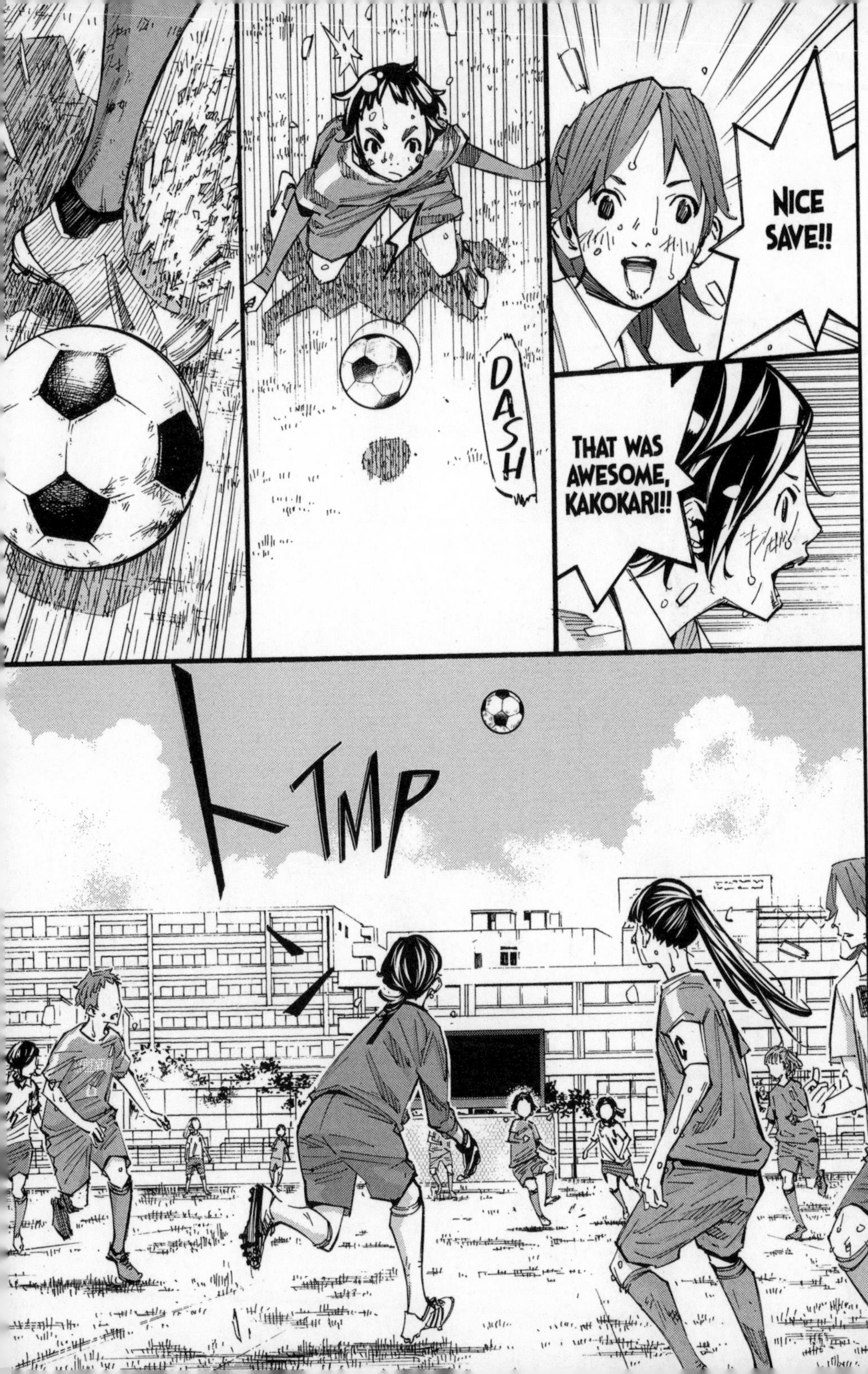
NICE SAVE!!
THAT WAS AWESOME, KAKOKARI!!!
DASH
TMP

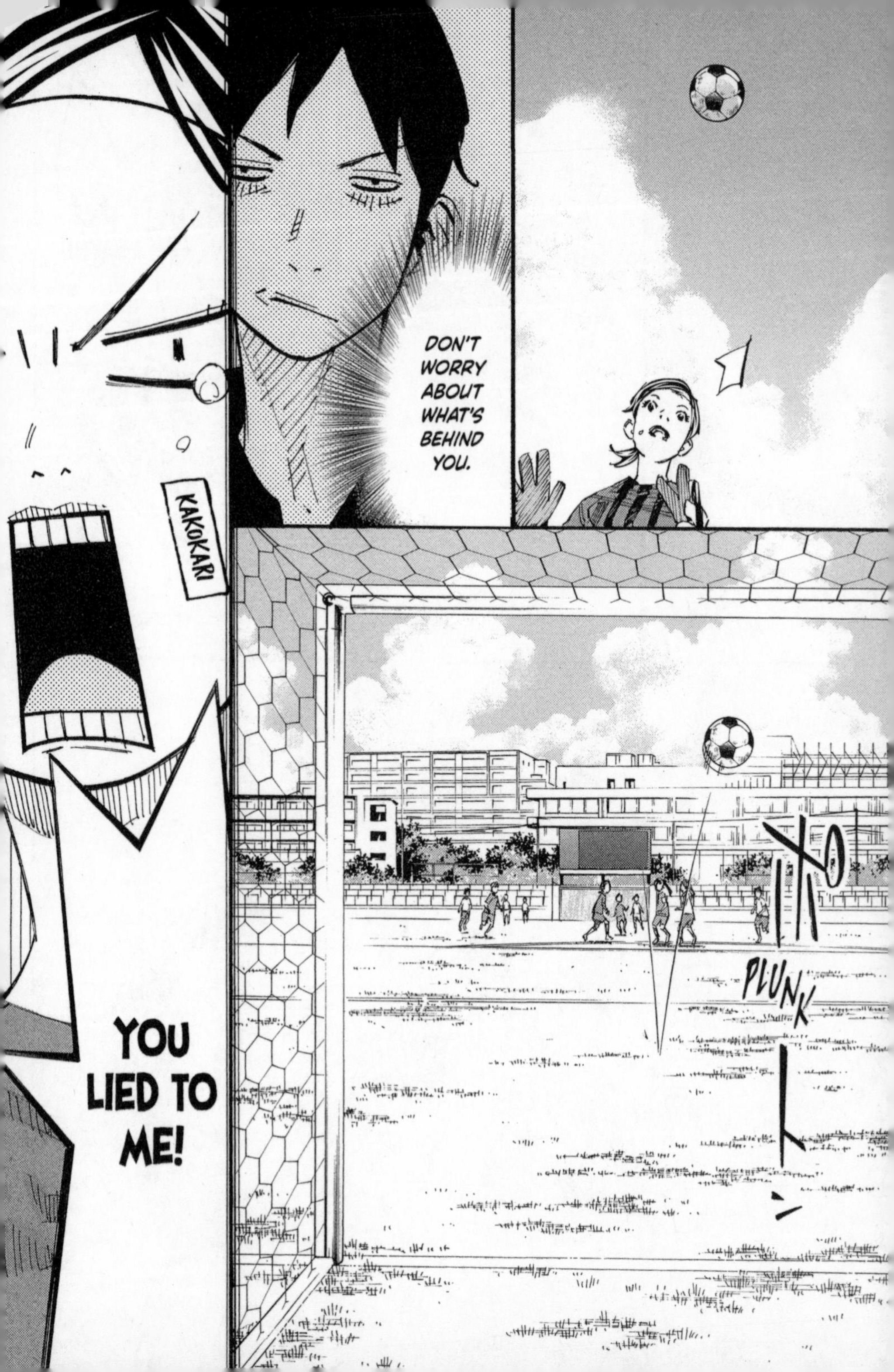

DON'T WORRY ABOUT WHAT'S BEHIND YOU.
PLUNK
KAKOKARI
YOU LIED TO ME!

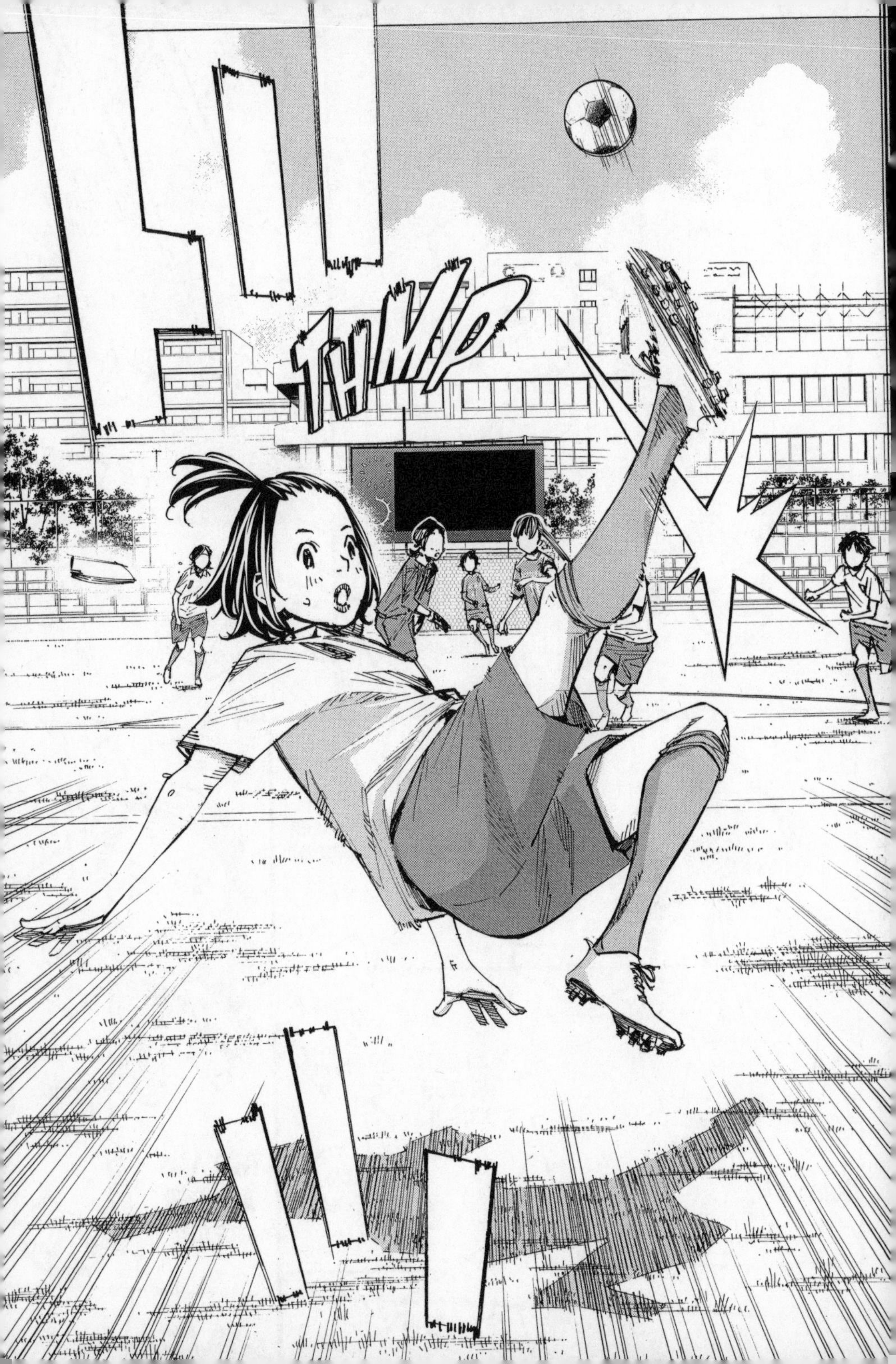
THUMP

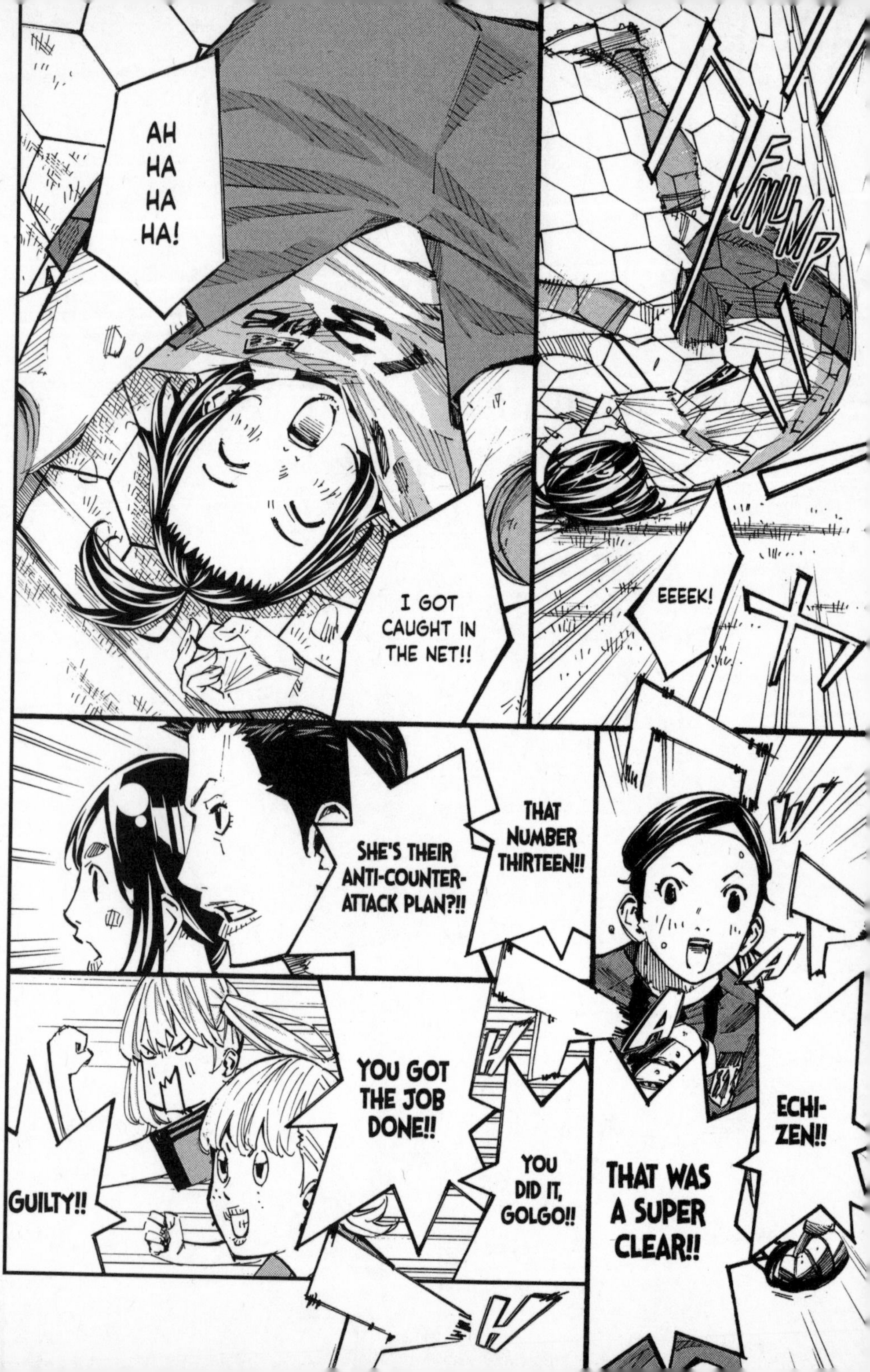
FWUMP
EEEEK!
AH HA HA HA!
I GOT CAUGHT IN THE NET!!
THAT NUMBER THIRTEEN!!
SHE'S THEIR ANTI-COUNTER-ATTACK PLAN?!!
ECHI-ZEN!!
THAT WAS A SUPER CLEAR!!
YOU DID IT, GOLGO!!
YOU GOT THE JOB DONE!!
GUILTY!!

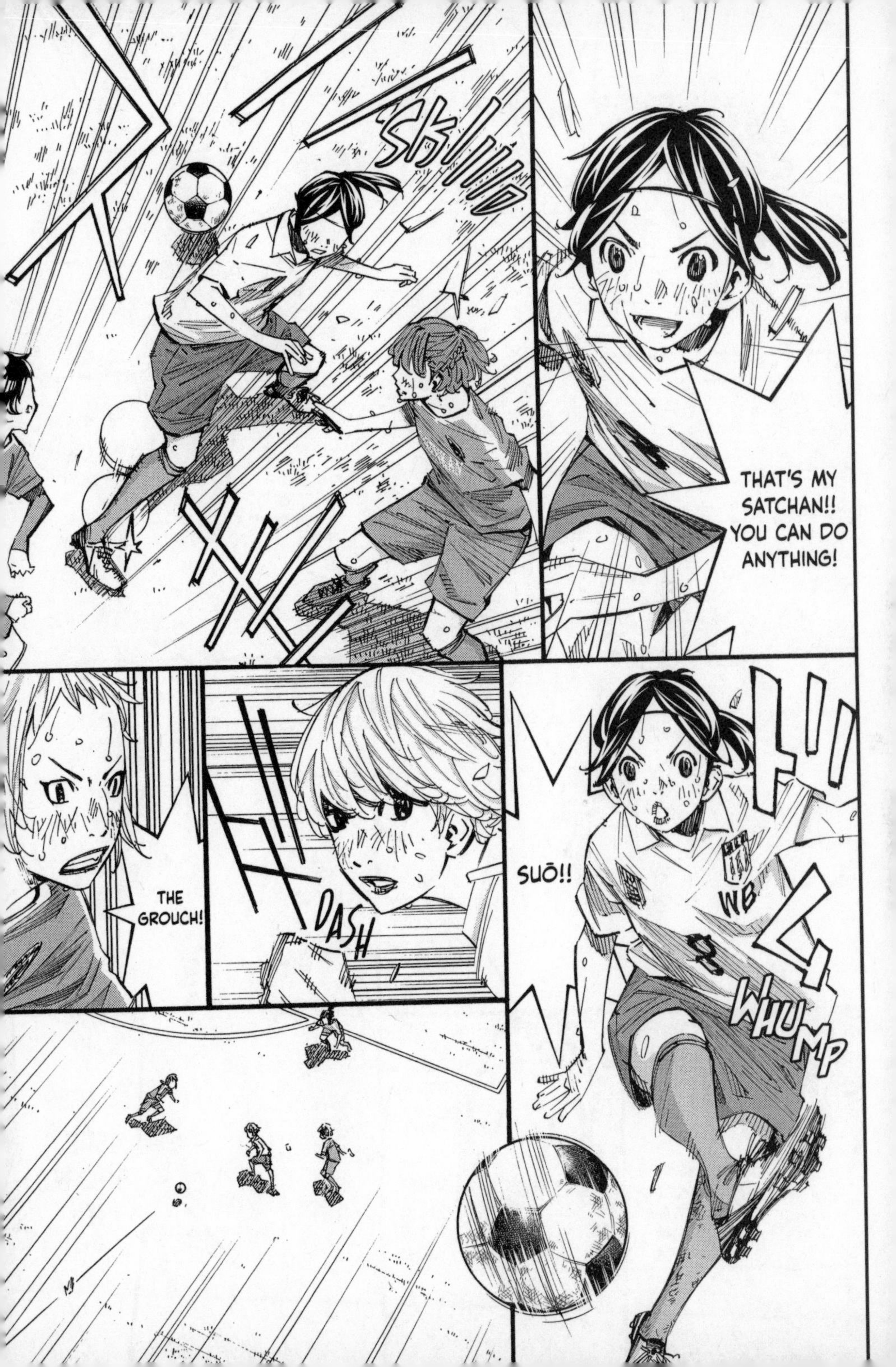
THAT'S MY SATCHAN!! YOU CAN DO ANYTHING!
SKIIIID
SUŌ!!
WHUMP
DASH
THE GROUCH!

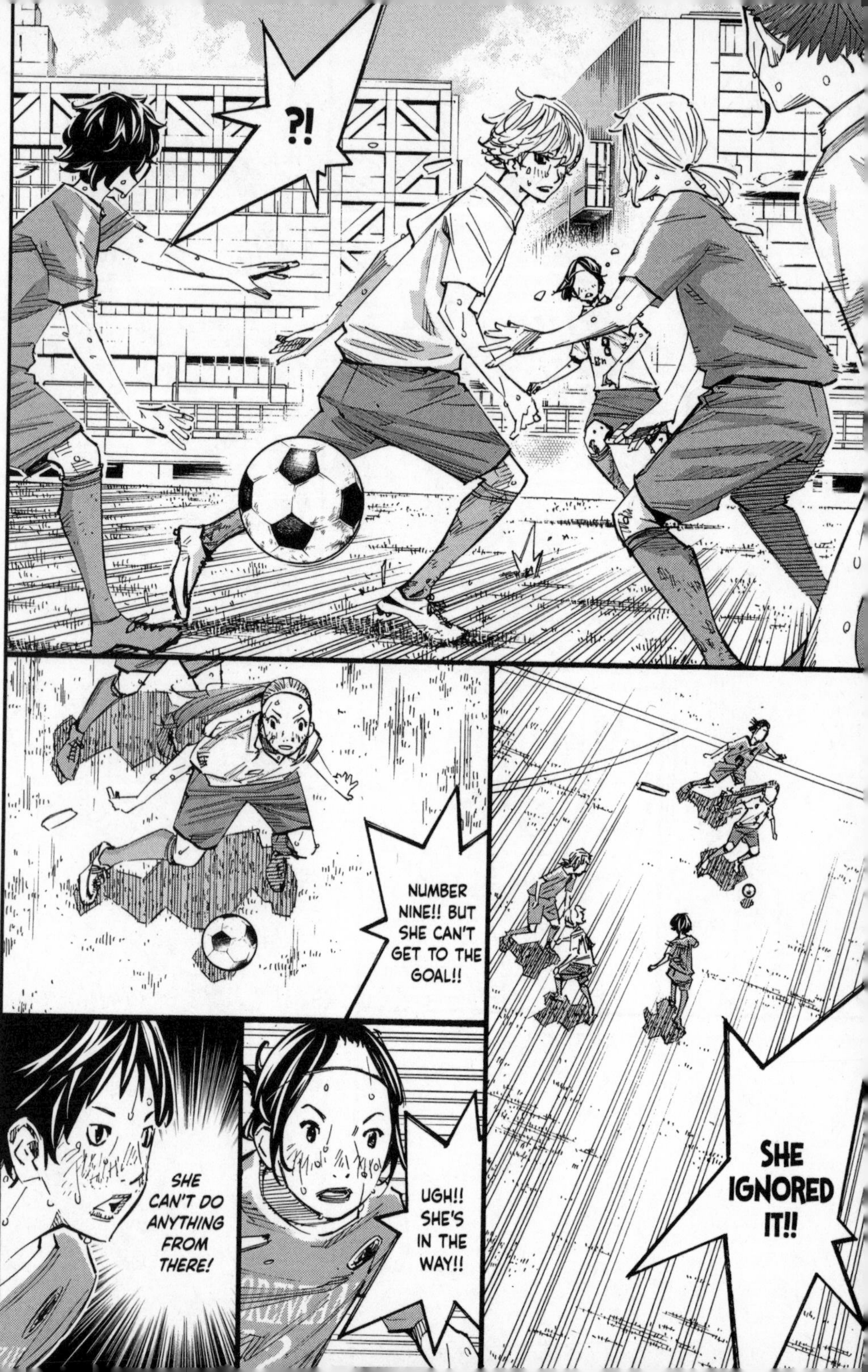
?!
SHE IGNORED IT!!
NUMBER NINE!! BUT SHE CAN'T GET TO THE GOAL!!
UGH!! SHE'S IN THE WAY!!
SHE CAN'T DO ANYTHING FROM THERE!

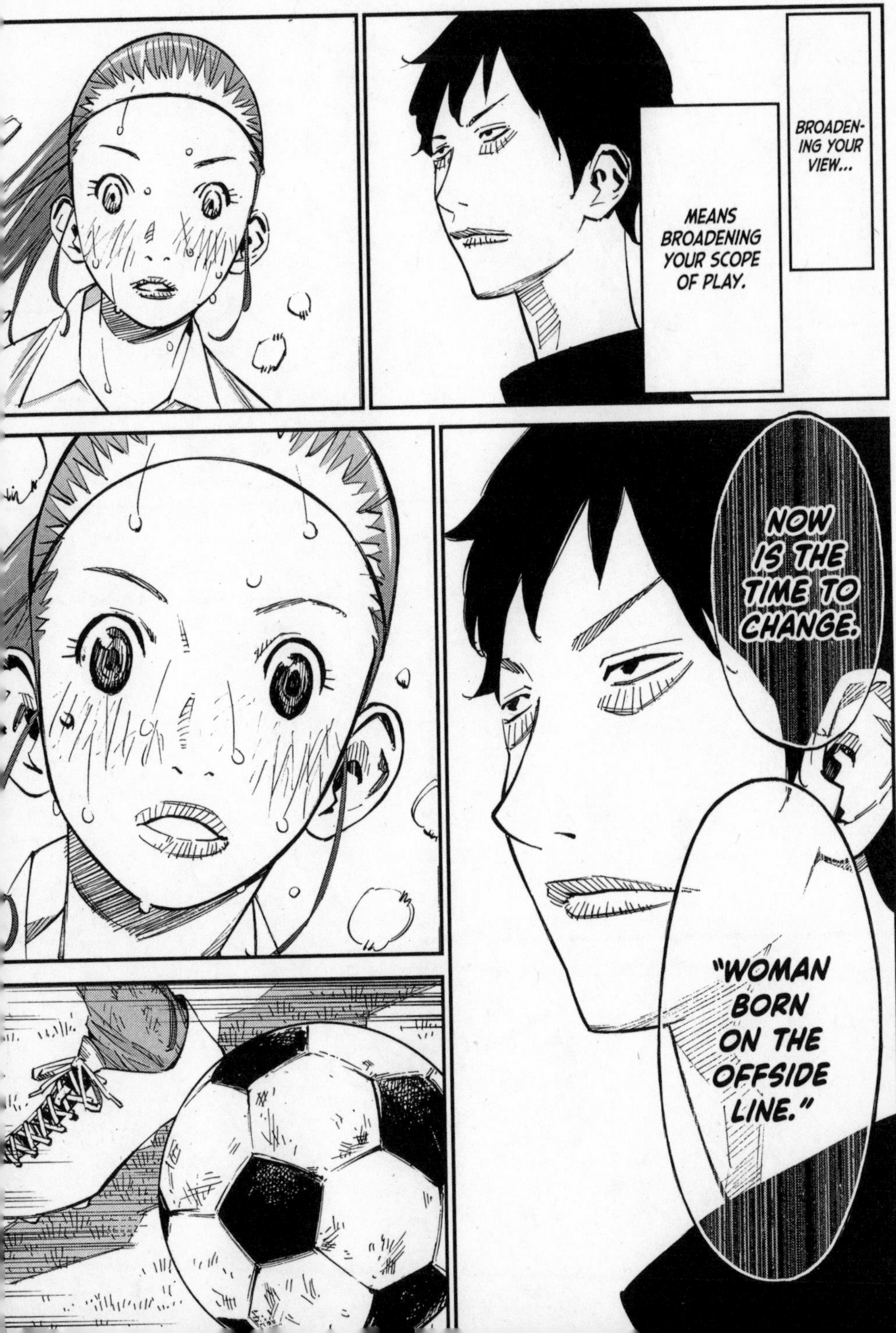
BROADENING YOUR VIEW...
MEANS BROADENING YOUR SCOPE OF PLAY.
NOW IS THE TIME TO CHANGE.
"WOMAN BORN ON THE OFFSIDE LINE."

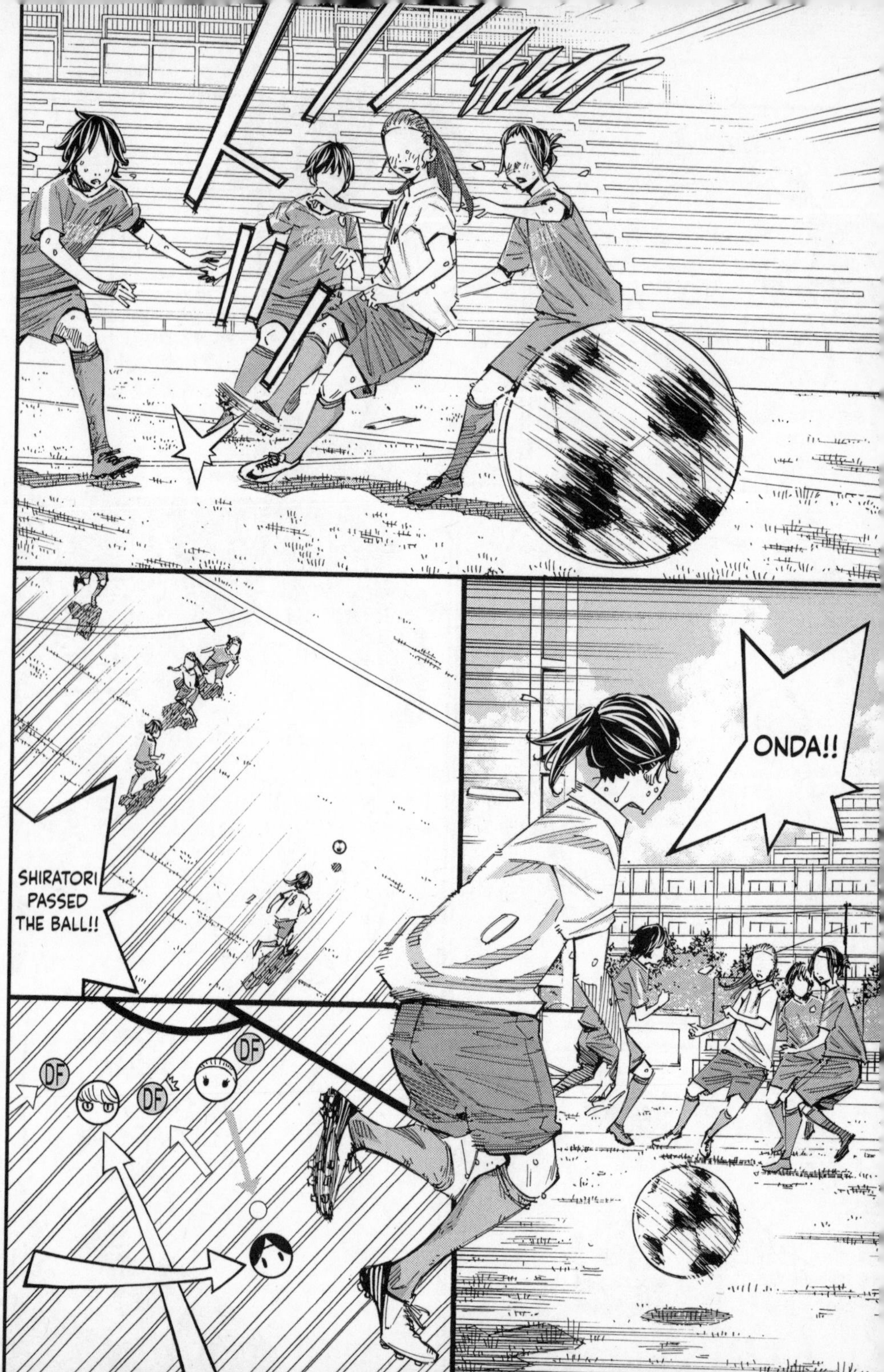
ONDA!!
SHIRATORI PASSED THE BALL!!
DF
DF
DF

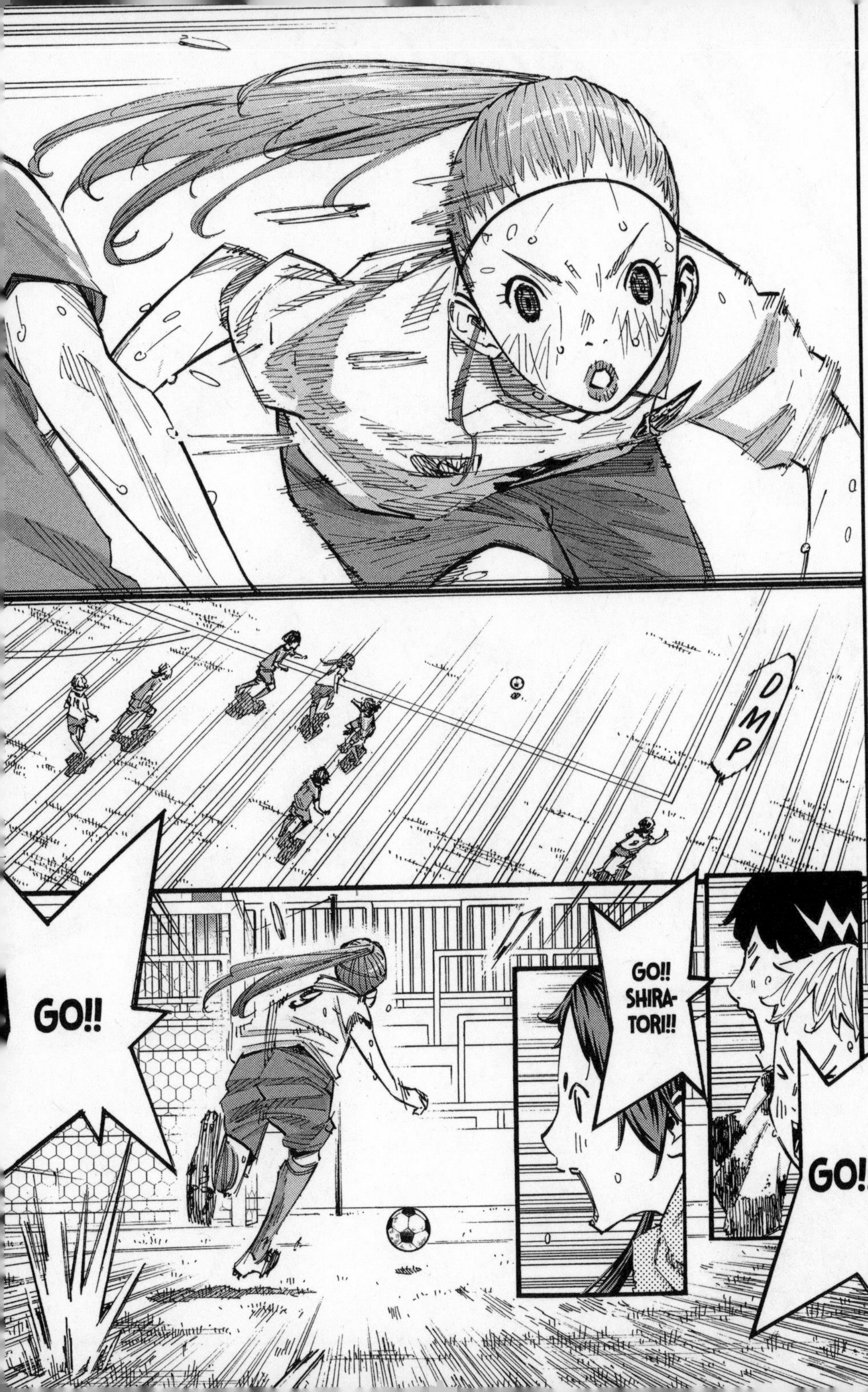
DMP
GO!! SHIRA-TORI!!!
GO!!
GO!!

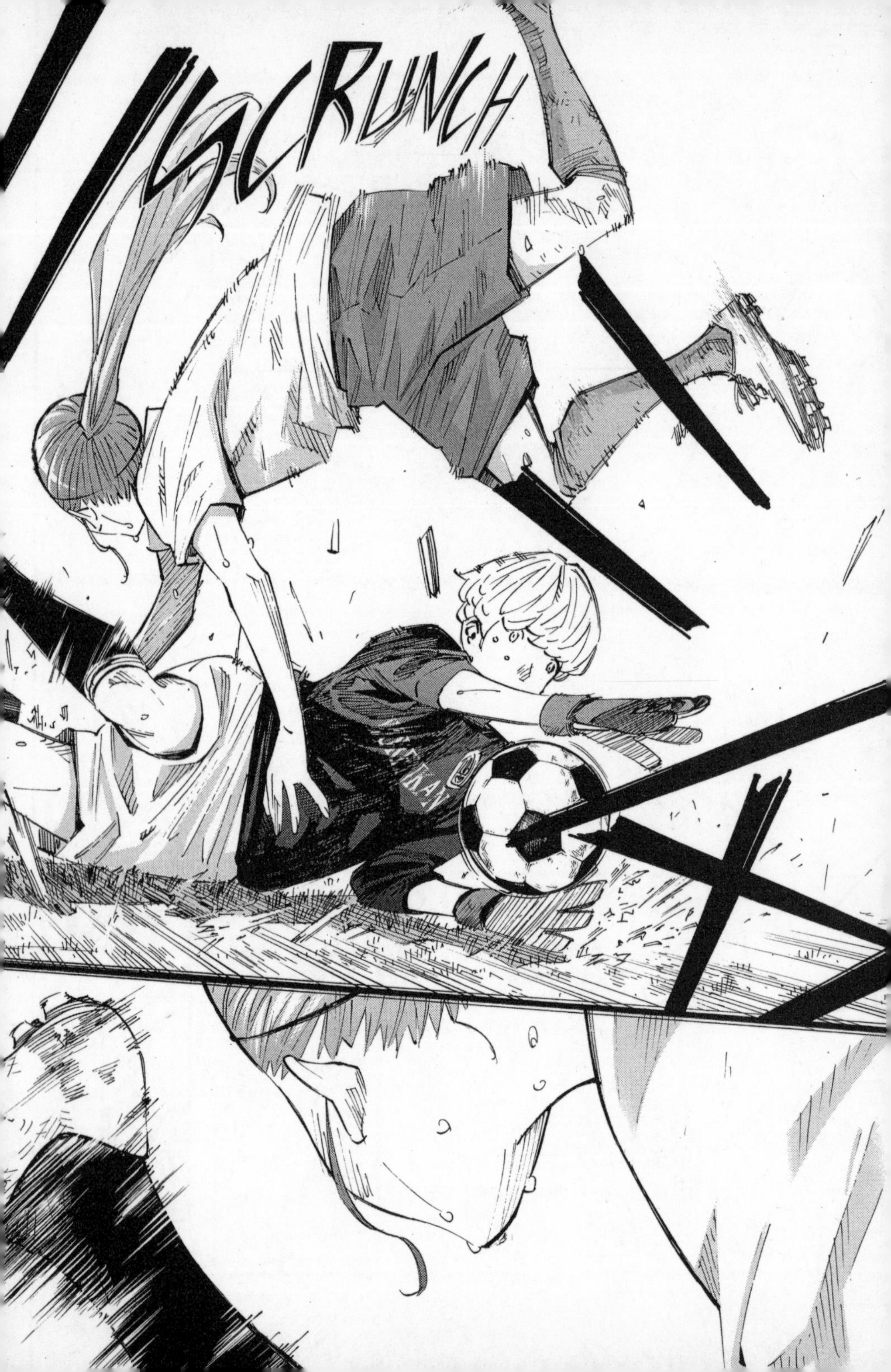
SCRUNCH

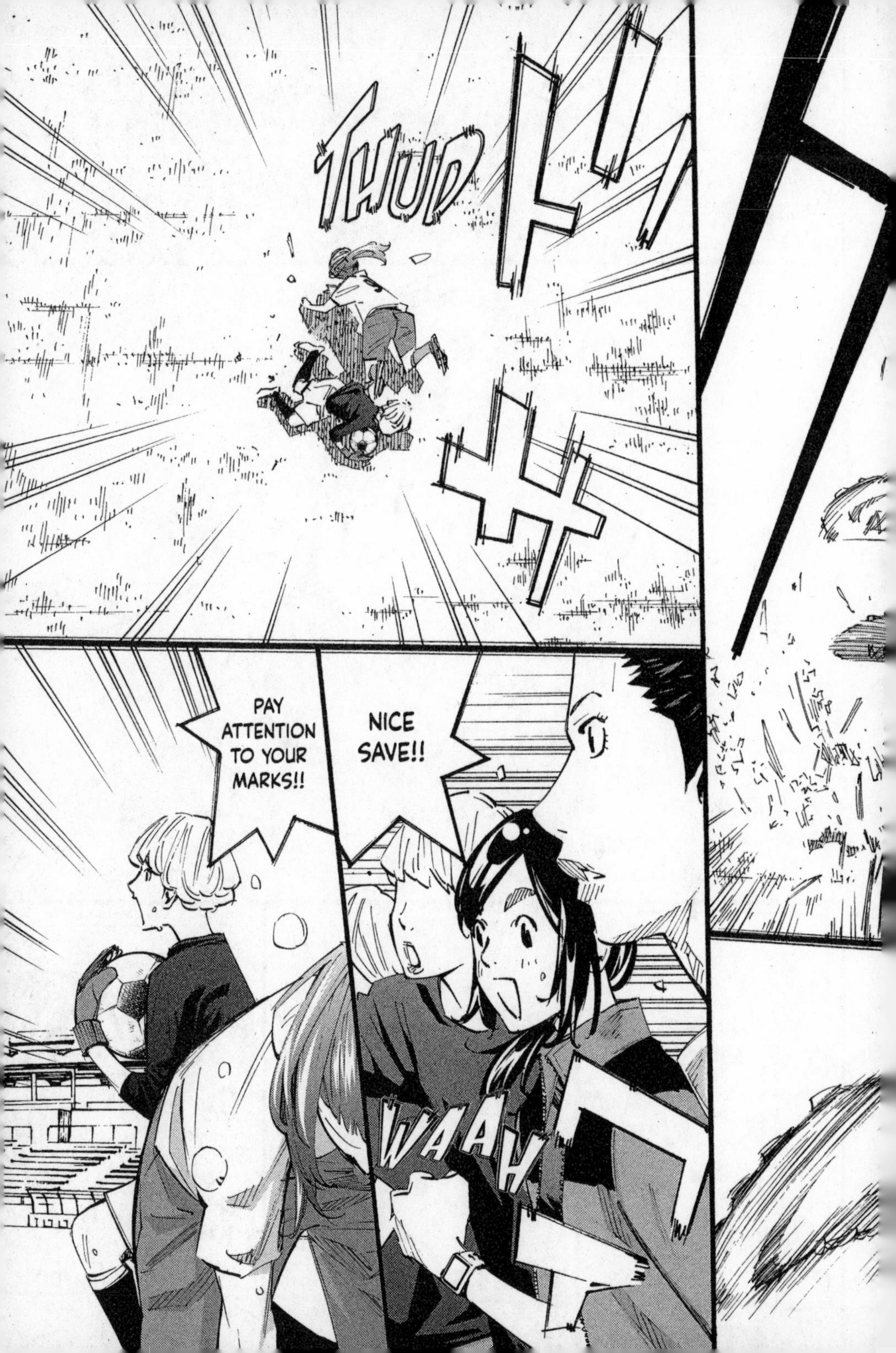
THUD
NICE SAVE!!
WAAH
PAY ATTENTION TO YOUR MARKS!!

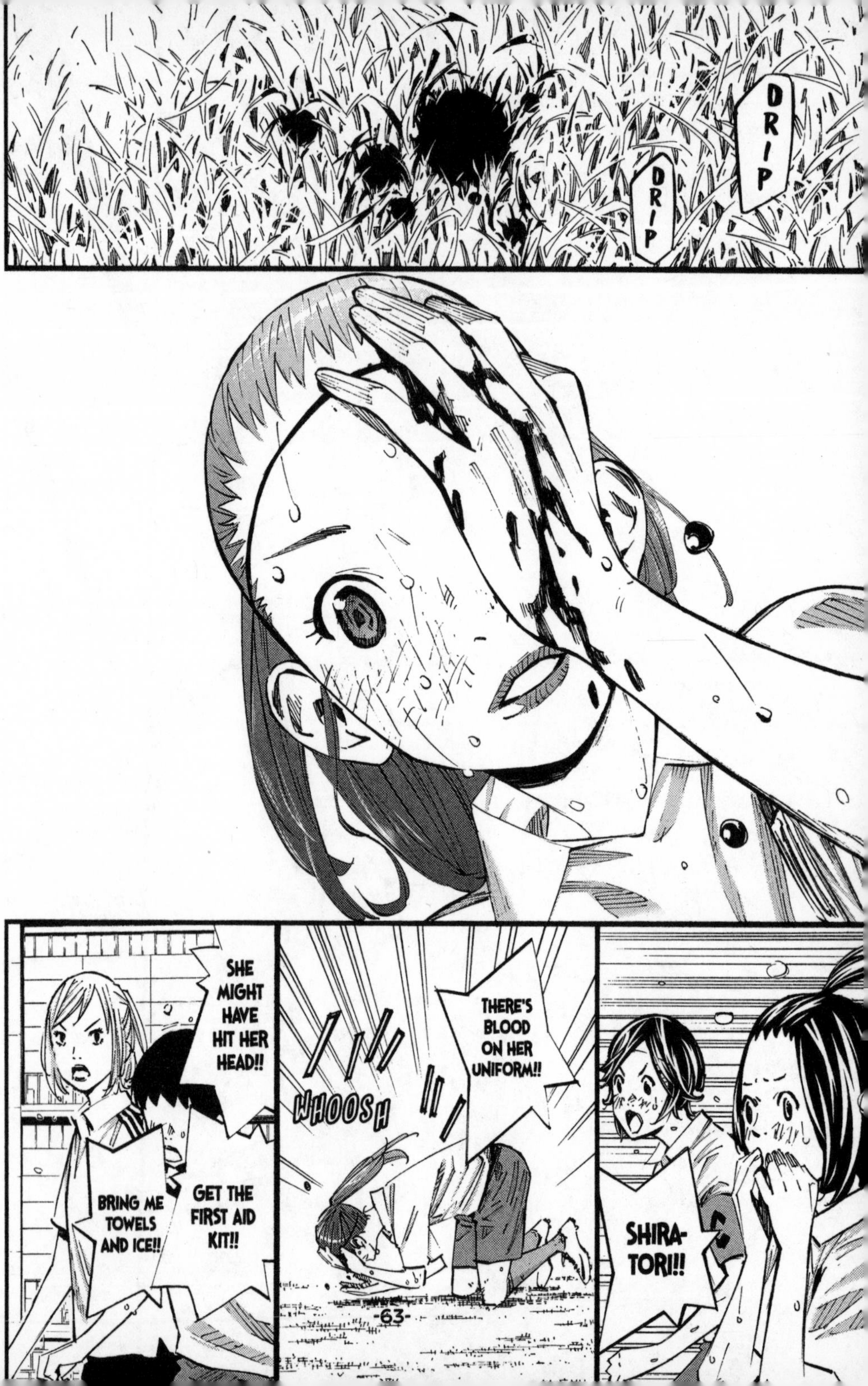
DRIP
DRIP
SHIRA-TORI!!
THERE'S BLOOD ON HER UNIFORM!!
WHOOSH
SHE MIGHT HAVE HIT HER HEAD!!
GET THE FIRST AID KIT!!
BRING ME TOWELS AND ICE!!

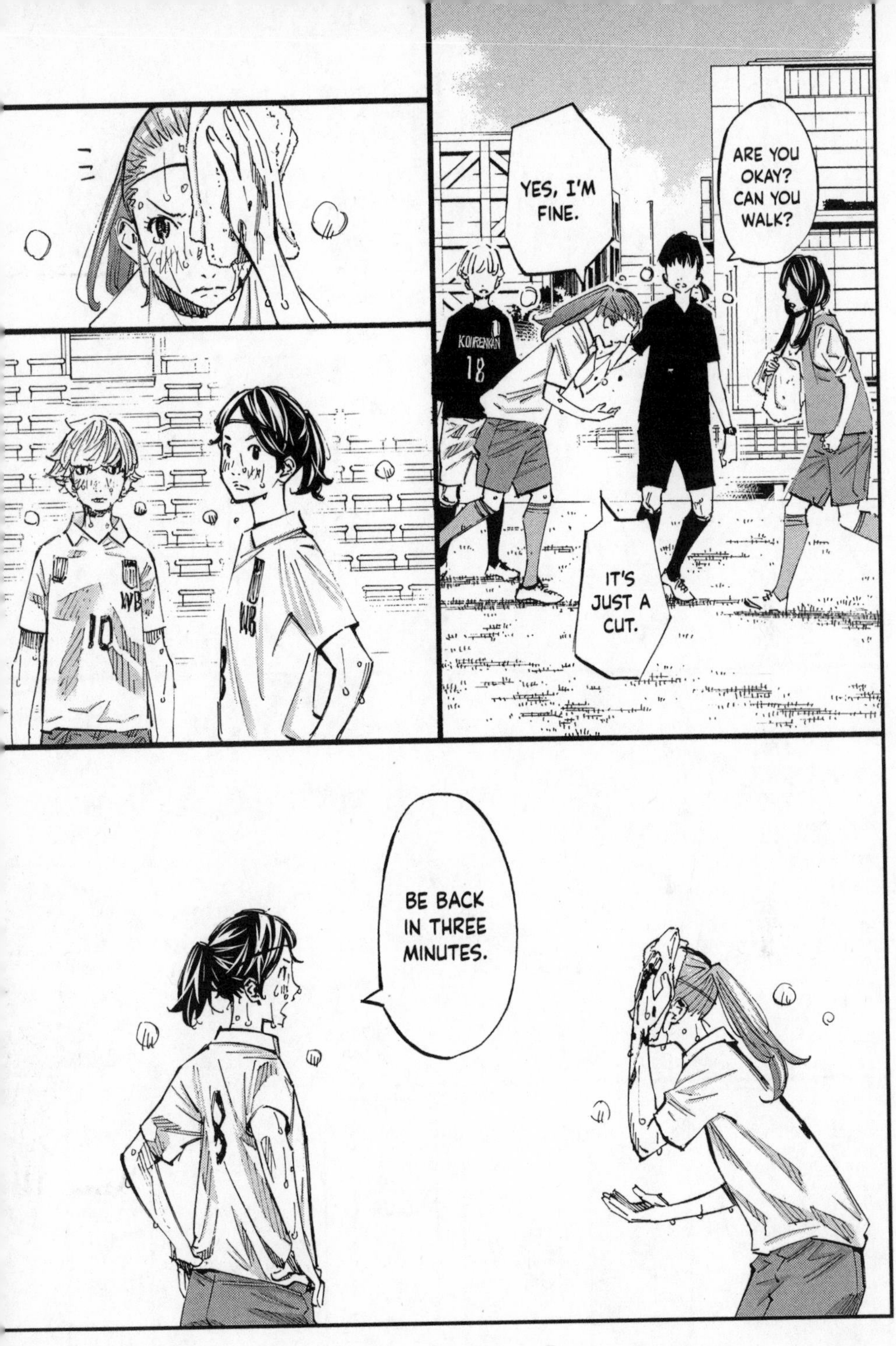
ARE YOU OKAY? CAN YOU WALK?
YES, I'M FINE.
IT'S JUST A CUT.
BE BACK IN THREE MINUTES.

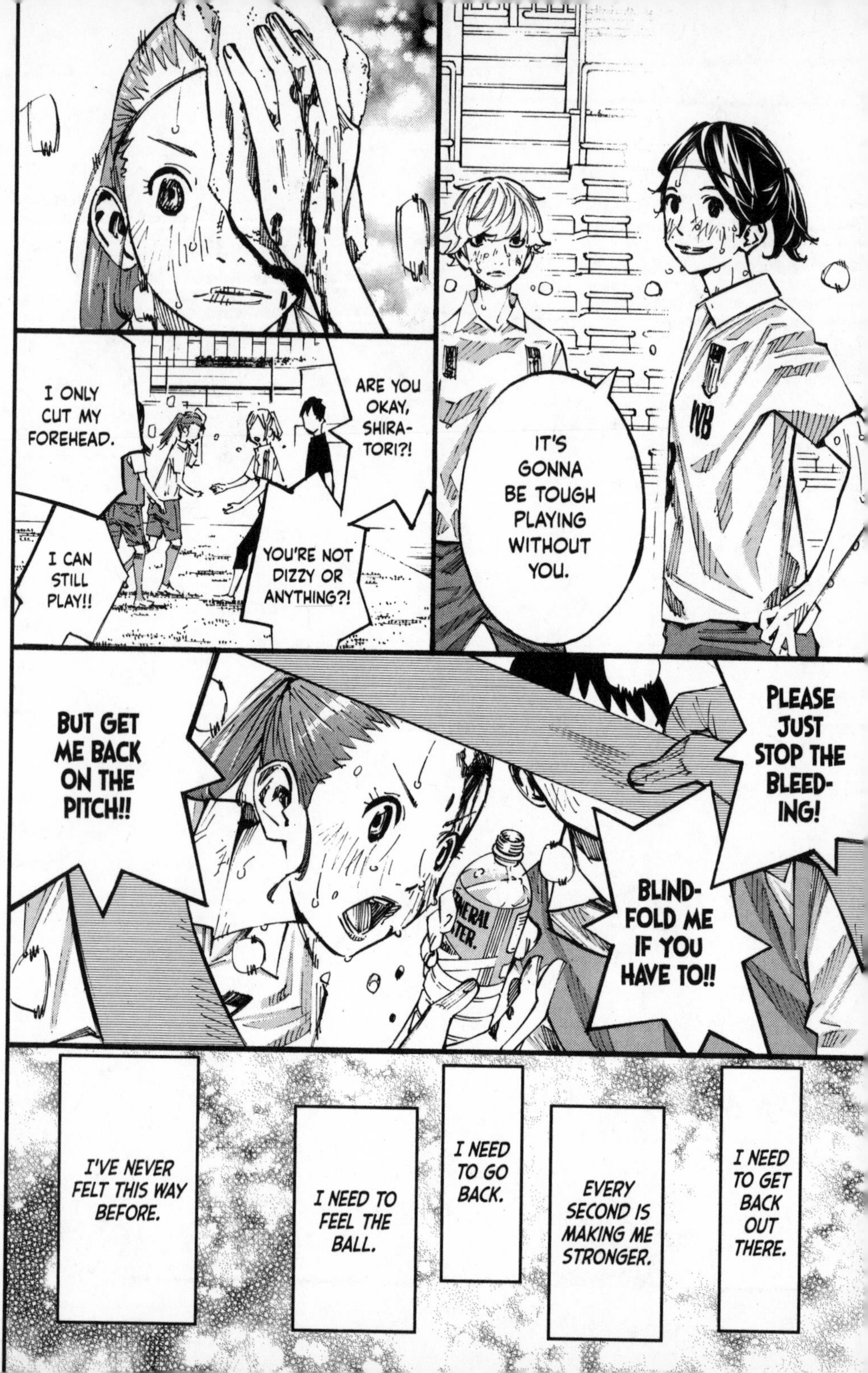
IT'S GONNA BE TOUGH PLAYING WITHOUT YOU.
ARE YOU OKAY, SHIRATORI?!
YOU'RE NOT DIZZY OR ANYTHING?!
I ONLY CUT MY FOREHEAD.
I CAN STILL PLAY!!
PLEASE JUST STOP THE BLEEDING!
BLINDFOLD ME IF YOU HAVE TO!!
BUT GET ME BACK ON THE PITCH!!
I NEED TO GET BACK OUT THERE.
EVERY SECOND IS MAKING ME STRONGER.
I NEED TO GO BACK.
I NEED TO FEEL THE BALL.
I'VE NEVER FELT THIS WAY BEFORE.

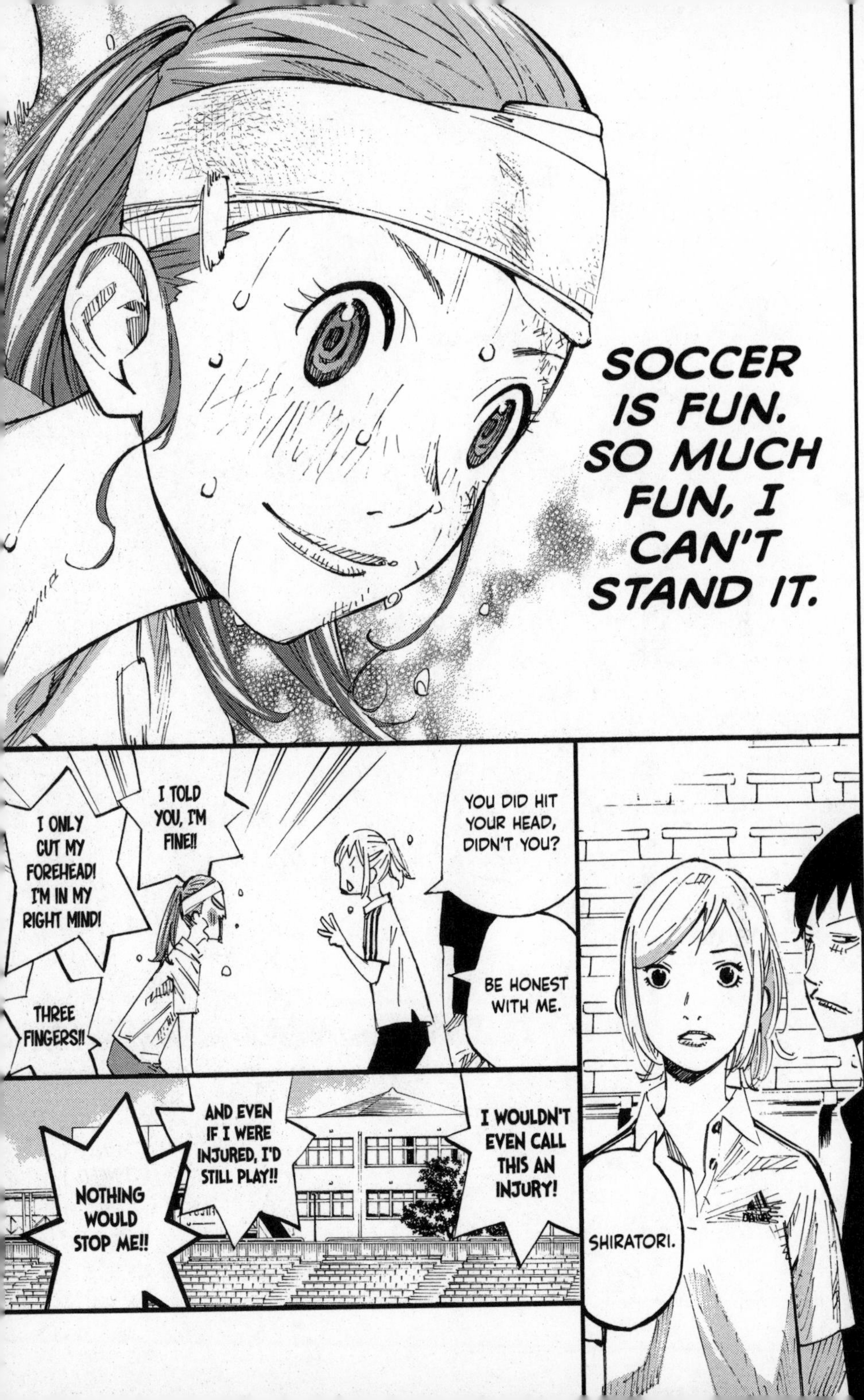
SOCCER IS FUN. SO MUCH FUN, I CAN'T STAND IT.
SHIRATORI.
YOU DID HIT YOUR HEAD, DIDN'T YOU?
BE HONEST WITH ME.
I TOLD YOU, I'M FINE!!
I ONLY CUT MY FOREHEAD! I'M IN MY RIGHT MIND!
THREE FINGERS!!
I WOULDN'T EVEN CALL THIS AN INJURY!
AND EVEN IF I WERE INJURED, I'D STILL PLAY!!
NOTHING WOULD STOP ME!!

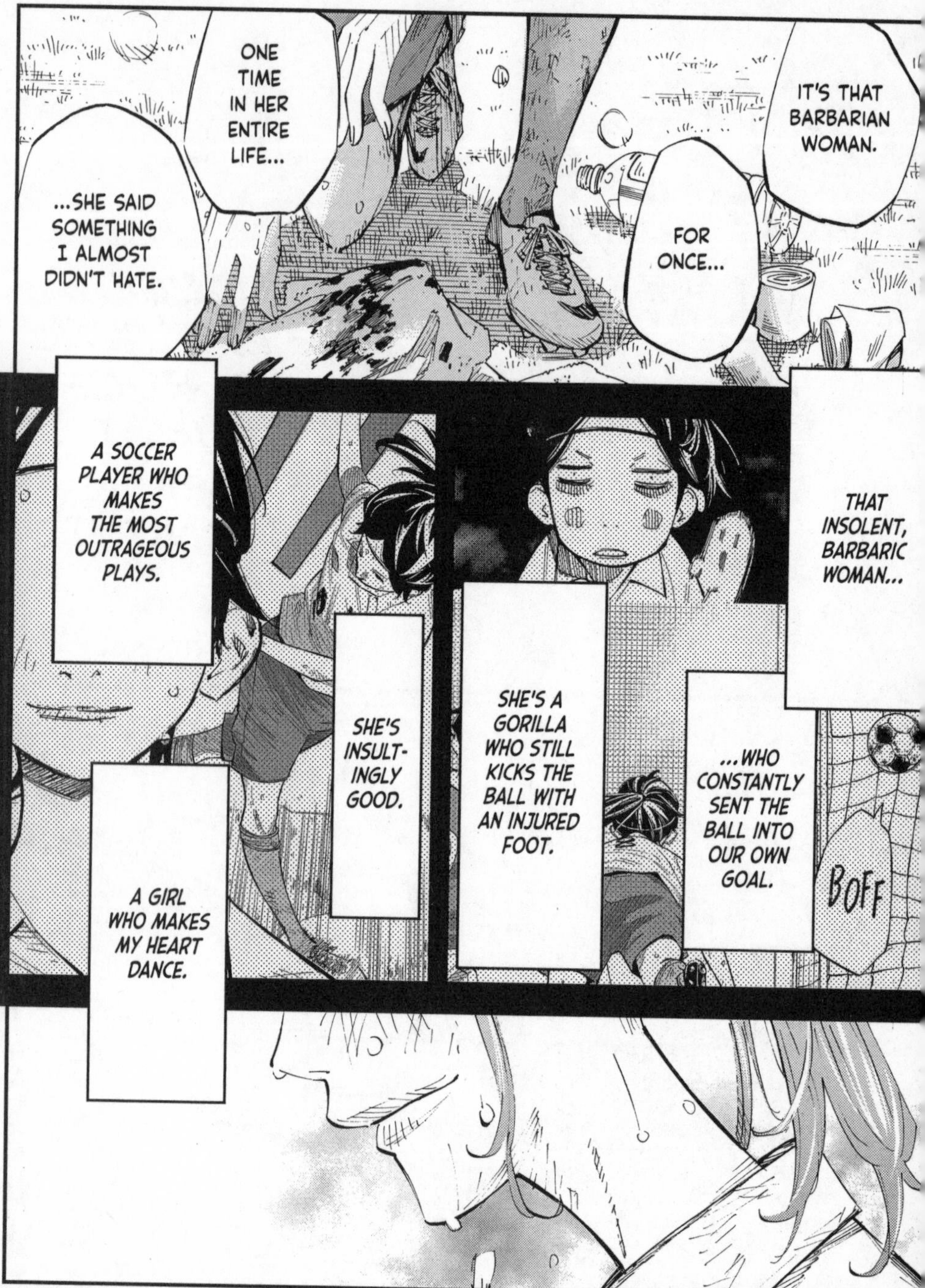
IT'S THAT BARBARIAN WOMAN.
FOR ONCE...
ONE TIME IN HER ENTIRE LIFE...
...SHE SAID SOMETHING I ALMOST DIDN'T HATE.
THAT INSOLENT, BARBARIC WOMAN...
...WHO CONSTANTLY SENT THE BALL INTO OUR OWN GOAL.
BOFF
SHE'S A GORILLA WHO STILL KICKS THE BALL WITH AN INJURED FOOT.
A SOCCER PLAYER WHO MAKES THE MOST OUTRAGEOUS PLAYS.
SHE'S INSULT-INGLY GOOD.
A GIRL WHO MAKES MY HEART DANCE.

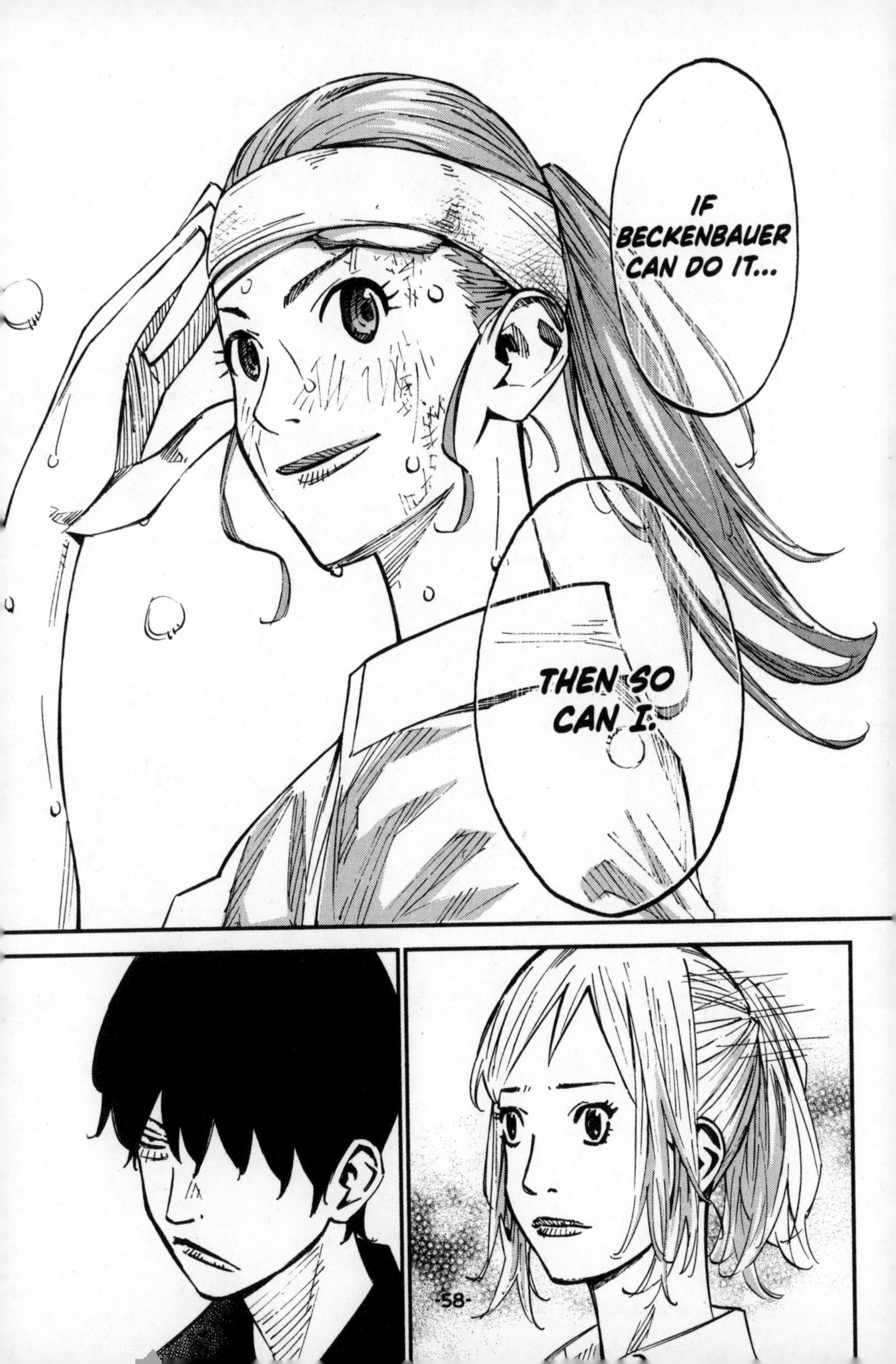
IF BECKENBAUER CAN DO IT...
THEN SO CAN I.

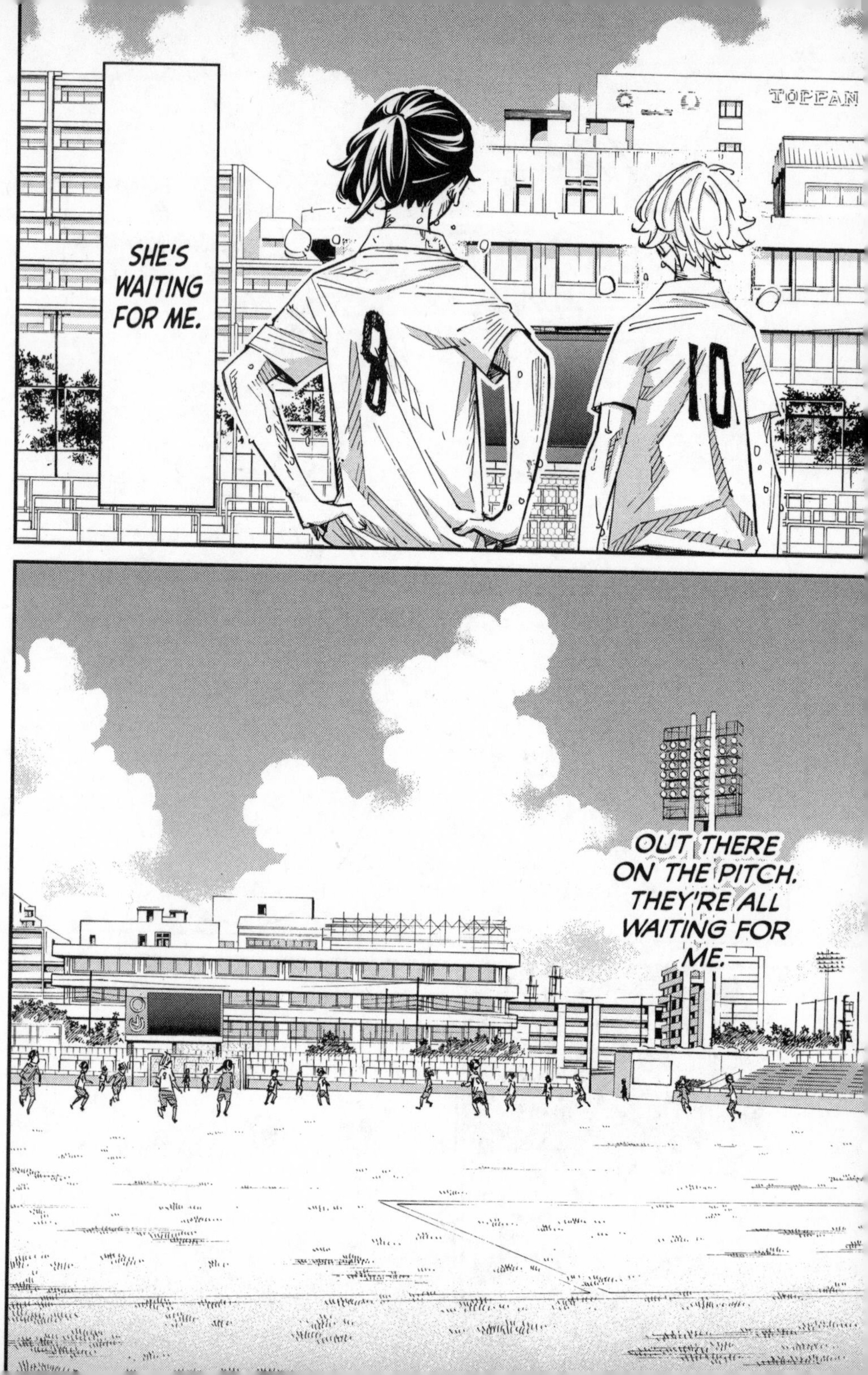
TOPPAN
SHE'S WAITING FOR ME.
OUT THERE ON THE PITCH. THEY'RE ALL WAITING FOR ME.

Farewell, My Dear Cramer

Farewell, My Dear Cramer

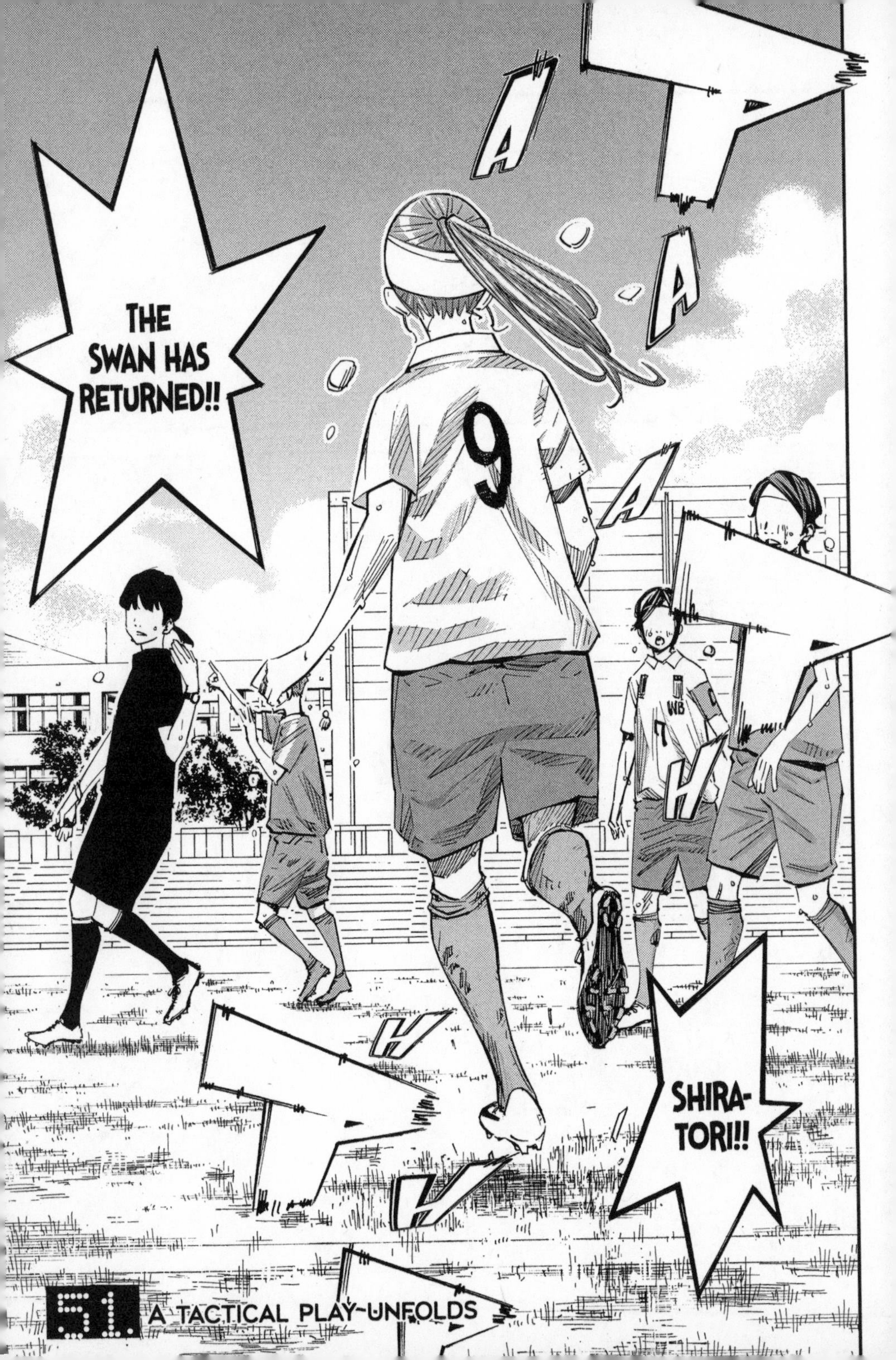
THE SWAN HAS RETURNED!!
SHIRA-TORI!!
51. A TACTICAL PLAY UNFOLDS

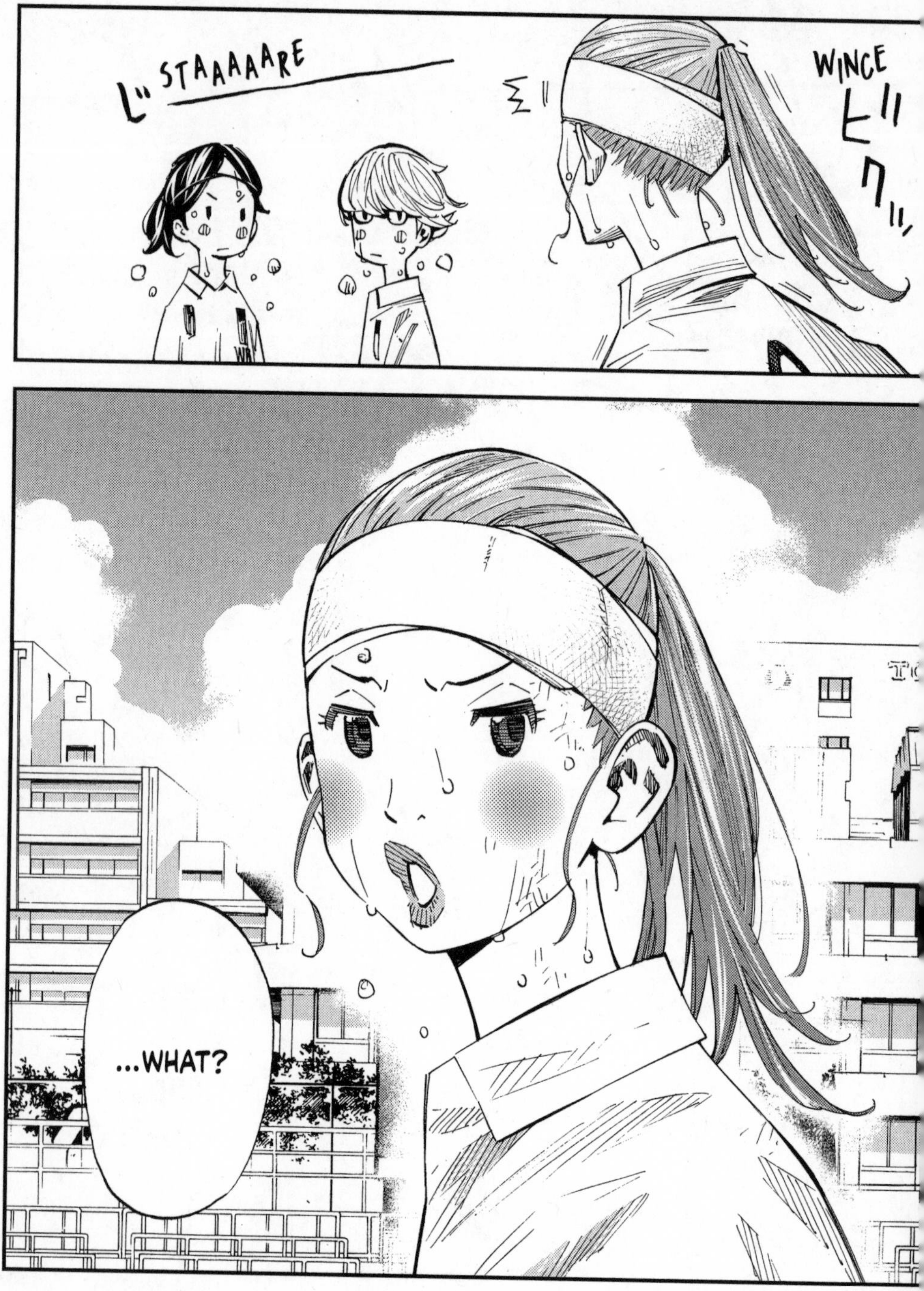
WINCE
ビクッ
じぃ STAAAAARE
...WHAT?

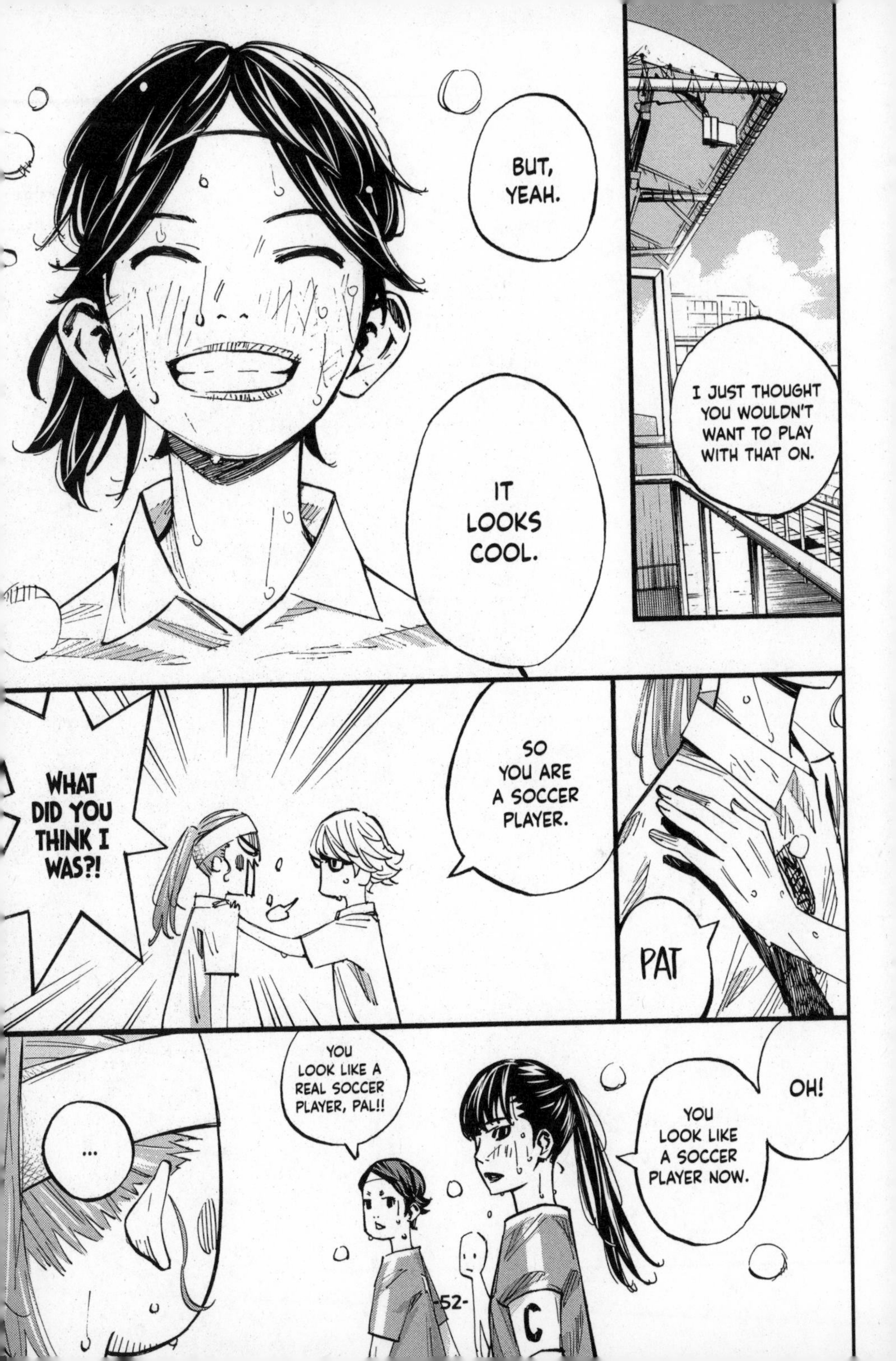
I JUST THOUGHT YOU WOULDN'T WANT TO PLAY WITH THAT ON.
BUT, YEAH.
IT LOOKS COOL.
PAT
SO YOU ARE A SOCCER PLAYER.
WHAT DID YOU THINK I WAS?!
OH!
YOU LOOK LIKE A SOCCER PLAYER NOW.
YOU LOOK LIKE A REAL SOCCER PLAYER, PAL!!
...

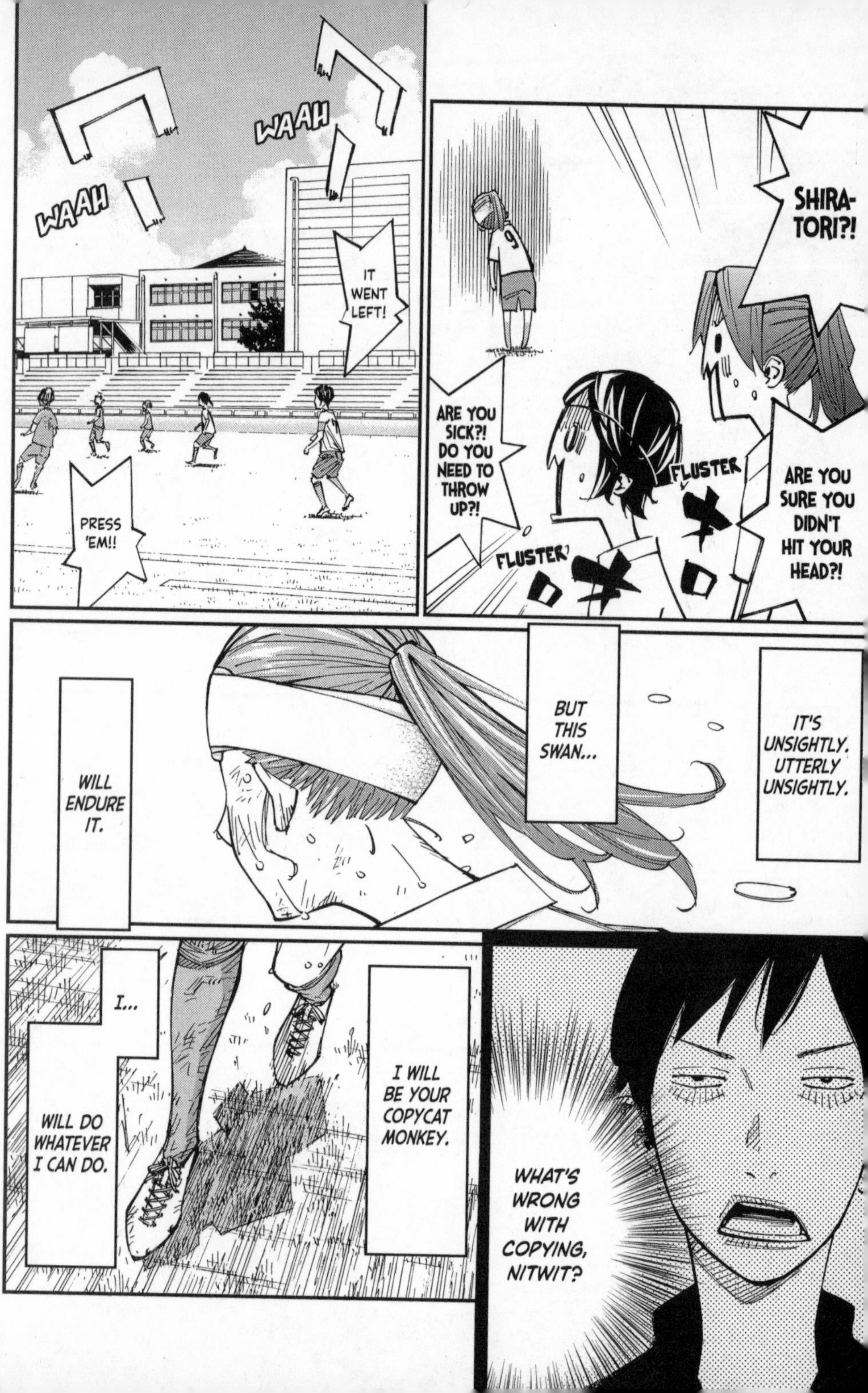
SHIRA-TORI?!
ARE YOU SURE YOU DIDN'T HIT YOUR HEAD?!
FLUSTER
FLUSTER
ARE YOU SICK?! DO YOU NEED TO THROW UP?!
WAAH
WAAH
IT WENT LEFT!
PRESS 'EM!!
IT'S UNSIGHTLY. UTTERLY UNSIGHTLY.
BUT THIS SWAN...
WILL ENDURE IT.
WHAT'S WRONG WITH COPYING, NITWIT?
I WILL BE YOUR COPYCAT MONKEY.
I...
WILL DO WHATEVER I CAN DO.

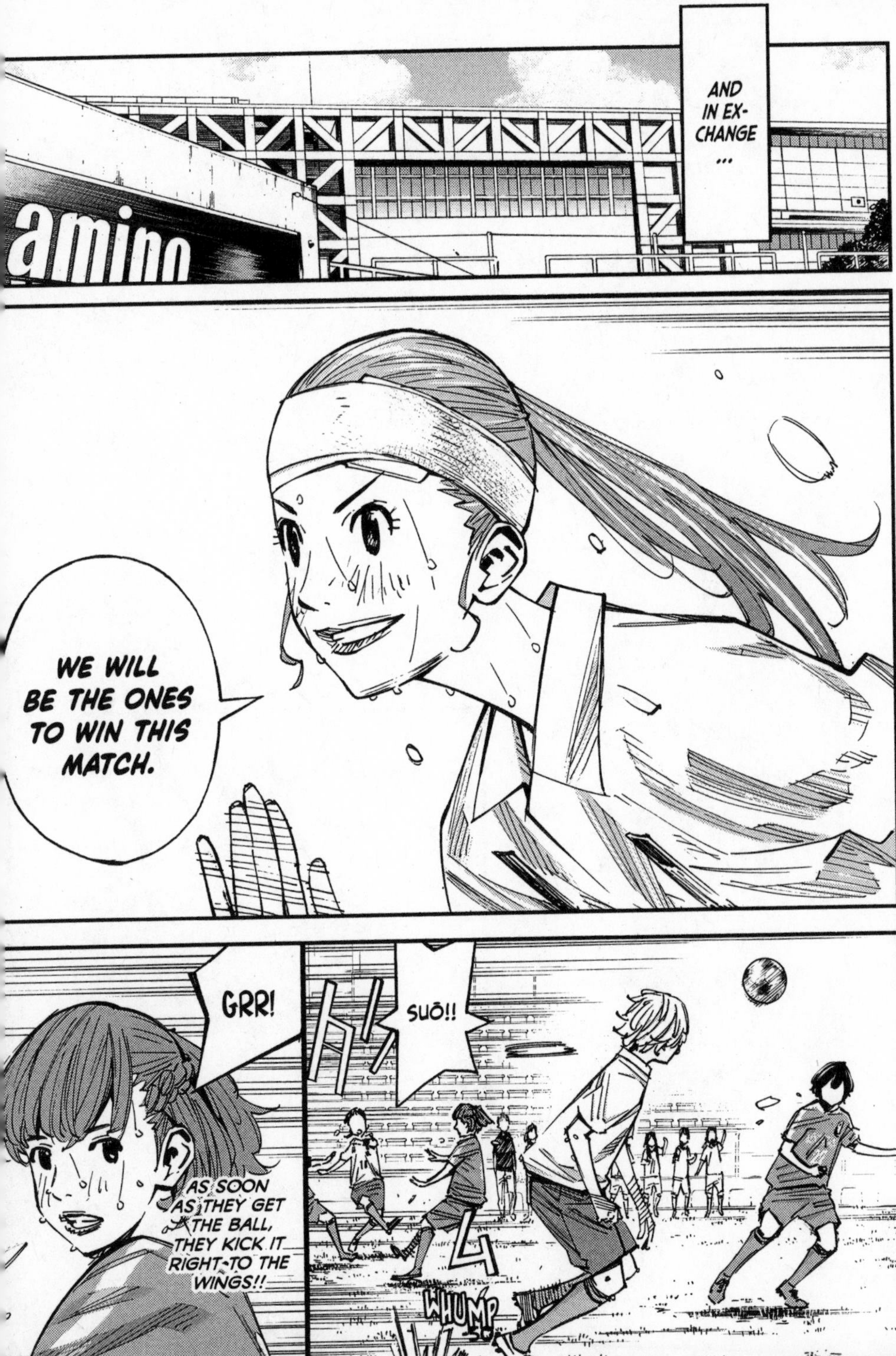

AND IN EX-CHANGE ...
amino
WE WILL BE THE ONES TO WIN THIS MATCH.
SUŌ!!
WHUMP
GRR!
AS SOON AS THEY GET THE BALL, THEY KICK IT RIGHT TO THE WINGS!!

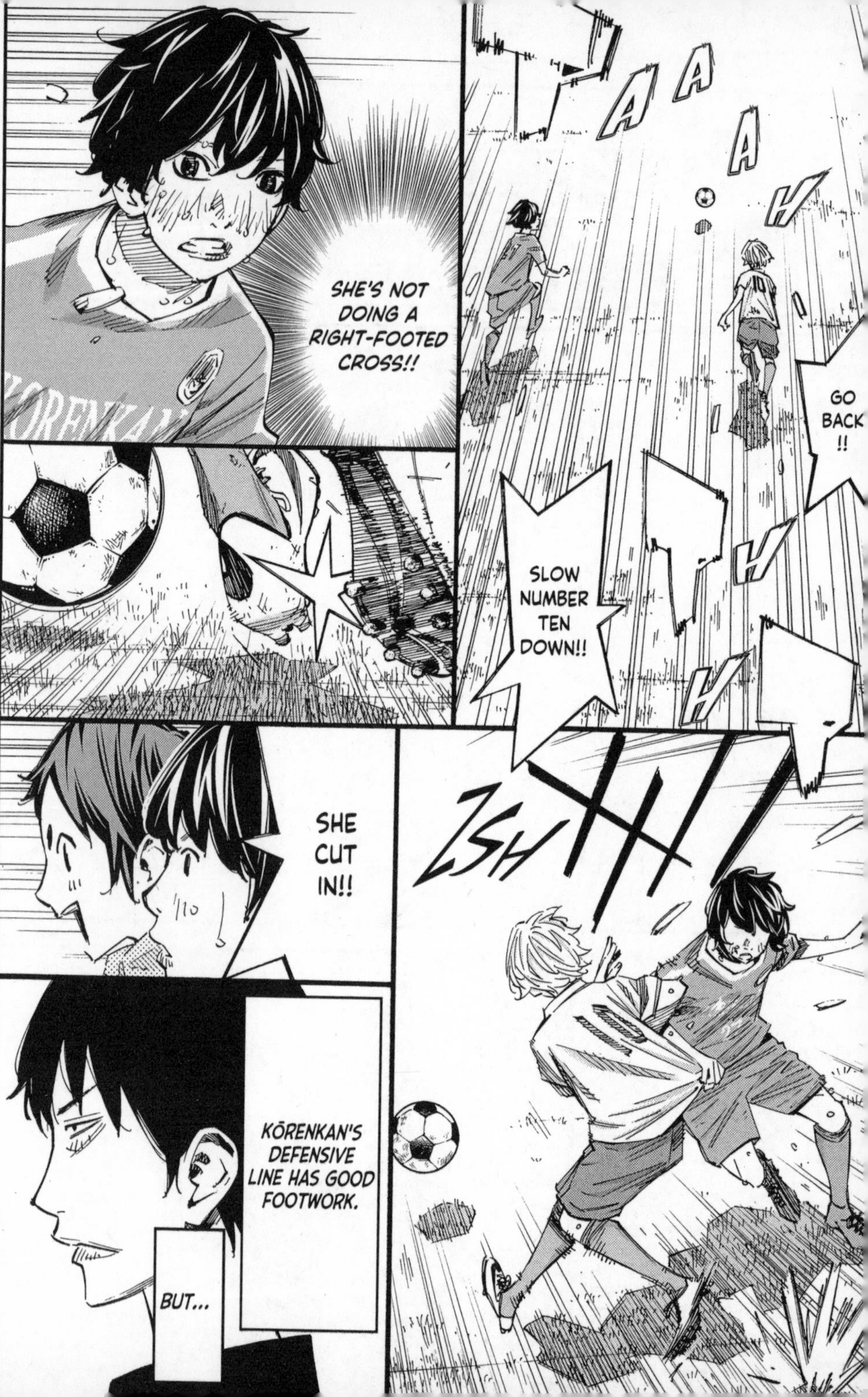
AAAAHHH
GO BACK!!
SLOW NUMBER TEN DOWN!!
SHE'S NOT DOING A RIGHT-FOOTED CROSS!!
KORENKAN
ZSHH
SHE CUT IN!!
KŌRENKAN'S DEFENSIVE LINE HAS GOOD FOOTWORK.
BUT...

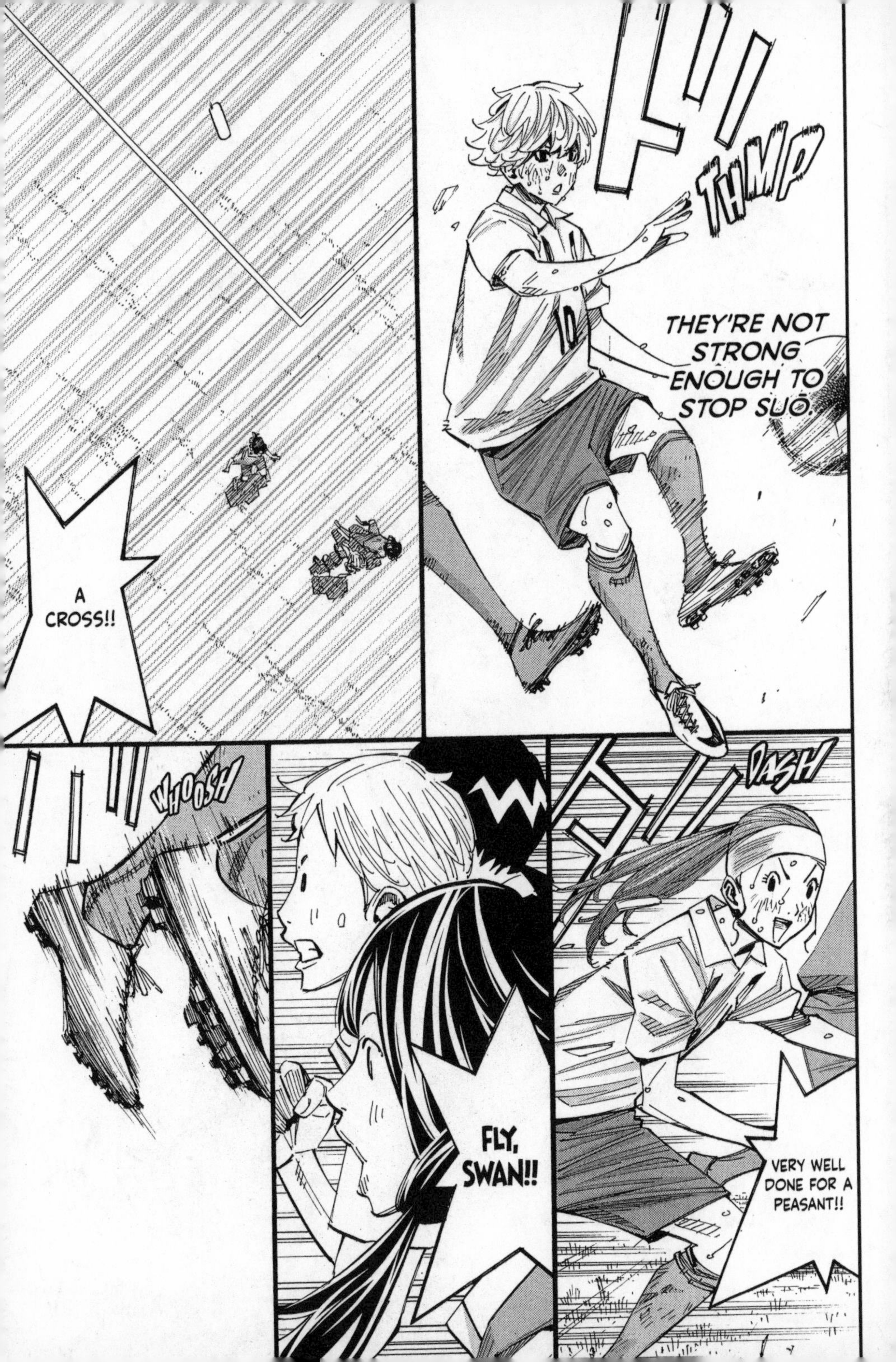
THMP
THEY'RE NOT STRONG ENOUGH TO STOP SUO.
A CROSS!!
DASH
VERY WELL DONE FOR A PEASANT!!
FLY, SWAN!!
WHOOSH

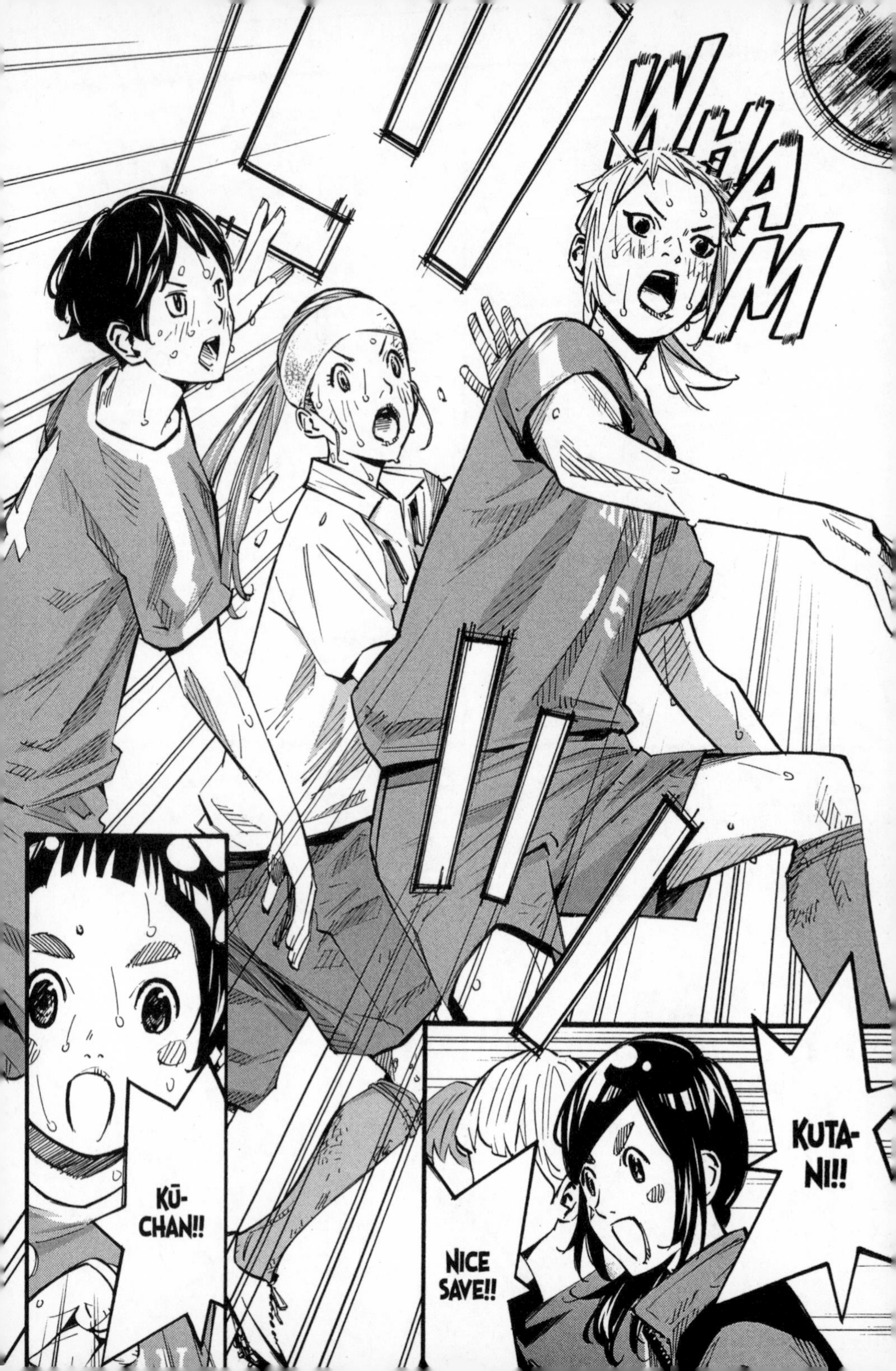
WHAM
KUTA-NI!!
NICE SAVE!!
KŪ-CHAN!!

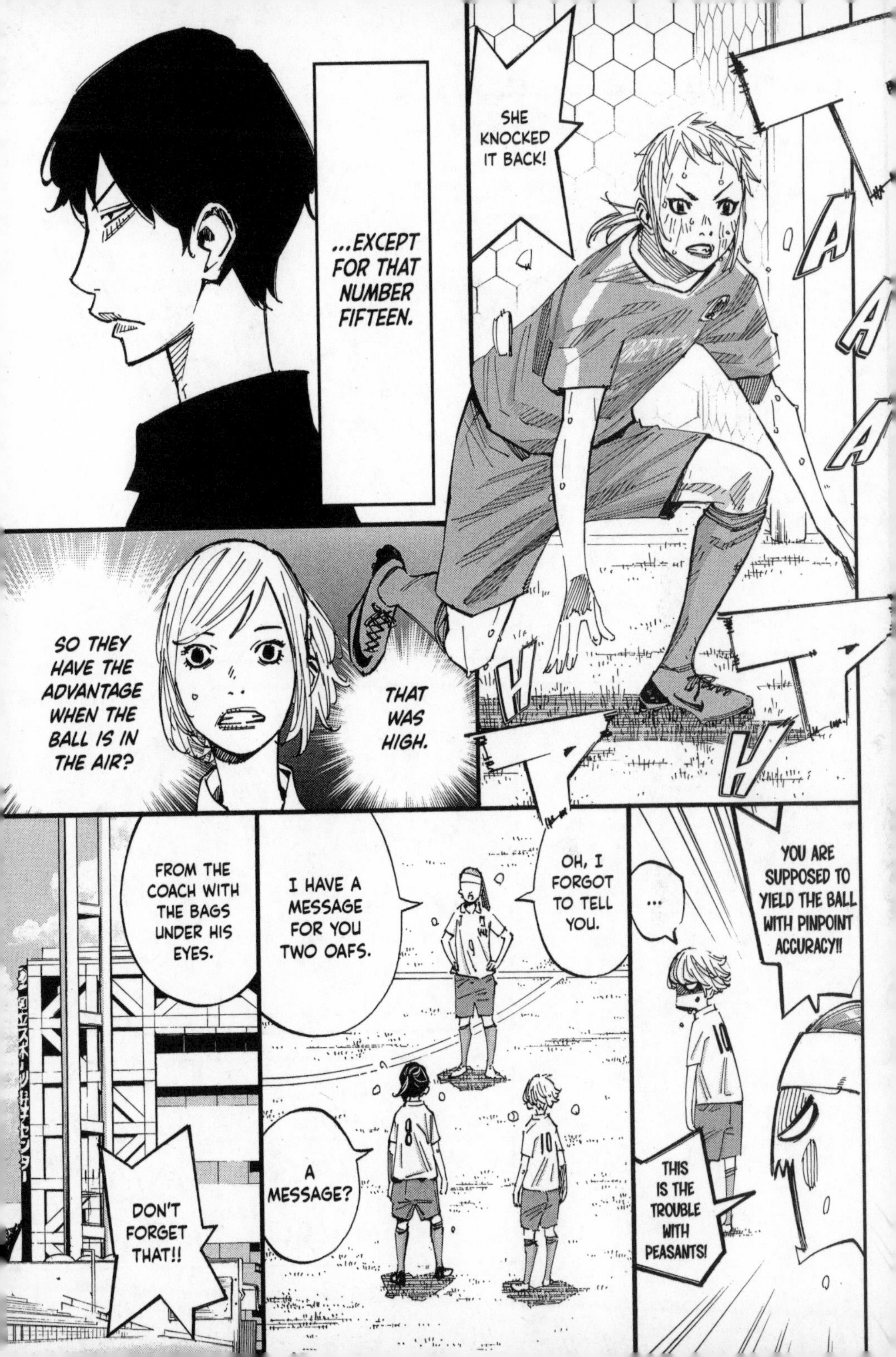

SHE KNOCKED IT BACK!
...EXCEPT FOR THAT NUMBER FIFTEEN.
THAT WAS HIGH.
SO THEY HAVE THE ADVANTAGE WHEN THE BALL IS IN THE AIR?
YOU ARE SUPPOSED TO YIELD THE BALL WITH PINPOINT ACCURACY!!
...
THIS IS THE TROUBLE WITH PEASANTS!
OH, I FORGOT TO TELL YOU.
I HAVE A MESSAGE FOR YOU TWO OAFS.
A MESSAGE?
FROM THE COACH WITH THE BAGS UNDER HIS EYES.
DON'T FORGET THAT!!

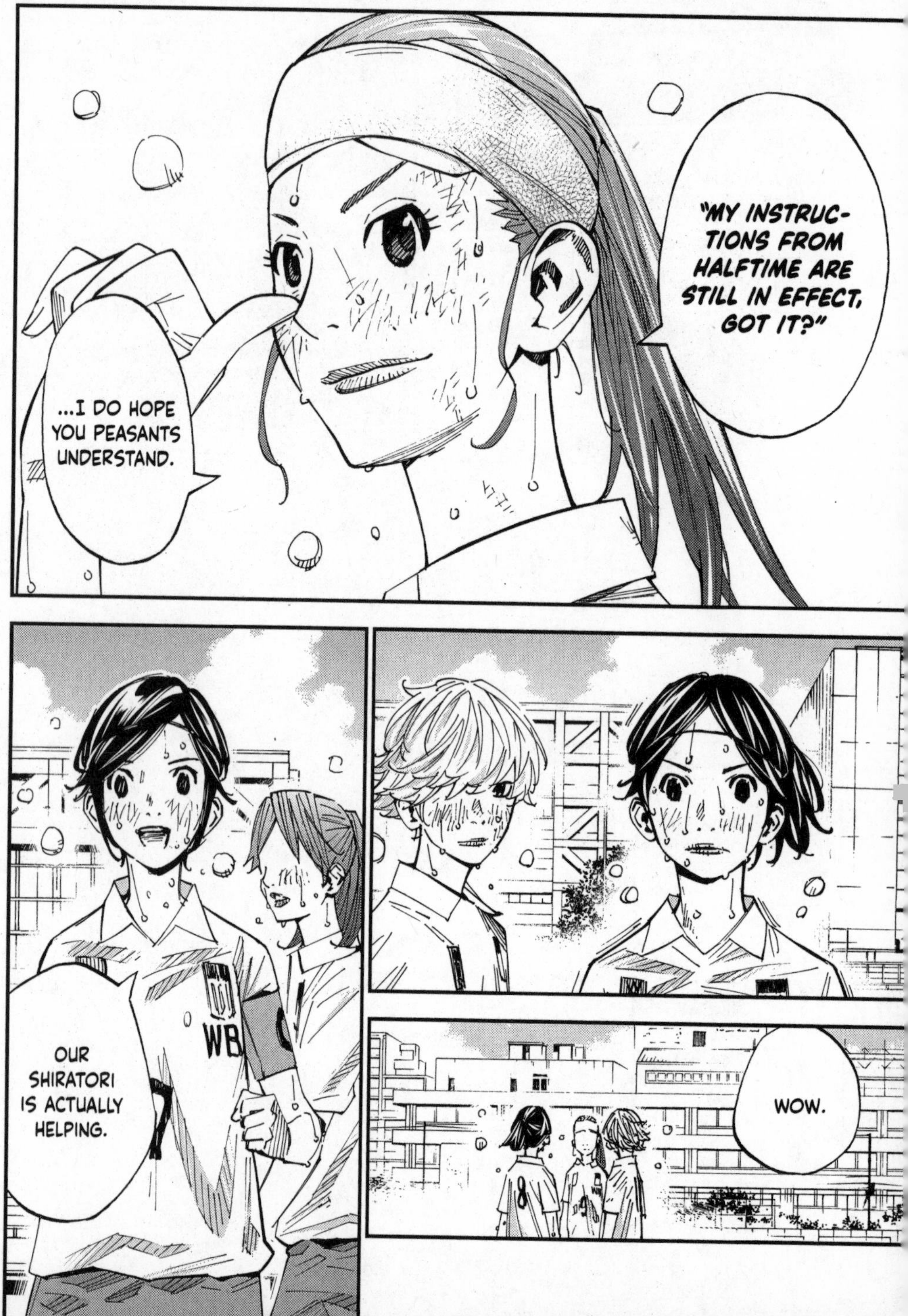
"MY INSTRUC-TIONS FROM HALFTIME ARE STILL IN EFFECT, GOT IT?"
...I DO HOPE YOU PEASANTS UNDERSTAND.
WOW.
OUR SHIRATORI IS ACTUALLY HELPING.

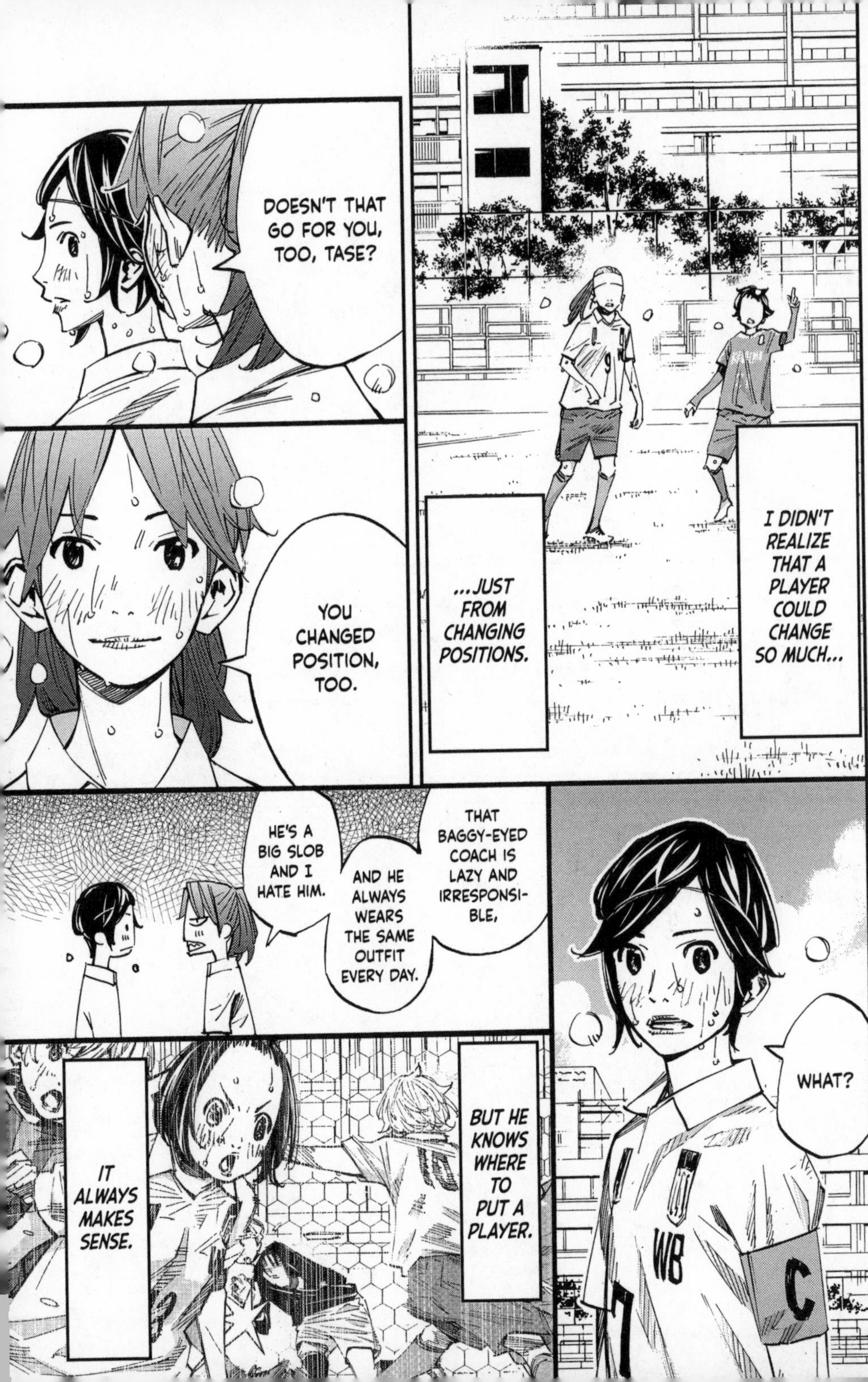
I DIDN'T REALIZE THAT A PLAYER COULD CHANGE SO MUCH...
...JUST FROM CHANGING POSITIONS.
DOESN'T THAT GO FOR YOU, TOO, TASE?
YOU CHANGED POSITION, TOO.
WHAT?
THAT BAGGY-EYED COACH IS LAZY AND IRRESPONSI-BLE,
AND HE ALWAYS WEARS THE SAME OUTFIT EVERY DAY.
HE'S A BIG SLOB AND I HATE HIM.
BUT HE KNOWS WHERE TO PUT A PLAYER.
IT ALWAYS MAKES SENSE.

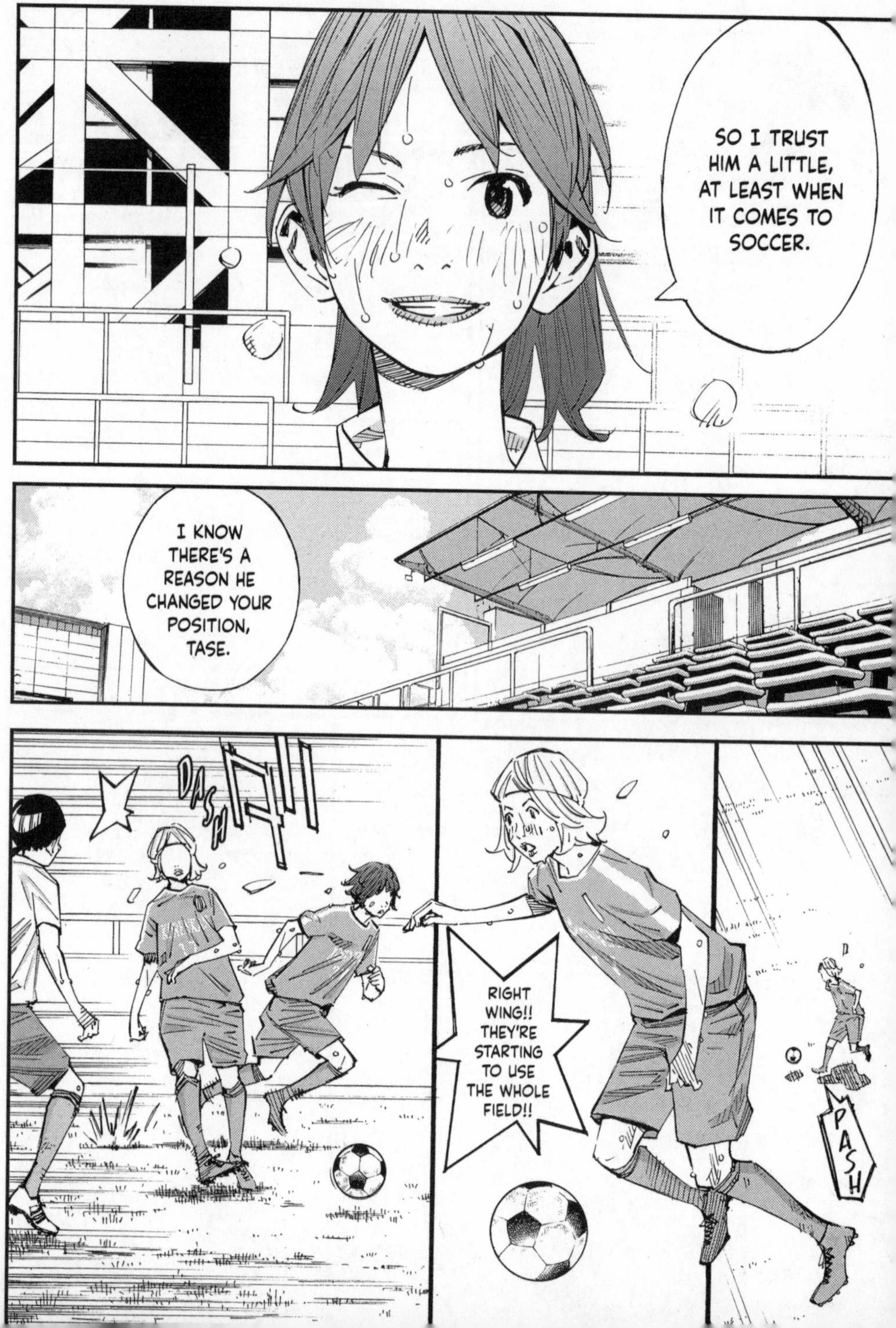
SO I TRUST HIM A LITTLE, AT LEAST WHEN IT COMES TO SOCCER.
I KNOW THERE'S A REASON HE CHANGED YOUR POSITION, TASE.
PASH
RIGHT WING!! THEY'RE STARTING TO USE THE WHOLE FIELD!!
DASH

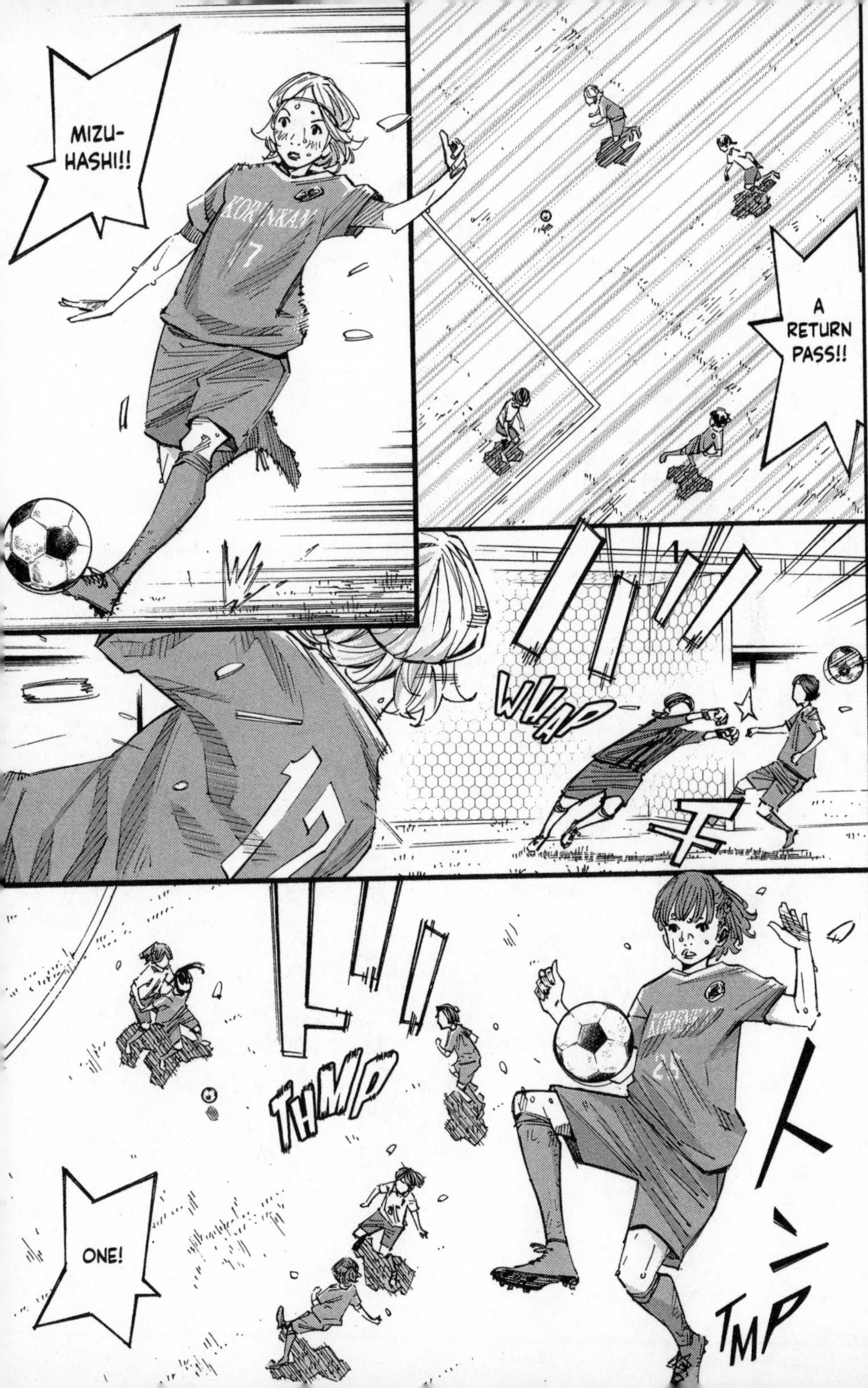
A RETURN PASS!!
MIZU-HASHI!!!
WHAP
TMP
THMP
ONE!

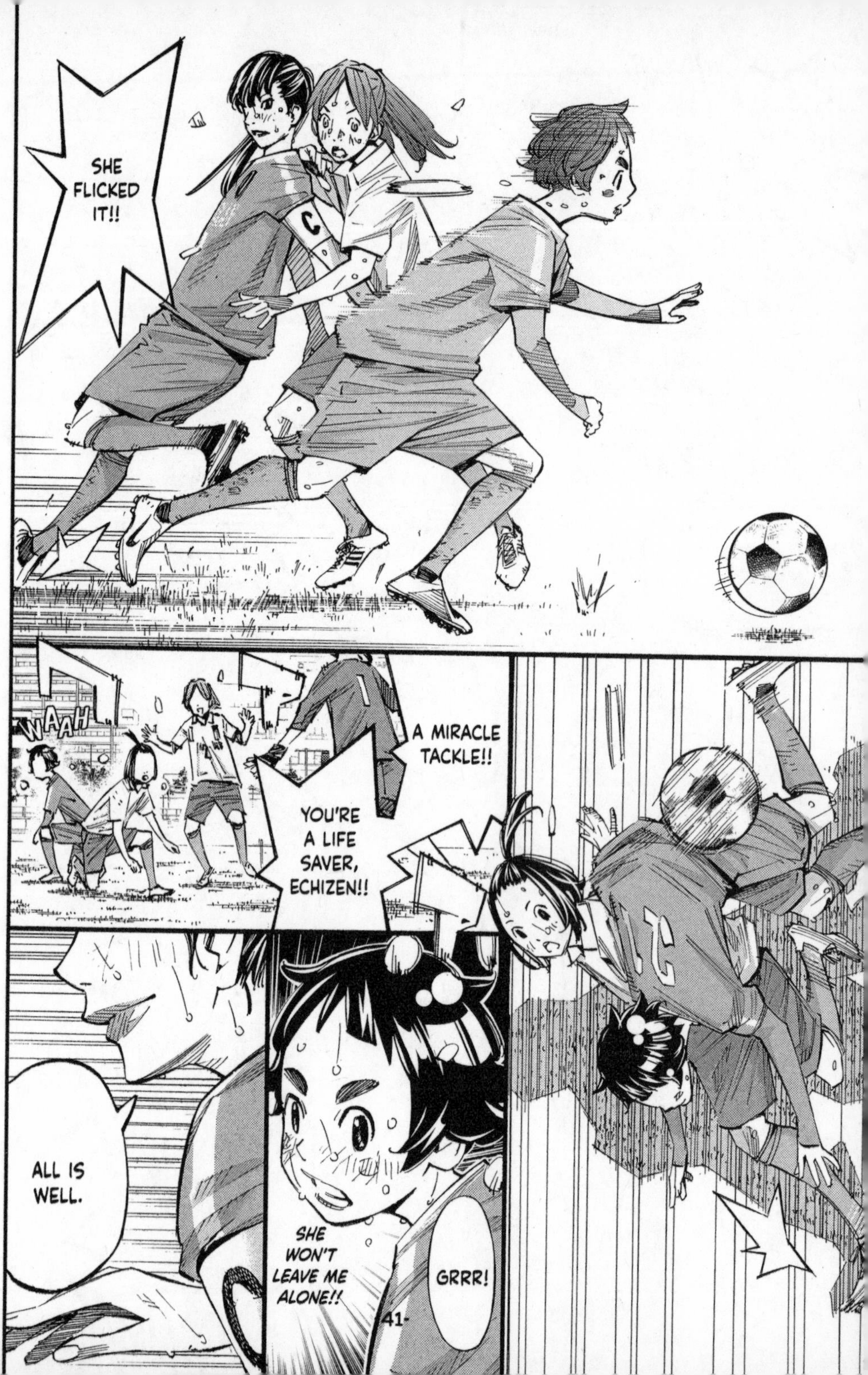
SHE FLICKED IT!!
A MIRACLE TACKLE!!
YOU'RE A LIFE SAVER, ECHIZEN!!
WAAAH
GRRR!
SHE WON'T LEAVE ME ALONE!!
ALL IS WELL.

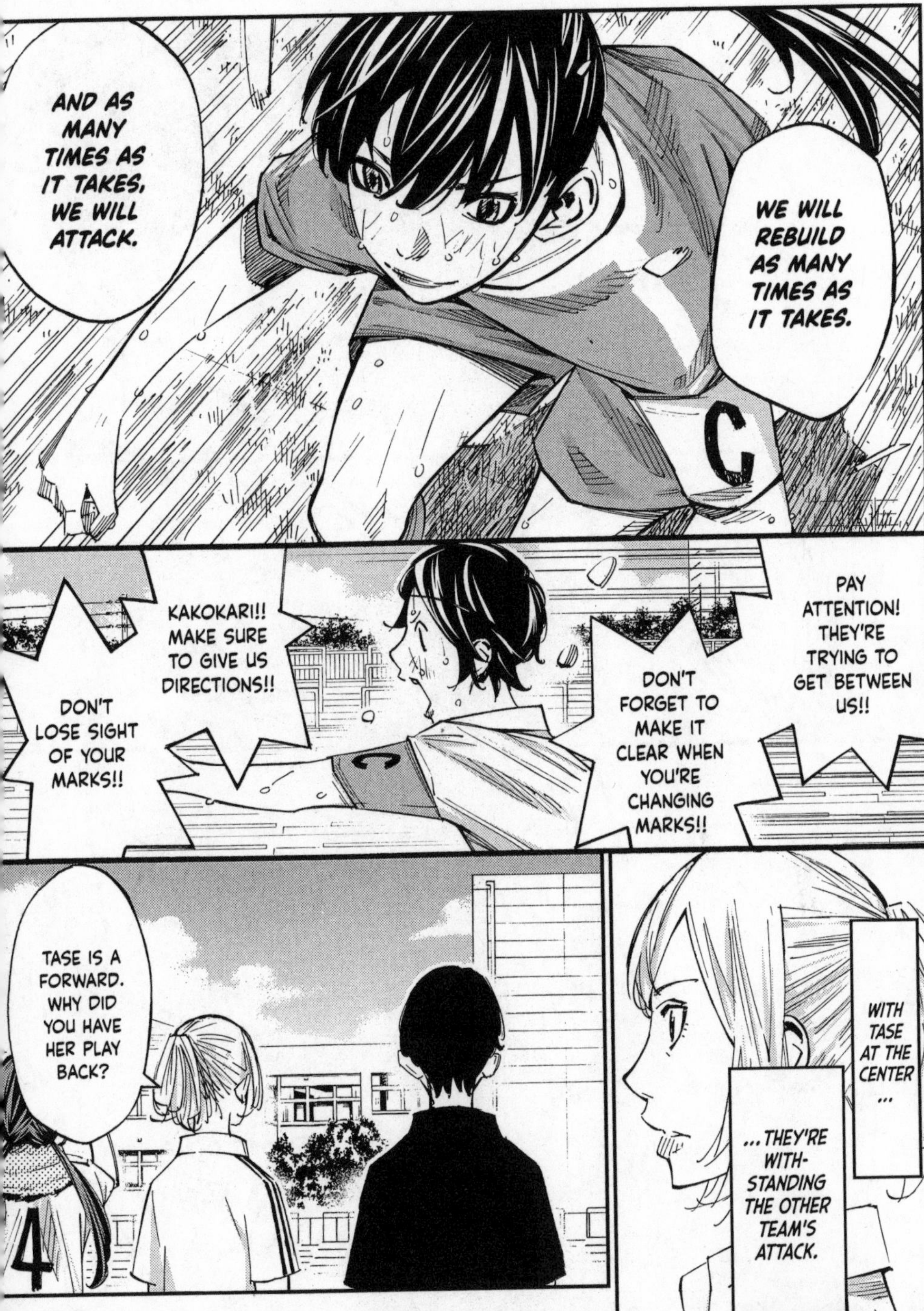
WE WILL REBUILD AS MANY TIMES AS IT TAKES.
AND AS MANY TIMES AS IT TAKES, WE WILL ATTACK.
PAY ATTENTION! THEY'RE TRYING TO GET BETWEEN US!!
DON'T FORGET TO MAKE IT CLEAR WHEN YOU'RE CHANGING MARKS!!
KAKOKARI!! MAKE SURE TO GIVE US DIRECTIONS!!
DON'T LOSE SIGHT OF YOUR MARKS!!
WITH TASE AT THE CENTER ...
...THEY'RE WITH-STANDING THE OTHER TEAM'S ATTACK.
TASE IS A FORWARD. WHY DID YOU HAVE HER PLAY BACK?

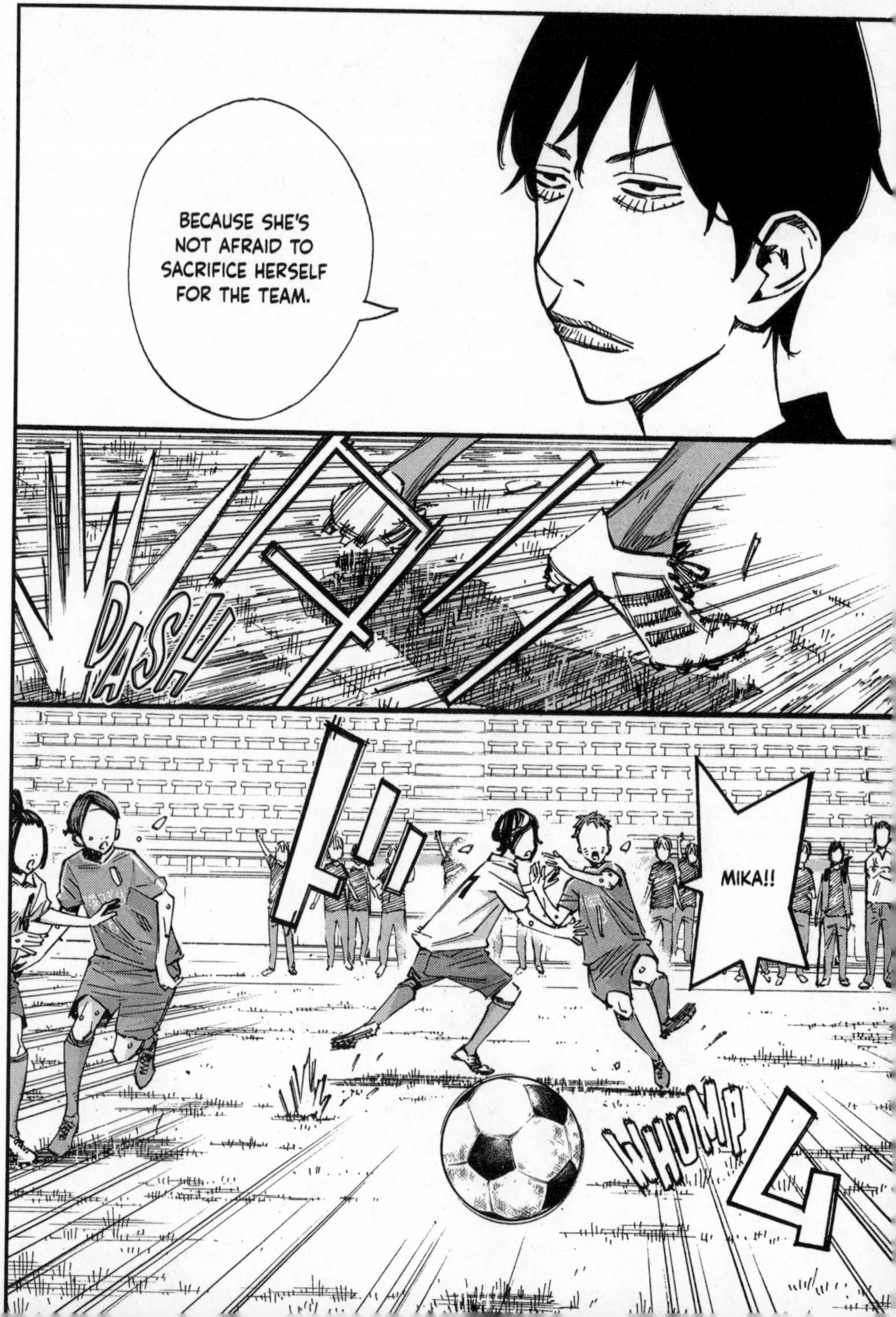
BECAUSE SHE'S NOT AFRAID TO SACRIFICE HERSELF FOR THE TEAM.
PASH
MIKA!!
WHOMP

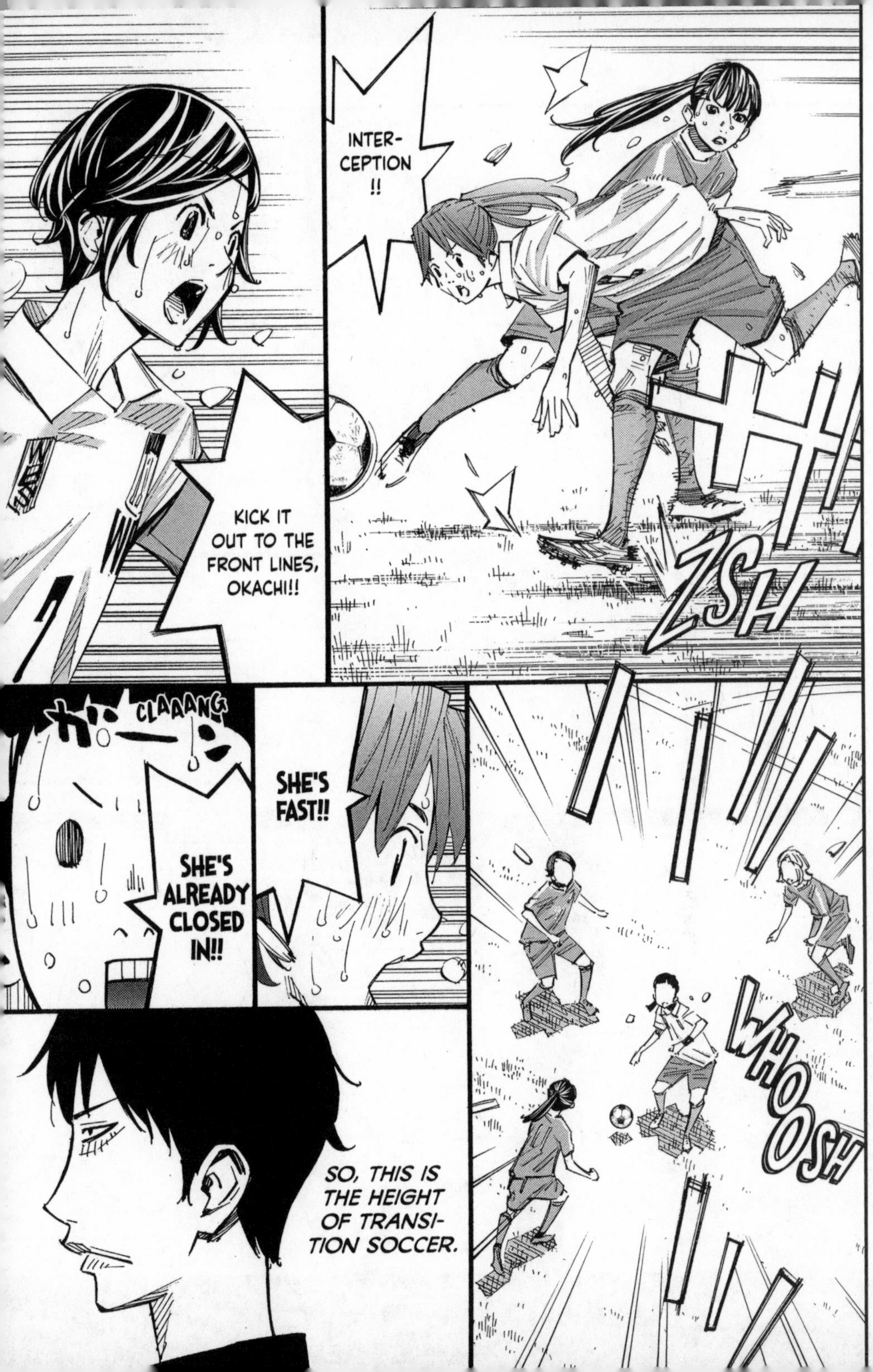
INTER-
CEPTION
!!
ZSH
KICK IT OUT TO THE FRONT LINES, OKACHI!!
WHOOSH
SHE'S FAST!!
CLAAANG
SHE'S ALREADY CLOSED IN!!
SO, THIS IS THE HEIGHT OF TRANSI-TION SOCCER.

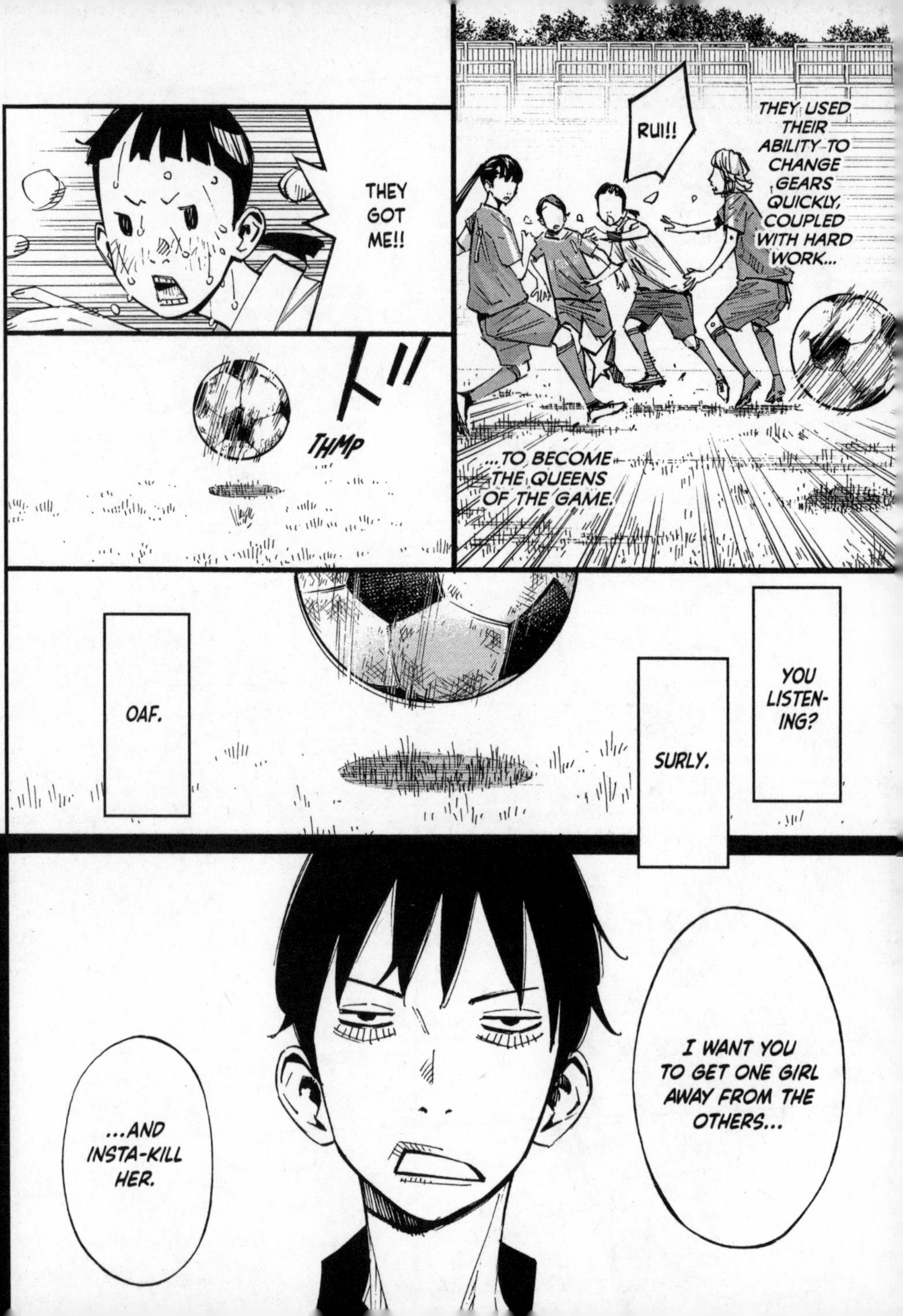
THEY USED THEIR ABILITY TO CHANGE GEARS QUICKLY, COUPLED WITH HARD WORK...
RUI!!
...TO BECOME THE QUEENS OF THE GAME.
THEY GOT ME!!
ドッ
THMP
YOU LISTENING?
SURLY.
OAF.
I WANT YOU TO GET ONE GIRL AWAY FROM THE OTHERS...
...AND INSTA-KILL HER.

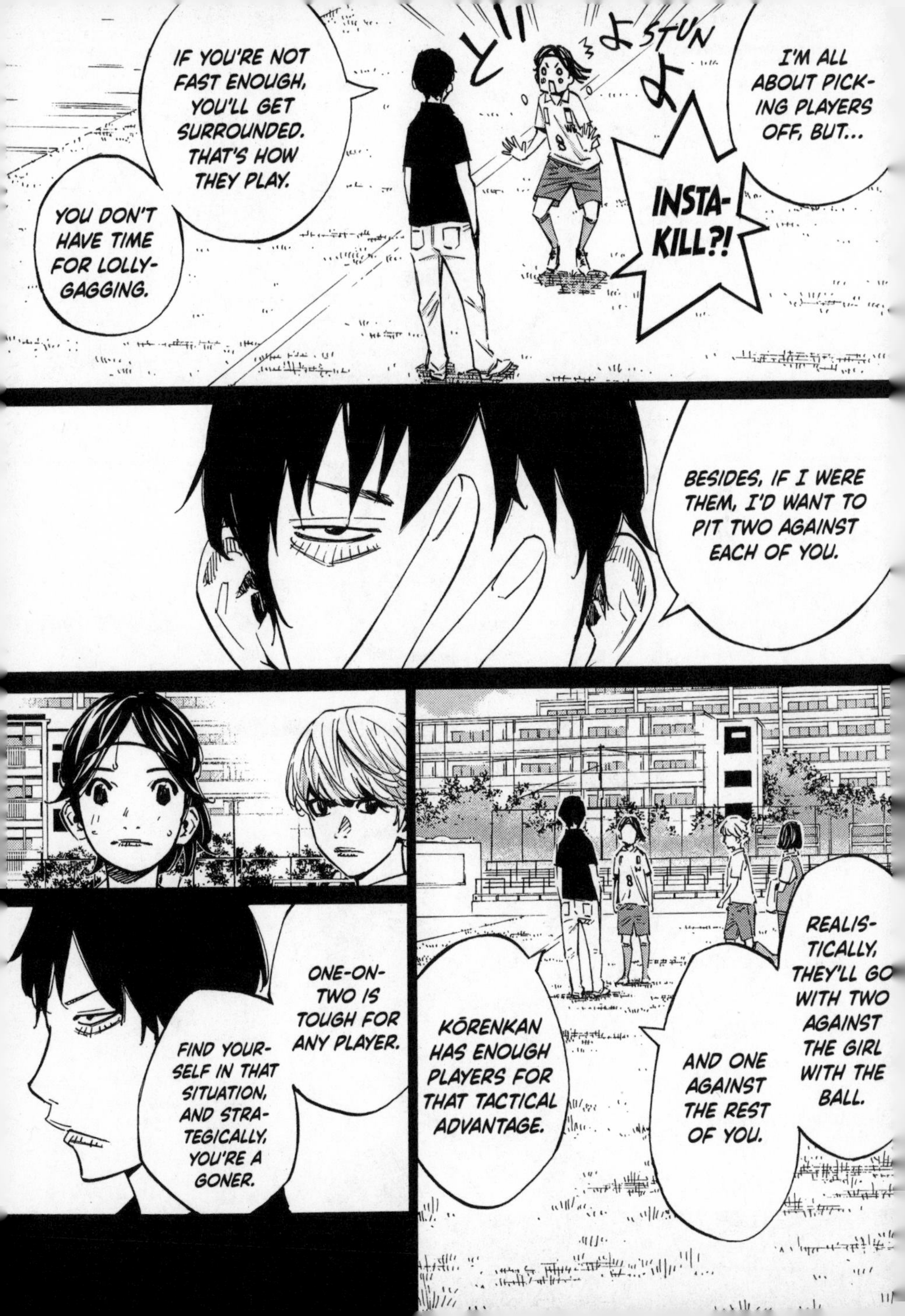

I'M ALL ABOUT PICKING PLAYERS OFF, BUT...
STUN
INSTA-KILL?!
IF YOU'RE NOT FAST ENOUGH, YOU'LL GET SURROUNDED. THAT'S HOW THEY PLAY.
YOU DON'T HAVE TIME FOR LOLLYGAGGING.
BESIDES, IF I WERE THEM, I'D WANT TO PIT TWO AGAINST EACH OF YOU.
REALISTICALLY, THEY'LL GO WITH TWO AGAINST THE GIRL WITH THE BALL.
AND ONE AGAINST THE REST OF YOU.
KŌRENKAN HAS ENOUGH PLAYERS FOR THAT TACTICAL ADVANTAGE.
ONE-ON-TWO IS TOUGH FOR ANY PLAYER.
FIND YOURSELF IN THAT SITUATION, AND STRATEGICALLY, YOU'RE A GONER.

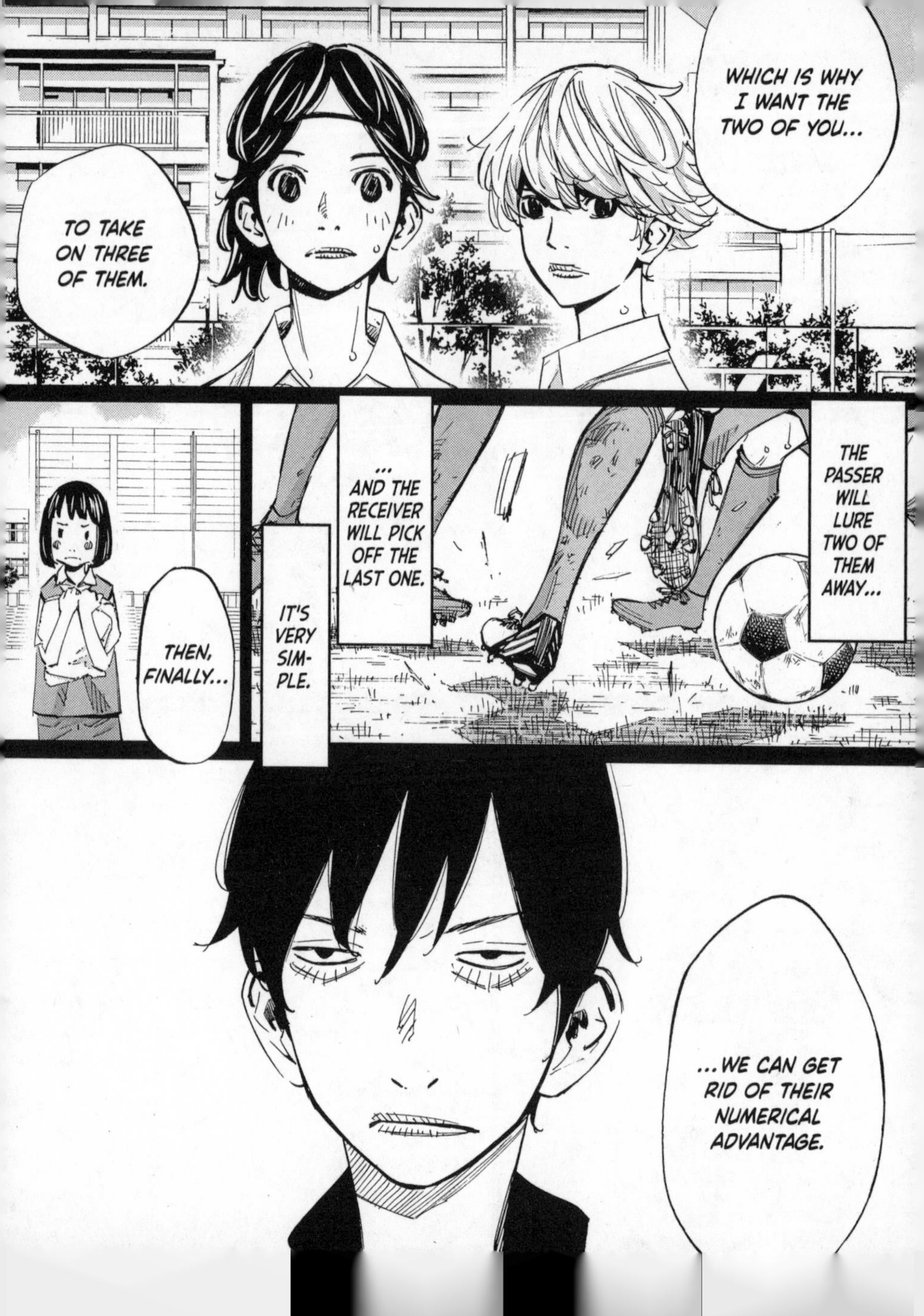
WHICH IS WHY I WANT THE TWO OF YOU...
TO TAKE ON THREE OF THEM.
THE PASSER WILL LURE TWO OF THEM AWAY...
...AND THE RECEIVER WILL PICK OFF THE LAST ONE.
IT'S VERY SIM-PLE.
THEN, FINALLY...
...WE CAN GET RID OF THEIR NUMERICAL ADVANTAGE.

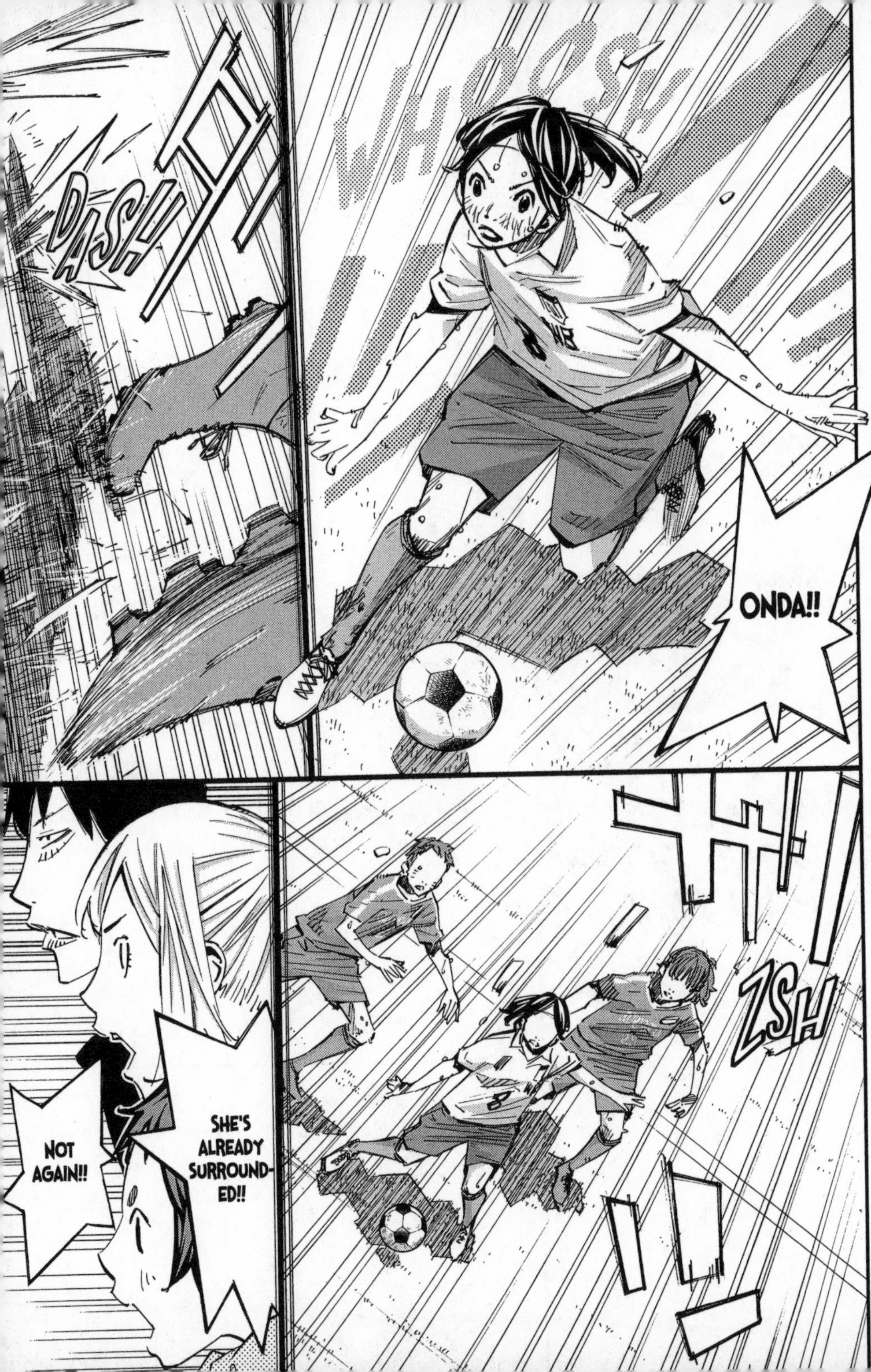
WHOOSH
ONDA!!
DASH
ZSH
SHE'S ALREADY SURROUND-ED!!
NOT AGAIN!!

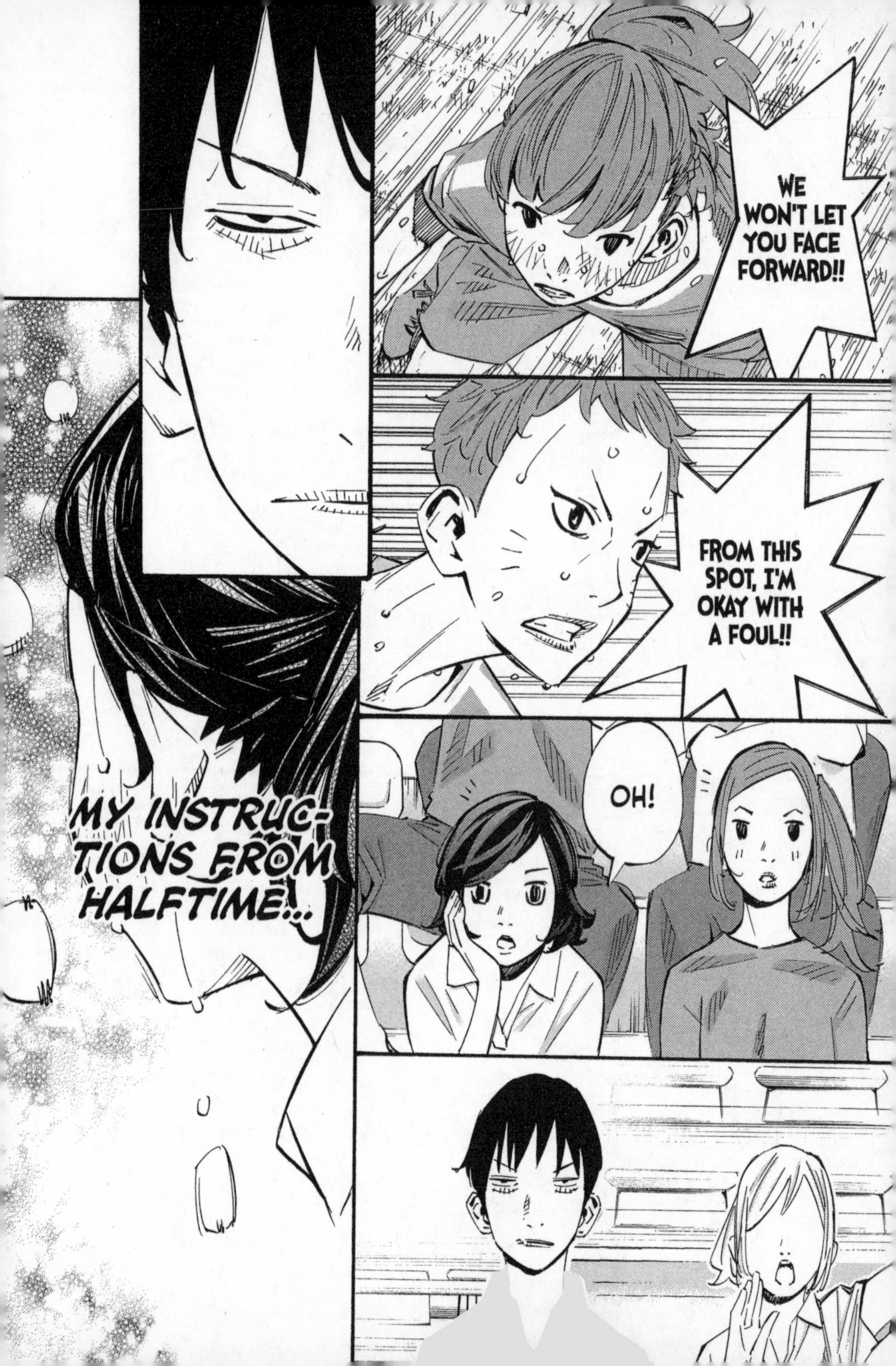
WE WON'T LET YOU FACE FORWARD!!
FROM THIS SPOT, I'M OKAY WITH A FOUL!!
OH!
MY INSTRUC-TIONS FROM HALFTIME...

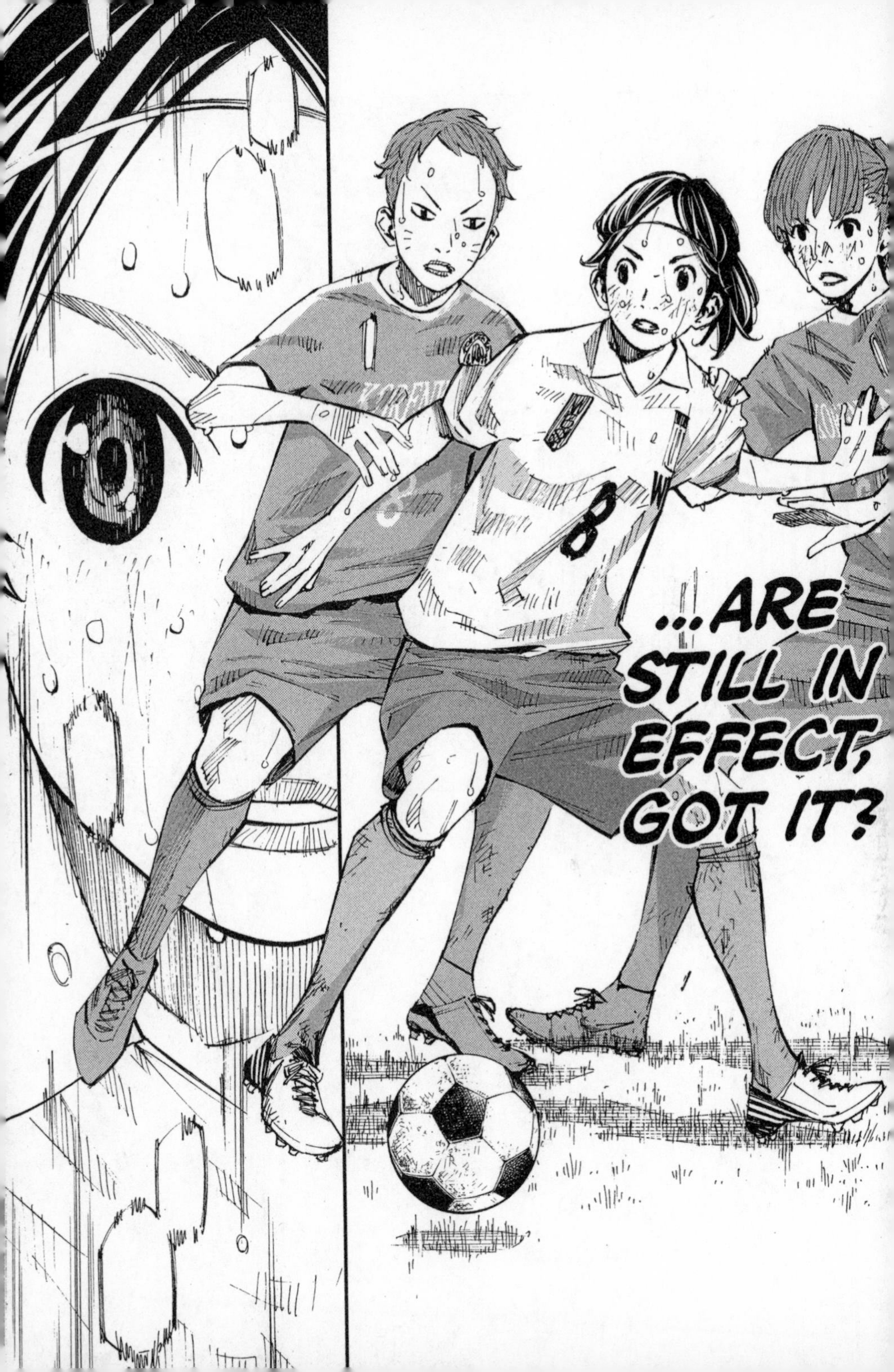
...ARE STILL IN EFFECT, GOT IT?

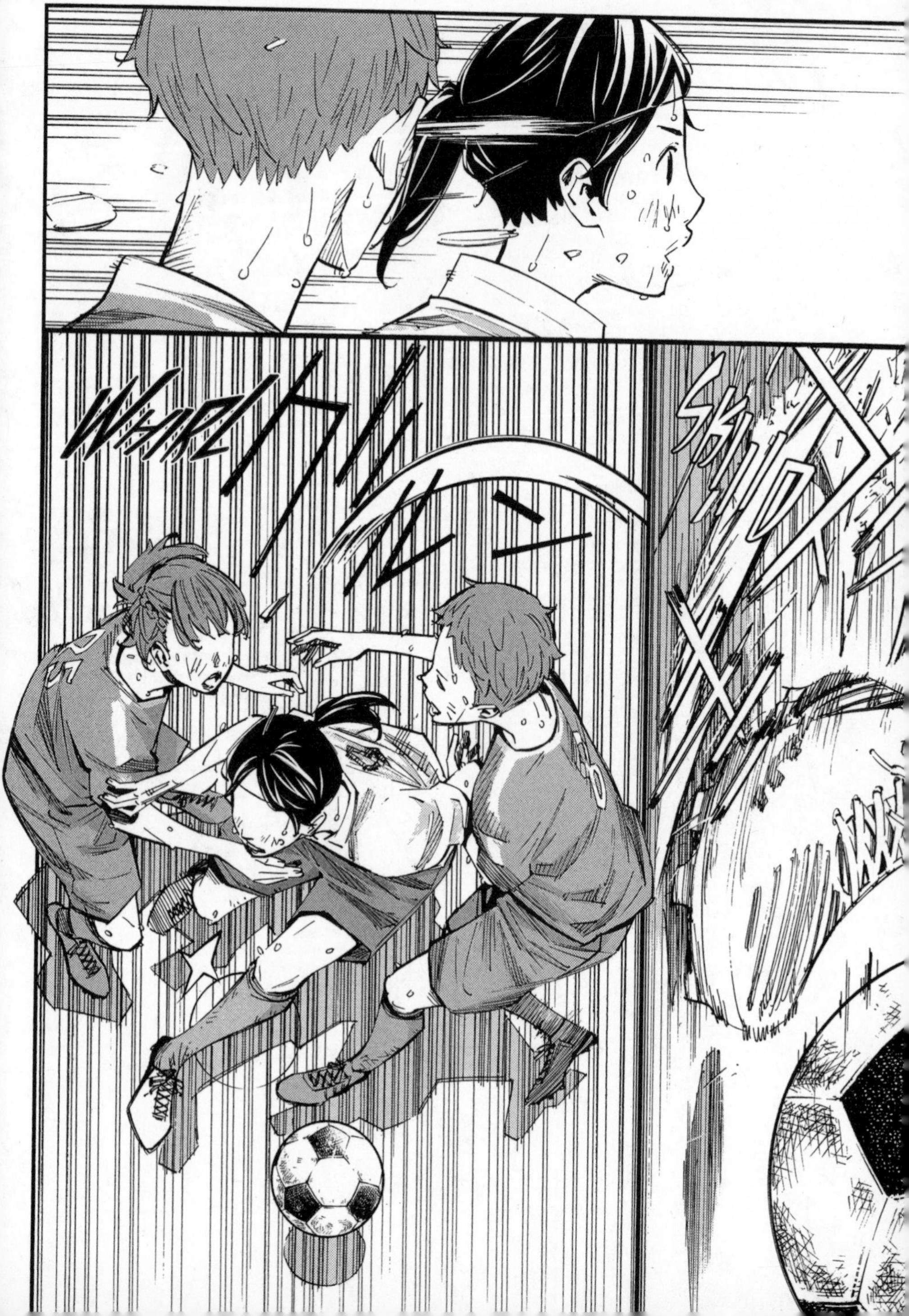
SKID
WHIRL

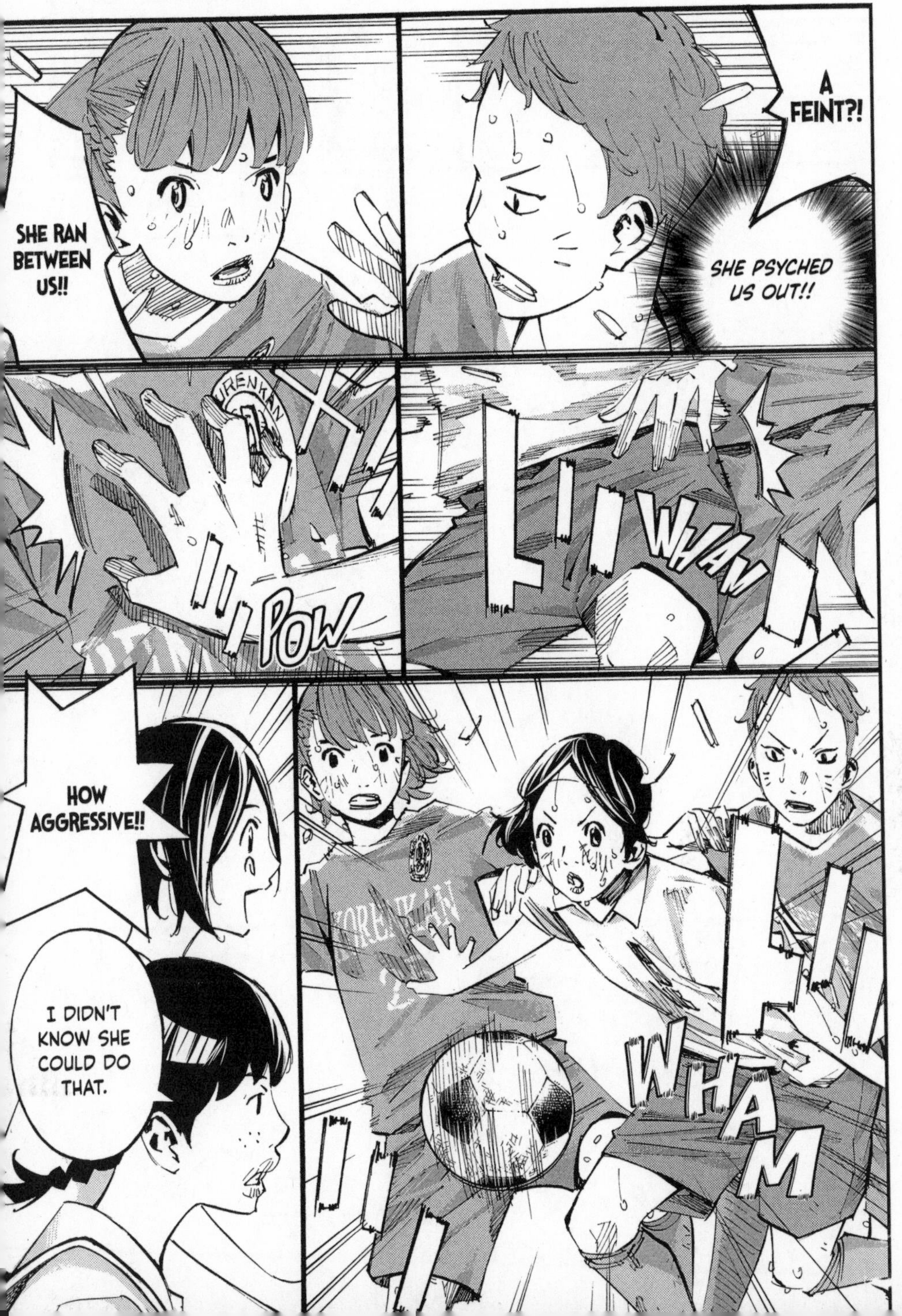
A FEINT?!
SHE PSYCHED US OUT!!
SHE RAN BETWEEN US!!
WHAM
POW
WHAM
HOW AGGRESSIVE!!
I DIDN'T KNOW SHE COULD DO THAT.

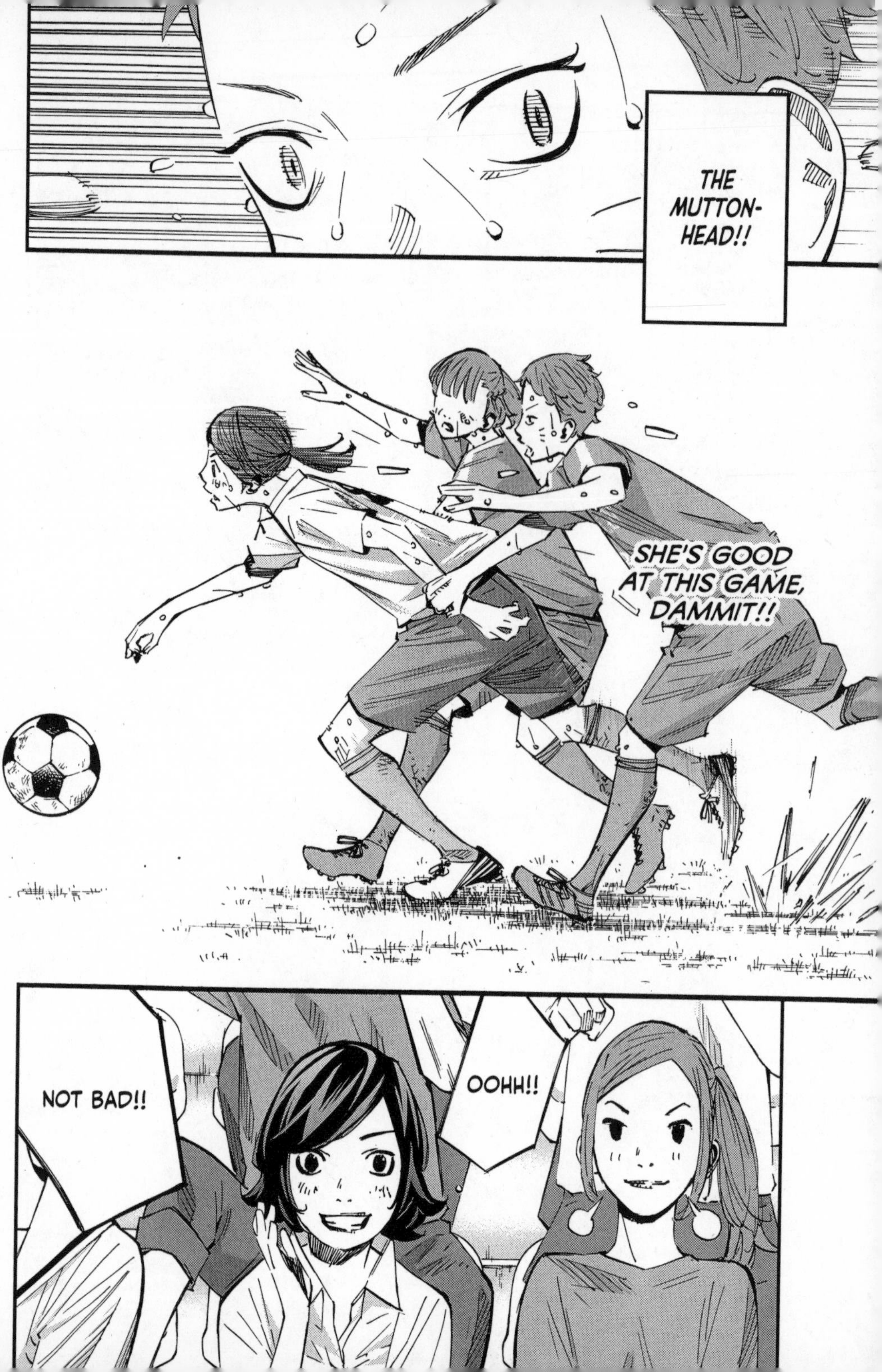
THE MUTTON-HEAD!!
SHE'S GOOD AT THIS GAME, DAMMIT!!
OOHH!!
NOT BAD!!

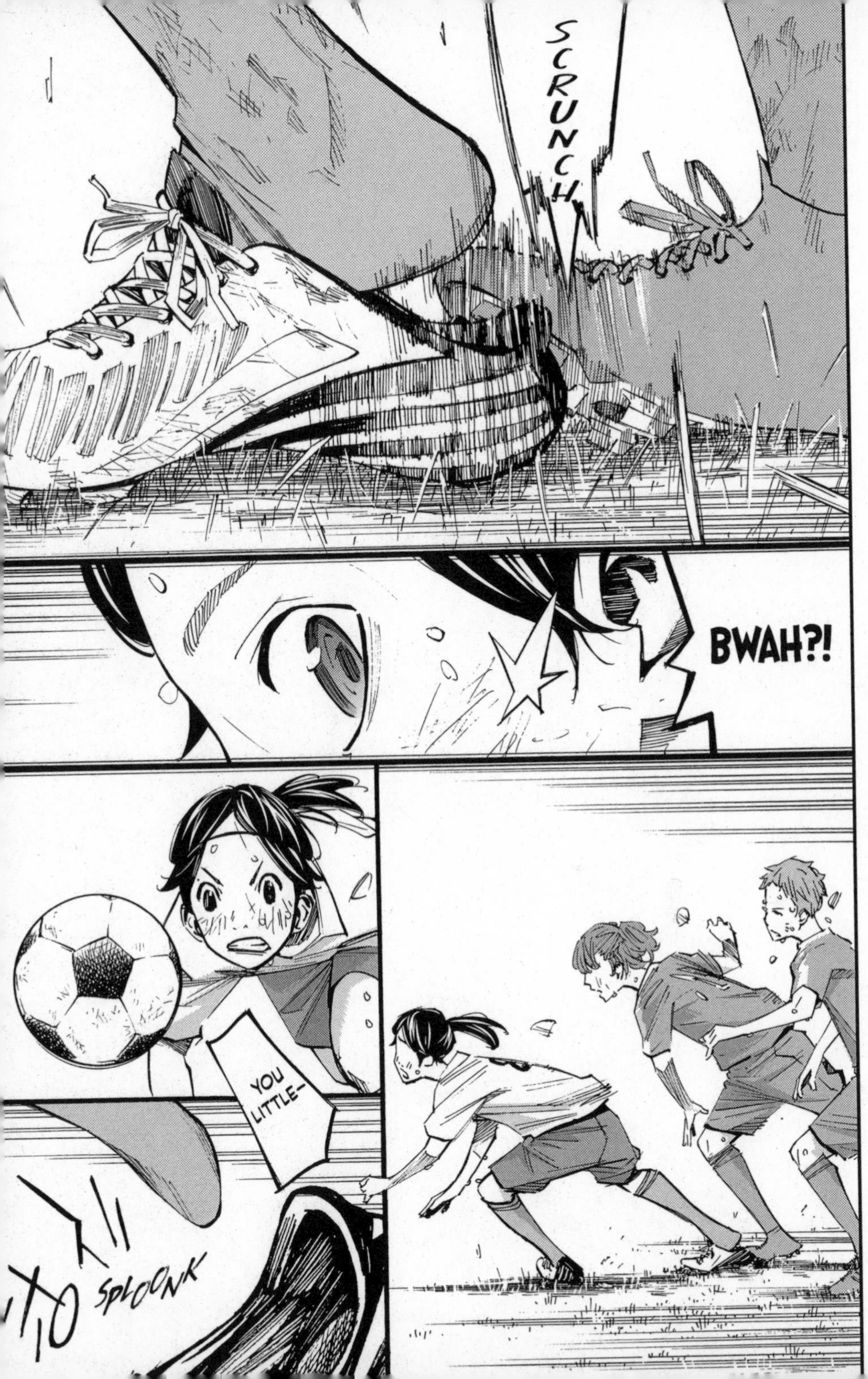

SCRUNCH
BWAH?!
YOU LITTLE-
SPLOONK

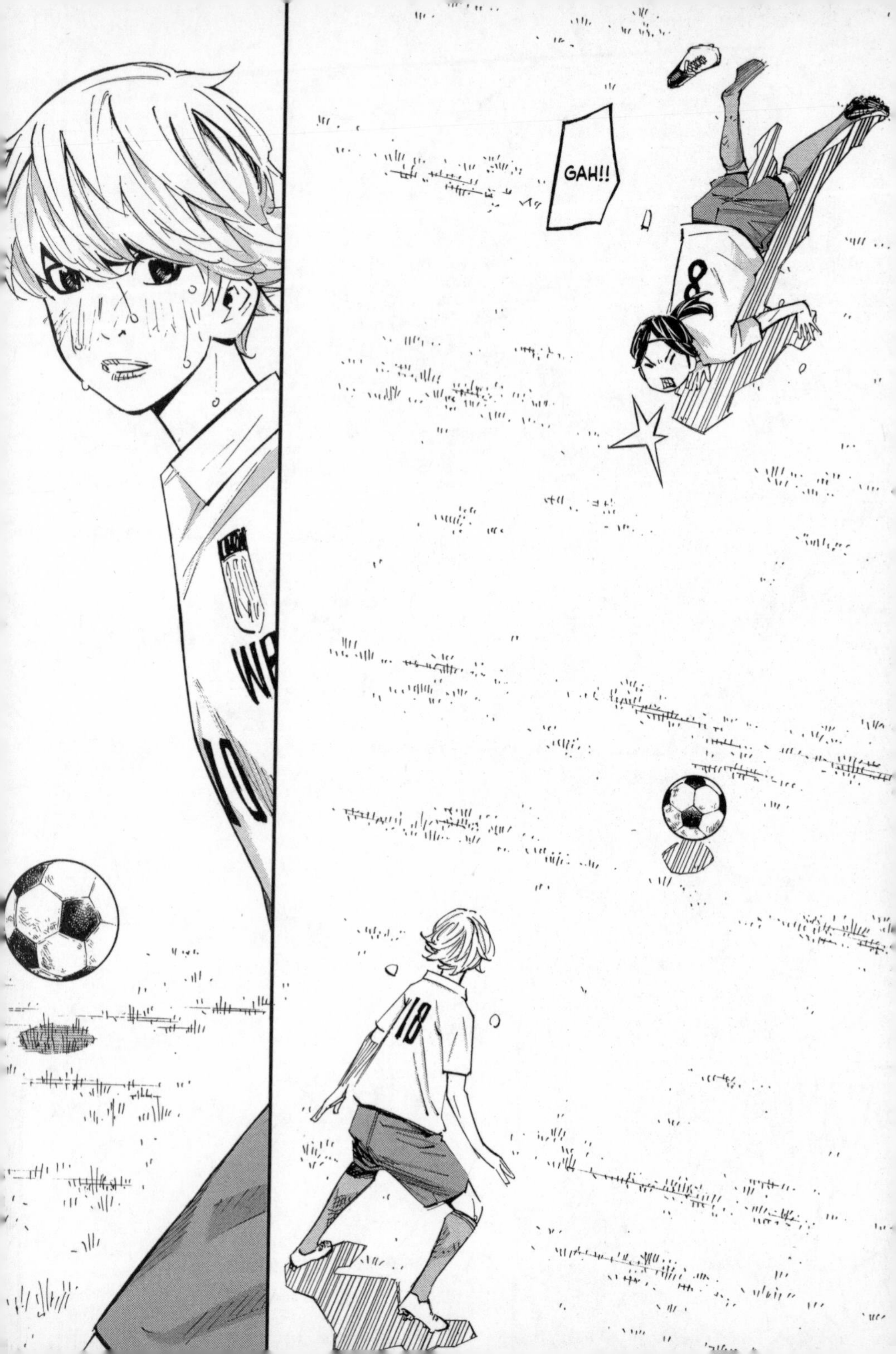
GAH!!

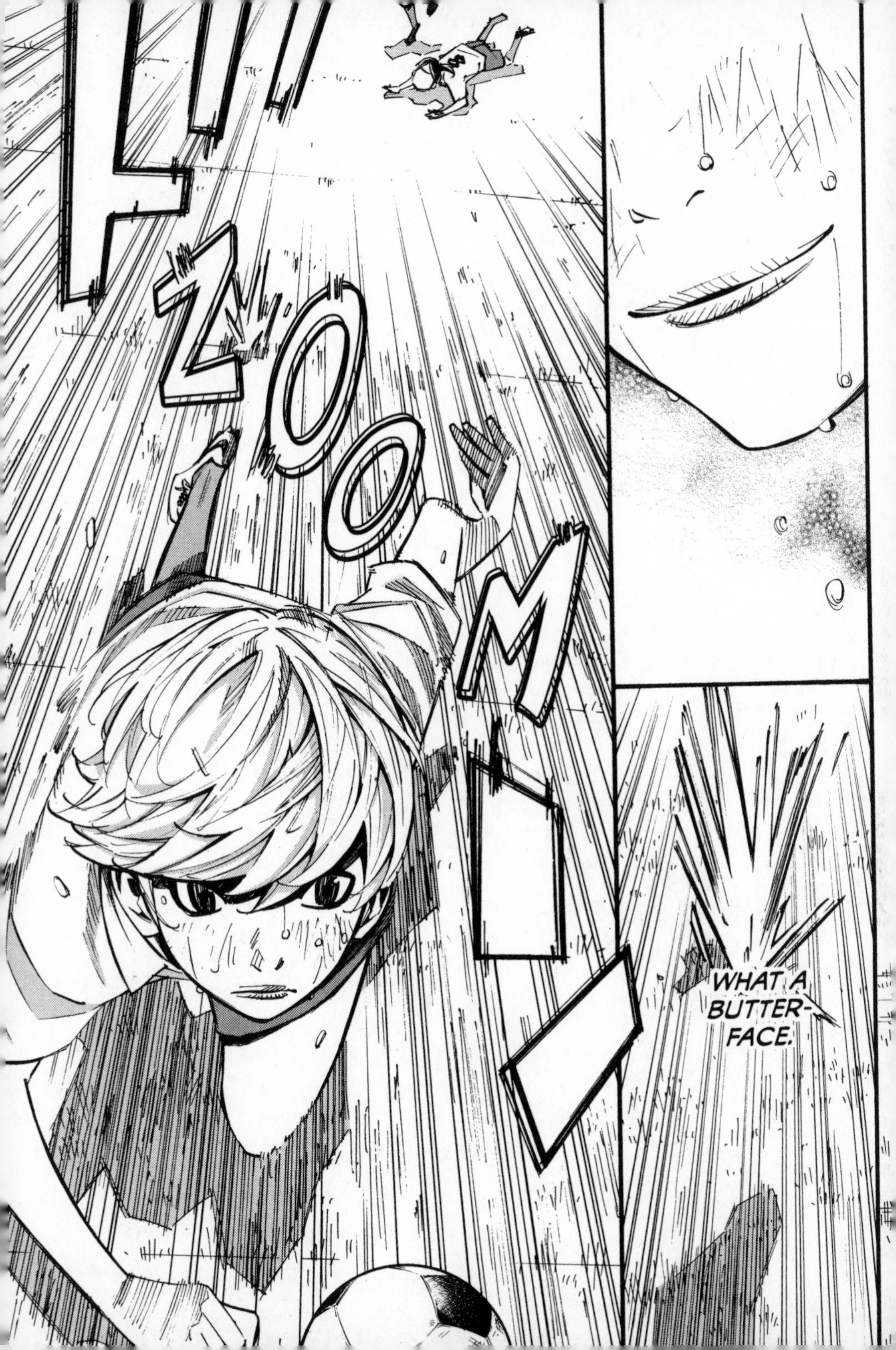
WHAT A BUTTER-FACE.
ZOOOM

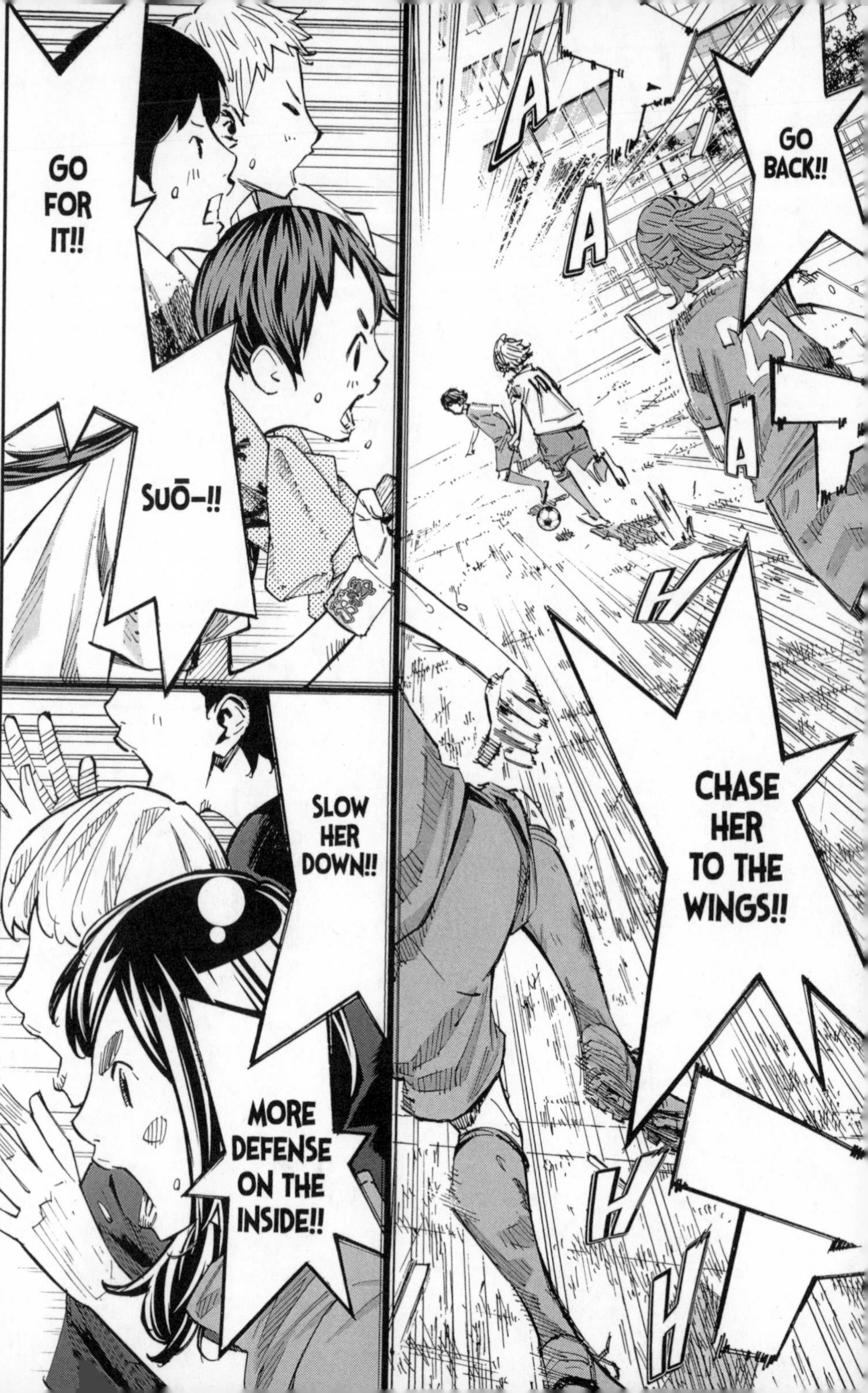
AAAHHHH
GO BACK!!
CHASE HER TO THE WINGS!!
GO FOR IT!!
SUŌ-!!
SLOW HER DOWN!!
MORE DEFENSE ON THE INSIDE!!

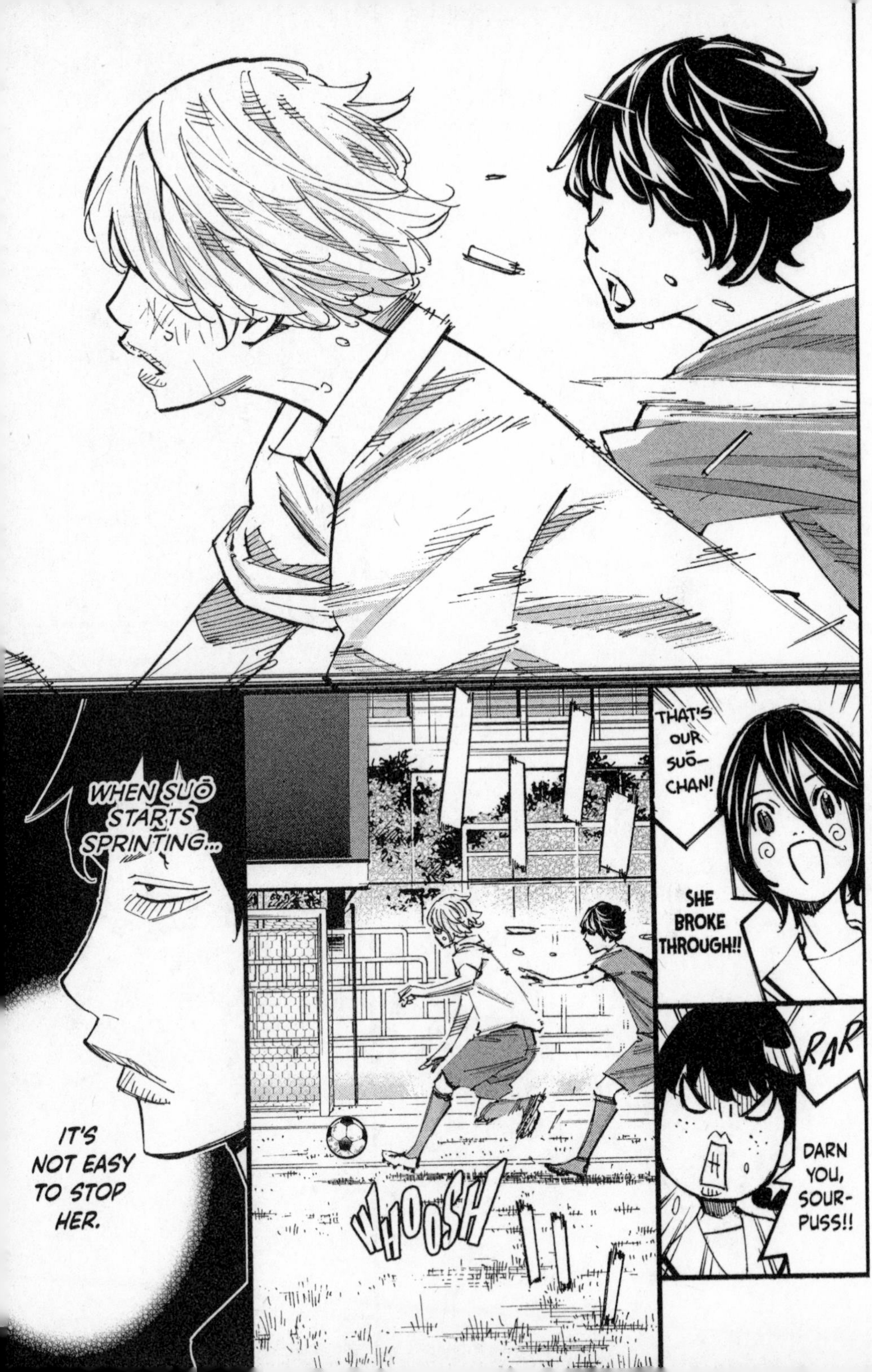
THAT'S OUR SUŌ-CHAN!
SHE BROKE THROUGH!!
RAR
DARN YOU, SOUR-PUSS!!
WHOOSH
WHEN SUŌ STARTS SPRINTING...
IT'S NOT EASY TO STOP HER.

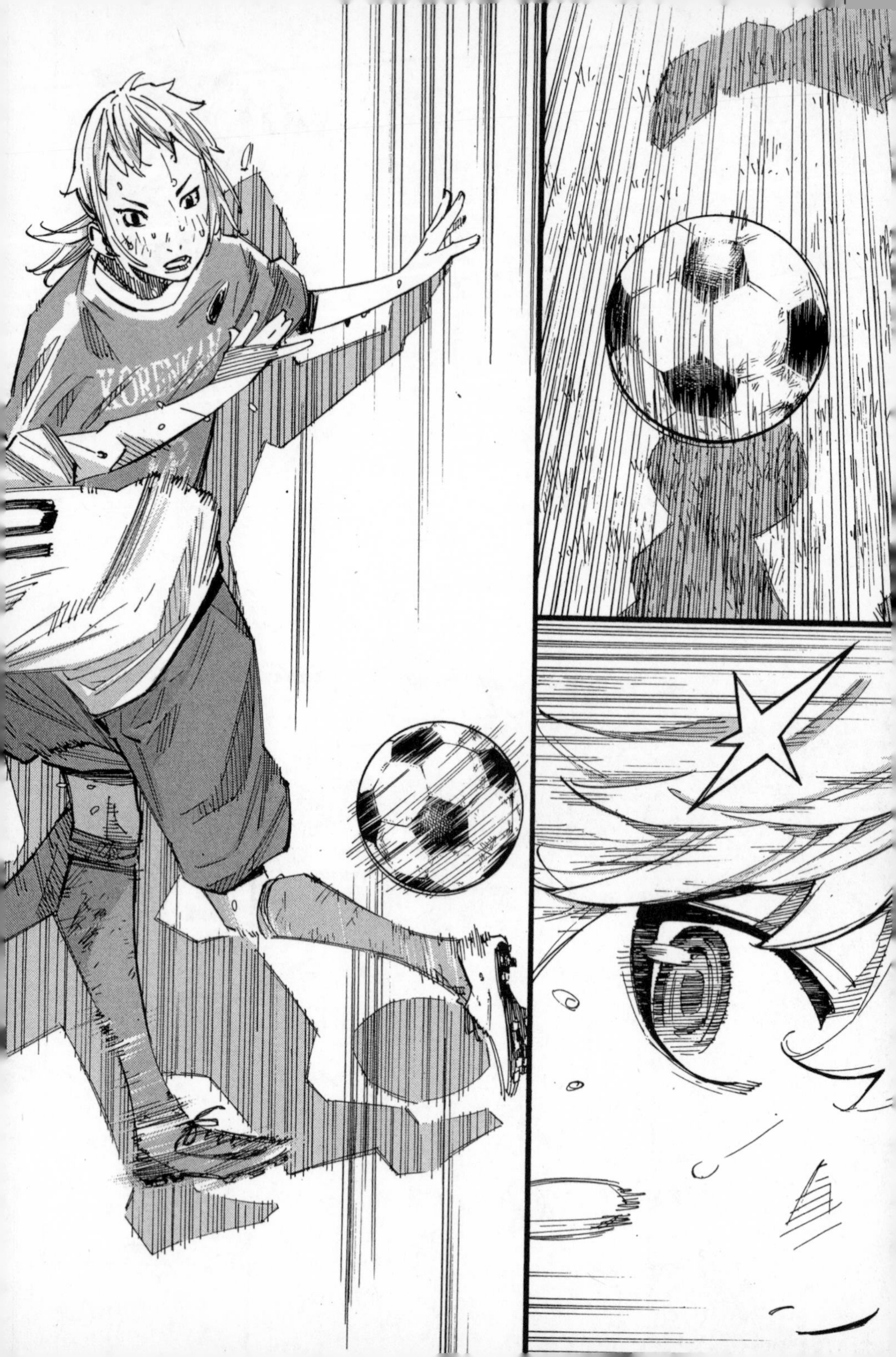
KORENKAN

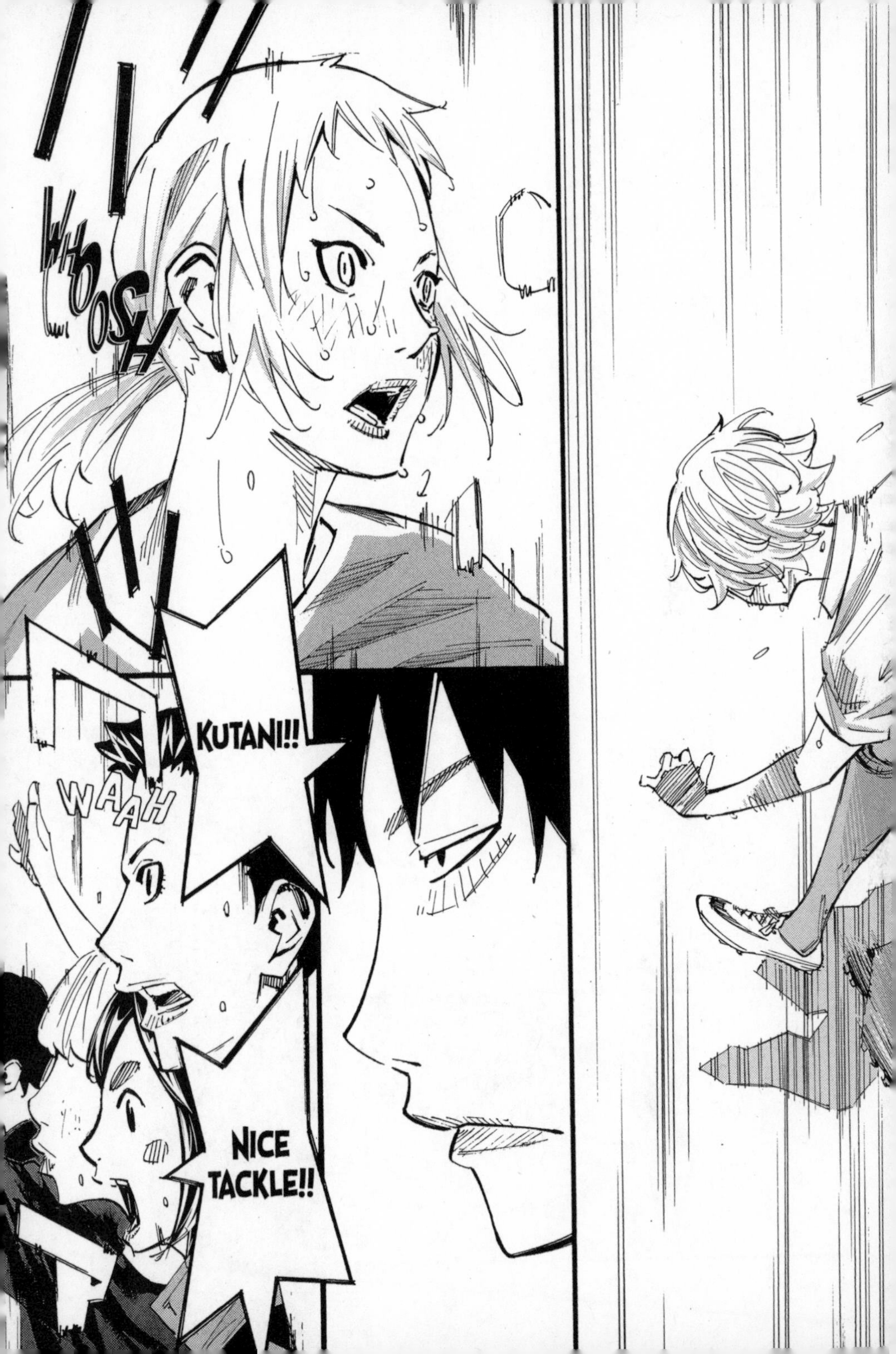
WHOOSH
KUTANI!!
WAAH
NICE TACKLE!!

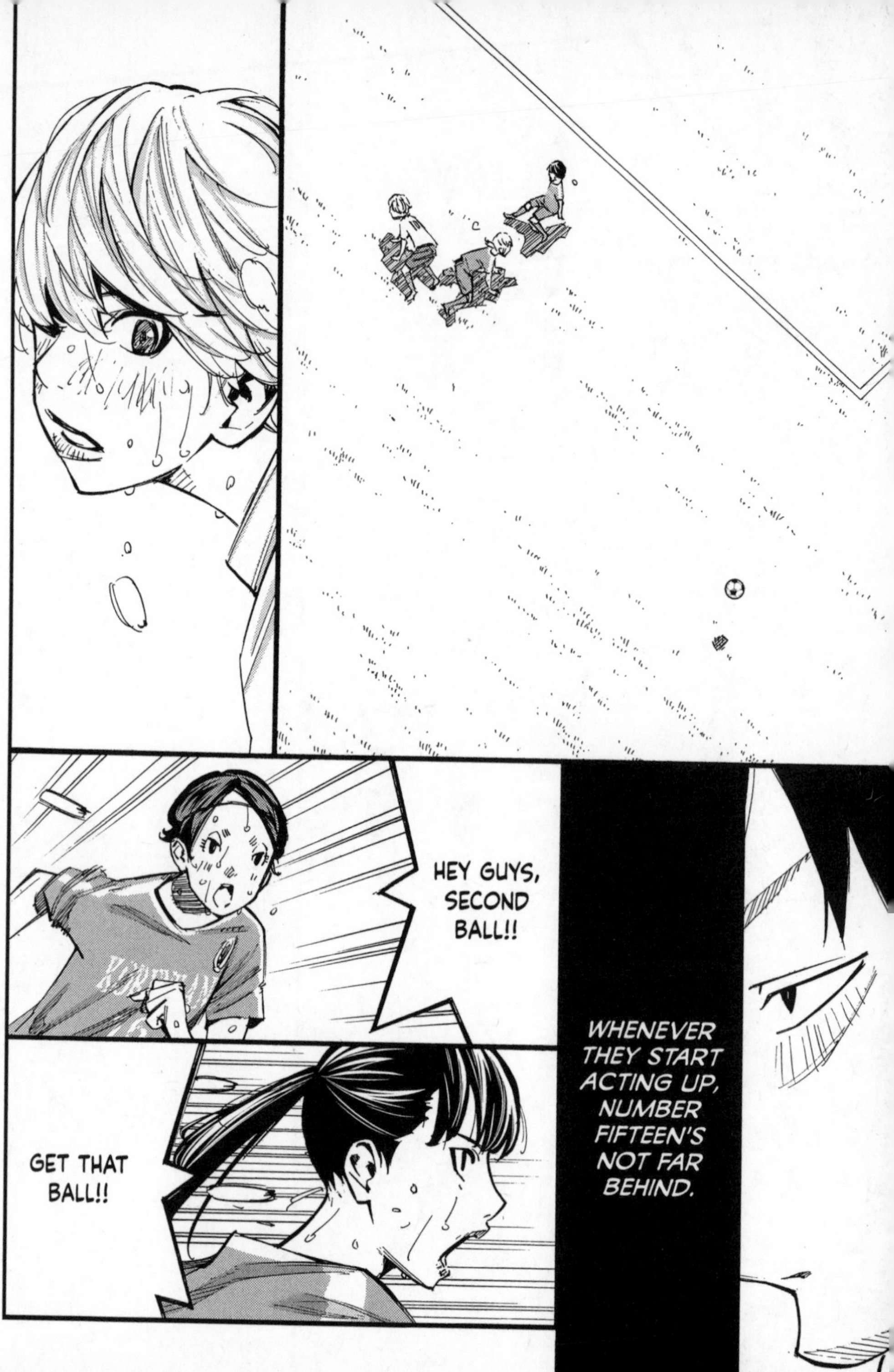
WHENEVER THEY START ACTING UP, NUMBER FIFTEEN'S NOT FAR BEHIND.
HEY GUYS, SECOND BALL!!
GET THAT BALL!!

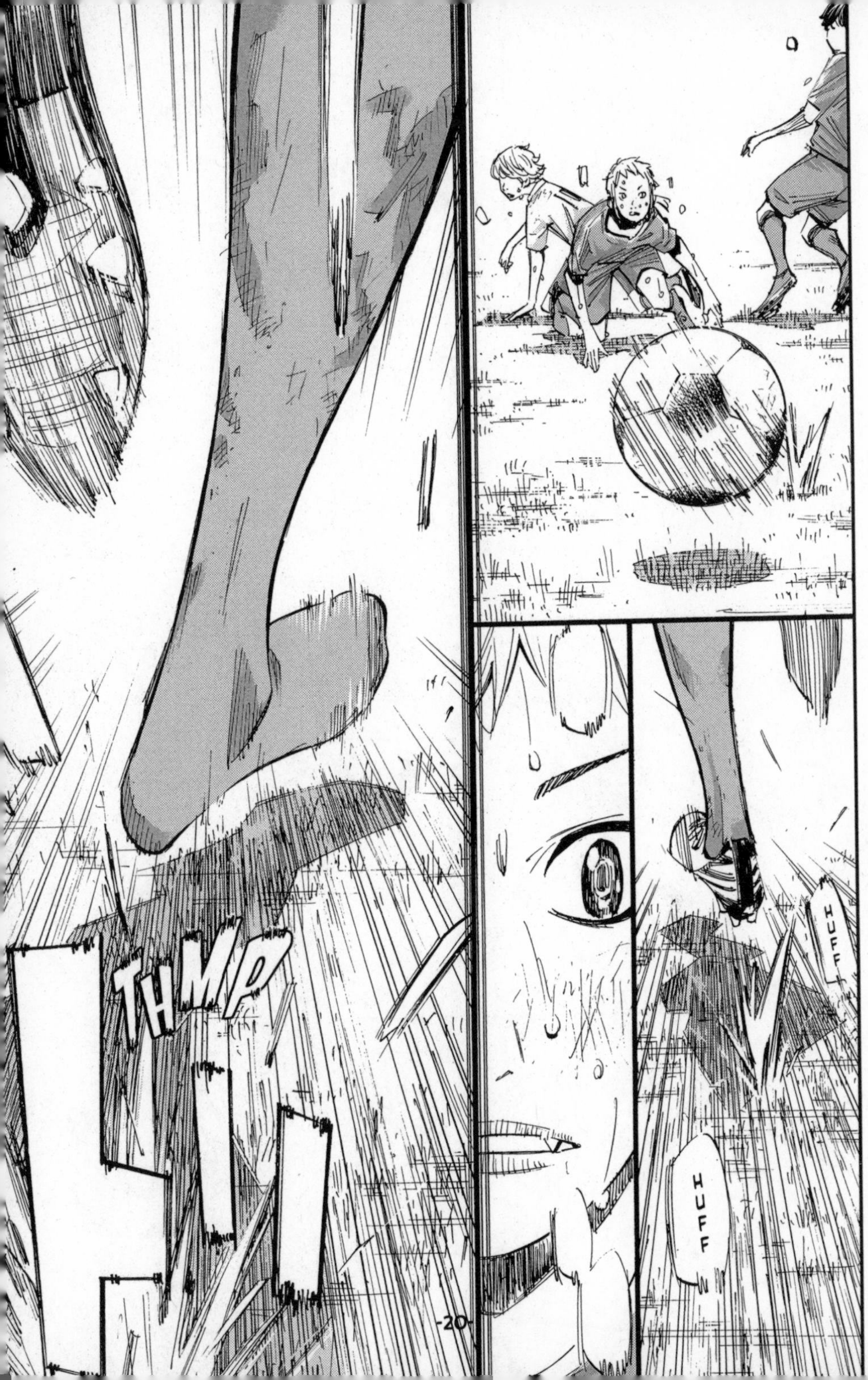
HUFF
HUFF
THMP

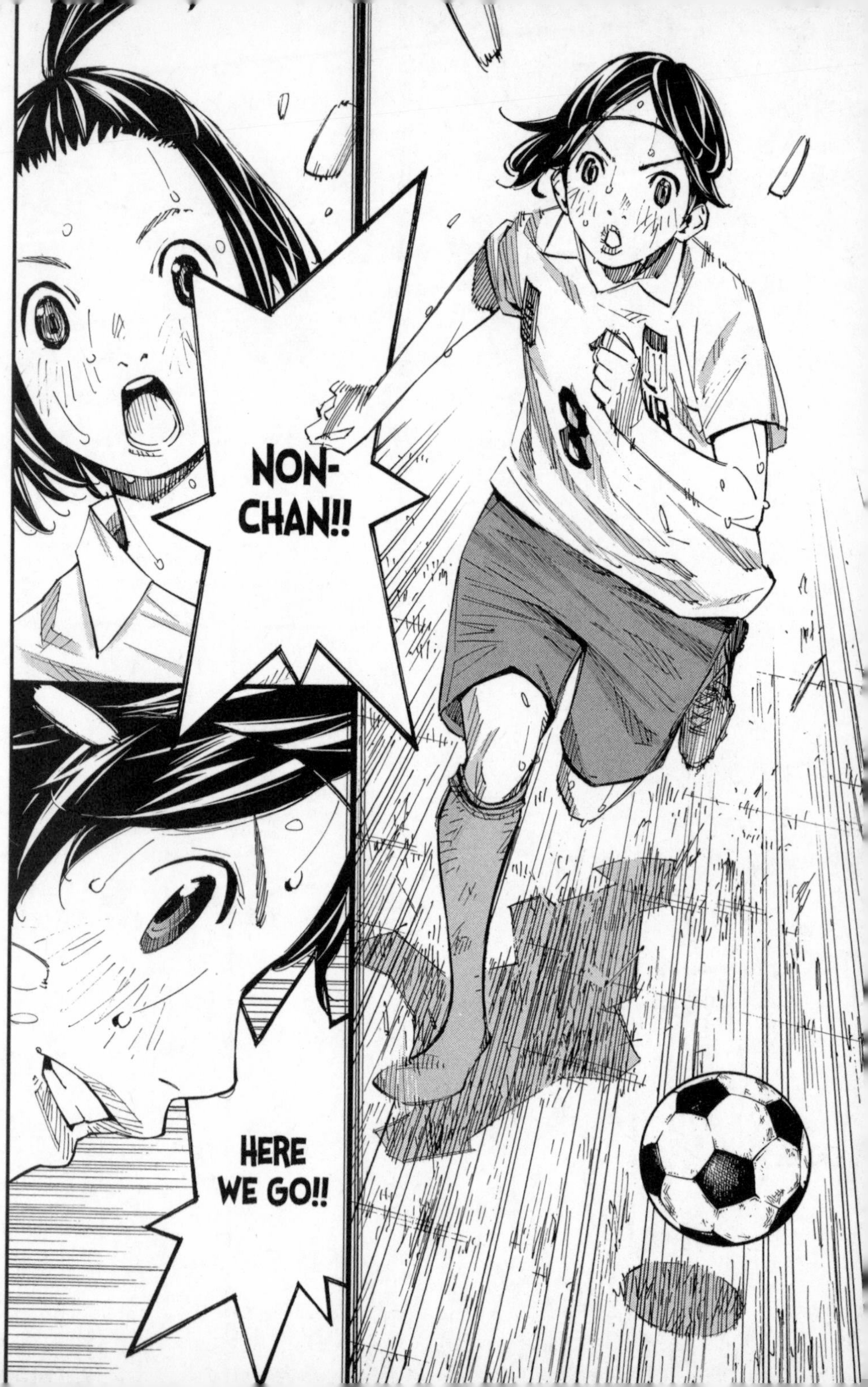
NON-CHAN!!
HERE WE GO!!

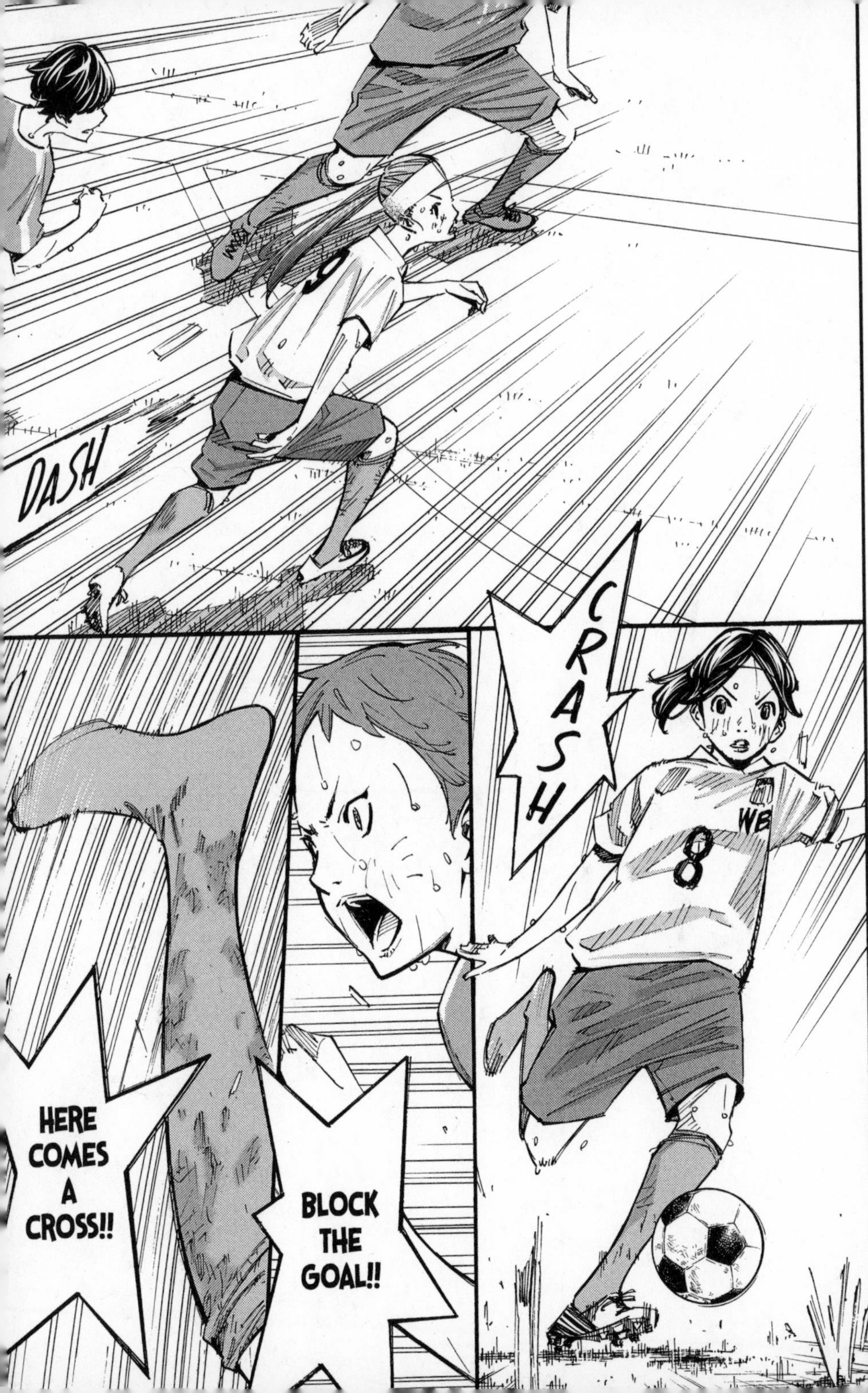
DASH
CRASH
BLOCK THE GOAL!!
HERE COMES A CROSS!!

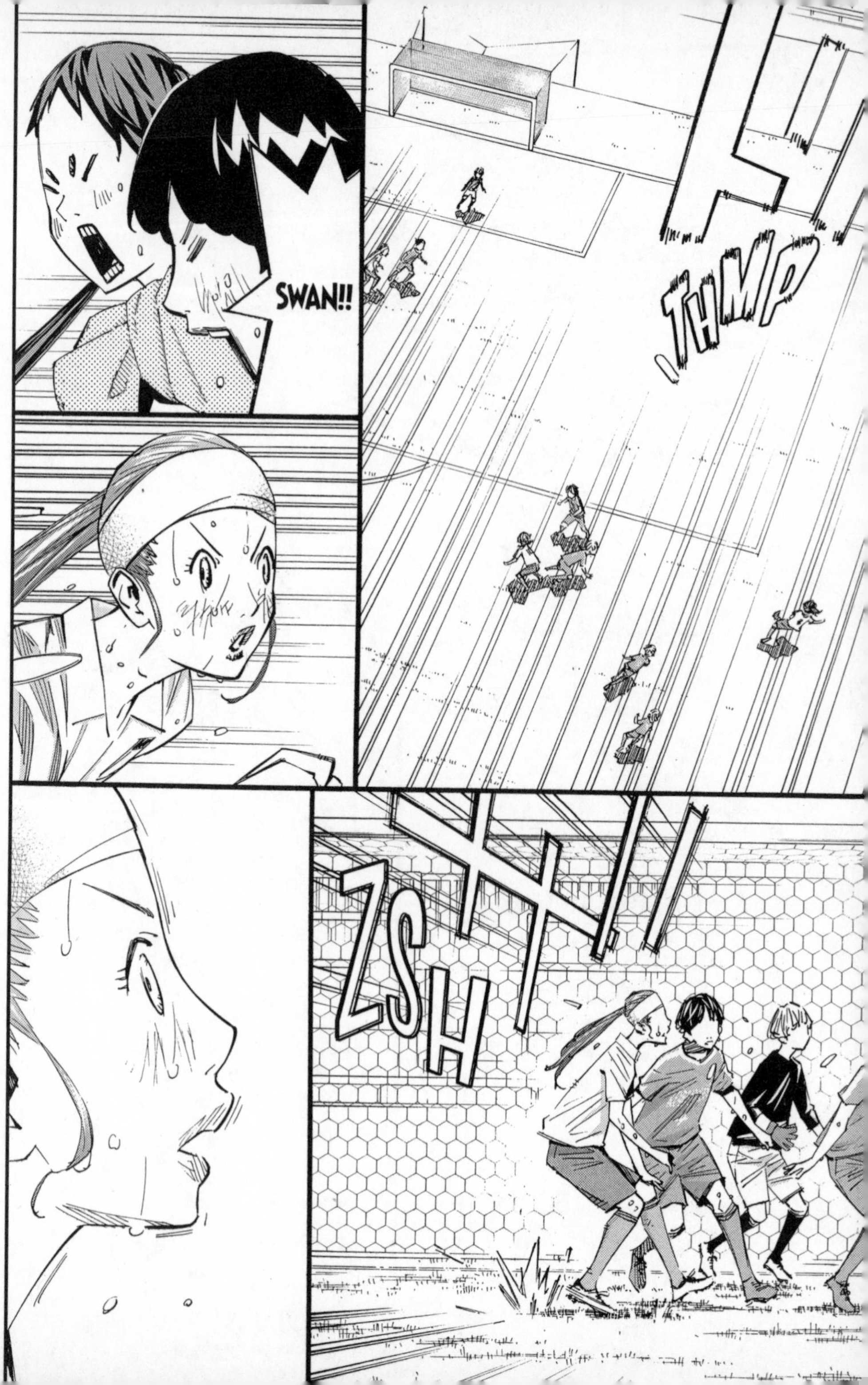
THMP
SWAN!!
ZSH

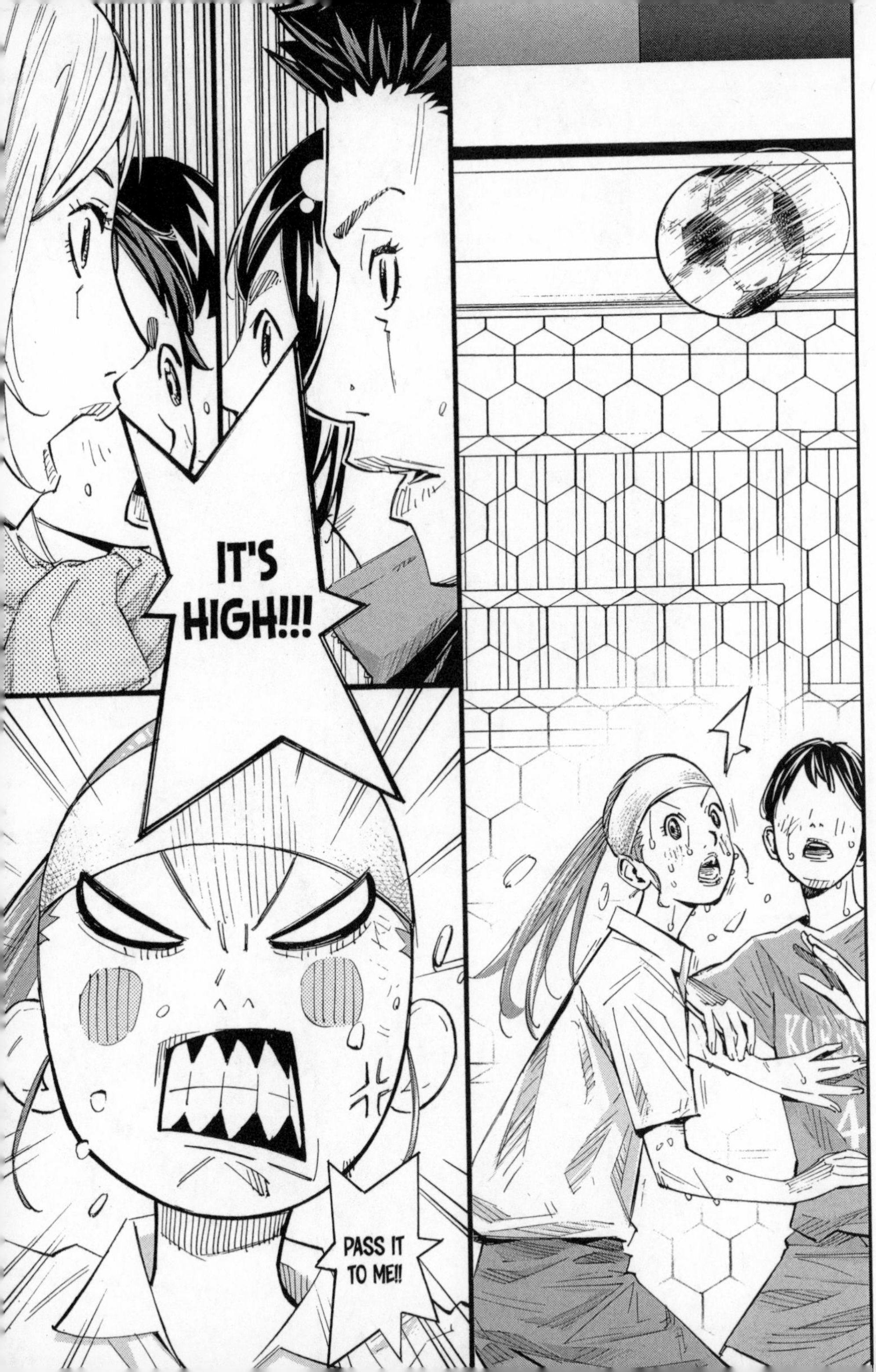
IT'S HIGH!!!
PASS IT TO ME!!

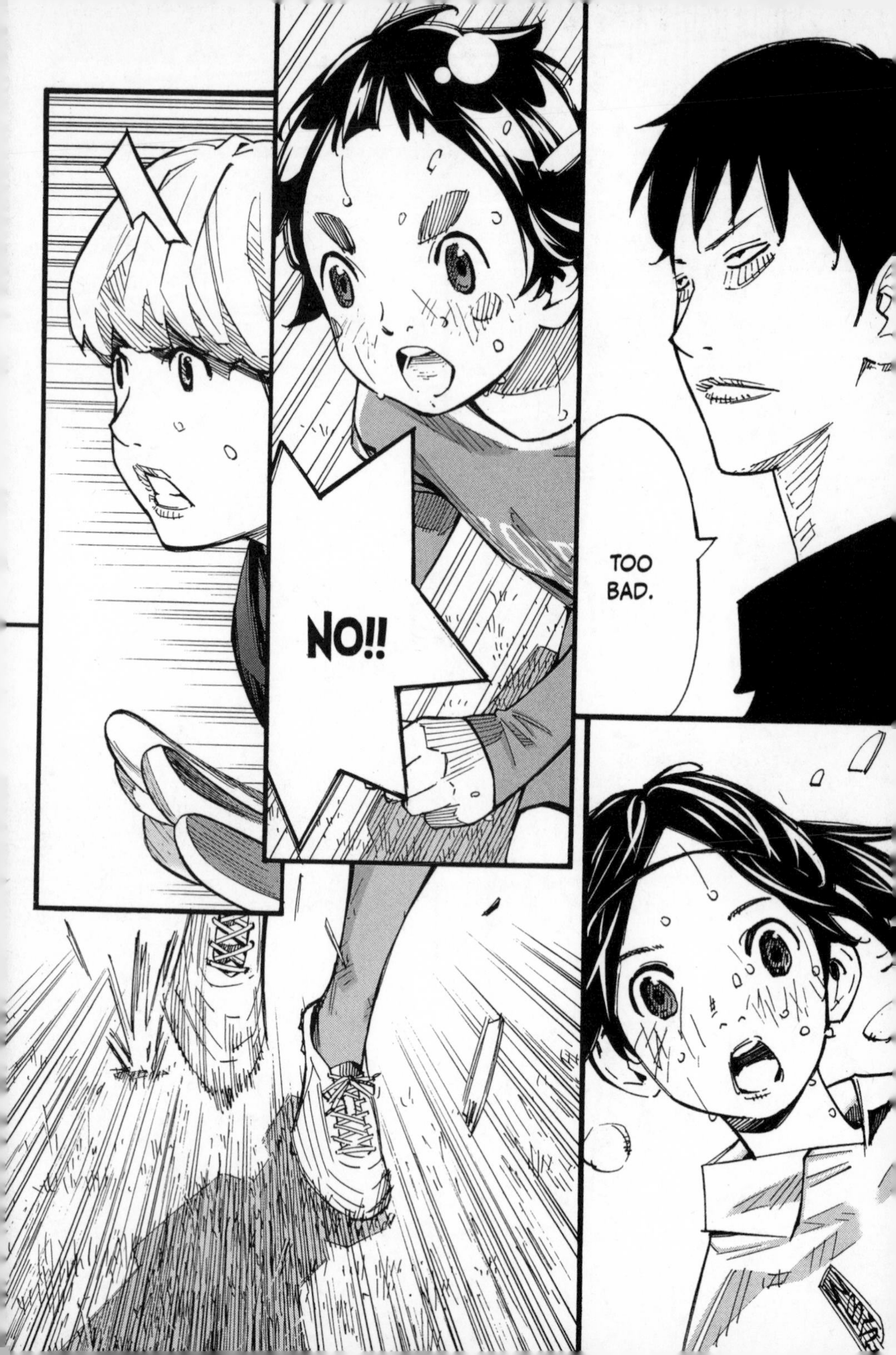
TOO BAD.
NO!!

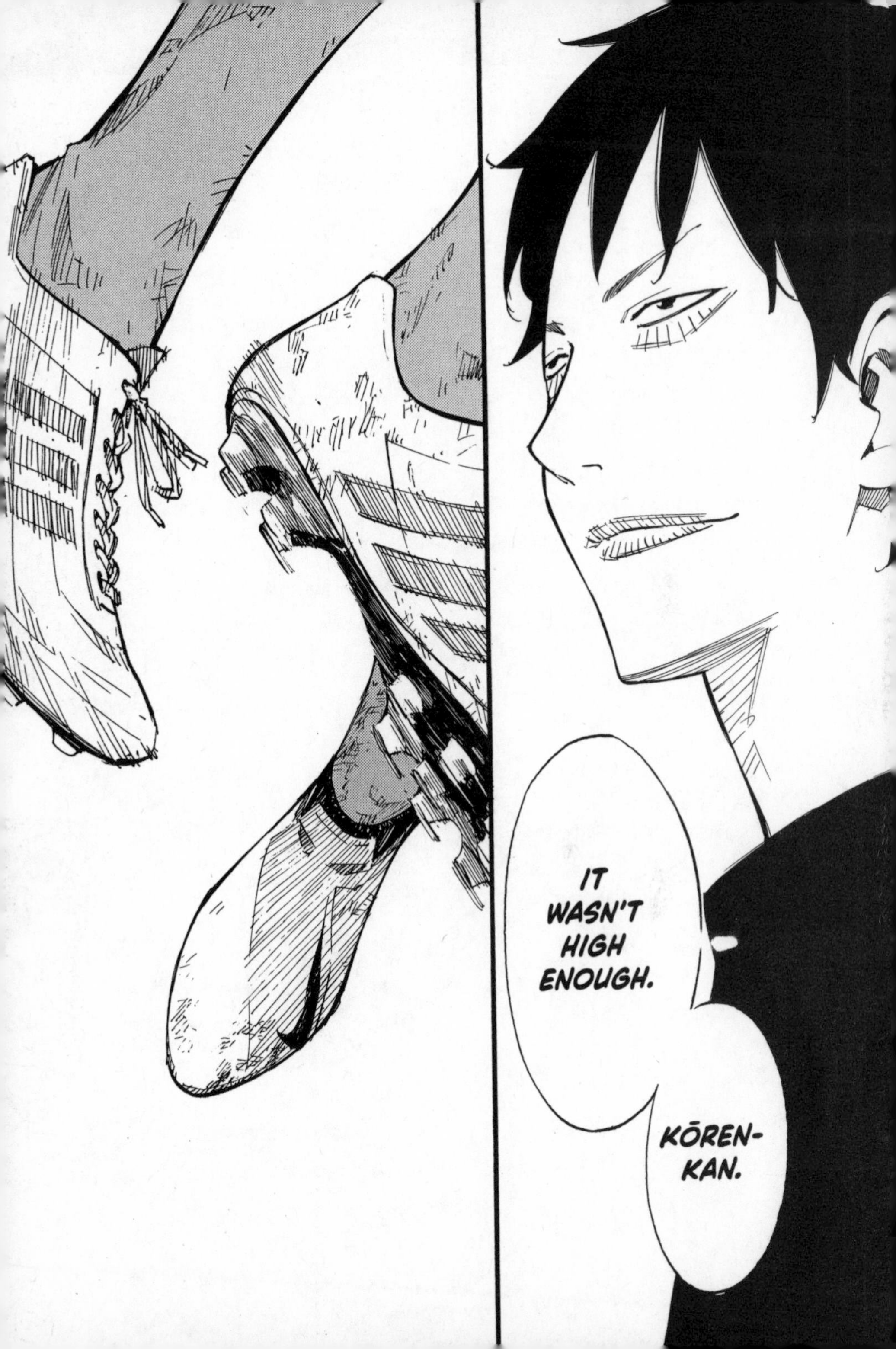
IT WASN'T HIGH ENOUGH.
KŌREN-KAN.

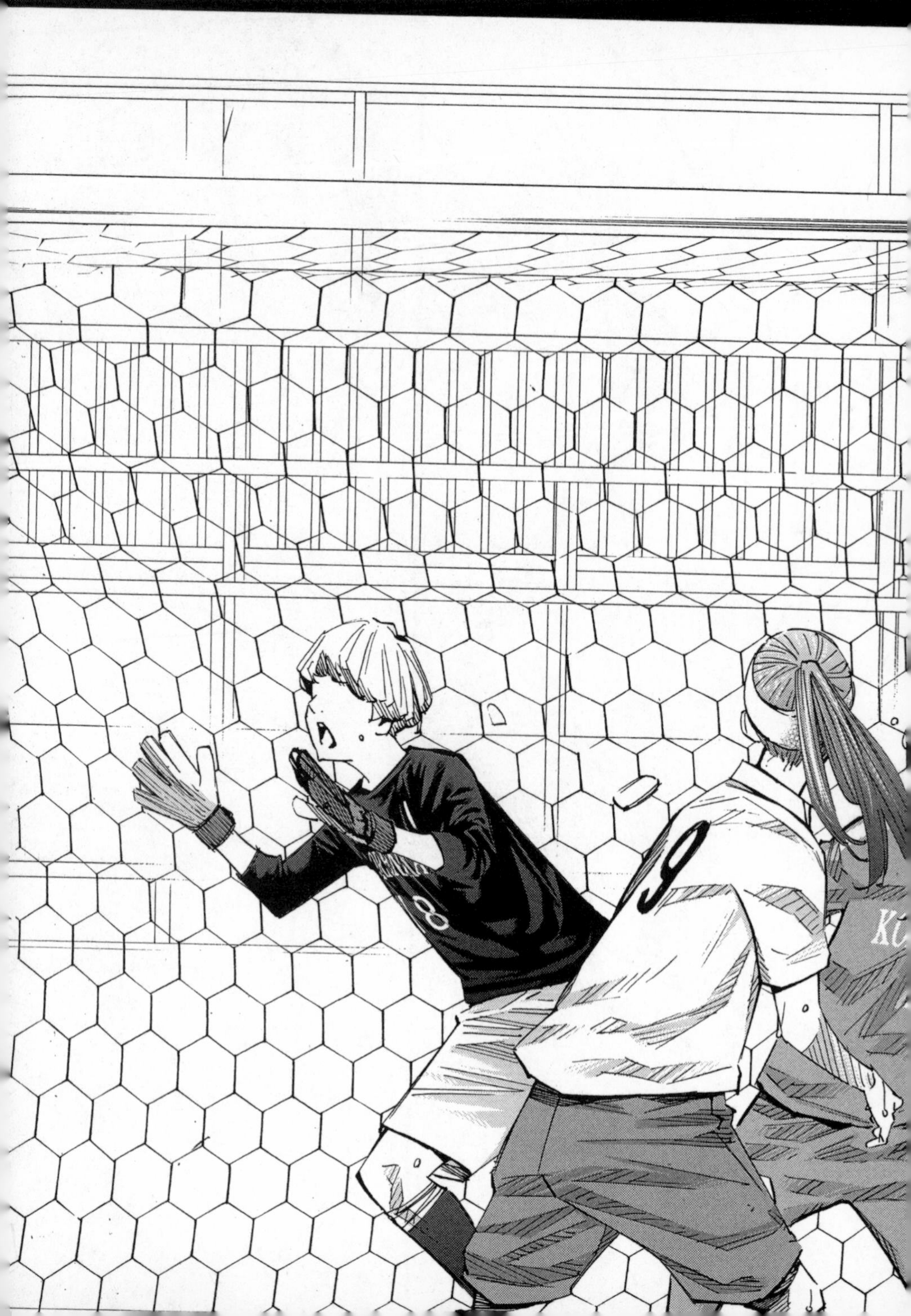

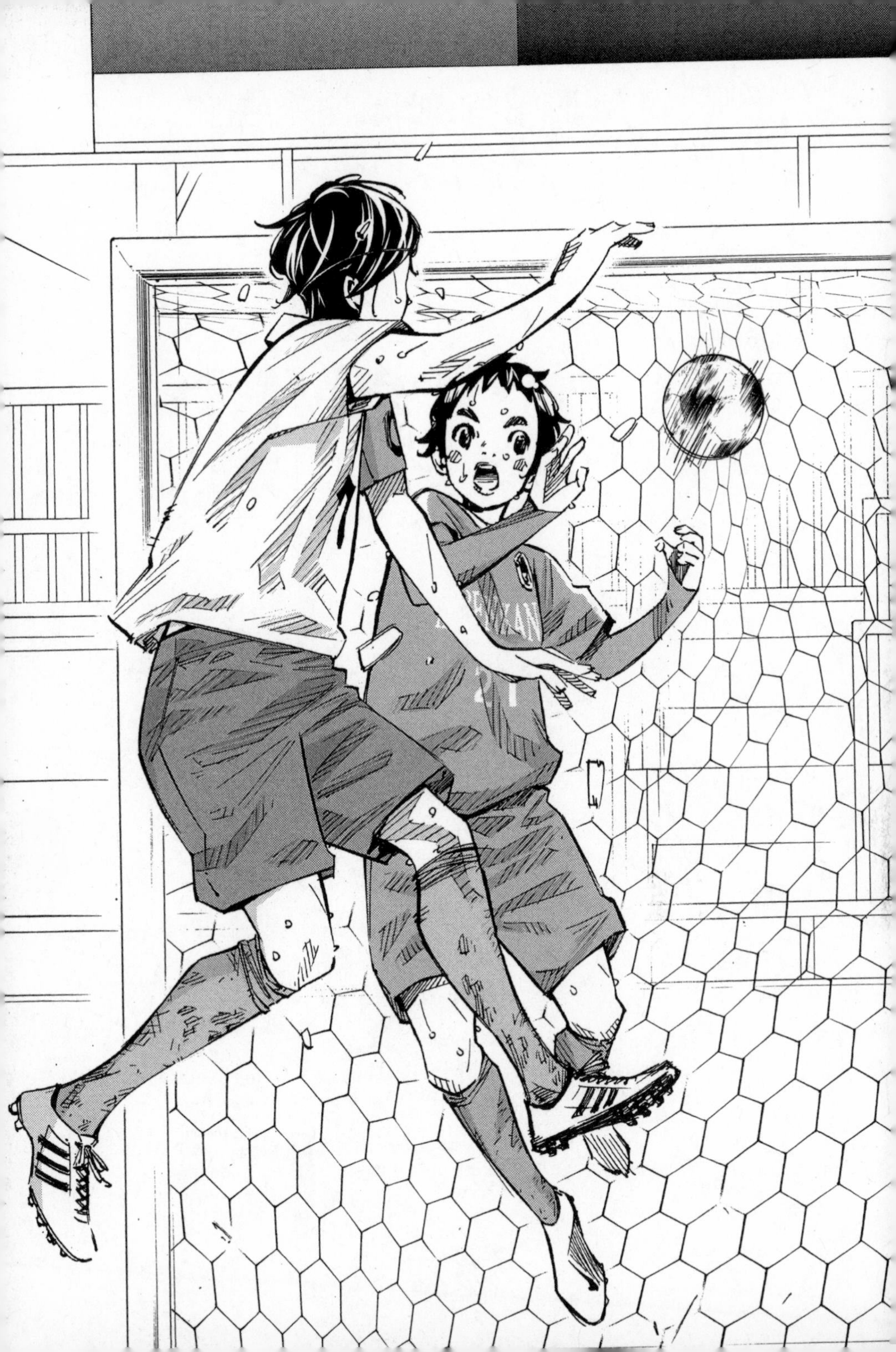

The art-deco cyberpunk classic from the creators of *xxxHOLiC* and *Cardcaptor Sakura*!

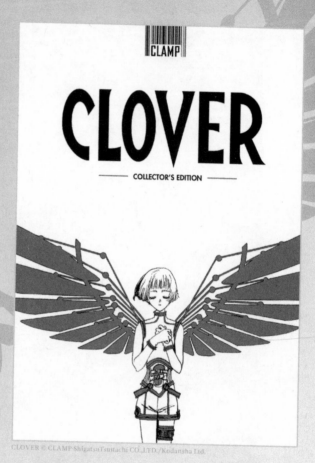

"Starred Review. This experimental sci-fi work from CLAMP reads like a romantic version of *AKIRA*."
—Publishers Weekly

CLAMP
CLOVER
COLLECTOR'S EDITION

Su was born into a bleak future, where the government keeps tight control over children with magical powers—codenamed "Clovers." With Su being the only "four-leaf" Clover in the world, she has been kept isolated nearly her whole life. Can ex-military agent Kazuhiko deliver her to the happiness she seeks? Experience the complete series in this hardcover edition, which also includes over twenty pages of ravishing color art!

KC KODANSHA COMICS

THE WORLD OF CLAMP!

Cardcaptor Sakura
Collector's Edition

Cardcaptor Sakura:
Clear Card

Magic Knight Rayearth
25th Anniversary Box Set

Chobits

TSUBASA Omnibus

TSUBASA WoRLD CHRoNiCLE

xxxHOLiC Omnibus

xxxHOLiC Rei

CLOVER Collector's Edition

Kodansha Comics welcomes you to explore the expansive world of CLAMP, the all-female artist collective that has produced some of the most acclaimed manga of the century. Our growing catalog includes icons like *Cardcaptor Sakura* and *Magic Knight Rayearth*, each crafted with CLAMP's one-of-a-kind style and characters!

"Clever, sassy, and original....*xxxHOLiC* has the inherent hallmarks of a runaway hit."
—NewType magazine

Beautifully seductive artwork and uniquely Japanese depictions of the supernatural will hypnotize CLAMP fans!

xxxHOLiC © CLAMP-ShigatsuTsuitachi CO.,LTD./Kodansha Ltd.
xxxHOLiC Rei © CLAMP-ShigatsuTsuitachi CO.,LTD./Kodansha Ltd.

Kimihiro Watanuki is haunted by visions of ghosts and spirits. He seeks help from a mysterious woman named Yuko, who claims she can help. However, Watanuki must work for Yuko in order to pay for her aid. Soon Watanuki finds himself employed in Yuko's shop, where he sees things and meets customers that are stranger than anything he could have ever imagined.

Young characters and steampunk setting, like *Howl's Moving Castle* and *Battle Angel Alita*

Beyond the Clouds © 2018 Nicke / Ki-oon

A boy with a talent for machines and a mysterious girl whose wings he's fixed will take you beyond the clouds! In the tradition of the high-flying, resonant adventure stories of Studio Ghibli comes a gorgeous tale about the longing of young hearts for adventure and friendship!

PERFECT WORLD

Rie Aruga

A TOUCHING NEW SERIES ABOUT LOVE AND COPING WITH DISABILITY

An office party reunites Tsugumi with her high school crush Itsuki. He's realized his dream of becoming an architect, but along the way, he experienced a spinal injury that put him in a wheelchair. Now Tsugumi's rekindled feelings will butt up against prejudices she never considered — and Itsuki will have to decide if he's ready to let someone into his heart...

"Depicts with great delicacy and courage the difficulties some with disabilities experience getting involved in romantic relationships... Rie Aruga refuses to romanticize, pushing her heroine to face the reality of disability. She invites her readers to the same tasks of empathy, knowledge and recognition."
—Slate.fr

"An important entry [in manga romance]... The emotional core of both plot and characters indicates thoughtfulness... [Aruga's] research is readily apparent in the text and artwork, making this feel like a real story."
—Anime News Network

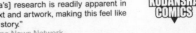

KC/ KODANSHA COMICS

A SMART, NEW ROMANTIC COMEDY FOR FANS OF *SHORTCAKE CAKE* AND *TERRACE HOUSE!*

A romance manga starring high school girl Meeko, who learns to live on her own in a boarding house whose living room is home to the odd (but handsome) Matsunaga-san. She begins to adjust to her new life away from her parents, but Meeko soon learns that no matter how far away from home she is, she's still a young girl at heart — especially when she finds herself falling for Matsunaga-san.

THE SWEET SCENT OF LOVE IS IN THE AIR! FOR FANS OF OFFBEAT ROMANCES LIKE *WOTAKOI*

Sweat and Soap © Kintetsu Yamada / Kodansha Ltd.

In an office romance, there's a fine line between sexy and awkward... and that line is where Asako — a woman who sweats copiously — meets Koutarou — a perfume developer who can't get enough of Asako's, er, scent. Don't miss a romcom manga like no other!

The adorable new odd-couple cat comedy manga from the creator of the beloved *Chi's Sweet Home*, in full color!

Sue & Tai-chan

Konami Kanata

Sue is an aging housecat who's looking forward to living out her life in peace... but her plans change when the mischievous black tomcat Tai-chan enters the picture! Hey! Sue never signed up to be a catsitter! *Sue & Tai-chan* is the latest from the reigning meow-narch of cute kitty comics, Konami Kanata.

KC
KODANSHA
COMICS

MRTW

A Kodansha Comics Trade Paperback Original
Sayonara, Football 13 copyright © 2020 Naoshi Arakawa
English translation copyright © 2022 Naoshi Arakawa

© Nike © Adidas Japan © Puma Japan K.K.

All rights reserved.

Published in the United States by Kodansha Comics, an imprint of
Kodansha USA Publishing, LLC, New York.

Publication rights for this English edition arranged through
Kodansha Ltd., Tokyo.

First published in Japan in 2020 by Kodansha Ltd., Tokyo
as *Sayonara watashi no Cramer,* volume 11.

ISBN 978-1-64651-592-9

Printed in the United States of America.

www.kodansha.us

9 8 7 6 5 4 3 2 1
Translation: Alethea and Athena Nibley
Lettering: Nicole Roderick
Editing: Michal Zuckerman
Kodansha Comics edition cover design by Adam Del Re

Publisher: Kiichiro Sugawara

Director of publishing services: Ben Applegate
Director of publishing operations: Dave Barrett
Associate director of publishing operations: Stephen Pakula
Publishing services managing editors: Madison Salters, Alanna Ruse, with Grace Chen
Senior production manager: Angela Zurlo
Logo and character art ©Kodansha USA Publishing, LLC

NOV · 6 2023